**The Organization
of American Historians
and the Writing and Teaching
of American History**

The Organization
of American Historians
and the Writing and Teaching
of American History

EDITED BY
RICHARD S. KIRKENDALL

UNIVERSITY PRESS

OXFORD
UNIVERSITY PRESS

Oxford University Press, Inc., publishes works that further
Oxford University's objective of excellence
in research, scholarship, and education.

Oxford   New York
Auckland   Cape Town   Dar es Salaam   Hong Kong   Karachi
Kuala Lumpur   Madrid   Melbourne   Mexico City   Nairobi
New Delhi   Shanghai   Taipei   Toronto

With offices in
Argentina   Austria   Brazil   Chile   Czech Republic   France   Greece
Guatemala   Hungary   Italy   Japan   Poland   Portugal   Singapore
South Korea   Switzerland   Thailand   Turkey   Ukraine   Vietnam

Copyright © 2011 by Oxford University Press, Inc.

Published by Oxford University Press, Inc.
198 Madison Avenue, New York, NY 10016

www.oup.com

Oxford is a registered trademark of Oxford University Press

All rights reserved. No part of this publication may be reproduced,
stored in a retrieval system, or transmitted, in any form or by any means,
electronic, mechanical, photocopying, recording, or otherwise,
without the prior permission of Oxford University Press.

Library of Congress Cataloging-in-Publication Data
The Organization of American Historians and the writing and
teaching of American history / edited by Richard S. Kirkendall.
   p. cm.
Includes bibliographical references.
ISBN 978-0-19-979056-2 – ISBN 978-0-19-979057-9 (pbk.)
1. Organization of American Historians—History.
2. Mississippi Valley Historical Association—History.
3. United States—History—Study and teaching.
4. United States—Historiography.
5. Curriculum planning—United States—History.
6. Education—Curricula—United States—History.
I. Kirkendall, Richard Stewart, 1928–
E172.O74O74   2011
973.007—dc22   2010037521

9 8 7 6 5 4 3 2 1

Printed in the United States of America
on acid-free paper

To the Members of the OAH
Past, Present, and Future

Acknowledgments

This book originated in a special committee—the Centennial Committee—of the Organization of American Historians, authorized by the group's Executive Board in the fall of 2003 to plan the celebration of the one-hundredth birthday of the OAH. Working in collaboration with Jacquelyn Dowd Hall and James O. Horton, the group's presidents in 2003–2004, Lee Formwalt, then the Executive Director, recruited Ron Briley, Paul Hutton, Juli A. Jones, William E. Leuchtenburg, Anne Firor Scott, and Deborah Gray White; I served as chair. We made a number of proposals but soon devoted most of our attention to the development of a series of panels for the 2007 meeting that would explore the history of the OAH and its predecessor, the Mississippi Valley Historical Association. Each committee member made contributions, helping to design the program, shape the panels, and suggest participants. Lee assisted us from beginning to end; several members of the OAH staff—Kara Hamm, John Dichtl, Amy Stark, Jason Groth, Michael Regoli, and Annette Windhorn—helped us in many ways, and the president, Richard White, and the Program Committee for the 2007 meeting, co-chaired by Peggy Pascoe and John Mack Faragher, also contributed.

The thought of publishing a history emerged early. Lee was the first person to suggest it, and Joan Catapano, the associate director and editor-in-chief of the University of Illinois Press, offered encouragement and assistance. After the 2007 meeting, I called upon the contributors to the centennial panels to prepare their presentations for publication. Nearly all were able to do so. I am deeply grateful to them and to all of the people who helped to shape this discussion of the history of the MVHA-OAH, including two anonymous reviewers.

People at my home base, the History Department of the University of Washington, also contributed to the making of this book. Carolyn Chaffee, Cassandra Bermel, Jeri Park, Stefanie Starkovich, and Jennifer Weiss of the department's staff and Joseph Wycoff, at the time a doctoral candidate, enabled me to respond to computer challenges. Kent Guy, the chair, helped with a grant.

I also wish to thank those who participated in the first stage of this project, the 2007 meeting, but whose schedules prevented them from contributing to this book: Robert Ferrell, Ira Berlin, Suzanne Lebsock, Heather Huyck, David McMillen, John Hope Franklin, and Mary Frances Berry.

In the late stages of the development of the book, Oxford's Susan Ferber proved to be a superb editor. I enjoyed working with her even though we were separated by 3,000 miles and forced to communicate by e-mail. I am deeply grateful for her many contributions. At the production stage, she turned me over to Joellyn Ausanka, who also supplied work of high quality and was a good communicator over the many miles separating New York City from Seattle. I am grateful.

From beginning to end of my work on the book, my wife, Kathleen, supplied loving encouragement, and now I am pleased to thank her.

Contents

Introduction, 3

PART I THE INSTITUTIONAL AND POLITICAL HISTORY OF THE MVHA–OAH

1. The Rise of a Modern and Democratic Learned Society, 13
   Stanley N. Katz

2. The Mississippi Valley Historical Association, 1907–1952, 17
   Michael Kammen

3. From the MVHA to the OAH, 1951–1981, 33
   Richard S. Kirkendall

4. The OAH in Troublesome Times, 1980–2000, 49
   Arnita A. Jones

5. One Hundred Years of History: Extraordinary Change, Persistent Challenges, 59
   William H. Chafe

PART II THE MVHA–OAH AND THE FIELDS OF HISTORY

6. The Most Appropriate Subjects for Study, 65
   William E. Leuchtenburg

7. The Persistence of Political History, 67
   James T. Patterson

8. The Continental Empire and the Global Power, 75
   Richard S. Kirkendall

9. Economic History and American Historians: From Integration to Segregation in One Century, 92
   Gavin Wright

10. The Battle for Military History: Success or Failure?, 101
    Edward M. Coffman

11   The Challenges to Traditional Histories, **111**
     Joan Hoff

12   Social History and Intellectual History, **125**
     James T. Kloppenberg

13   The Long and Influential Life of Social History in the
     MVHR and the *JAH*, **127**
     Stephanie J. Shaw

14   The *MVHR*, the *JAH*, and Intellectual History:
     From Margin to Mainstream, **146**
     David A. Hollinger

15   Immigration and the Tattered Narrative of Progressive History, **155**
     John Bodnar

16   The Slow Rise to Prominence of African American History, **169**
     Arvarh E. Strickland and Richard S. Kirkendall

17   Women's History: From Neglect to Prominence
     and to Integration, **188**
     Alice Kessler-Harris

18   The Presence of Native American History, **198**
     Frederick E. Hoxie

19   The Wild One: Environmental History as Redheaded Stepchild, **208**
     Karl Brooks

20   The History That Dare Not Speak Its Name, **217**
     Kathy Peiss

21   How Discipline Change Happens, **228**
     Thomas Bender

     PART III EDITING THE JOURNAL

22   A Learned Journal Adjusts to Change, **237**
     Lewis C. Perry

23   Editing and the Challenges of Specialization, Audiences,
     Sites of Practice, **243**
     David Thelen

24   Putting Together American History, **252**
     Joanne Meyerowitz

25   Becoming the Editor, **259**
     Edward T. Linenthal

PART IV THE MVHA–OAH AND THE TEACHING OF HISTORY

26 The Shouldering of Responsibilities, 265
    Gary B. Nash

27 The MVHA and Teaching: A Strained Relationship, 267
    Ron Briley

28 Why a Focus on Teaching Day?, 275
    Marjorie Bingham

29 The OAH and the Community College Professoriate, 279
    Charles A. Zappia

30 The Recent Years, 287
    Timothy N. Thurber

31 A Plea for Equality, 292
    Leon F. Litwack

PART V THE MVHA–OAH AND PUBLIC HISTORY

32 Public History: Past and Present, 301
    Spencer R. Crew

33 Historians in the Federal Government, 306
    Donald A. Ritchie

34 Discovering Public History in an Unlikely Place:
    UC, Santa Barbara, 1976 and After, 317
    Otis L. Graham Jr.

35 Public History and the Academy: A Continuum of Practice, 323
    Marla R. Miller

PART VI PRESIDENTIAL MEMORIES

36 The Sitting President Looks On—Uncomfortably, 331
    Richard White

37 The Transformation of the Annual Meeting, 333
    Richard W. Leopold (1912–2006)

38 The Warm Memories of a Life Member, 337
    Carl Degler

39 The Third Woman in the Presidency, 341
    Anne Firor Scott

40 The OAH in Philadelphia: The Musical, 344
    Leon F. Litwack

41 History's Public Function, 347
Eric Foner

42 The OAH in St. Louis: The Protest, 351
David Montgomery

Afterword, 357
Katherine Mandusic Finley

Appendix: The Officers, 1907–2012, **361**

Notes on Contributors, **365**

The Organization of American Historians and the Writing and Teaching of American History

Introduction

From March 29 to April 1, 2007, thousands of historians gathered in Minneapolis to attend the annual meeting of the Organization of American Historians (OAH). Not merely another meeting, this one marked the group's centennial. This rich collection of essays emerges from that occasion. In addition to looking at what the OAH is and how it has developed, the essays trace the writing of American history over the past century.

The organization was born out of a discussion among directors of Midwestern historical societies, who named the group the Mississippi Valley Historical Association (MVHA) and decided that the promotion of historical research should be its top priority. During the early years, Frederick Jackson Turner's idea of the importance of the American West loomed large in the MVHA, and members discussed, among other things, whether history could be scientific, could be used for social betterment, and should be popularized.

After midcentury, the group changed in a number of ways. Membership grew rapidly for a time, and in 1965, leaders and members changed the name to Organization of American Historians. Soon, African American and women historians challenged the domination of the OAH by white men, and beginning in the 1970s, the OAH became increasingly concerned about the status and role of history in American life, the teaching of history in the schools and colleges, and jobs for historians. By the 1990s, the OAH had developed a staff headed by a full-time executive officer and had been drawn into "culture wars" that included debate in the public arena over how history was being and should be written and taught.

In five early chapters, three historians, Michael Kammen, Arnita Jones, and I, tell this story, and two others, Stanley Katz and William Chafe, muse about the OAH and democracy. Katz suggests that this historical group has become a modern and democratic learned society, and Chafe notes that, throughout the past century, professional historians have struggled over whether they should seek scientific detachment and objectivity or engage in advocacy to advance the principles of a democratic society.

Then the book focuses over many chapters on the contributions of the OAH to the development of historical fields. It begins with four—political history, foreign relations, economic history, and military history—which, William Leuchtenburg reports, the founders regarded as the most appropriate subjects for study. Political history was a prominent feature of the MVHA's major publication, the *Mississippi Valley Historical Review (MVHR)* throughout its long life (1914 to 1964), and James Patterson contests the charge that the field has died out in the OAH and its *Journal of American History (JAH)*. The history of diplomacy and other foreign relations has also always been treated as important by the *MVHR* and *JAH*, and many of the articles in this field dealt with issues central to the history of a large region and then a big nation.

The chapter on economic history tells a quite different story. This field has been largely segregated from the mainstream of American history in recent years after being a prominent part of the *MVHR* from the beginning and especially important in the profession from the 1930s to the 1950s before being pulled and pushed into the discipline of economics. Gavin Wright hopes for a blending of economic and historical perspectives, a breaking down of the walls of segregation.

The chapter on military history begins with a battle for acceptance of the field by other professional historians. Although that effort has enjoyed some success and military history is much admired and read outside of academe and among undergraduates in colleges and universities, its practitioners have generally not regarded the OAH as supportive. Nevertheless, Edward Coffman concludes that the "future appears to be brighter than some military historians think."

Joan Hoff notes that general readers admire these traditional fields more than professional historians do. She writes of a systematic crisis in the profession and questions how the discipline as a whole has dealt with the powerful challenge to the traditional fields from postmodern theories and deconstructionist methodologies. She finds within the field of U.S. foreign policy the basis for a mediating role between the challengers and the traditionalists and ends with a call for more analysis of a traditional kind of American domestic and foreign policy.

A half century and more ago, historians combined social and intellectual history into one course. More recently, the topics were separated, but this book, James Kloppenberg points out, returns "to the older, and wiser, tradition of joining together thought and practice, ideas and behavior, as aspects of the single, albeit multifaceted, reality that all of us American historians study."

Following this observation, Stephanie Shaw shows that social history has had a long life in the *MVHR* and *JAH* and has transformed the discipline in important ways. The field appeared in the *Review* "almost from the beginning," although early on most of the articles provided "more social content than social history." The 1940s was a turning point in which historians began to write history from the "bottom up." Yet, Shaw maintains, "the mandates of 'the new social history' would not be completely fulfilled until well into the 1980s," but by now, the field "has undoubtedly come of age."

Chapter 14 shifts the focus to intellectual history, a field that was integrated into the mainstream of the discipline in the 1950s. Scholars outside the historical profession, David Hollinger informs us, did most of the early writing on the history of thinking, but the demonstration that ideas could be studied in their social contexts made the field attractive to American historians. Early on, the intellectual historians split, with one group emphasizing popular ideas, the other, sophisticated ones, but in time, the latter approach came to dominate the field. Over the past half century, Hollinger points out, the *Review* and the *Journal* have published many important essays on intellectual history, most of them in recent years written from an internationalist perspective.

Turning our attention to immigration, John Bodnar sets up the subject with two presidential addresses, one to the MVHA in 1944, the other to the OAH fifty-four years later. He then focuses on some of the broad transformations in the ways historians have approached immigration and related topics. The Progressive view of the course U.S. history was taking portrayed immigration as a "form of uplift and improvement" and "upheld a faith in assimilation and the progressive potential of the nation. . . ." Beginning in the 1950s, this view was challenged and gave way first to one that emphasized intolerance and divisiveness and portrayed assimilation as relatively easy only for white people. Another interpretation suggested that integration of the foreign-born was most often the result of coercion by powerful forces of patriotism and racism that immigrants had to struggle against.

African American history very slowly gained acceptance within the Mississippi Valley Historical Association, but now, as Arvarh Strickland and I show, the field is one of the major ones in the OAH. In the early years, attention was confined to the book review section and largely devoted to the work of Carter Woodson. Not until 1945 did the magazine carry its first article by an African American historian. Six years later, an African American appeared for the first time on the program of the annual meeting; and in 1953, the meeting devoted its first full session to African American history. In the 1960s, the historical profession felt the heavy demand for change in race relations; African American history gained recognition as a viable field for study and research, and the prominence of the field now offers evidence of the democratization of the OAH.

For a long period, a small number of women were active in the MVHA but there were no papers on women at the annual meetings and only two articles on women in the *MVHR*, one of them by a man. This situation prevailed until the eve of the 1970s. Reflecting the rising influence of the feminist movement, the *JAH* began to publish articles and the annual meeting began to offer papers on women, most of them written by women. By the 1980s, the *JAH* left no doubt that the historical profession had changed, and by the 1990s, articles on women gave way to ones on gender and the history of women moved into the mainstream. Now, Alice Keller-Harris concludes, women's history "has fulfilled its promise of fostering a history of 'all the people,'" and the OAH has "fully participated in this process."

Another history contrasts sharply with African American history. As Frederick Hoxie surprisingly discovers, presence rather than neglect dominates Native American history within the MVHA and OAH from the earliest years. There have been changes, including a sharp decline in the attention paid to frontier topics, an "explosion of interest" in the field at the annual meetings since 1969, and the rise of new themes, including "zones of contact." Hoxie proposes that the story reflects the democratization process in the OAH and suggests we have been learning to think about Indian people historically and have come to understand that they are not deficient and, therefore, unimportant or irrelevant to the continent's history and do not need to be supervised and taken care of.

The book emphasizes neglect in its appraisal of the MVHA-OAH relationship with environmental history. In the early period, Karl Brooks suggests, *Mississippi Valley Historical Review* (*MVHR*) editors recognized that place matters to people, but later editors, especially in the postwar period, did not give the field the encouragement they did to the new social history. The essay's explanation for the failure to supply the help emphasizes the *Journal*'s "conviction that people came first, last, and always." Refusal to endorse environmental history's legitimacy until the 1990s and to bring it together with other fields prevented the discipline from becoming as strong as it could now be, Brooks argues.

The history of sexuality, Kathy Peiss reports, was virtually absent from the MVHA-OAH before the 1970s and did not regularly appear until the 1990s. Historians were slower to take up this topic than practitioners of several other disciplines, and some historians presented their findings in other vehicles. In the *JAH*, the first article did not appear until 1968; the first session at an annual meeting followed in 1971, but very little else showed up in either site during the next two decades. Acceptance and legitimacy within the OAH did not come until the 1990s. What more needs to be done to grow this field? Peiss's list includes the recommendation that the profession should define historical significance.

In the final essay on the fields of history, Thomas Bender speculates about the course of the discipline since 1907. Attempting to explain why historical specialties gain recognition at different times, he suggests that a field needs more time to become ready for publication in a broad journal than a specialized one, and champions of new fields must persuade others that their subjects are historically significant and capable of reshaping the mainstream narrative. After expressing concern about a weakening of the OAH's connection with the study of institutional power, Bender concludes that the essayists offer a starting point for discussion of how learned societies change and grow.

The issues of submission and rejection raised by Bender, among others, demand research that the contributors were not asked to do. They drew mainly on two sets of sources: published ones—mainly the *MVHR* and the *JAH*—and memories. To deal with what articles historians sent in and how they were appraised, researchers would need to explore the OAH's archives. It would be a huge as well as important task, better left for other, more sharply focused, studies.

Contributors in Part II refer more than once to the role of journal editors in shaping the writing of American history. In the next part, the editors speak for themselves, telling readers about their goals and their accomplishments. Coming to office in 1978, Lewis Perry felt a strong responsibility for protecting the *JAH*'s great scholarly reputation and finding and publishing good examples of the new scholarship. Looking back, he now feels quite pleased with the results.

The long-serving David Thelen tells us that when he began he recognized he had much to learn about the *JAH* and the practice of American history. He hoped to make that practice more democratic and polled the readers about what they wanted. They persuaded him to publish new kinds of essays on what historians outside as well as inside academic institutions and around the world were doing.

Joanne Meyerowitz takes us inside the job to describe what editors, as opposed to academic historians, usually do. From her editor's perch, she concluded that the much-discussed "fragmentation" of American history is a "myth." She also discusses the digital landscape's impact on journal publication, what initiatives she pioneered, and what might lie ahead.

The current editor, Edward Linenthal, muses on his connections with his predecessors and the *JAH*'s move into its second century.

In Part IV, the book moves away from research and editing to teaching. Gary Nash calls attention to what has been seen as a serious shortcoming over much of the first century of the MVAH and OAH: their neglect of the quality of history teaching in the schools. He goes on to note recent efforts to strengthen contact and cooperation among history educators of different levels.

Ron Briley shows that soon after its establishment, the MVHA expressed interest in the teaching of American history but then paid little attention to history in the schools until 1937 when a "Teachers' Section" was added to the

MVHR. It survived, however, only to 1949. By then, Briley concludes, the MVHA saw itself as a researchers' club separated from teachers of history in the schools.

Marjorie Bingham hones in on what she calls "the new era" of the OAH when history teaching became a central concern. She looks closely at one sign of change: the Focus on Teaching Day, arguing that it emerged from both a reform movement to encourage academically sound and creative history teaching and the OAH leadership's desire to recruit a new pool of members.

Charles Zappia discusses what he designates "the purest teaching institutions in the world of higher education: the community colleges." A professor in one of those colleges, he narrates the inclusion of these teachers in the early 1990s and efforts by the OAH, beginning at the end of that decade, to break down walls between community college historians and other members of the historical profession.

Timothy Thurber reviews the OAH's transformation from "a primarily scholarly organization to a more broadly-based professional body that views teaching as central to its mission." The evidence offered includes the OAH's establishment of the *Magazine of History* in 1985, its heavy involvement in the Teaching American History Grant Program, begun in 2001, and the pedagogical materials it provides in the *JAH* and on the Web site.

In a broad review of how American history has been taught, Leon Litwack blames historians for the low quality of history classroom education taught during World War II and much of the Cold War, He sees improvements with the rise of new histories, beginning in the 1960s. Deploring the present-day attack on the public schools, he calls upon the OAH to join in a battle for equality in educational opportunities.

In the 1970s, a new name was given to long-established ways of practicing history. The name was public history, which referred to the wide scope of historical work done outside of academic venues, and Part V devotes four chapters to it.

Spencer Crew explores the "clash of values" between academic and public historians. He defines the similarities and differences between them and the reasons for the formation of separate organizations for public historians and suggests that the American Historical Association (AHA) responded more positively to the challenge from public historians than the OAH has until recently.

Employees of the federal government have been doing historical work since 1861 and have facilitated historical work in countless ways. Academic historians, Donald Ritchie reminds us, have dominated the MVHA-OAH over nearly its entire lifetime. The marginalization of federal historians for many years led to the formation in 1979 of the Society for History in the Federal Government. The OAH soon began to better accommodate these historians, and at the end of its first century chose one of them to serve as its president.

An academic participant in the public history movement, Otis Graham, discusses the pioneering public history program at the University of California, Santa Barbara, where the term was coined and the National Council on Public History was founded. He offers a complex interpretation of the relations between the OAH and the movement, suggesting that, beginning in the late 1970s, the OAH often reached out to the public historians and made some progress. He also comments that many academics need to pay more attention to what public historians can offer.

Marla Miller challenges the very idea that a great divide separates "public" from "conventional" historians. She blames institutional factors for the gaps that do exist but writes that the OAH "has maintained an ongoing (if sometimes comparatively marginal) interest in public history issues over its entire hundred year history." She urges historians to focus on the "common ground" that unites them "because the crisis that faces the discipline is shared by all of us." The crisis she sees is a widespread neglect of history, based upon doubts about the value of historical study.

In the book's final part, several former presidents reflect on their experiences with the MVHA-OAH and testify to the diversity among the historians elected to the office. Richard White, the first to do so, expresses his admiration for his predecessors, recalling them as historians who had influenced him and "whose thinking about the American past had burst the bounds of the academy and influenced popular culture." Richard Leopold charts the changes in the annual meetings, beginning in 1938, indicating that he did not always equate change with progress. Carl Degler recalls the differences between the MVHA and the OAH, including the great difference in the size of the annual meetings, and plots some of the organizational and intellectual changes, such as the establishment of the program of Distinguished Lecturers. Anne Scott, the third woman to serve, recalls her presidency as a "crisis ridden year" and wonders why the OAH has never confronted the question of criteria for its presidents. Grading her performance a B-, she ends with advice and a warning for her successors.

Leon Litwack writes with enthusiasm of his annual meeting in 1987. A unique event, it began with an opening session that featured Pete Seeger and emphasized the importance of music in understanding the diversity of expression in America and ended, Litwack writes, with "hundreds of historians . . . rockin' and rollin' to the finest R&B and Rock n' Roll—on tape." In his presidential commentary, Eric Foner emphasizes two themes: the expansion during the 1990s of the OAH's public role and "history's sudden emergence as a 'wedge issue' in the so-called culture wars." David Montgomery, who served in 2000, provides a richly detailed and peopled account of an unusual annual meeting, held in St. Louis, when the OAH and a hotel chain clashed over charges of racial discrimination by the chain against African American patrons.

He compares the episode with the decision during the 1950s against holding a meeting in New Orleans. This time, all OAH business was rapidly moved out of the headquarters hotel. The episode was, he concludes, "a lesson in what cooperation can accomplish."

The book ends with comments from the new executive director, Katherine Finley, on present-day challenges and the OAH's responses to them.

The history of the OAH, this book shows us, is a complex and dynamic story that demonstrates a century-long movement toward democracy. The increasing diversity in membership, leadership, and the agenda supports this interpretation, underscoring the recognition of historical participants in the American story who once were largely ignored.

Have the recently recognized participants in American history displaced the people and fields that dominated the earlier life of the MVHA-OAH? Contributors to the book deny there has been that much change. They point out that political and diplomatic history and the elites of politics and foreign relations still populate the pages of the *JAH* and specialists in those fields continue to be prominent in the OAH. Economic history, by contrast, has become weak in this location, a somewhat puzzling development to students of American history who know that the decisions and behaviors of the corporate elite affect the lives of all Americans as well as millions of people elsewhere.

One hundred years and counting, the OAH continues to serve both the historical profession and society's need to understand American history. In its next century, the OAH will respond to ongoing changes in historical scholarship and teaching, and its members will adapt creatively to the forces that impact their writing about the past. Even now, new fields are emerging, including the history of capitalism, which seems likely to enlarge attention to the importance of corporate elites. The new fields are broadening and deepening U.S. history and will become parts of the OAH's future, and as new fields take shape, this group, with its wide responsibilities, will encourage and promote mergers among them and with long-established ways of looking at American history.

Part I

THE INSTITUTIONAL AND POLITICAL HISTORY OF THE MVHA–OAH

1

The Rise of a Modern and Democratic Learned Society

Stanley N. Katz

The Mississippi Valley Historical Association–Organization of American Historians (MVHA–OAH) has played a central role in my life as an historian of the United States for nearly half a century, but the impressive centennial celebrations in 2007 reminded me that I have only been around for the second act of one of the best long-running historical shows in town.

I feel, however, as though I had been recruited to the profession by the founders of the OAH, since my first PhD seminar teacher was Frederick Merk, who was introduced to the then new Mississippi Valley History Association (MVHA) by his mentor, Frederick Jackson Turner. Talk about a heritage! Indeed, the nicest professional compliment I have ever received came from Mr. Merk (his students never called him either "Professor" or "Fred," no matter how long they had known him). When as a Harvard assistant professor I went to tell Mr. Merk that I had been appointed an assistant professor at the University of Wisconsin (from whence came both Merk and Turner), he beamed and said, "Stan, the wheel has come full circle." I probably should have retired right then, since it couldn't get any better than that.

For Turner, Merk, and me the center of the universe was somewhere within walking distance of the Mississippi River—I had been raised in Chicago and Merk just north of Madison, and we thought that the University of Wisconsin was the Center of Historical Inquiry about the United States. Certainly there were other fine institutions, but still . . .

Indeed our organization was not called the Mississippi Valley Historical Association for nothing. As Michael Kammen's essay points out, the initial call was for "improved communication and cooperation among state historical agencies located between the Appalachian Mountains and the Rockies. Emphasis would always be placed upon the space defined by three great rivers: the Ohio, the Mississippi, and the Missouri." There are some important truths hidden here. The first is that the OAH was originally founded to bring together public historical societies, agencies that were invisible to the more highly privatized cultural and educational life of the northeastern part of the United States. These societies were central educational and research institutions in the Midwest, however, and their drive to associate has contributed a lasting sense of public mission to the MVHA and the OAH. It must have been the instinct that American history was somehow integral to the intellectual life of interior America, less connected as it was in those days to the rest of the world (and especially to Europe). The original instinct was also related to the mission of the historical societies to build major collections of historical source materials—and for much of its history I would describe the orientation of the MVHA-OAH as quintessentially positivist. Mr. Merk and his peers were what one awed graduate student friend of mine called "fact men."

So the MVHA emerged as a regional effort, but not in reaction to the eastern intellectual bias of the American Historical Association (AHA), though that feeling did emerge after it became clear that the new professional organization was condescended to by the barely older AHA. Still, the OAH has always been careful to see that western history and southern history were given equal pride of place to the Atlantic seaboard region. It was quintessentially the organization of Fredrick Jackson Turner, who dominated its proceedings and consciousness for many years. Although Turner had moved from Wisconsin to Harvard, and then retired to a Cape Cod cottage in Madison, he symbolized the history of the frontier and of the ever-new America. Another early hallmark of the MVHA was its commitment to the teaching of American history at all levels. This was partly a characteristic professional response of the era, and acknowledgment of the responsibility of the professoriate for public education, and partly a characteristic of the sorts of men (they were almost all men, alas) who had gathered around the flag of American history.

The final feature of the early history of the OAH that impresses me was the social interaction and conviviality of the annual meeting—dinners, golf outings, and the like. I can still visualize the large oblong photographs of MVHA dinners at various universities and spas. Each depicted a large room full of round tables around which sat men (and an occasional woman in an evening gown) dressed in black tie, and clearly ready to launch into a substantial feast. I do not have a similar memory of meals at the OAH in the 1960s and thereafter!

In full confession, although I was one of the modernizers, I voted against the change of name from Mississippi Valley Historical Association to Organization of American Historians in 1964, making me one of the 661 reactionaries on the losing end of the vote. The new name is clearly a better description of who we are and what we do, and there is plenty to forget about a fairly small organization composed almost entirely of white males. Still, as a Midwesterner, a refugee from the University of Wisconsin, and a "fact man," I loved the old, more intimate society and its steamboat logo.

During the 1960s and 1970s, the OAH struggled to reinvent the MVHA as a modern and democratic learned society. The OAH grew substantially in membership and budget, and it expanded the range of its activities beyond the *Journal* and annual meeting, which had been virtually the entirety of its early ambitions. The *Mississippi Valley Historical Review (MVHR)* became the *Journal of American History (JAH)* in 1964 and soon solidified its position as the preeminent serial in the field. Women and African Americans began to assume their rightful roles in the OAH. In short, it grew with the enormous post-Sputnik expansion of the American academy, and the astonishing growth in the number of graduate students and (ultimately) faculty in the American history field. And it saw its opportunities and responsibilities much more broadly than the MVHA, especially with regard to the teaching of U.S. history in the schools. The same was true of outreach to what we now call public history—history as conducted professionally outside the academy—and the OAH gracefully enhanced its range and vision.

Not all the growing pains were painless, however. I remember very well and with considerable anguish the 1976 controversy over the rejection of the proposed seminar by Herbert Aptheker at Yale. A joint committee of the OAH and AHA had reported that the available evidence did not sustain the charge that the Yale historians had acted as they did for political rather than professional reasons, and the OAH Executive Board voted to sustain what I considered at the time a whitewash of Yale's behavior by a vote of 11 to 4. I was one of the four dissenters on the question, and I will never forget the afternoon before the vote on which Ken Stampp and Frank Freidel, two close and valued friends, took Bob Wiebe and myself for a drink to try to convince us that Vann Woodward, Aptheker's leading critic, was, like us, a good old boy, who could not have intended ill. This was of course part of the larger set of tensions that rocked all the major learned societies during the Vietnam War era.

But the major trends of institutional development were (and are) altogether positive. We continued the collaboration with the AHA and other historical and archival organizations. The number of publications expanded, most particularly with the creation of the *Magazine of History*, enabling OAH better to serve history teachers. Internationalization was spearheaded by important reforms of the *Journal* by editor David Thelen and the OAH by president Linda Kerber. But the recent years were also years during which American history became embroiled in the so-called Culture Wars, and one of the important challenges to the national American history society has been to navigate a professionally responsible path through the problems created by the continuing politicization of our national history.

Let me conclude by saying how fortunate the OAH has been over the years in its leadership—the elected presidents (and other officers), the professional executives who have guided our multifold activities, and the *Journal* editors who have created and maintained the most important serial publication on American history in the world. I suppose the success of the OAH is that, while it has become truly national and international, it is still located on the campus of Indiana University in Bloomington, smack in the middle of the Mississippi Valley. That pleases me a lot.

2

The Mississippi Valley Historical Association, 1907–1952

Michael Kammen

At the invitation of Clarence S. Paine, Secretary of the Nebraska State Historical Society, the directors of seven state historical institutions met in Lincoln in October 1907 in order to discuss improved communication and cooperation among state historical agencies located between the Appalachian Mountains and the Rockies, which is how the Mississippi Valley came to be defined geographically for organizational purposes. Emphasis would always be placed upon the space defined by three great rivers: the Ohio, the Mississippi, and the Missouri. States represented at the formative meeting included Minnesota, Iowa, Missouri, Kansas, and Nebraska.[1]

A few in that initial group argued for the organization of a conference of superintendents of state historical societies and directors of historical activities in the Mississippi Valley, but Paine successfully insisted upon the creation of a much more inclusive *association* of anyone interested in the history of the region, regardless of institutional affiliation or academic background. Two months later the group met again in Madison at the State Historical Society, which became an important base of operations in the years ahead.[2] Paine, born in Eden Prairie Township in Minnesota, became Secretary-Treasurer of the new MVHA and served with vigor and efficiency until his death in 1916, whereupon his wife, Clara Paine, succeeded him in that role and served until 1952, when illness and age incapacitated her. Her son, also Clarence, served for one year in an acting capacity, and then James C. Olson took over in 1953. The position (and hence the records) remained based in Lincoln during these early decades.[3]

Word of the new association spread swiftly. By the time the first annual meeting gathered at Lake Minnetonka in June 1908, eighty members had joined. Clarence W. Alvord, one of the initial group, the second president, and managing editor of the *Mississippi Valley Historical Review* for a decade following its inception in 1914, declared, "Here in the extreme north of the Mississippi Valley may be traced the transformation of foreign communities into American." Immigration and Americanization as thematic concerns, however, would not be nearly so central to the organization's mission during its first generation than the promotion of "historical research and the collection and conservation of historical material in these western states."[4]

It is noteworthy that so many of the most prominent early leaders of the MVHA devoted significant effort to building major collections of primary sources for their states and regions. Edward E. Dale established the Western historical research collections at the University of Oklahoma. Theodore Blegen did much on behalf of collection development at the James Ford Bell Library of the University of Minnesota. Tom Clark earned recognition as the "father" of Special Collections and Archives at the University of Kentucky in Lexington. He roamed the state "rescuing priceless documents and papers from decay and destruction." And Elmer Ellis created the Western historical manuscript collection as part of the University of Missouri library.[5]

A top priority for the MVHA continued to be improved connections among state historical agencies and institutions. Consequently many of the earliest leaders were not academics with a university base but top administrators of state historical societies and archives. Special attention to state and local history remained prominent at annual meetings throughout the first half of the twentieth century, along with teachers' meetings and attention to textbook development.[6] Most of the early meetings were held jointly with other groups that were based in or near the venue of the annual gathering. The ninth meeting, held at Nashville in 1916, typically involved joint sessions with the Tennessee Historical Society, the Ohio Valley Historical Association, and the Tennessee History Teachers Association.

It was always my impression—shared by others, I believe—that the MVHA came into being in response to eastern snobbery and professional domination by the AHA and its neglect of Western and Southern history. That is only partially valid and did not really emerge as a *widely* shared sentiment until after the AHA responded suspiciously and quite negatively to the inception of the MVHA. The AHA flatly opposed the creation of a new and independent historical organization, preferring instead that it become a Midwestern branch of the AHA, like the Pacific Coast Branch. Moreover, the AHA wanted to restrict membership in the MVHA to historical societies only. When the founding group rejected that idea out of hand, the AHA refused to cooperate; so in 1909 the two groups did not meet at the same place, as the founders had at Madison in 1907.[7] Although the AHA soon relented, thereafter leaders of the MVHA would bristle at the controlling mindset of the AHA, and tensions flared into the open during the years following 1913, six years after the founding of the MVHA. For an extended period beginning in 1911, however, the MVHA held a one-day gathering in conjunction with the AHA's December meeting.[8]

Starting in 1913, Frederic Bancroft (former librarian of the State Department) and Dr. Dunbar Rowland, head of the Department of Archives and History in Mississippi and an active figure in the MVHA, led a revolt against the leadership of the AHA on the grounds that it maintained excessively tight control as a self-co-opting group.[9] Bancroft, Rowland, and their disgruntled sympathizers, mainly located in the South and West, demanded "means for better eliciting the general opinion" of members and choosing officers. In 1914 they requested a plan "by which the activities, control, and government of the association may be made more liberal and more responsive to the needs of the rapidly increasing membership of the association." That motion lost by a vote of 88 to 31, and precipitated increasing disillusionment on the part of westerners who shared a more democratic ethos and also found it increasingly difficult to attend meetings held in the East immediately following Christmas.[10] Rowland was elected president of the MVHA for 1914–1915, and the tenth annual meeting took place in New Orleans in April 1915. Although the MVHA continued to hold a one-day gathering at the AHA convention for many years, relations between the established association and the newcomer remained uneasy for quite some time.[11]

In the "News and Comments" section of the *MVHR* for September 1915, Alvord wrote, "The July number of the *American Historical Review* contains comparatively little of interest in the field of western history." In his proud announcement of the *MVHR*'s debut issue fifteen months earlier, Alvord had referred to its constituency as "the fraternity of western historians,"[12] which is precisely how the early members envisioned themselves.

Even so, presidential addresses by leaders of the MVHA often quoted from or acknowledged the important work done by leaders of the AHA; and members of the MVHA, with their strong commitment to teaching what they called "modern history," or even "recent history," had a notable, ongoing admiration for the so-called New History advocated by James Harvey Robinson of Columbia. Clarence W. Alvord published an essay in praise of Robinson's New History in 1912.[13] Orin G. Libby, Theodore C. Blegen, and Elmer Ellis, presidents of the MVHA in 1910, 1947, and 1951, respectively, each taught twentieth-century U.S. history and acknowledged Robinson's influence. Because so many members of the MVHA were sympathetic to the Progressive movement, they liked the idea that historical knowledge should be selected, organized, and applied in the interest of social betterment. In May 1922 when the MVHA met in Iowa City, the gathering seemed quite thrilled to hear after-dinner remarks from Robinson himself.[14]

The principal object of anti-eastern antipathy was Harvard's Edward Channing and his multivolume *History of the United States*. Channing openly disapproved of Frederick Jackson Turner's emphasis on the West and the frontier, and referred to the historically significant East with chauvinistic pride as

Cisappalachia. When Channing paid a visit to the University of Wisconsin, he declared that he "was glad to be out in this neck of the woods," which did not go over particularly well in Madison.[15] Members of the MVHA regarded Channing as a hopeless New England provincial. When Clarence W. Alvord wrote the lead review of Channing's fifth volume (covering 1815–1848) for the *MVHR* in 1922, he made several wry remarks about Channing's arch references to Cisappalachia as well as the author's footnote referring readers to works by Turner for "a radically different view."[16] Alvord added that "one vital factor in the development of the west—it is not the only one—is entirely omitted from the volume. The reader will find on consulting the index only two references to the Indians; one is in a note on Indian treaties, which is placed at the end of a chapter, and the other is a short description of California Indians." Alvord made it very clear that for the period from 1815 to 1848, such willful ignorance of Indian policy and activities was inexcusable.[17]

Content analysis of the *MVHR* during the first half of the twentieth century makes abundantly clear that members and contributors had considerable interest in white-Indian contact and Native American history. On the other hand, there is very little evidence of African American history, except for some exceedingly laudatory remarks about the Dunning "school" of writing about Reconstruction, along with considerable praise for Ulrich B. Phillips, the best known apologist for slavery, as a notable democrat because he would speak to *everyone* when traveling to conventions by train and deliberately chose to ride coach.[18] An interest in social history emerged surprisingly early and predates the usual attribution of initiative to Arthur M. Schlesinger and his doctoral students at Harvard during the mid- and later 1930s. As early as 1917 Frederic L. Paxson devoted his presidential address to "The Rise of Sport, 1876–1893," and Paxson (then at Wisconsin, later at Berkeley) was best known as a Turnerian historian of the West. When Solon J. Buck appealed for social history in his 1923 address, he defined it as "the history of the people" and linked it to the study of local communities.[19]

During the early decades of the twentieth century prominent members of the AHA could not agree on whether history was a science or could be pursued in a scientific manner.[20] Clarence W. Alvord, perhaps the single most influential figure during the formative years, received praise for laying the foundation for the production of a "scientific history" of the state of Illinois in conjunction with the 1918 centennial of its admission to the Union. He insisted upon the need for "scientific interpretation" of information concerning state history.[21]

Writing an essay titled "The Science of History" in 1914, however, Alvord sounded far more traditional and circumspect. With both the social and natural sciences in mind, he categorically rejected the notion that history could ever be scientific like the natural sciences. Then, comparing the historian's vocation with that of the sociologist, he warned against generalizing about "universal forces" or seeking to disclose the "laws of social dynamics." He added that "the historian contents himself with disclosing the causal relations of the successive movements in the evolution of human society; but even here the science is subject to important limitations for the use of experiment is impossible." He insisted that history is "not a science of pure induction and never can be," and declared that history is concerned with the particular rather than the general. Therefore, "the limitations of the science of history are very real."[22]

In Solon J. Buck's presidential review of "The Progress and Possibilities of Mississippi Valley History" (1923), he observed that historical societies in the Valley, with one or two exceptions, "were largely antiquarian institutions, performing, it is true, a valuable service for posterity in collecting and preserving some of the materials for the history of their communities, but having little conception of the scientific method in history." He then credited Frederick Jackson Turner with altering that lamentable situation.[23] Explicit discussions of what the "scientific method" and "scientific interpretation" actually entailed were not often articulated; it was assumed that most practitioners understood just what was required: relentless fact-gathering and then objectivity in organizing and analyzing the materials. Peter Novick has succinctly summarized what the scientific method meant to historians at the turn of the century: "Science must be rigidly factual and empirical, shunning hypothesis; the scientific venture was scrupulously neutral on larger questions of end and meaning; and, if systematically pursued, it might ultimately produce a comprehensive, 'definitive' history."[24]

No guessing, no suggesting, no induction. Just the well-ordered facts followed by plausible and sustainable explanations. A few of the MVHA leaders had, after all, received their PhD's during the late nineteenth century from The Johns Hopkins University during the regime of Herbert Baxter Adams, a leading champion of this kind of history.[25]

To move to a discussion of a historian of great influence on the MVHA, I need to call attention to extracts written by two well-known (and oft-quoted) figures in American historical writing. The first is from Alexis de Tocqueville's *Democracy in America* (1840): "The men daily occupying the Mississippi valleys are inferior in every respect to the Americans who inhabit the former boundaries of the Union. And yet they are already having a great influence in its councils and they undertake the government of public affairs before they have learned to govern themselves." Tocqueville then added a reassuring footnote, however: "It is true that this is only a temporary danger. I have no doubt that, with time, society in the West will settle down and become as stable as that on the Atlantic seaboard."[26]

Seventy years later Frederick Jackson Turner, having just decided to leave the University of Wisconsin for Harvard, addressed the third annual meeting of the MVHA, held in Iowa City, on "The Significance of the Mississippi Valley in American History." His assessment was more sweeping, and certainly more sanguine than that of the French visitor who did, after all, reach as far as Green Bay, Wisconsin, in 1832. Turner declared that "the Mississippi Valley has been the especial home of democracy. Born of free land and the pioneer spirit, nurtured in the ideas of the Revolution, and finding free play for these ideas in the freedom of the wilderness, democracy showed itself in the earliest utterances of the men of the Western Waters and it has persisted there."[27]

I cite these two observations not so much to illustrate Tocqueville's partiality to the settled Northeast or Turner's abiding faith in frontier democracy, both of which are familiar, but because democratization and Turner himself would become two of the most prominent motifs of the nascent historical organization. When we examine the published *Proceedings* of the MVHA and then the *MVHR*, no other figure dominates, personally and intellectually, as much as Turner. Many of the early presidents had been his students at Wisconsin and Harvard, including Solon J. Buck (1922–1923), Louise Phelps Kellogg (1930–1931), and Charles H. Ambler (1942–1943). Frederic L. Paxson served the MVHA in that capacity in 1916–1917, and at the annual meeting of the American Historical Association in 1932 he presented a paper titled "A Generation of the Frontier Hypothesis."[28]

In 1939 William O. Lynch of Indiana University devoted his presidential address in Memphis to "The Mississippi Valley and Its History," an elaboration of the Turner thesis with numerous references to staunch American champions of democracy.[29] As late as 1951 when Elmer Ellis of the University of Missouri delivered his presidential address in Cincinnati, "The Profession of Historian," he paid lavish tribute to Turner, who had died in 1932, and mentioned no other scholar by name. Ellis had been an undergraduate student of Orin G. Libby at the University of North Dakota; and Libby, who served as the third president of the MVHA, had been an early Turner disciple and collaborator at Madison. Three other MVHA presidents had also been Turner students: Isaac J. Cox of Northwestern (president in 1913–1914), Joseph Schafer of the State Historical Society of Wisconsin (1926–1927), and Merle Curti, the Turner Professor at the University of Wisconsin (1951–1952).[30]

These connections tell only part of the tale. Turner's influence was ubiquitous and persistent. The eleventh annual meeting took place in the Twin Cities in May 1918, hosted by the Minnesota Historical Society and the University of Minnesota. On Saturday morning, May 10, twenty of Turner's former students gave a breakfast in his honor at the St. Paul Hotel. Later that day Turner gave the dedicatory address, "Middle Western Pioneer Democracy," at the brand new building of the Minnesota Historical Society, and supper was served in its galleries. After that the facility was open for inspection.[31]

Lavish kudos for Turner appear hither and yon throughout the first forty-five years of the *Proceedings* and the *Review*,[32] but the most engaging narrative in praise of Turner—indeed, a wry idealization—appears in a memoir written by Edward Everett Dale of Oklahoma, who served as president of the MVHA in 1936–1937. His address for that meeting, called "The Cow Country in Transition," dealt with the Great Plains. Six years later, however, he published in the *Review* a memoir of going to Harvard as a greenhorn in 1913 to take an MA degree with Turner and eventually returning intermittently from Oklahoma to complete the PhD between 1916 and 1922.[33]

Turner had a summer cottage in the tiny village of Hancock, Maine, where his prime obsession was fishing rather than scholarship. In the summer of 1918 Dale returned to Cambridge to work on his dissertation and decided that he needed consultation with his mentor. He proceeded to Hancock, unannounced, and when he arrived the Turners had no choice but to greet him cordially. They even invited him to dinner the next evening. When Dale reappeared, Turner became apologetic, explaining that he had been fishing and had some flounders in the icebox. But he had forgotten that it was the maid's day off, so they would have to go to a hotel for dinner. Let Dale tell the rest of the tale:

> This prompted me to offer a suggestion. I said, "Professor Turner, the first lesson which a cowboy learns is that he has two choices: he can either cook or starve. I have always preferred to cook, so if you would like to have flounders for supper it will be a pleasure to go into the kitchen and fry them and prepare supper."
>
> Turner's face brightened. "Let's do it!" he said. "I think it would be fun." I repaired to the kitchen, donned an apron which Mrs. Turner provided, and proceeded to make a pan of biscuits—praying all the time that my hand had not lost its cunning—and to fry the flounders. They were all dressed and ready for cooking, and required only to be salted a little and rolled in flour and dropped in the skillet of sizzling hot fat. It was war time, and the Turner cupboard was a bit scanty on lard, but there was enough to do. Good fortune was with me. The biscuits came out of the oven light and flaky, and their rich brown color matched that of the fried flounders. I also made a pot of coffee and, with the addition of jelly and pickles, we sat down to a real feast.
>
> Turner was apparently in high spirits. When Mrs. Turner expressed regret that it was Mary Ann's afternoon out and, in consequence, the guest had to cook his own supper, Turner exclaimed, "I am glad she's gone. Mary Ann in her palmiest days never fried flounders or made biscuits like these!"

Dale ended up staying at Hancock Point for more than a week and met with Turner every day except one when Dale crossed over to Mount Desert to visit Bar Harbor and climb the mountains behind it. Although Dale depicts himself as a naïve cowboy totally out of his element in New England, when he successfully defended his dissertation in 1922, his committee consisted of Turner, Albert Bushnell Hart, Charles McIlwain, and Charles Homer Haskins, a fairly formidable group. Like so many other historians of his generation, he was a Turner disciple first and last. Late in his career he presented a paper at the annual meeting of the MVHA in 1947 titled "Two Mississippi Valley Frontiers."[34]

Teaching history at all levels became a major priority of the annual meeting from the outset, and two traditions emerged early: joint meetings with organizations devoted to teaching; and special sessions set aside to discuss new developments and possible innovations in teaching history, social studies, and civics. This seems all the more noteworthy because Article 2 in the MVHA constitution did not mention teaching. It simply declared that "The object of the Association shall be to promote historical study and research and to secure cooperation between the historical societies and the departments of history of the Mississippi Valley."[35] In 1947 the MVHR discontinued its Teachers' Section,[36] but in subsequent years the commitment to sessions devoted to teaching remained a standard element of the annual meeting, usually reserved for Saturdays when secondary school teachers were most likely to attend.[37]

Due to the tireless letter-writing campaigns of Clarence S. Paine, the founding secretary, membership climbed from 7 in 1907 to 80 at the first annual meeting, then to nearly 600 by 1910, and 1,213 in 1914 but fell to 840 in 1923. The early years were financially precarious because individuals often joined nominally but failed to pay their dues, which initially were one dollar per year. A major fund-raising campaign had to be undertaken to launch the MVHR in 1914, and generous support from the University of Illinois essentially made it possible. Membership eventually reached 1,600 individuals by the years following World War II but then leveled off for more than a decade.[38]

The executive committee tried its best to vary the venues for the annual meeting, though in the early years it was dependent on organizations and universities to extend invitations to host the gatherings and provide hospitality, which ran the gamut from meals to sightseeing. In 1915 when the meeting took place in New Orleans, members coming from the north were met at Memphis and traveled together to Jackson, Mississippi where they were the guests of Dr. and Mrs. Dunbar Rowland. On the return trip from the Crescent City, many made visits to Natchez and Vicksburg. The 1925 meeting in Detroit included a trip to the Clements Library at the University of Michigan as well as an invitation to Dearborn to view the Americana collections of Henry Ford and tour his River Rouge plant. I have found no commentary on how the historians got along with Henry Ford, or vice versa.[39]

Despite the desire for diversity and opportunities to see unfamiliar historic sites, certain venues were most accessible and provided the widest range of collaborative institutions. St. Louis hosted meetings four times between 1909 and 1944, and Chicago four times between 1911 and 1952. Minneapolis/St. Paul,

Madison, and New Orleans each had three, followed by two visits to Iowa City, Cincinnati, Lexington, Oklahoma City, and Lincoln. Certain universities exercised an unusual degree of influence because of their distinguished reputations and close ties with the state historical societies. Madison, Wisconsin, would become pre-eminent in this respect because of Turner's legacy and the presence for periods of time of Paxson, Libby, Hicks, plus Milo M. Quaife and Joseph Shafer at the Historical Society.

Opportunities for social interaction and conviviality supply us with some amusing glimpses into the ways that members liked to wind down following a day of serious sessions. (It should be noted, however, that this was also true of the AHA, especially during its early decades.)[40] At New Orleans in 1915 a reception was scheduled for the Library at Tulane, but "this reception proved so interesting that the evening program was entirely dispensed with, partly owing to the fact that the principal speaker of the evening, General John Lee Webster, was unable to be present."[41] Five years later the organization would meet in Greencastle, Indiana, hosted by DePauw University and Purdue. A possible visit to the Tippecanoe battleground is mentioned in the *MVHR*'s call, but we also learn that the Greencastle golf club "has generously offered free use of its course to visiting members who care to play, and automobiles will be provided to carry players to the links, 'after the afternoon meetings,' the chairman is careful to specify."[42]

My favorite account concerns the twenty-third annual meeting, held at Chattanooga in the spring of 1930. Many members had never been there before, so the superb vista from Lookout Mountain and the nearby Civil War battle sites became major attractions. According to future president W.O. Lynch, the annual dinner took place on Thursday evening:

> At this banquet no one was required to wrestle with a serious thought. The weighty problems that have troubled older historical investigators for many years and which younger men now attack as if their very existence had never before been discovered—these were ignored or forgotten. E. E. Dale of Oklahoma University, the chairman on this occasion, measured up to his responsibility. From his ample stock of humorous (and really new) stories, he supplied the company present with a few of his best which were received with evident appreciation.[43]

There were also many serious moments at the annual meetings, however. For illustrations, I would include three presidential addresses: "The Blundering Generation" by James G. Randall of Illinois, a Lincoln scholar, delivered at Omaha on May 2, 1940, and suggesting that wars could be avoided; Clarence E. Carter's "The United States and Documentary History Publication" (April 1938), a progenitor for those concerned about the National Historical Publications and Records Commission (NHPRC); and "The Democratic Theme in American Historical Literature," given by Merle Curti in Chicago on April 18, 1952. Curti's talk was symptomatic of a motif that runs through so many discussions and concerns that characterized the initial decades of the MVHA: the democratic impulse in American society, politics, and culture.[44]

Presentations at the annual meetings were not ordinarily political in tone, but several notable exceptions stand out. Arthur C. Cole taught at four universities (ranging from Illinois to Brooklyn College), served the MVHA as managing editor of the *Review* from 1931 to 1940, and as president in 1940–1941. His politics were libertarian, he was active in the ACLU, and he wrote positively about the abolitionists during the 1920s and 1930s when doing so was very unfashionable.[45] Dwight L. Dumond, who served as president in 1948–1949, was quite impassioned on behalf of the abolitionists, and concluded his presidential address on April 15, 1949, by condemning political apathy among the young and the repression of activism on behalf of social justice. His particular provocation at that time was the requirement of state loyalty oaths for teachers, and he singled out Wisconsin and Minnesota with praise for resisting the nationwide epidemic. Dumond flourished in the role of historian as moral critic. As he declared near the end of his address: "Free inquiry and discussion is so outraged by Teacher Oath laws and circumscribed by the rules and regulations of boards, regents, and administrators, that the interest of students in public questions and their ability to make sound judgments are almost completely paralyzed. This is a matter of grave concern."[46]

That 1949 meeting, which took place in Madison, had a special format because the program committee decided to have a theme that would represent the new global challenges and responsibilities that arose in the wake of World War II. They chose "The Mississippi Valley: Its Changing Relations with the Nation and the World" and sessions were organized accordingly. In addition, the University of Wisconsin's Committee on the Study of American Civilization arranged for a major symposium on regionalism to be held in conjunction with the MVHA. The American Civilization group and its chosen topic was also a sign of the times because 1949 would mark the birth of the American Studies Association and its new journal, *American Quarterly*. Appeals for new approaches to the cultural history of the United States had been heard intermittently throughout the 1940s, and they reached a crescendo in 1949. The convention held at Madison enjoyed the largest attendance in the history of the Association during the first half of the twentieth century: 530 registered members, 200 wives [sic], local historians, teachers, and nonregistered members.[47]

Two major issues that became divisive in nature emerged quite early in the MVHA's history. Both have long since been resolved, though not in ways that might have been envisioned a century ago.

Between 1909 and 1914, especially, Benjamin F. Shambaugh, one of the founding members and superintendent of the State Historical Society of Iowa, made an appeal for what he called applied history. He admired and sought to enhance the "application of scientific knowledge in the practical affairs of men and communities." Believing that "knowledge of the past throws light on the present and the future," he wanted to make historical information systematically available to legislators and others so that they could make wiser policy decisions and write well-informed laws.[48]

Clarence Alvord listened at the second annual meeting of the MVHA in 1909 when Shambaugh presented a paper urging his colleagues to consider seriously his recommendations. In 1915 Alvord, former president and then managing editor of the newly born *Review*, wrote an extended editorial undermining any notion of applied history by oddly ignoring or distorting the basic rationale that Shambaugh had offered. He lamented that journalists and social scientists,

> in urging the alteration of existing social or political institutions, have too often referred with an air of finality to the supposed lessons of certain isolated parts of past history. More than a few of them have openly avowed and many more in their manner of writing history have implied, that the key to human history is to be found in some single principle—in economic environment, or in psychological analysis of the heroes of the past.[49]

After launching an attack on monocausal explanations in historical inquiry, and pleading that the past be studied for its own sake, Alvord asserted his basic point: "the trained historian of the present . . . is conscious that in approaching the past he endeavors to strip himself of all preconceptions and prejudices inherent or acquired." Like Richard Hofstadter half a century later,[50] Alvord appealed for a deeper sense of complexity in historical explanation:

> while the shortness of time and the vastness of the material to be mastered sometimes compels him to separate a single factor from the rest, he tries never to forget that in studying it apart he is merely preparing for a complete reconstruction of the whole in which each factor shall bear its proper relation to the rest.[51]

Alvord became so concerned about popularized and present-minded misuses of history that he ended up misconstruing what Shambaugh had envisioned, so that these two pioneering figures in the Association's formative years essentially talked past one another. Although Alvord made some clearly unexceptionable points, what Shambaugh had in mind seems to have anticipated at least *some* aspects of what we today call public history. Shambaugh's basic goal seems to have been historically informed policy decisions and legislation. Like James Harvey Robinson, whose *New History* he so admired, Shambaugh viewed history as an agency for social betterment.[52]

Alvord's concern about the distortion of historical knowledge for simplistic purposes of popularization connects to the other early controversy that divided the founders. When they met initially in Lincoln and then Madison for organizational purposes late in 1907, Clarence Paine and others intended to reach and influence a broad and democratized audience. Consequently, collecting documents, writing scholarly works, but also *popularizing* the past were proposed as the central mission of the MVHA. Alvord successfully insisted that the phrase "and popularize" be deleted from the mandate and, therefore, from the constitution of the organization. Although the name of John Fiske was not explicitly mentioned, that independent author of numerous widely read histories of the United States was surely a prime exemplar of just what Alvord wanted serious professionals to avoid. In addition to commanding a very broad audience, Fiske (1842–1901) was a Social Darwinist who believed that generalized scientific laws could be derived from historical knowledge.[53]

Yet Solon J. Buck, almost as influential as Alvord, and his successor as managing editor of the *Review*, called for special attention to local history because of its wide appeal. In his presidential address in 1923 Buck declared that "another method of reaching the people in large numbers, of interesting them in history, and of giving them some smattering of useful or entertaining information is the publication of historical material in the newspapers." He pleaded for "varied programs including scholarly papers, popular addresses, discussions of historical work, and entertainment features if the public is to be attracted."[54]

Those words largely fell upon deaf ears. For decades to come, members of the MVHA would pursue scholarship and teaching but largely ignore the lay public. In Theodore Blegen's presidential address in 1944 he lamented that "too many scholars, engulfed by their specialization, seem to write mainly if not only for their long-suffering colleagues, yet curiously cherish the hope that the public will buy their books,"[55] anticipating the frequent and highly vocal appeals of our own time.[56] Clarence Paine and Solon J. Buck would feel vindicated. How intriguing it would be if we could have a verbatim account of the intense discussion that took place a century ago at the Nebraska State Historical Society, and then following Buck's address at the ninth annual meeting, held in Oklahoma City on March 29, 1923. Applied history has become a meaningful reality, and history for Everyman does happen, though not so often, still, as some of us might like.

Having invoked an extract from Tocqueville's *Democracy in America*, I find it appropriate to conclude with one. Early in his first volume (1835) he wrote the following:

> At the end of the last century, bold pioneers began to penetrate the valleys of the Mississippi, which was akin to a new discovery of America. Soon the bulk of emigrants moved there and unknown societies rose from the desert. States whose names had not even existed a few years before lined up with the states of the American Union and, in the West, democracy reached the extremes of its development.[57]

That last sentence, but especially its concluding clause, anticipated the single most pervasive motif at the annual meetings and in publications by MVHA members during its first forty-five years: that the apogee of American democracy developed historically in the trans-Appalachian West.

NOTES

1. *Mississippi Valley Historical Review* (*MVHR*) 10 (Sept. 1923): 111–12. For detailed and engaging accounts of the founding and early years, see James L. Sellers, "Before We Were Members—the MVHA," *MVHR* 40 (June 1955): 3–24, and especially Ian Tyrrell, "Public at the Creation: Place, Memory, and Historical Practice in the Mississippi Valley Historical Association, 1907–1950," *Journal of American History* 94 (June 2007): 19–46. Tyrrell's admirable essay overlaps with this one in some respects, but there are also some significantly different emphases. Tyrrell regards the widely accepted geographical definition of the region as "tendentious" (25) for reasons that remain unclear.

2. *MVHR* 10 (Sept. 1923): 111–12; Theodore C. Blegen, "Our Widening Province," *MVHR* 31 (June 1944): 3.

3. *MVHR* 4 (June 1917): 137–38; *MVHR* 10 (Sept. 1923): 112.

4. Both quotations in Blegen, "Our Widening Province," 4.

5. See John E. Kleber, ed., *Thomas D. Clark of Kentucky: An Uncommon Life in the Commonwealth* (Lexington: University Press of Kentucky, 2003), 6–7; Theodore C. Blegen, "A Glorious Court," in *Book Collecting and Scholarship*, by Theodore C. Blegen et al., 3–23 (Minneapolis: University of Minnesota Press, 1954).

6. See Solon J. Buck, "The Progress and Possibilities of Mississippi Valley History," *MVHR* 10 (June 1923): 5–20.

7. John R. Wunder, "The Founding Years of the OAH," *OAH Newsletter* 34 (Nov. 2006): 6.

8. See Ellen Fitzpatrick, *History's Memory: Writing America's Past, 1880–1980* (Cambridge, MA: Harvard University Press, 2002), 81.

9. The best accounts will be found in Ray Allen Billington, *Frederick Jackson Turner: Historian, Scholar, Teacher* (New York: Oxford University Press, 1973), 337–43, and Allan G. Bogue, *Frederick Jackson Turner: Strange Roads Going Down* (Norman: University of Oklahoma Press, 1998), 306–19. Bogue suggests that anti-northeastern sentiments predated 1913. See 306, 311.

10. *Annual Report of the American Historical Association for the Year 1913* (Washington, DC, 1914), I, 49; *Annual Report . . . 1914* (Washington, DC, 1916), I, 49–50; *Annual Report . . . 1915* (Washington, DC, 1917), 52–54. See John D. Hicks, *My Life with History: An Autobiography* (Lincoln: University of Nebraska Press, 1968), 313.

11. See Herbert A. Kellar, "The Historian and Life," *MVHR* 34 (June 1947): 26. By 1913 objections began to be raised that the "best" papers presented at the annual meeting of the MVHA ended up in the *American Historical Review* rather than in the *Proceedings* of the MVHA. See *Proceedings* 6 (1913): 43.

12. *MVHR* 2 (Sept. 1915): 304; ibid., 1 (June 1914): 157.

13. Alvord, "The New History," *The Nation* 94 (May 9, 1912): 385–90. The tradition of having a presidential address at the annual meeting seems to have begun in 1916. Prior to that, the presidents simply presented papers as part of regular sessions.

14. See Lester B. Shippee, "A Voice Crying," *MVHR* 22 (June 1935): 8–15; Luther V. Hendricks, *James Harvey Robinson: Teacher of History* (New York: King's Crown Press, 1946), 20; *MVHR* 9 (Mar. 1923): 109.

15. Late in 1910, just after Turner moved from Wisconsin to Harvard, Reuben Gold Thwaites wrote Turner a bemused letter from Madison referring to it as "this neck of the woods"! Quoted in Richard Hofstadter, *The Progressive Historians: Turner, Beard, Parrington* (New York: Alfred A. Knopf, 1968), 80.

16. Early in his career, while still at Wisconsin, Turner had written a very critical review of Channing's U.S. history textbook for schools. Channing never forgave him. See Billington, *Frederick Jackson Turner*, 177–78.

17. Kellar, "The Historian and Life," 24–25; Alvord's review in MVHR 8 (Mar. 1922): 377–80.

18. Kellar, "The Historian and Life," 12–13.

19. Paxson, "The Rise of Sport, 1876–1893," MVHR 4 (Sept. 1917): 143–68; Buck, "The Progress and Possibilities of Mississippi Valley History," MVHR 10 (June 1923): 6.

20. See Herman Ausubel, *Historians and Their Craft: A Study of the Presidential Addresses of the American Historical Association, 1884–1945* (New York: Columbia University Press, 1950), chs. 6 and 7, esp. 219; Deborah L. Haines, "Scientific History as a Teaching Method: The Formative Years," *Journal of American History* 63 (Mar. 1977): 892–912.

21. Solon J. Buck, "Clarence Walworth Alvord, Historian," MVHR 15 (Dec. 1928): 311, 314, 316.

22. Alvord, "The Science of History," *Popular Science Monthly* 84 (May 1914): 490–99.

23. Buck, "The Progress and Possibilities of Mississippi Valley History," 5–6.

24. Novick, *That Noble Dream: The "Objectivity Question" and the American Historical Profession* (New York: Cambridge University Press, 1988), 33–37, the quotation at 37.

25. James A. Woodburn (1856–1943), president of the MVHA in 1925–1926, received his PhD at Hopkins in 1890, and Beverly W. Bond, president in 1930–1931, earned his PhD at Hopkins in 1905. Frederick Jackson Turner received his PhD from Hopkins in 1889.

26. Alexis de Tocqueville, *Democracy in America*, trans. Gerald E. Bevan, ed. Isaac Kramnick (New York: Penguin, 2003), 442–43.

27. Fredrick J. Turner, *The Frontier in American History* (New York: Henry Holt, 1953), 190. The address was given at 8 P.M. on Thursday, May 26, 1910. It was not a presidential address. In fact, in 1910 Turner served as president of the American Historical Association.

28. Paxson, "A Generation of the Frontier Hypothesis," *Pacific Historical Review* 2 (Mar. 1933): 34–51.

29. Lynch, "The Mississippi Valley and Its History," MVHR 26 (June 1939): 3–20. See also Arthur C. Cole, "The Passing of the Frontier," MVHR 5 (Dec. 1918): 288–312. In a retrospective content analysis of the MVHR in 1957, John W. Caughey declared that Turner was "absent" from the *Review* during its first four decades. That is hardly correct. His influence was frequently felt. Caughey, "Under Our Strange Device: A Review of the 'Review,'" MVHR 44 (Dec. 1957): 520. The first "personal" notice ever to appear in the *Review* announced that Turner planned to retire from Harvard in 1924 and quoted him as saying, "I hope to do some writing when I end my teaching." MVHR 10 (Sept. 1923): 205.

30. Elmer Ellis, "The Profession of Historian," MVHR 38 (June 1951): 3–20; Gilbert C. Fite, ed., *Elmer Ellis: Teacher, Scholar, and Administrator* (Columbia: University of Missouri Press, 1961), 19–22, 24–27. See John R. Wunder, ed., *Historians of the American Frontier: A Bio-Bibliographical Sourcebook* (Westport, CT: Greenwood, 1988).

31. *Proceedings of the MVHA* 9 (1919): 346; *MVHR* 5 (June 1918): 113. At the MVHA dinner held in conjunction with the AHA annual meeting in 1920, Turner received lavish praise. He was persuaded to address the group afterward on his "early flirtations with western history." Two hundred fifty people appeared rather than the thirty or so for whom he had prepared informal remarks!

32. See, e.g., Solon J. Buck, "The Progress and Possibilities of Mississippi Valley History," *MVHR* 10 (June 1923): 6.

33. "Memories of Frederick Jackson Turner," *MVHR* 30 (Dec. 1943): 339–58. The first major revisionist essay to offer an alternative vision to Turner's began in a politely deferential way. See Arthur M. Schlesinger, "The City in American Civilization," *MVHR* 27 (June 1940): 43–66.

34. Edward Everett Dale, "Memories of Frederick Jackson Turner" is reprinted in *Frontier Historian: The Life and Work of Edward Everett Dale*, ed. Arrell M. Gibson (Norman: University of Oklahoma Press, 1975), the quotation at 342–43. "Two Mississippi Valley Frontiers" appears in ibid., 72–99.

35. It should be noted that in 1907 the founders took the constitution of the Pacific Coast Branch of the AHA as their model!

36. See Novick, *That Noble Dream*, 368; Caughey, "Under Our Strange Device," 521.

37. See Elmer Ellis, "The Profession of Historian," 8, 20.

38. The *Review* became the *Journal of American History* in June 1964, the month I received my PhD. In 1938 the *MVHR* added a subtitle: *A Journal of American History*.

39. *MVHR* 12 (Sept. 1925): 261.

40. See Rebecca Conard, *Benjamin Shambaugh and the Intellectual Foundations of Public History* (Iowa City: University of Iowa Press, 2002), 1.

41. *Proceedings of the MVHA* 8 (1914–1915): 30.

42. *MVHR* 6 (Mar. 1920): 601.

43. *MVHR* 17 (Sept. 1930): 305.

44. Curti, "The Democratic Theme in American Historical Literature," *MVHR* 39 (June 1952): 3–28. See also Herbert A. Kellar, "The Historian and Life," *MVHR* 34 (June 1947): 26–27.

45. See Hans Trefousse, ed., *Toward a New View of America: Essays in Honor of Arthur C. Cole* (New York: Burt Franklin, 1977), vi–viii.

46. Dwight L. Dumond, "The Mississippi Valley of Decision," *MVHR* 36 (June 1949): 24–25.

47. Ray A. Billington, "The Forty-Second Annual Meeting of the Mississippi Valley Historical Association," *MVHR* 36 (Sept. 1949): 283–300; the attendance at 284.

48. Benjamin Shambaugh, "Applied History," *Proceedings of the MVHA for the Year 1908–1909*, II (Cedar Rapids, IA, 1910), 137–38. See also Shambaugh's pamphlet, *Applied History* (Iowa City, 1912).

49. [Alvord], "News and Comments," *MVHR* 2 (Sept. 1915): 303.

50. See Hofstadter, *Progressive Historians*, 442.

51. [Alvord], "News and Comments," 304. In 1968 Hofstadter observed that "an engaging and moving simplicity, accessible to the casual reader of history, has given way to a new awareness of the multiplicity of forces," a striking echo of Alvord. Quoted in *Progressive Historians*, 442.

52. Shambaugh, *Applied History*, 10–12; and see Conard, *Shambaugh*. Although Shambaugh taught frontier history at the University of Iowa, he was actually a member

of the Political Science Department there. During the late nineteenth century, leading scholars at Johns Hopkins University believed that national progress demanded instruction in history and public affairs in order to achieve social and political reform. Shambaugh surely was aware of that movement. See Raymond J. Cunningham, "Scientia Pro Patria: Herbert Baxter Adams and Mugwump Academic Reform at Johns Hopkins, 1876–1901," *Prospects* 15 (1990): 109–44.

53. Sellers, "Before We Were Members," 8; Milton Berman, *John Fiske: The Evolution of a Popularizer* (Cambridge, MA: Harvard University Press, 1961), 209–12, 218–19.

54. Buck, "Progress and Possibilities of Mississippi Valley History," 16–17. For an expansive emphasis on this trend, see Ian Tyrrell, *Historians in Public: The Practice of American History, 1890–1970* (Chicago: University of Chicago Press, 2005).

55. See Sellers, "Before We Were Members—the MVHA," 21–22; Blegen, "Our Widening Province," 18.

56. See, for example, Joyce Appleby, "The Power of History," in Appleby, *A Restless Past: History and the American Public* (Lanham, MD: Rowman & Littlefield, 2005), 133–51. For this and related matters, see the valuable book by Tyrrell, *Historians in Public*, esp. 1–8, 171, 219–21.

57. Tocqueville, *Democracy in America*, 64.

3

From the MVHA to the OAH, 1951–1981

Richard S. Kirkendall

For the MVHA–OAH, the 1960s and 1970s were years of transformation, not least in name. What had been only an association became an organization, and while the association's name suggested it was only regional in scope, the new name proclaimed that it was truly national. By the late 1960s, the Organization of American Historians (OAH) was much larger than the Mississippi Valley Historical Association (MVHA) had been only a few years before. Furthermore, during the 1970s, two groups of historians—women and African Americans—became more actively involved and influential than they had been in the days of the MVHA, and the OAH, while continuing to emphasize scholarship, paid more attention than before to two closely linked issues: the status of history in American life and schools, and jobs for historians.

Before the transformation began, the MVHA was small in size and in the scope of its activities. It had approximately 2,500 individual members and institutional subscribers in 1951. The annual budget for the early 1950s included income of only $16,000, most of it from dues and subscriptions, and disbursements of $14,000, nearly all of it for the printing of *The Mississippi Valley Historical Review*.[1] The MVHA devoted itself to two major activities: publishing the *Review* and holding the annual meeting. Although the content of both ranged over the whole of American history, all meetings were held in the Valley, no farther east than Pittsburgh, never west of Denver.[2] The *Review* devoted most of its pages to articles and reviews. The annual meeting, which attracted 400 to 700 historians each year during the 1950s, offered twenty to thirty events, chiefly sessions focused on scholarly papers.[3]

For most of the 1950s, the annual meetings flowed smoothly. The business meetings dealt with such issues as the National Park Service's efforts on behalf of historical sites and the welfare of the National Archives, for which resolutions of support passed easily. Concerns of the larger society, such as the Red Scare, penetrated the business meetings, but the historians present spoke out about them, as in the California Oath Controversy, only when such concerns directly impacted the lives of their professional colleagues. On one occasion, the Executive Committee praised its chairman for having "met exceptionally troubled times with . . . the realization that an association of historians should be primarily an association of scholars."[4]

Occasionally, the meetings did not go as planned. The business meeting in 1951 included a heated debate over the meeting site for the following year. New Orleans had been chosen, but there, hotels discriminated against African Americans. Incoming president Merle Curti announced that he would not give his address in a hotel that discriminated, and the debaters shifted the meeting to Chicago. After that, the MVHA held a racially integrated meeting in Lexington, Kentucky in 1953, and then, in 1955, the Executive Committee decided to meet only in places that guaranteed there would be no discrimination.[5]

Two political leaders also troubled the waters. In St. Louis in 1955, a dinner speaker, President Harry S. Truman, failed to show up, provoking the city's *Post-Dispatch* to assert that the former president had "stood up his best friends" and forcing members to seek compensation in a "smoker" in the Anheuser-Busch Rathskeller. Later in the decade, Senator John F. Kennedy backed out, causing the MVHA to cancel a dinner and raising doubts about the desirability of putting prominent politicians on the program.[6]

Inside the MVHA, a power structure of several parts made the big decisions.[7] An Executive Committee, with wide ranging authority, including the selection of the secretary-treasurer and the editor, consisted of the president, the vice president, the secretary-treasurer, the editor, six former presidents, and nine elected members. The editor selected the nine members of the Editorial Board; he and his board chose the articles for the *Review*, and he selected the books for review and the reviewers. Members of a Nominating Committee nominated the president, the vice president, candidates for the elected positions, and its own successors, and the vice president chose the members of the committee that developed the program for the annual meeting.

In 1955, reformers persuaded the Executive Committee and the business meeting to revise the constitution. In addition to reducing the number of ex-presidents on the Executive Committee, the revisions required the Nominating Committee to solicit suggestions from the members and to put forward two or more candidates for open positions on the Executive and Nominating Committees, and the revisions shifted these elections from the business meeting to the membership via a mail ballot. The Nominating Committee continued to choose only one person for the vice presidency; the vice president continued to be the person nominated as the next president, and the business meeting continued to elect these two officers, the president and the vice president, although sixty or more members of the MVHA could, by petition, challenge the Nominating Committee's choices.[8]

Men—white men, academic men—dominated this structure during the 1950s and on into the 1960s.[9] With one exception, the presidents from Elmer Ellis and Merle Curti at the beginning of the 1950s to Avery O. Craven and John W. Caughey in the mid-1960s fit this definition. The exception was Ray Allen Billington, who had recently moved from Northwestern University to the Huntington Library. The three editors during this period—Wendell Holmes Stephenson, William C. Binkley, and Oscar Winther—were also academic men, as were nearly all members of the Executive Committee, the Editorial Board, and the Nominating and Program committees.

Only a small number of women occupied positions in the governing structure. Two women—Jeannette Nichols and Bessie Pierce—did serve three-year terms on the Executive Committee during the first half of the 1950s, but no women succeeded them for many years; only three served on the Nominating Committee, the Editorial Board, and the Program Committee during the 1950s; none did during the early 1960s.

The presence of African Americans in the MVHA was even smaller. Only one—John Hope Franklin—served in the governing structure. He held positions on the Executive Committee, the Editorial Board, and the Program Committee in the late 1950s and early 1960s.

Two historians from outside the academic world—James C. Olson and William D. Aeschbacher—served as secretary-treasurer. The director of the Nebraska State Historical Society, Olson held the part-time MVHA job from 1953 to 1956, and Aeschbacher did so for a decade (1956–1966) while directing the Nebraska Society and then the Eisenhower Library. A few other nonacademic historians occupied positions on the Executive Committee, the Editorial Board, and the Nominating Committee.

The academics knew that historians outside the colleges and universities were doing important work. In his presidential address in 1951, Ellis, a professor at the University of Missouri, called attention to that work and predicted a steady expansion of opportunities for historians in historical societies, government agencies, and business corporations, as well as in higher education. The *Review* publicized the development of the territorial-papers project by Clarence E. Carter, a historian based in the National Archives, and Richard Leopold of Northwestern University called attention in reviews and an article to the great importance of the *Foreign Relations Series* published by historians in the United States State Department.[10]

By the 1960s, the academic institutions in which most members and nearly all leaders of the Association worked were developing rapidly, and their growth impacted the MVHA quite powerfully. As the colleges and universities expanded, history departments and their graduate and undergraduate enrollments did so as well. That enabled the MVHA to acquire greater resources. The members and subscribers grew from less than 3,500 in 1958 to nearly

7,200 in 1964; attendance at the annual meeting exceeded 1,400 that year, and income rose to nearly $57,000 in 1963–1964. Advertising contributed to that increase, because the rapid expansion of higher education stimulated the growth of the publishing industry. Acquiring a much larger market for history textbooks, the publishers sharply increased their purchase of advertising space in the *Review* and the printed program. The MVHA had earned only $1,300 from this source in 1950–1951 but obtained over $12,000 in 1963–1964.

With resources increasing, the MVHA became more ambitious. In 1959, the Executive Committee applied for membership in the American Council of Learned Societies. Three years later, the Program Committee, while keeping the sessions it arranged at nineteen, enlarged the program by inviting other societies to arrange additional sessions, and the response raised the number of regular and joint sessions and meal-time events to thirty-five by 1964. By then, the Executive Committee had established a Committee on the Future.[11]

In this new situation, the members changed the names of their major publication and the society. The issue had come up during World War II when some members called for a name that fitted the MVHA's national scope in both interest and members. The effort failed and did so again in 1951 and 1959, but after that, the pressure for change gained force. The content of the annual meetings and the *Review* testified that most members focused on the nation rather than on the region, as the champions of change, such as Paul Gates of Cornell University and John Caughey of the University of California, Los Angeles, pointed out. Furthermore, New York and California ranked, respectively, first and second in number of members and subscribers, having displaced Illinois, the state that occupied the top position before the late 1950s. Furthermore, most of the presidents from 1956 to 1965, beginning with Edward E. Kirkland of Bowdoin College in Brunswick, Maine, were based outside the Mississippi Valley.[12]

The name changes came in 1964 and 1965. At the end of 1963, the Executive Committee accepted a recommendation from its Committee on the Future to rename the MVHA's major publication *The Journal of American History*. The justification offered was "an awareness not only of the growing nationally distributed membership in the Association but a recognition of a decided shift in contributor emphasis from regional to nationally-oriented history." The members agreed in a mail ballot, and the change took effect with the June 1964 issue, the first number of volume fifty one.[13]

Then the focus shifted to the MVHA itself. In April 1964, the Executive Committee accepted another proposal from the Committee on the Future and unanimously recommended a favorable vote on this question: "Shall the name of the Association be changed to Organization of American Historians?" The rationale, presented by the chair of the Executive Committee, Ray Billington, emphasized that the MVHA had "become in effect the national organization of American historians" and noted that, although early on, 83 percent of the articles in the *Review* "dealt with the Mississippi Valley," now only 10 percent "reflect this interest." The old name had, the argument maintained, become "increasingly outmoded," had "handicapped the Association's expansion," and had "stigmatized" it with various people "as a regional society undeserving of rank among national scholarly bodies." The voters agreed by a large margin—2,595 to 661—and the change began on the final day of the 1965 meeting in Kansas City. Four years later, the OAH began to hold meetings outside the Valley and also became a member of the American Council of Learned Societies. Advocates of a new name had promised that it would elevate the group's status.[14]

For several years, the OAH functioned much as the MVHA had. Men, most of them white and academic, continued to run things. During its first five years, only two nonacademic historians served on what was now called the Executive Board; only one on the Editorial Board; one on the Program Committee. No women served in any of the four major places, and John Hope Franklin was the only African American who held a position in them.

In 1966, nonacademic historians lost an important position when Aeschbacher moved from the Eisenhower Library to the University of Utah and took the post of secretary-treasurer with him. Soon after he left Utah in 1968 to become chair of the history department at the University of Cincinnati, his job was split into two parts. He continued on as treasurer; Charles Peterson and David Miller of the University of Utah served brief terms as secretary, and then Thomas D. Clark of Indiana University took over as executive secretary on July 1, 1970.

During these years, the OAH continued to prosper and, for a time, to grow. By the end of 1966, it had nearly 12,000 members and subscribers. The 1970 meeting, the first one on the Pacific Coast, attracted about 1,800 historians. Annual income of the OAH increased to over $137,000 late in the decade, in part because of the continuing growth of advertising revenue as advertisers, mainly publishers, purchased space in the *Journal* and the annual meeting program.

In an expansive mood, the OAH developed new committees and enlarged the *Journal (JAH)*. The new committees included ones on both research and teaching and on how the OAH might expand its activities and develop a more effective "administrative governing apparatus."[15] Pressured by what the new editor, Martin Ridge, called a "swelling tide of scholarship," the *JAH* enjoyed sharp increases in manuscript submissions, from 191 in 1964–1965 to 300 four years later, and in books worthy of review. By the end of the decade, the publication had grown from less than 850 pages to more than 1,000.[16]

The OAH also expanded its collaboration with the American Historical Association (AHA). In 1966, a Joint Committee on Textbook Pressures, which had been established earlier to "lessen the pressures for conformity that exist in the textbook field," submitted a strong statement reporting that various groups "demand *their* interpretation of American life" and proclaiming that the "highest commitment of authors, teachers, and publishers is to diffuse historical knowledge in as unbiased form as they are able."[17] At the same time, a Joint Committee for the Defense of the Rights of Historians under the First Amendment rallied successfully to the aid of an author, Sylvester K. Stevens, whose interpretation of Henry Clay Frick had provoked Frick's daughter to sue the historian.[18]

Then, at the end of the decade, the OAH and the AHA established another joint committee. Initially designed to reestablish the National Archives as an independent agency and to improve access to government records, it soon added another goal: better relations between historians and archivists. Those relationships had been damaged by critics of the Franklin D. Roosevelt Library, so the two societies invited the Society of American Archivists to join the Joint Committee on the Historian and the Federal Government, renaming it the Joint Committee on Historians and Archives and later the Joint Committee on Historians and Archivists.[19]

The business meetings remained brief and quiet events. Some members had pressed for bold moves into the political arena, but dominant opinion held that action should be limited to matters of professional concern. In the late 1960s, that opinion regarded speaking out on issues of importance for the National Archives as a much needed and an appropriate political act. Here, the pressing issues concerned restoration of its status as an independent agency and continuation of the archivist of the United States as a nonpolitical appointee.[20]

In 1970, however, a radical caucus demanded that the OAH go much farther, and the business meeting was not brief, not quiet. It ran from midafternoon until midnight with a break for dinner, attendance reached as high as 400, and participants heatedly debated a series of large issues. The caucus had submitted a petition nominating Daniel Yamshon, identified as a graduate student, to run against the Nominating Committee's choice for the vice presidency, Richard Hofstadter. After hearing the challengers call for large-scale changes in the OAH and in historians, the members present voted by written ballot and then turned to a series of resolutions from the group. The first one called upon the OAH to take several steps regarding women historians and women's history, including the appointment of a committee "to deal with matters affecting the status of women in the historical profession," and the members accepted the resolution. After the failure of two resolutions reflecting the left's critique of universities and another advocating the establishment of an OAH "committee to review cases where the academic freedom of teachers and students of history may have been infringed," the majority favored a substitute, calling for reliance on the executive secretary and the American Association of University Professors for action on behalf of academic freedom.

Then, the meeting turned to the most controversial subject: the Vietnam War. The resolution from the caucus called upon the OAH to demand "the immediate withdrawal of all American troops from Vietnam and Southeast Asia, the immediate end of the domestic colonization of black, brown, red, and yellow people, and the release of all political prisoners." An alternate resolution declared that "the OAH as an organization of scholars must not attempt to commit its members on such issues unless they directly concern the teaching and study of history"; it passed, but so did a motion declaring that "we, a majority of the membership present at [an] OAH meeting, oppose American intervention in Vietnam and call for immediate withdrawal of American troops from Vietnam."[21]

In the long run, the proposal for a women's committee was the most significant consequence of the 1970 business meeting. The written ballots elected Richard Hofstadter by a large majority, but cancer deprived him of his opportunity to serve, and the resolutions on the war nullified one another. In contrast, the women's committee quickly became an unusually active group.

Chaired first by Anne Firor Scott, then by Nancy Weiss, and then by D'Ann Campbell, and composed mostly of women, the new committee moved along several lines during its first decade. They included promotion of equal opportunities for women in the OAH and the historical profession and promotion also of research, writing, and teaching on the history of women, including black women. The committee also produced a roster of historians of women, distributed models for part-time appointments and maternity leaves, and developed guidelines for the job-interviewing process at annual meetings. It obtained grants for conferences, including one on the integration of the history of women into history survey courses.[22]

From time to time, the committee called attention to the progress of women in the OAH. The process began in 1970 with the election of Willie Lee Rose to the Executive Board, the first woman chosen for that place in nearly two decades. In the following eight years, eight women followed Rose onto that board. The voters also elected Betty Fladeland to the Nominating Committee in 1971. She became its chair, and from 1974 to 1979, six women were elected to it. Mary Young served a term on the Editorial Board and chaired a Program Committee, and three other women served on that committee. Then, Linda Kerber chaired it for the 1980 meeting; three women worked with her, and three held positions on this committee for 1981.

In 1978, the enlarged importance of women in the OAH encouraged the Executive Board to decide against meeting in states that refused to ratify the Equal Rights Amendment. The state of Missouri challenged the National Organization for Women, arguing that it had championed a boycott and thus violated the antitrust law. Called upon to testify in the case, the executive secretary denied that the OAH was part of a conspiracy and maintained instead that "the decisive consideration was concern about discrimination against women historians."[23]

The African American presence in the OAH also increased during the decade. An early sign was the election of Edgar A. Toppin to the Executive Board in 1971. Mary Frances Berry followed him in 1974; Nathan Huggins did so in 1978. Other evidence of change included Arvarh Strickland's election to the Nominating Board in 1973 and John Bracey's election to it in 1978. In addition, Earl Thorpe, Jimmie Franklin, Mary Berry, John Blassingame, and Darlene Clark Hine served terms on the Program Committee.

During these years, a controversy erupted within the OAH about the qualifications and treatment of a historian of the left. In 1976, petitioners represented by Jesse Lemisch called for an investigation of a claim that the Yale History Department had violated the academic freedom of Herbert Aptheker, a Communist, in denying him an opportunity to teach a student-sponsored seminar on the Yale campus, and members in a mail ballot authorized the OAH to investigate. The Joint Committee on the Defense of the Rights of Historians, composed of the two presidents, the two executive officers, and two other members of the OAH and AHA, worked on the issue for well over a year. They sent letters of inquiry to the participants in the dispute and received helpful responses from a diverse group of people, although the principle of confidentiality limited some responses. The committee concluded that the available evidence did not sustain the charge that the Yale historians acted as they did for political rather than professional reasons. The AHA Council agreed, and the OAH Executive Board concluded, in an eleven-to-four vote, "that on the basis of the data sought by the Committee and made available to it, the Findings are reasonable."

The issue dominated the 1978 business meeting and led to other OAH actions. At the meeting, Mark Naison introduced a resolution arguing that the "inadequacy" of the report "necessitates the appointment of a balanced and representative [OAH] Committee . . . fully empowered to give this and other academic freedom cases the attention they deserve"; Kenneth Stampp, who served on the committee as the OAH president, proposed a substitute, accepting the action of the Executive Board, and it was adopted, sending the issue to the members via a mail ballot. In a low-turnout contest, the voters endorsed the substitute, 272 to 167.

During the following year, the OAH returned to this area of concern. The executive secretary testified in a district court case as an expert witness on behalf of a historian who, after informing his students of his membership in the Progressive Labor Party and of his Communist political beliefs, lost a university position. The Executive Board and the business meeting authorized establishment of an OAH committee to investigate charges about violations of historians' rights.[24]

Elections to the presidency from 1973 to 1981 testified to the OAH's growing diversity. John Hope Franklin moved onto the presidential line in 1973 and became the first African American president in 1974. Two representatives of the left, Eugene Genovese and William Appleman Williams, became presidents: Genovese in 1978 and Williams in 1980. Then, in 1981, Gerda Lerner became the first woman chosen for the office in half a century and only the second in the society's seventy-four years.

Diversity was not the only issue that came to the forefront during the 1970s. Another concerned the teaching of history and grew to include the status of history throughout American life. Over the years, some members had pressed for more attention to teaching and teachers, and for many years, the MVHA had a teachers' section that arranged at least one session for each annual meeting. In 1959, disappointed with the results, the Executive Committee had taken over responsibility for this area. By the end of the 1960s, a Committee on History in the Schools and Colleges had been established, and in the early 1970s, the programs of the annual meetings increased the attention paid to teaching, teacher training, textbooks, and other related matters.[25]

Then, the OAH tried to do more. Thomas D. Clark had taken over as executive secretary in 1970 with authority to make the job a big one. He brought rich experience to the task, including terms as president of the MVHA and chair of its Executive Committee and of the Committee on the Future. The OAH now had, for the first time, its own headquarters and staff, located at Indiana University where the *Journal* had been based for several years. Intending to serve only briefly, he hoped to help the OAH become a more "effective instrument." Although he regarded the promotion of scholarship as the top priority, he called for action in other areas, including the reform of graduate education so that recipients of the PhD would be prepared to hold jobs outside the academy. He also proposed an investigation of history teaching in the schools and colleges, arguing that, to act effectively, the OAH needed more facts than it had. The Executive Board endorsed his proposal.[26]

In the summer of 1973, I succeeded Clark as executive secretary, and during the next two years, I organized a nation-wide fact-gathering ad hoc committee and prepared a report, published in the *JAH* in 1975, on "The Status of History in the Schools." It argued "that history is in crisis and that history's crisis is not merely a part of the large difficulties of academic life at the present time. History's crisis has proportions of its own." According to the report, confidence in history's "usefulness for the individual and for society" and interest in it were "not nearly as widespread and strong among students, educational administrators, and politicians" as they had been only a few years before. The report called upon the profession to face these "facts," develop "solutions," and demonstrate "the value of historical perspective and historical comparisons and the importance of a sense of time and of place."[27]

The OAH followed up on this widely publicized and debated report. The ad hoc committee continued to report on developments around the nation. The Program Committee for the 1976 meeting sought, in the words of its chair, Alden T. Vaughn, to pay more than "lip service to the methods and materials of teaching" and "allotted a sizeable portion of its program to historical pedagogy." The Committee on History in the Schools and Colleges developed plans for a History Education Center to promote collaboration among classroom historians on all levels, experiments in teaching, and the reformation of public attitudes. The executive secretary participated in a variety of efforts, including the growth of History Day from a local to a regional and, then, a national event. A new media committee confidently encouraged historians to make and use films and brought about the establishment of an award for the making of films on American history.[28]

Included in the 1975 report was a call for "action by those who are served well by history as well as those who suffer most severely from its troubles." The latter referred to unemployed historians. A job crisis had emerged early in the decade, threatening the health of the profession as well as the welfare of individuals. Illustrative of the problem, the recently established job registry at the 1973 annual meeting listed 416 job seekers and only 34 jobs. Several forces, including budgetary problems in higher education, produced the crisis and discouraged people from entering graduate programs in history, encouraged others to drop out, and produced a class of unemployed and underemployed professionals.[29]

The OAH had to respond. It had begun to do so as early as 1971 when the Program Committee presented two sessions that recognized the crisis. The next year, Tom Clark reported on the unfavorable imbalance between new PhD historians and job openings in higher education, and he suggested that the profession must seek alternative positions and devise programs to create those positions. Before he left office in 1973, the business meeting passed a resolution, originating with the Midwest Radical Historians Caucus, calling for action on the job crisis by the OAH and the United States Congress. The Executive Board and the new executive secretary followed up in several ways, including the establishment of a Committee on Non-Teaching Opportunities for Historians, chaired by a government historian, Wayne Rasmussen. It hurriedly developed a guide to nonteaching jobs and ways of obtaining them.[30]

The crisis did not go away. At the annual meetings, job seekers continued to far outweigh the number of jobs listed. In 1976, the ratio was 290 to 74. That year, Frank Freidel devoted his presidential address to "the over-production of doctorates, many of whom are unable to find employment in academic institutions or in history-related occupations." A biographer of Franklin Roosevelt,

Freidel was not a pessimist. "The historical profession is in a state of crisis," he proclaimed, "and it is one of our most salutary American traditions in time of crisis to seek new opportunities. . . . Should not this bicentennial year," he asked, "mark the beginning of an enlarged and even more useful role for this nation's historians?" He outlined what needed to be done and called attention to an effort, begun in 1975–1976 by the OAH, the AHA, and other historical organizations, to attack the problem. This was the National Coordinating Committee for the Promotion of History and the Employment of Historians, the NCC.[31]

The NCC hoped to elevate the status of history in American life and expand job opportunities for historians. It employed a full-time director, Arnita Jones, built an elaborate structure consisting of a number of historical societies, resource groups concerned with areas of employment, and state organizations, and collected and disseminated information relevant to its aims. "Both painful adjustments and exciting new directions appear on the professional horizon," Jones observed. "Whether historians face more of the one than the other can be a result of choice as much as circumstance."[32]

Unfortunately, NCC fund-raising did not go well, forcing the committee to turn to the historical organizations in its ranks to provide support out of their own budgets. The OAH began to contribute in 1979, doing so even though it had money problems of its own. Those problems resulted, in part, from the job crisis and the consequent decline in enrollments in graduate programs, for the OAH had depended heavily on graduate students for its new members. From a high of approximately 12,000 members and subscribers in the early 1970s, the total dropped by nearly 1,000 before the end of the decade. Declining library budgets also contributed to the money problems by persuading some libraries to drop their subscriptions to the *JAH*. Still further, advertising by publishers in the *Journal* and the annual program fell off as undergraduate enrollments in history classes, sales of history textbooks, and attendance at the annual meetings declined. Attendance dropped below 1,600 more than once. At the same time, the expenditure side of the budget faced irresistible pressure to rise, some of it coming from the great inflation of the 1970s, some from expanding programs. Illustrative of the latter, the *JAH* moved above 1,350 pages in 1978–1979. The economic difficulties forced the OAH to raise dues more than once and to tap the trust account. Fortunately, an upturn in memberships beginning in 1979 and an increase in dues the next year produced a nearly balanced budget by 1981.[33]

Throughout these difficult years, the OAH tried to narrow the gap between historians working in academic institutions and those employed in other places. The latter represented a still-active job market that academics and their students needed to learn how to tap. The Program Committees organized sessions on such topics as "Non-Teaching Careers in History" and "Placement of

History Graduates, Recruitment of Archivists—Complementary Problems," and it placed more nonacademics on the program than before. Furthermore, several nonacademic historians—Lucille Kane, Richard Brown, Francis Jennings, Glenn Porter, and Morton Sosna—obtained positions on the Program Committee, the Nominating Board, the Executive Board, and the Editorial Board. In 1977, Richard W. Leopold devoted his presidential address to the great importance for historians of several government agencies, and four years later, the OAH established an award named for him and given to a historian employed by a government agency.[34]

Beginning in the mid-1970s, the new OAH *Newsletter* publicized historians who were responding creatively to the job crisis. They included the people who established a historical office in the United States Senate and those who built companies that employed historians to write histories, set up archives, and perform other professional services for business firms and other employers. Some historians featured in the *Newsletter*, including Robert Kelley of the University of California at Santa Barbara, created new graduate programs. Kelley also gave historians working outside the schools, colleges, and universities a new name. He called them public historians. Some historians disliked the term and suggested alternatives, but it caught on inside and outside the OAH.[35]

In spite of these many efforts, the OAH, by the late 1970s, had not yet become as attractive as it needed to be. "We should continue to serve scholarship but should also find ways to make the results of research in American history more useful to other people—to teachers of American history on all levels, to historians in museums and historic preservation programs, to people in the media who are concerned with historical themes, to planners and decision makers in the public and private sectors, to the reading public and other groups," I suggested in 1978. If we would do these things, I assumed, we would solve our membership problem. "Membership in the OAH," I proposed, "should become indispensable to all people with a serious interest in the study of American history."[36]

To at least one public historian, David Clary of the U.S. Forest Service, the efforts by the OAH to reach out appeared woefully inadequate. He wrote a forceful essay for the *Newsletter* in 1979 and spoke out at a business meeting that year, charging that research-oriented historians in the large universities still dominated the OAH and that explained its decline. It treated others, the historians working outside academia and the teachers in the schools and small colleges, as second class, he maintained, and must change its ways to revitalize itself.[37]

For Clary, the recent history of the OAH contained too much continuity, not enough change, and there surely were continuities in that history. Scholarship had always been the top priority, and it continued to be. All the people chosen for the presidency in the 1970s and early 1980s, from David Potter to

Gerda Lerner, had made major contributions as scholars. Scholarship continued to dominate the *Journal* as edited by both Martin Ridge and then Lewis Perry, the programs of the annual meetings, and the several prizes awarded at them. Most resolutions passed at the business meetings concerned such matters as access to government records and the protection and strengthening of research institutions such as the National Archives, the presidential libraries, and the Library of Congress. Furthermore, one OAH-sponsored project sought to give researchers a new tool: a guide to American newspapers. All of this assumed that everything historians did depended on the quality of scholarship the profession produced, and that scholarship was or should be basic to the teaching that historians performed in and out of classrooms and to their other work in public arenas.

Nevertheless, the OAH did respond to Clary's challenge. The business meeting in 1979, although tabling his resolution, endorsed another calling for a committee to study how nonacademic historians could be drawn into the OAH in larger numbers. The new committee, called the Special Committee on Public Historians and composed of three such historians, quickly made a number of recommendations that gained support from the Executive Board. They included the expansion of opportunities within the OAH for historians working outside the academic community and led to the establishment of a permanent Committee on Public History.[38]

There were other signs of a willingness to change. The presidents of 1980–1981—William Appleman Williams and Gerda Lerner—promoted change as well as represented it. Both of them grappled creatively with the job crisis and the money problems, and Lerner offered the members an ambitious agenda.[39] The search in 1980 for a new executive secretary was conducted by two committees, one representing the Indiana University history department, the other, the OAH. The latter committee was composed of five people: one public historian as well as four academics, two women in addition to three men, one African American. They recommended an academic, Joan Hoff, who took on the job in 1981.[40]

In my final report as executive secretary (April 3, 1981), I insisted that "the OAH has earned even more support from American historians and other people with a strong interest in American history," but I admitted that "much remains to be done to make the OAH more useful and fully worthy of its name."[41] Although a large part of the past continued to be a major feature of the present, the OAH had changed in important ways. It had transformed itself in two stages over two decades. In the 1960s, it grew in size and changed its name and the name of its major publication, and in the 1970s, although the growth stopped, it became more diverse in its membership and leadership and gave more attention to some major issues, most notably the status of history in American life and jobs for historians. Throughout the decade, many people in the OAH tried to make it truly *the* Organization of American historians, composed and representative of all historians focused on American history. Much remained to be accomplished, but a start had been made.

NOTES

1. On members, subscribers, and budgets, see the *Mississippi Valley Historical Review* (MVHR), *Journal of American History* (JAH), and *Newsletter* (NL), especially the minutes of the business meetings and the reports of the secretary-treasurer, the treasurer, and the executive secretary.

2. James L. Sellers, "The Semi-Centennial of the Mississippi Valley Historical Association," *MVHR* 44 (Dec. 1957): 516–17.

3. On the annual meetings, see the reports of the chair of the program committee, the secretary-treasurer, and the executive secretary.

4. *MVHR* 42 (Sept. 1955): 401.

5. *MVHR* 38 (June 1951): 154, (Sept. 1951): 367–68, 372–73; 39 (Sept. 1952): 393–95; 40 (Sept. 1953): 309; 41 (Sept. 1954): 389–92, 395; Ray Allen Billington, "From Association to Organization: The OAH in the 'Bad Old Days,'" *JAH* 65 (June 1978): 78–79; Thomas D. Clark, "Our Roots Flourished in the Valley," *JAH* 65 (June 1978): 94, 96.

6. *MVHR* 42 (Sept. 1955): 305, 398; 45 (Sept. 1958): 300–301.

7. On the structure, see "The Constitution," *MVHR* 42 (Sept. 1955): 405.

8. On the reformers, see Billington, "The OAH," 83. The quote is from Sellers, "The Semi-Centennial," 515.

9. On the members of the structure, see the early pages of each issue of the *MVHR* and *JAH* and also the *NL* after it became available in 1973.

10. Elmer Ellis, "The Profession of Historian," *MVHR* 38 (June 1951): 3–20; Clarence Carter, "The Territorial Papers of the United States: A Review and a Commentary," *MVHR* 42 (Dec. 1955): 510–24; Richard Leopold, "*The Foreign Relations Series*: A Centennial Estimate," *MVHR* 49 (Mar. 1963): 595–612.

11. *MVHR* 46 (Sept. 1959): 382; 48 (Mar. 1962): 760–61; 49 (Sept. 1962) 291–92, 405, (Mar. 1963): 747–48; 50 (Sept. 1963): 351; *JAH* 51 (Sept. 1964): 263; 52 (Sept. 1965): 456; 54 (Sept. 1967): 351–52.

12. *MVHR* 38 (Sept. 1951): 365, 370; 39 (Sept. 1952) 390; 40 (June 1953): 23; 41 (Sept. 1954): 289–90, 394; 44 (Mar. 1958): 535; 45 (Sept. 1958): 380–381; 46 (Sept. 1959): 383–84, 386–87, (Mar. 1960): 769–71; 47 (Sept. 1960) 391, (Mar. 1961): 769–71; 49 (Dec. 1962): 402; 50 (Sept. 1963): 353; *JAH* 54 (Sept. 1967: 343, 346–49; 65 (June 1978): 99–100.

13. *MVHA* 50 (June 1963): 170, (Sept. 1963): 350, 351, 352, 354, 357; *JAH* 51 (June 1964): 166, (Sept. 1964): 358–59; 65 (June 1978): 101–2.

14. *JAH* 51 (Sept. 1964): 351–52, 360–61; 52 (Sept. 1965): 339, 456, 459; 54 (Sept. 1967): 339; 57 (Sept. 1970): 510; 63 (Sept. 1976): 507; 64 (June 1977): 21–22, (Sept. 1977): 538.

15. *JAH* 55 (Sept. 1968): 452–53, 460–61; 56 (Sept. 1969): 457.

16. *JAH* 51 (Sept. 1964): 361; 52 (Sept. 1965): 457–59, 468; 54 (Sept. 1967): 485; 56 (Sept. 1969): 462.

17. *MVHR* 48 (Sept. 1961): 378; 49 (Sept. 1962): 399, 403; *JAH* 54 (Mar. 1968): 977–80.

18. *JAH* 52 (Sept. 1965): 461; 53 (Sept. 1966): 441, 667; 54 (Sept. 1967): 478-79, (Dec. 1967): 739; 55 (Sept. 1968): 460.

19. *JAH* 58 (June 1971): 299, (Sept. 1971): 538-39, 542; 60 (Sept. 1973): 551-52, (Dec. 1973): 714; 64 (June 1977): 7, 13, 21-22, (Sept. 1977): 549; 65 (Sept. 1978): 576; *NL* 2 (July 1974): 3-4.

20. *MVHR* 48 (Sept. 1961): 378-79; *JAH* 55 (Sept. 1968): 462; 56 (Sept. 1969): 455-56.

21. "Minutes of the Business Meeting of the Organization of American Historians," April 17, 1970, *JAH* 57 (Sept. 1970): 516-27.

22. *JAH* 58 (Sept. 1971): 542, 554-56; 60 (Sept. 1973): 555, 562; 61 (Sept. 1974): 580, 587; 62 (Sept. 1975): 509; 65 (Sept. 1978): 572; *NL* 2 (July 1974): 4 (Jan. 1975): 4-5; 3 (July 1975): 2, (Jan. 1976): 12; 5 (Jan. 1978): 5; 6 (July 1978): 9, 14, (January 1979): 5, 6; 7 (July 1979): 3, (Jan. 1980): 15; 8 (July 1980): 13-14, (Oct. 1980): 3-4, 14; 9 (July 1981): 23.

23. *JAH* 65 (Sept. 1978): 566; *NL* 6 (Jan. 1979); 7 (July 1979): 3, 6.

24. *JAH* 63 (Sept. 1976): 522; 64 (Sept. 1977): 538-39; 65 (Sept. 1978): 566, 576-80, (Dec. 1978): 873: *NL* 4 (July 1976): 3-6; 5 (Jan. 1978) insert; 6 (July 1978): insert; (Jan. 1979): 1, 5; 7 (July 1979): 2, 3, 6.

25. *JAH* 57 (Sept. 1970): 373-79, 512-13; 58 (Dec. 1971): 696; 60 (Sept. 1973): 388-90, (Dec. 1973) 747-48.

26. *JAH* 57 (Sept. 1970): 509; 58 (Sept. 1971): 537-40, 546-47; 59 (Sept. 1972): 517, 518; 60 (Sept. 1973): 549-51, 553, 561, 565; 61 (Sept. 1974): 576; 65 (June 1978): 105-7.

27. *JAH* 61 (Sept. 1974): 577-78; 62 (Sept. 1975): 509, 557-70; 63 (Sept. 1976): 509.

28. *JAH* 63 (Sept. 1976): 509, 519-20; 64 (Sept. 1977): 537-38, 549, (Mar. 1978): 1186; 65 (Sept. 1978): 565, 576; *NL* 2 (Jan. 1975): 4; 3 (July 1975): 2, (Jan. 1976):5-7; 4 (July 1976): 7-9; 5 (July 1977): 3, 6, 8-9; 6 (July 1978): 9-10, (Jan. 1979): 3, 4, 9; 7 (July 1979): 6, (Jan. 1980): 2-3, 6, 13; 8 (July 1980): 16-17, (Oct. 1980): 8-9; 9 (Jan. 1981): 5, (July 1981): 4-6, 19-24.

29. *JAH* 60 (Sept. 1973): 561; 62 (Sept. 1975): 509, 519; 63 (Sept. 1976): 520, 521.

30. *JAH* 58 (Dec. 1971): 695-96; 59 (Sept. 1972): 517; 60 (Sept. 1973): 556-58; 61 (Sept. 1974): 578-80; 62 (Sept. 1975): 508-9, 511; *NL* 2 (Jan. 1975): 4; 3 (Jan. 1976): 12.

31. Freidel, "American Historians: A Bicentennial Appraisal," *JAH* 63 (June 1976): 5, 20. On the ratio between jobs and job seekers at the 1976 meeting, see *JAH* 63 (Sept. 1976): 515.

32. *JAH* 63 (Sept. 1976): 509; 64 (Sept. 1977): 538, 549-50; 65 (Sept. 1978): 565; *NL* 5 (July 1977): 3, 6-7; 6 (July 1978): 5-7, (Jan. 1979): 7-8, insert; 8 (July 1980): 15, (Oct. 1980): 3; 9 (Jan. 1981): 12-13; (July 1981): 24-25.

33. The pages of the *JAH* and the *NL* from 1973 to 1981 offer abundant testimony on the money problems and the efforts to solve them.

34. Leopold, "The Historian and the Federal Government," *JAH* 64 (June 1977): 5-23; *NL* 9 (July 1981): 5-6.

35. *NL* 3 (Jan. 1976): 7-9; 7 (Jan. 1980) 8, 10-13; 8 (July 1980): 4, 7, (Oct. 1980): 10; 9 (Jan. 1981): 13, (July 1981): 4.

36. *JAH* 65 (Sept. 1978): 567; see also *NL* 7 (July 1979), 6; 9 (July 1981): 11-12.

37. Clary, "The Scope of the Profession," *NL* 6 (Jan. 1979): 8–9; 7 (July 1979): 3–4.
38. *NL* 7 (Jan. 1980): 7–10; 8 (July 1980): 4; 9 (Jan. 1981): 13–14, (July 1981): 4.
39. *NL* 8 (July 1980): 8, (Oct. 1980): 2–3; 9 (July 1981): 3, 7, 14–15, 24.
40. *NL* 9 (January 1981): 10, (July 1981): 1–2.
41. *NL* 9 (July 1981): 13.

4

The OAH in Troublesome Times, 1980–2000

Arnita A. Jones

The history of the Organization of American Historians (OAH) since 1980 offers an extraordinary amount of continuity, even as there has been, inevitably, substantial change. I speak from some experience on this point, for I first became closely acquainted with the OAH more than thirty years ago, in 1977, when I was appointed the staff associate for the National Coordinating Committee for the Promotion of History. Housed at the American Historical Association in Washington, the NCC, as it soon came to be known, was a new, cooperative effort on the part of AHA and OAH, and several other major historical associations to address several problems besetting the historical profession, chief among them the lack of jobs for new PhDs and the sorry state of teaching in the nation's school.

It did not take me long to realize that the problems the NCC was established to address were not new, nor was the fledgling coalition the first effort to address them. History instruction in primary and secondary schools had, for example, been a serious concern of the old MVHA until midcentury. Attacks by Allan Nevins and others in *The New York Times* in 1943 prompted OAH to form a joint committee with AHA and the National Council on Social Studies to defend history, just as criticism of textbooks during the McCarthy era created another round of concern. However, at most, these episodes were passing distractions while the great expansion of higher education in the early postwar decades focused historians' attention further away from the problems of the schools.

By the 1970s, however, under the leadership of Richard Kirkendall, the OAH had begun again to focus serious attention on the problem of history teaching in the schools. A new Committee on the Status of History in the Schools completed a major report in 1975, which drew the attention of many academic historians back to K-12 education. When I began my term as executive secretary at the OAH in 1988 I found that this renewed effort had continued unabated. Along with the AHA and the National Council for Social Studies, the OAH had created the History Teaching Alliance, which sponsored collaborative efforts between precollegiate and university historians to focus on research and teaching, providing a model for today's "Teaching American History" grants now supported by the U.S. Department of Education at $120 million per year. Leaders of the OAH were also active in the Bradley Commission on History Education as well as the National Commission on Social Studies in the Schools, both of which produced influential reports in the late 1980s. The most durable of these efforts, however, and the one most closely connected to scholarship in the field, was initiated by Joan Hoff. She was successful in gaining support from the Rockefeller Foundation to launch the *Magazine of History*, a publication designed to bring new research to K-12 teachers in a form they could readily use in the classroom. The *Magazine* is now in its twenty-first year, has been used by thousands of teachers, and has, I believe, been firmly integrated into the life and work of the OAH.[1]

The story of the OAH and history outside the academy is somewhat similar. Although the founders of the MVHA came from the midwestern historical societies, over the years academic concerns came to dominate. By the late 1970s, though, this pattern had slowly begun to change as public history—a label that covered degree programs, locations of employment for historians, as well as the work that many historians did outside the classroom—came to be a more significant factor within the profession. No one was more supportive of this development than Richard Kirkendall, who made the annual meeting program, the *OAH Newsletter*, and other resources of the OAH accessible to these ideas while he himself actively promoted them. His supportive presence at early assemblies of federal historians meant a great deal to the founders of the Society for History in the Federal Government in 1979 as it did to those from historical societies, consulting groups, and others who established the National Council on Public History in that same year. These relationships continued on through the 1980s under his successor, Joan Hoff, with frequent joint annual meetings between the National Council on Public History (NCPH) and OAH beginning in Los Angeles in 1984.

Strengthening the bond between OAH and public history was the close relationship between the OAH and the National Park Service (NPS), which also began during the mid-1980s. This started with a special grant from the Landmarks Commission for an identification of women's history sites in the parks, and it continued with the involvement of OAH in the development of a thematic framework for history in the parks and, later, in several conferences at NPS park sites, such as Edison National Park, Seneca Falls, and the Booker T. Washington birthplace. Page Miller, who had replaced me at the NCC in 1980, was a key player in some of these efforts, as were congressional staffer and historian Heather Huyck, who provided critical expertise on the U.S. House of Representatives subcommittee on Parks and Public Lands, and Dwight Pitcaithley, who served from 1995 to 2005 as the chief historian of the NPS. Within a few years, the OAH was able to formalize this relationship with an official cooperative agreement that has led to the participation of hundreds of academic scholars in the historical programs of the National Parks, an effort that continues to bear fruit today.

More must be said about the National Coordinating Committee for the Promotion of History, which OAH staunchly supported from its beginnings and which continues to be the OAH's primary advocacy effort. Originally the focus of the NCC was twofold: providing outreach from academia to history professionals in nonacademic jobs and organizing around issues of education in the states. Page Miller, who directed the NCC for twenty years, was able to transform this somewhat scattershot set of initiatives into a highly effective collaborative effort. True, OAH and other history organizations had been taking stands on certain issues of interest to historians over the years—establishment of a National Archives and the National Historical Publications Commission, for example—but the idea of employing a lobbyist was somewhat beyond the pale. In the 1980s, advocacy was embraced, an outcome that would not have happened without the staunch support of OAH leaders.

A turning point came in 1981 when President Ronald Reagan decided to dismantle the National Endowments for the Arts and for the Humanities. Founded in 1965, the NEH had in just a few years become a major source of support for scholarly research and programming in history, and the prospect of its loss galvanized scholars across an array of disciplines. Just as the National Humanities Alliance (OAH did not join until some years later) and the Consortium of Social Science Associations were formed in these years, historians also saw the need to speak up and defend the federal programs critical to their disciplines. Miller, at the nexus of a broad coalition of historical groups, ranging from archivists to state historical societies to small groups representing specialized sub-fields, did not miss the opportunity to enable the NCC to weigh in on critical needs. Chief among these needs, along with assuring the survival of the NEH, were the winning of independence for the National Archives and Records Administration from the General Services Administration in 1984, the establishment of the Advisory Commission for Historical Diplomatic Documentation at the Department of State, and the strengthening of connections between National Park Service professionals and historians in higher education.

The OAH and the historical profession have been fortunate in Miller's successors, first Bruce Craig and now Leland White, both experienced lobbyists with training in history. All have faced the task of addressing a daunting number of issues with modest resources. There is no budget for taking members of

Congress golfing in Scotland, or hiring a public relations company to launch a major ad campaign on behalf of a particular issue. Instead, the members of the OAH, both through their sustained financial support and through their personal participation in the advocacy process, have played and continue to play a major role.

Changes in the profession and changes in the OAH clearly had implications for the structure of the OAH itself. Throughout its lifetime, MVHA was located at the Nebraska Historical Society, which provided administrative support for the small Association. By 1970, it had grown much larger, successfully claimed a national mission, changed its name, and acquired a permanent staff and location for both its journal and executive offices at Indiana University.

These developments were not without growing pains. Tom Clark, who managed the transition to Bloomington in the summer of 1970, wrote to a new president, Edmund Morgan, the next year: "One of the reasons that I consented to accept appointment as Executive Secretary was to develop a degree of efficiency in the operation of this central office, and that I have been able to do. I have had to try and educate the members of the committees and of the Executive Board that the operation of the office is a domain all its own; otherwise we would be in complete chaos. You haven't seen the angry complaints about inefficiency of operation which came in the past."[2] Clark looked forward to the appointment of his successor, but he cautioned John Higham, OAH president in 1973–1974, that, though the relationship with Indiana University was quite satisfactory, it was also delicate, relying on informal understandings rather than carefully vetted contracts. He urged careful planning for the future, noting that his successor's appointment would be similar to his own, that is, split between the OAH and the history department: "the administrative details of this office have become more numerous almost by the month and I do not see anything in the future to indicate that there will be a leveling off."[3] He believed that, if the board wanted the OAH to grow further, it would need to provide additional staff or more time for the executive secretary.

The answer was both. By the middle of the 1970s, the office had grown to five full-time and two part-time staff members, in addition to the executive secretary. It had taken on publication of the *OAH Newsletter* as well as efforts to address growing problems of the historical profession. An infusion of fresh energy in the person of Joan Hoff in 1981, as well as the employment of additional staff during the next several years, allowed not only for maintenance of the many programs members had come to expect from the OAH but the beginning of new ones, including the publication of the *Magazine of History*. With support from the Fund for the Improvement of Postsecondary Education, the OAH also introduced a much needed effort to help departments of history by providing teams of consultants to support their planning and review efforts and by establishing a council of history-department chairs with its own special newsletter. Money was ever tight, and new demands had to be met with efforts to identify new sources of funding. To supplement membership dues and foundation support, the OAH also established a highly successful lectureship series, which continues today. In those years the OAH also raised several hundred thousand dollars to create the Fund for American History, which supports new initiatives in the field.

Joan Hoff's departure from the position of executive secretary in 1989 brought to a head the staffing problems so frankly described by Thomas Clark. Two failed national searches to replace Hoff led the OAH Executive Board in 1991 to form a special committee for reviewing the office of the executive secretary and consider what should be done.[4] In 1993, after serving in an acting capacity for several years, I became the first full-time executive secretary (later executive director) of the OAH, and in 1999, when Lee Formwalt was appointed executive director, the full-time status was retained and the staff had grown substantially since Clark established the Bloomington office.

The 1990s were years of building on the important legacies left by my predecessors. Two of those—the *Magazine of History* and the outreach efforts to public historians—were my highest priorities, not only because we stood to gain members from those communities but also because they offered the prospect of disseminating to a much wider audience the abundantly rich scholarship that a new generation of historians of the United States was producing at that time. The schools and the public history institutions, including museums, historical societies, the national parks, and increasingly film and other media, are the places where millions of citizens find their history, and it seemed to me that the largest national association devoted to the history of the United States was obliged to do its best to connect those institutions with the historical scholarship that our members were producing.

There were several important new initiatives in the 1990s as well. Early in my tenure at OAH, I began to hear from historians in community colleges who felt isolated from their peers in the discipline and who wanted to find a home within the OAH. Larry Levine, President of the OAH in 1993–1994, made the project his own after participating in two special meetings with community-college historians during his presidential year. Levine appointed a task force to work with historians from this rapidly growing sector of higher education by assessing their needs and undertaking a special survey to find ways to more fully include them in the life of the association.[5]

Closely related to the interests and concerns of community-college historians was the problem of the rapidly growing number of historians in part-time teaching positions, most (though not all) working part time, not by choice, and under conditions that limited their accessibility to students and created difficulties for their research and scholarship. This problem was and is endemic to higher education and not one easily amenable to efforts by one or two disciplinary associations. However, the OAH, together with the American Historical Association, the Modern Language Association, the American Political Science Association, and other groups have been able to shine some light on the growth of casual labor in academe and urge departments to do their best to follow "best practices" that have been developed to ameliorate the impact of this situation. Most recently the OAH and AHA have established guidelines for departments about the equitable treatment of part-timers.

The 1990s were also the years of the "internationalization" of the OAH. The first impetus in this direction came from UCLA historian Joyce Appleby, who dropped by my office in Bloomington shortly after being named president-elect of the OAH. She was a woman with a plan. We created a program committee that included historians from outside the United States and made room on the program itself for dozens of scholars from abroad. No sooner had I begun to worry about how we would pay for all this when she volunteered to seek—successfully as it turned out—grants from the MacArthur Foundation, the Marshall Fund, and the United States Information Agency.

At the 1992 annual meeting and during the year that followed, ideas were engendered and connections made that set in motion a larger effort to "internationalize" the OAH. The *Journal of American History*, under the leadership of editor David Thelen, established an international board of contributing editors and began regularly including and reviewing the work of scholars of American history abroad. Appleby, her appetite whetted by the enormously successful meeting in Chicago, went on to launch a successful lobbying campaign to earmark the United States Information Agency budget for the establishment of libraries of American history abroad, that is, libraries that would be located in universities and would contain the best of new books and journals in the field. Linda Kerber, one of her successors as president, established a program for the regular exchange of scholars of American history between the United States and Japan. And from 1997 to 2000, thanks to board member Thomas Bender, the OAH collaborated with the International Center for Advanced Studies at New York University on a series of conferences that culminated in an influential publication on "Rethinking American History in a Global Age."[6]

The 1980s and 1990s were years of growth and solid achievement for the OAH. But they were also years of great frustration and concern. Just as the OAH had become a national organization with a professional staff and an increasingly well-defined mission, something else was happening in American society. History was becoming popular, and the public was finding the exhibits and programs of historical societies, museums, and the national parks increasingly attractive. Agencies that supported this public programming—the National Endowment for the Humanities chief among them, but also major private agencies such as the Rockefeller, Mellon, and Ford Foundations—were concerned that what they supported should reflect research in the disciplines and standards of sound scholarship. At the same time, academic historians were drawn more and more to the possibility of reaching audiences beyond the classroom. Historians and their publics, however, were not always quite ready for each other.

The earliest stage in the "culture wars" focused less on history in particular than on higher education in general. Conservative political commentators Allan Bloom (*Closing of the American Mind*), Charles Sykes (*Profscam*), Roger Kimball (*Tenured Radicals*), and Dinesh D'Souza (*Illiberal Education*) attacked higher education faculty for being politically correct, and NEH chairs William Bennett and Lynne Cheney produced a series of reports critical of both higher education and humanities scholarship. Initially, Cheney exempted the work of museums and historical societies, characterizing these institutions as a parallel school not yet corrupted by politically correct scholarship. That would soon change.

Tensions grew between historians and their audiences in the early 1990s. The much anticipated Columbian quincentenary prompted a debate about whether the nation could or should commemorate the anniversary of Columbus's voyages from a multicultural perspective as opposed to a heroic narrative. Feathers were ruffled but ultimately the weight of scholarship seemed to carry the day on that issue, as was the case with a much criticized exhibit on the "The West as America" in the National Museum of American Art. National Park Service efforts to include up-to-date scholarship at iconic sites, such as Little Big Horn and Pearl Harbor, were also stirring up controversy, as did Colonial Williamsburg when it developed an exhibit depicting a slave auction. But two clashes—the highly publicized repudiation by then NEH chair Lynne Cheney of national history standards developed at the NEH during her tenure there and the Enola Gay controversy that led to the censure of a planned exhibit at the Smithsonian Institution's National Air and Space Museum—pitted scholars of American history against an enraged public, with the OAH squarely in the middle of both.

The Enola Gay museum exhibit's interpretive script reflected the substantial body of scholarship on the end of the Second World War, analyzing choices confronting President Harry Truman as he made the decision to drop the bomb and challenging traditional versions of how many American lives had been saved by avoiding a ground invasion. Not long before the exhibit was ready for public view in 1994, the Air Force Association challenged the Smithsonian's plans and launched a public attack against the exhibit, charging that it was politically correct, revisionist, and biased. Editorial writers and commentators around the country repeated these complaints for months so that, eventually, the U.S. Senate condemned the exhibit and it was withdrawn. During this time, the curators and administrators at the museum who had developed the exhibit asked the OAH for help and we tried to provide it, with informal advice as well as efforts to place before the public information about the soundness of the scholarship involved in its development. We put together a last-minute session on the exhibit and the controversy swirling around it, which subsequently became the basis of a special issue of the *Journal of American History*, and the OAH executive board also published a formal resolution of support. Eventually the controversy died down, but the Enola Gay remains on exhibit at the Smithsonian, a lone relic, with no historical interpretation of the events and decisions that it symbolizes.[7]

One of my most vivid memories from the mid-1990s was arriving in an Albuquerque hotel to join a meeting of the OAH Executive Board and finding our president, Gary Nash, stunned, reading from a column by Lynne Cheney that had just appeared in the *Wall Street Journal*. She had resigned her NEH position soon after the 1992 presidential election, and in that column she launched a pre-emptive strike on the soon-to-be-released history standards, castigating them as politically correct and pursuing a revisionist agenda. Admitting that she had signed off on an earlier grant to the National Center for History in the Schools at UCLA to begin preparation of the standards, Cheney claimed that the 1992 elections had "unleashed the forces of political correctness" and urged those who shared her view to oppose their certification. Nash, who directed the UCLA Center and the Standards project, had worked closely with Cheney and her staff at NEH to develop them, and now, understandably felt betrayed.[8]

As a matter of fact, the OAH had warmed to the idea of national standards only slowly. I had served, for example, in the early 1990s on the steering committee to develop the history framework for the National Assessment for Educational Progress (NAEP), but because members of the executive board were wary of federal government interference in what had been largely a state and local matter, I found it necessary to consult regularly with them and make it clear that my signing on to the final document was contingent on executive board approval. The NAEP assessment planning was contentious. I can remember one meeting that began with the moderator's admonishing the group to "leave your guns at the door," but, ultimately, it was successful. Still, the OAH board remained wary of the national standards project and was won over mainly by the high quality of work that Nash's center had done, as well as the potential of significantly improving precollegiate history education.[9]

In our efforts to defend the standards, however, we soon learned that we were poorly prepared to enter this kind of national debate. Our attempts to place op-ed pieces were in vain whereas Cheney's columns were reprinted in newspapers all over the country, as others took up her cause. Talk-show host Rush Limbaugh proposed that the standards be flushed down the toilet, and George Will complained that the standards miniaturized great men. In January of 1995 the U.S. Senate condemned the standards by a vote of ninety-nine to one.

The media furor eventually died down and was replaced by more reasonable coverage. Frank Rich's *New York Times* article, "Eating Her Offspring," in February of 1995 seemed to make a difference, as did the detailed *CQ Researcher* analysis by Kenneth Jost and his colleagues that appeared in September of 1995. Michael Kammen, who succeeded Nash as president of the OAH, secured a grant from the Rockefeller Foundation that allowed the OAH to make small grants to a number of history departments that were willing to work with educators and others in their states on implementing the standards. A revised version of the history standards were eventually salvaged by a commission convened by the Council on Basic Education and ultimately became the template for dozens of state history standards and curricula over the next few years.[10]

Here is another memory, this one from 1995: I was waiting in the U.S. Senate chamber for the confirmation hearing of John Carlin, former governor of Kansas, dairy farmer, and crony of President Bill Clinton, whose nomination to the post of Archivist of the United States had been opposed by the OAH and other history groups. We argued that this nomination violated the legislation establishing the Archives, which required a professional historian or archivist to be appointed to the post. In his introductory remarks, Carlin's home state Senator Robert Dole, then Senate Majority leader, acknowledged our opposition but dismissed it with the quip that "history is too important to be left to the historians." Later that day, John Carlin was unanimously confirmed by the senate as Archivist of the United States.

In the final analysis I firmly believe that historians have not and will not accept Senator Dole's judgment. The OAH and the historical profession weathered the culture wars and learned how better to explain what we do and why it is important. Members of the OAH did not draw back from participation in the public arena and have continued enthusiastically to work with teachers in the schools and present their work to public audiences. The OAH has seated itself firmly in the mainstream of these developments, even as it continues to foster, through its publications and recognition of excellence, the creation of new scholarship. I hope that all this work continues far into the future.

NOTES

1. Michael Regoli, "What a Difference Fifteen Years Makes," *OAH Magazine of History* 15 (Fall 2000).
2. Clark to Morgan, October 25, 1971, OAH Archives.
3. Clark to Higham, March 22, 1973, OAH Archives.
4. "Report of the Committee to Review the Office of the Executive Secretary," *OAH Newsletter* 20 (Nov. 1992): special supplement.

5. Charles A. Zappia, "Improving History Teaching and the Status of the Community College Historian," in *Community College Historians in the United States*, ed. Nadine Ishitani Hata (Bloomington, IN: Organization of American Historians, 1999).

6. Thomas Bender, *La Pietra Report* (Bloomington, IN: Organization of American Historians, 2000).

7. An excellent brief account of the controversy is Tony Capaccio and Uday Mohan, "Missing the Target: How the Media Mishandled the Smithsonian Enola Gay Controversy," *American Journalism Review* (July/August 1995): 19–26.

8. Lynne Cheney, "The End of History," *Wall Street Journal*, October 20, 1994.

9. Arnita A. Jones, "Our Stake in the History Standards," *Chronicle of Higher Education* (January 6, 1995): B 1–3.

10. Frank Rich, "Eating Her Offspring," *New York Times*, February 26, 1995; Kenneth Jost, "Teaching History," *CQ Researcher* 5 (Sept. 29, 1995): 849–72. For further accounts of the controversy, see Arnita A. Jones, "National Standards and Testing: A Challenge for U.S. Historians," *Council of Chairs Newsletter* 27/28 (August/October 1992); Gary Nash, Charlotte Crabtree and Ross E. Dunn, *History on Trial* (New York: Alfred A. Knopf, 1997), and Linda Symcox, *Whose History? The Struggle for National Standards in American History* (New York: Teachers College Press, 2002).

5

One Hundred Years of History
Extraordinary Change, Persistent Challenges

William H. Chafe

Chapters 2 to 4 eloquently testify to the courage, persistence, and vision of the Organization of American Historians from a small offshoot of the American Historical Association in 1907 to the largest organization of teachers and scholars of United States history in the world today.

Appropriately, all segments of the organization's history, from the Mississippi Valley Historical Association's early days to the issues confronting the contemporary Organization of American Historians, reflect a series of abiding tensions that suggest continuity as much as discontinuity over fundamental issues: Who do we, as an historical organization, represent? Is our role to be an elite assemblage of scholars from a narrow band of research universities or an inclusive body of practitioners of American history, ranging from high school and community college teachers to state and local archivists, military, state department, and national park service historians, as well as members of history departments at liberal arts colleges and universities? Should our professional standard of conduct be one of seeking scientific detachment and objectivity, or one of engaged advocacy for issues and constituencies that we see as important in advancing the principles of a democratic society? In some ways, these questions seem like a summary of the last decade's most pressing controversies. However, as each of these pieces shows, they actually represent challenges that have confronted historians of the United States for the entire century of our organization's existence.

Michael Kammen discusses the consistent issue of whether the MVHA should identify itself on a continuing basis by its difference from, and antipathy toward the AHA, and by its intention to be a "fraternity of western historians." Clearly, the role of Frederick Jackson Turner was pivotal to the latter question, and the experience some MVHA members had with Eastern condescension, especially from Harvard, continually reinforced the former instinct.

A second large issue was the dispute between MVHA leader Clarence Alvord's single-minded insistence on the need for a scientific interpretation of information in various state histories, on the one hand, and Turner's focus on the Mississippi Valley and the West more generally as "the special home of democracy." Although it might be possible to argue that there was no inherent contradiction between seeking objectivity and praising democracy, the reality was that these were two very different approaches to historical analysis, one consistent with a generation of progressive historians, the other with those focused on more detailed local histories.

A third and final issue was whether the MVHA would dwell on the scholarly findings of research scholars or broaden its reach to include all those who were interested in teaching history and developing innovative approaches to social studies, and those who practiced what would soon come to be called, however awkwardly, as public history.

As Kammen shows, these issues were never resolved definitively. The organization for most of its first half century remained small and still geographically focused. Increasingly, the MVHA spoke out on issues of free speech and public policy and seemed to lean more decisively toward the idea of a link existing between studying history and working for social betterment. The MVHA remained distinctly a white male club with a limited membership, but it was moving in a direction that would change all that.

Richard Kirkendall carries this story forward, tracing the emergence of the OAH, chronicling the burst of membership and support for the new organization that saw its constituency vault from a little more than 3,000 in 1957 to almost 12,000 a decade later. He makes abundantly clear that the major shift in the period from 1951 to 1981 was the much belated recognition of women and blacks in the organization's ranks and leadership. All this, in turn, reflected the turbulent history of the 1960s and 1970s when black history and women's history became defining priorities for a generation of graduate students, in the process helping to transform dramatically the writing and teaching of American history. In historical organizations generally, but especially in the OAH, this shift resulted in substantive differences in how programs at the annual meetings were developed, who was elected to the executive board and the leadership of the organization, and how actively and publicly the OAH took on an advocacy role on national issues of race and gender. During the period since 1981, those who, in the past, had been systematically excluded from leadership roles in the OAH became among its most prominent leaders, with many of the white males who came to occupy the presidency having scholarly interests that focused specifically on issues of gender and race.

The tensions between the AHA and the MVHR/OAH gave way to a new era of cooperation, particularly in the creation of new organizations such as the National Coordinating Committee for the Promotion of History (NCC).

Historians resisted pressures to make textbooks conform to preconceived political orthodoxy, worked to improve access to public records, created a Joint Committee on Historians and Archivists, and with increasing frequency, entered the political arena. By 1970, the annual meeting became a hotbed of activism, with competing resolutions on the Vietnam War, and a decisive breakthrough on endorsing action to achieve "equitable representation of women historians" in the OAH, as well as to "encourage research and instruction on the history of women in America." More and more women and blacks served in leadership positions, the OAH joined the boycott of convention sites in states that had not ratified the ERA, and issues of academic freedom often occupied a primary place on executive-board and business-meeting agendas. The organization's office grew in size, with the executive secretary assuming larger and larger responsibilities.

One of the ongoing issues of both the MVHA and the OAH remains a challenge: how to make teaching a more central focus of historians, and, just as important, how to generate bridges between those who taught American history to the largest numbers of people—high school teachers and community college instructors—and the scholars at universities and colleges who were writing most of the American history books. The 1970s were also the years when academic jobs for newly minted PhD's became scarce. Significantly, increasing attention went to jobs in what became amorphously called public history. New graduate programs emerged to train such public historians, and the OAH began to acknowledge the fact that it had not done an adequate job of reaching out to "teachers of American history on all levels, to historians in museums and historic preservation programs, to people in the media who are concerned with historical themes, to planners and decision makers in the public and private sectors."

Not surprisingly, as Arnita Jones documents in her essay on the two decades since 1980, these issues have continued to be a salient presence in the OAH. K-12 teaching, community colleges, the effort to improve the teaching of American history at all levels all became focal points for the OAH in these years. Simultaneously, internationalization became a primary concern, with David Thelen and Tom Bender providing decisive leadership in broadening the outreach of the OAH to historians of America who lived in other countries and cultures. Development of the *Magazine of American History* provided a critical vehicle for extending the insights and pedagogical experiences of OAH members to a constituency of teachers across the country at all levels. Under Larry Levine, a task force on community colleges highlighted the urgent need to expand the OAH's outreach to that constituency, and during my term as president, provision was made to restructure the executive board so that both community college and high school teachers would be represented in the organization's decision-making structure.

The "culture wars" of the 1990s made casualties of historians who had carefully worked on developing new standards for helping to teach history in the nation's schools; the historians were demeaning great men and exalting radical insurgencies, the critics said. In the meantime, museum exhibits like the Enola Gay came under attack for raising issues about the deliberations surrounding the decision to drop the atom bomb. Clearly, by now, the OAH was a fully engaged participant in issues of critical national import. Long gone were the initial divisions within the Mississippi Valley Historical Association over scientific history as opposed to engaged advocacy.

It is reassuring that the same important issues keep resurfacing. Who are we as historians? What is our role? Are we an inclusive organization that cares about all those who teach American history, or are we just professors at elite universities and colleges? And what does all this have to do with our definition as an institution and as a community? With the history recounted here as a guide, we can engage the current manifestations of these age-old questions with some sense of being part of a tradition of leadership and vision.

Early Leaders

Clarence Paine: the founder and the first secretary-treasurer (1907–1916).

Clarence Alvord: a founder, a president (1908–1909), and the first editor of the *Review* (1914–1923).

Clara S. Paine: the secretary-treasurer (1916–1952).

Louise P. Kellogg: the first woman president (1930–1931).

Reformers

Merle Curti: the president (1951–1952) who challenged racial segregation and is now recognized by book awards named for him in both intellectual and social history.

Thomas D. Clark: a president (1956–1957), a reformer, and the first executive secretary (1970–1973).

Paul W. Gates: a president (1961–1962) and an early champion of the change from a regional to a national name.

Ray Allen Billington: a president (1962–1963) and the leading promoter of the name change of 1965.

Representatives of a New Order

John Hope Franklin: the first African American president (1974–1975).

Joan Hoff: the first woman to serve as executive secretary (1981–1989).

Gerda Lerner: the second woman to serve as president (1981–1982); founder of the OAH Distinguished Lectureship Program, she is now recognized by the Lerner-Scott Prize in women's history.

Representatives of a New Order (continued)

Mary Frances Berry: the first African American woman to serve as president (1990–1991),

Joanne Meyerowitz: the first woman to serve as editor of the *JAH* (1999–2004).

Vicki L. Ruiz: the first Hispanic American president (2005–2006).

Part II

THE MVHA–OAH AND THE FIELDS OF HISTORY

6

The Most Appropriate Subjects for Study

William E. Leuchtenburg

The scholars who gathered at Lincoln, Nebraska, in 1907 to found the Mississippi Valley Historical Association would have considered political history, diplomatic history, economic history, and military history as, self-evidently, the most appropriate subjects for study. If they did not all fully believe that history is past politics, they assumed something much like that.

The very first issue of the *Mississippi Valley Historical Review* (MVHR) (June 1914) devoted two of its four articles to diplomatic history (including "Louisiana as a Factor in American Diplomacy"), and the first volume also found room for a political history piece ("The South and the Right of Secession in the Early Fifties") as well as a military history document ("William Clark's Journal of General Wayne's Campaign"). Economic history appeared as early as the first number of the second volume of the *MVHR* (June 1915) with an essay, "The Methods and Operations of the Scioto Group of Speculators." Consequently, the planning committee for the sessions on fields of history for the 2007 OAH convention never had a moment's doubts that these subjects belonged in a centennial program.

Yet, if some fanciful time-space vehicle contrived by Jules Verne (who had died only two years before the 1907 meeting) had transported the founders to the Minneapolis convention of 2007, they would have been disoriented. The change of the organization's name would probably have troubled them least, for "Mississippi Valley" embraces a huge expanse of the United States. One of the first MVHA meetings I spoke at was held in Pittsburgh. Many years later, I gave the opening address in Denver. And both Pittsburgh and Denver are in the Valley. Furthermore, though the name "Mississippi Valley Historical Association" suggests an affinity with provincial county antiquarian societies in Great Britain, the founders were nationalist enough in their interests to have been able to accommodate to the rubric of Organization of American Historians.

They would have found more disconcerting the content of the sessions. That was not caused by just the emergence of new fields (they could not have imagined in 1907 that historians would one day be engaged in "Queer Studies"), but also the broadened conception of traditional subjects, in good part because the world had changed so much over the course of a century. The political historian in 2007 wrote at a time when the national state had magnified exponentially. The economic historian assessed Gross Domestic Product in an era when the United States had become the mightiest economic power on earth. And, in contrast to an earlier period when the American army was smaller than that of Greece or Bulgaria, the military historian pursued his craft with acute awareness of the mammoth Pentagon and of a nuclear arsenal.

Much, though, would have been familiar to the visitors. Historians still wrote about political parties and elections, Congress and the Supreme Court, and a series of biographies of every one of the American presidents was well under way. Even William Henry Harrison and Millard Fillmore would get their due. Improbably, a biography of crusty John Adams had become a best-seller. Economic historians continued to mull over longstanding problems such as the nature of the business cycle. Military history was taught less than in past generations, but millions of Americans had recently sat enthralled before their television sets, night after night, watching a megadocumentary on the Civil War.

In sum, in this part of our book, the scholars called upon to contribute to a centennial history confront the challenge of delineating in a few pages the many and diverse currents in their specialties from the dawn of the twentieth century in the Edwardian era to the opening decade of a new millennium.

7

The Persistence of Political History

James T. Patterson

I accept a broad definition of political history that includes writing, not only about national politics and policy making, but also about state and local politics, political thought, political institutions, voting behavior, political movements, and many studies in legal and constitutional history. As Mark Leff observed in 1995, political history concerns the "development and impact of governmental institutions, along with the proximate influences on their actions."[1]

Using this broad definition, what can we say about political history when we look at the activities of the Mississippi Valley Historical Association/Organization of American Historians over the past 100 years? I will begin with a few impressionistic findings based on my surveying of movers and shakers in the organization over the years. Until well into the 1940s, the editors and presidents were likely to be men whose main interests were in western, midwestern, southern, and regional history. The frontier thesis exerted a strong influence. Every editor but one through 1978 (eleven in all, ending with Martin Ridge) was a specialist either in western (mostly midwestern) or regional (state) history. The one exception was a national political historian, Arthur Cole (1930–1941). This trend was broken only with the appointment of Lewis Perry in 1978.

Turning to presidents, we discover a similar pattern. Between 1907 and 1947, twenty-three of the MVHA's forty-one presidents specialized in frontier-related or regional/local history. I would classify fifteen other presidents as political historians, and three as specializing in diplomatic history during these forty-one years. Although these categories are unavoidably crude, one can say that all but a few of these presidents worked primarily in the fields of regional and/or political history. Regional/frontier historians, moreover, remained prominent for a good many years thereafter, with eleven of the next eighteen MVHA presidents so classifiable. Thus, of the first fifty-nine presidents, thirty-four fall into this broad category.

National political history, insofar as the MVHA presidency was concerned, was shut out between 1947 and 1964. But it then surged to the fore. During the 22 years between 1965 and 1986, nine presidents were political historians and four more were diplomatic historians. In 1965 the MVHA went national and became the OAH.

Since 1986, not one OAH president might be classified as primarily a national political or diplomatic historian. (Here, there is surely room for argument. These presidents include Eric Foner, William Chafe, Gary Nash, Joyce Appleby, and Linda Kerber, all of whom have written political history.) What *has* changed considerably over time is the emphasis (again, looking at presidents) on black-white race relations in recent years. Prior to 1986, only one president, John Hope Franklin, had focused primarily on black history, though a few others (James Randall, Dwight Dumond, and of course C. Vann Woodward) had published important works concerning aspects of race relations. Starting with Leon Litwack in 1986, the scholarship of fourteen of the next twenty-two presidents has been greatly engaged with racial matters.

The other major change over time regarding presidencies has to do with women's history. The second woman president (the first was Louise Kellogg in 1930) was Gerda Lerner in 1981. Eight women, most of them specialists in women's history, have followed her.[2]

Therefore, I offer three conclusions, none of which will surprise academic historians: first, within the MVHA political history was second in importance only to regional/frontier history before the early 1960s; second, political history rose in importance in the 1950s and eclipsed regional history by the mid-1960s and into the early 1970s; and third, political history, in turn, was eclipsed thereafter by social history, a broad category in which a race/class/gender paradigm has occupied center stage. The rise of social history stemmed in part from the power of the civil rights and women's movements, which exposed the neglect by older historians of many aspects of black and women's history. Contemporary political events, notably the Vietnam War and Watergate, also played a role in turning younger scholars away from the study of American statecraft, which appeared in those years to have lost its bearings. In contexts such as these, writing about the social world of rights-conscious reformers seemed far more important.[3]

In his presidential address to the OAH in 1986, William Leuchtenburg colorfully described this last eclipse. The field of political history, he said, had been overrun since the late 1960s by social history, and seemed to be in crisis. By the mid-1980s, he wrote, "the status of the political historian within the profession had sunk to somewhere between that of a faith healer and a chiropractor. Political historians were all right in a way, but you might not want to bring one home to meet the family."[4] Hugh Davis Graham, writing in 1993, found little to joke about. "The ranks of traditional political historians," he observed, "are depleted, their assumptions and methods discredited, along with the Great White Men whose careers they chronicled."[5]

This doleful conclusion, needless to say, had already seemed valid to political historians as early as the 1970s. Some political historians grumbled that the number of sessions devoted to political history had dwindled at historical conventions.[6] Scholars of American foreign and military affairs, perceiving social historians to have captured the OAH, virtually abandoned the *JAH*, submitting their work instead to journals such as *Diplomatic History*.[7] In addition, it was relatively rare that prominent political historians sent articles to the *JAH*.[8]

Many of us in political history *did* feel marginalized in those years, noting not only that the vogue for social and cultural history seemed all-powerful but also that some younger colleagues seemed to regard political historians as old-fashioned has-beens who were interested only in the maneuvering of white male elites. I remember vividly an OAH panel in Washington in 1995 (at which I was a speaker) concerned with the state of political history: more than 150 people turned out for it, surprising the organizers, jam-packing an overheated room, and spilling out into the corridors. Many of those in the audience appeared to hope that we panelists would reassure them and announce the worst was over. Though some on the panel maintained that there was nothing much to worry about, I could not and did not offer much optimism about the future.

Still, political historians remained resilient. Many senior scholars in the field continued to publish important work concerning national political events and people, and an impressive number of younger ones made auspicious debuts. (The list is quite long and need not be offered here.) Several OAH presidents after 1990—Eric Foner, Linda Kerber, Jacquelyn Dowd Hall, James Horton, and Michael Kammen—touched on political developments (broadly defined) in their presidential addresses. Undergraduates, as earlier, flocked to courses in political history. The general public snapped up political histories and biographies by David McCullough, Doris Kearns Goodwin, and others. The OAH supported efforts to promote public history.

Insofar as the *JAH* is a guide, it seems fair to say that political history has managed all right, even after the triumph of social history in the profession at large. I base this generalization on my own extensive (though nonexhaustive) examination of journal articles and reviews, and on reports and statistics from journal editors. In articles published and books reviewed, political histories consistently matched or outnumbered any other single broad category. Only the *MVHR*'s aforementioned focus prior to the 1950s on regional history—a focus swelled by reviews of a great many records and diaries by travelers, settlers, and military expeditions—outdid the presence of political history in the journal over time.

The considerable presence of political history was clear, for instance, in the very first *MVHR*, which, among other things, allotted space for a review of

Charles Beard's *An Economic Interpretation of the Constitution of the United States.* (The reviewer, Orin Libby, slammed it, concluding, "A little knowledge is as dangerous a thing in reform as in scholarship, and the professional agitator is always in search of some new statement or novel combination of facts, which may be twisted to support his particular end, by obliquity toward the existing order.")[9]

That first issue, as if proving the axiom that "History is past Politics, and Politics present History," also reviewed books by Henry Cabot Lodge, Grover Cleveland (two of his), and Elihu Root. The next issue carried a review of a book by William Howard Taft. Political history also loomed large in the journal thereafter. I estimate that roughly 25 percent of articles and 25 percent of books reviewed in the early years (between 1914 and the 1950s) fell into this category.

My survey of the journal in later years indicates that these trends persisted. Indeed, there was an upward blip in attention given to political history, to around 33 percent—both for articles and for books reviewed—in the late 1950s and 1960s, which were something of a Golden Age for political historians. This blip (like the later turn to social history) reflected trends in the culture at large, notably the growth of the state since the 1930s, World War II, and the Cold War. A related blip appeared a little later (in the 1970s and early 1980s), by which point some of the many political historians who had entered the profession after World War II had risen to prominence as officers within the OAH.

Scattered reports of journal editors confirm my impressionistic statistics about the steady importance of political history in the *JAH*. In September 1965 editor Oscar Winther (a colleague of mine at Indiana at the time) reported: "more [article] manuscripts [20 or more] were received on political history [for the first four issues of the *JAH*] than on any other topic; a slightly smaller number pertained to foreign policy and diplomacy." Next in order of importance (with ten or more each) were articles on reform, historiography, and social history. Then (with five to nine submissions each) came colonial, southern, military, immigration, religion, and business histories. Smaller numbers dealt with intellectual history, literature, the frontier, the city, labor, and slavery.[10]

Eleven years later, in 1976, editor Martin Ridge (who had also been a colleague of mine) reported that the *JAH* had received 317 articles that year, of which 13 were accepted. Most of the submitted articles, Ridge observed, "were classified as political, economic, and diplomatic."[11]

I have been unable to find data on submissions to the *JAH* between 1984 and 2000. Therefore, I cannot answer an important question: Did the widely lamented marginalization of political history in these years discourage such submissions? What I can say is that political history in the *JAH* by no means suffered the contemporary fate of diplomatic or military history. Though the journal began featuring a good many roundtables on aspects of social history (as well as sections on film and museum exhibitions), it continued to include political historians on its editorial board, to solicit articles for roundtable discussions of political history, and to publish peer-reviewed essays in political history that crossed the transom.

There were two reasons for this situation, which may have offered moderate encouragement to political historians. Notwithstanding grim warnings from their undergraduate professors, students continued to enter graduate school to work in political history. Many of them, moving beyond narratives that concentrated on the actions of political elites, sought to write broader political histories that would link grass-roots, "bottom-up" social and cultural developments to political responses at higher levels. Highly acclaimed publications by Lizabeth Cohen and Thomas Sugrue provide good examples of this tendency.[12] Some older historians, too, attempted to integrate social and cultural developments with political action. Recognizing this trend, Leuchtenburg emphasized in 1986 that political historians were paying special attention to what he called "underlying structures of society and long-developing processes of change." Some, seeking to "bring the state back in," were looking carefully at institutional developments. Forging connections with sociologists and political scientists, they often published in new journals such as *Studies in American Political Development* (1986) and the *Journal of Policy History* (1989).

Many social and economic historians, although writing history that included the "bottom up," understood that they could not tell a complete story, especially about events since the rise of the state in the 1930s, without bringing political ideas, campaigns, and programs strongly into their narratives. What the state did, after all, mattered. So it was that historians such as Linda Gordon, Sonya Michel, and Alice Kessler-Harris, to mention only a few scholars among the many who have written about social policy involving women, published work that merged social developments and political activity.[13]

Political history has not recovered the high academic status it once had. Given the clout it had in its heyday, this is not surprising. Moreover, the discipline of history has undergone considerable fragmentation since the 1960s: no single specialty, of the many that have sprung into being, can dominate the landscape.[14] And newly minted PhDs, whose work focuses tightly on elite actors or on events divorced from a larger social context, are likely to have trouble advancing in the profession. Who among us would strongly encourage a graduate student to write such a thesis? But there *is* a great deal of excellent work being done in the field, defined broadly, and morale among political historians seems to have improved, at least slightly, since the 1990s. Joanne Meyerowitz, *JAH* editor from 1999 to 2004, wrote me to say that political history "consistently ranked first, as the subfield with the most submissions."[15] Editor Edward Linenthal's annual report for 2005–2006 noted (concerning article submissions) that "favorite subject areas, in descending order, are political, social, cultural, African American, labor and working-class, American Indian, and race."[16]

For the years from 2000 through 2006, Melissa Beaver of the OAH office confirmed the strength of political history. During these seven years, the *JAH* reviewed a total of 4,056 books, or nearly 600 per year. Of these, 1,584, or 39 percent, were classified by the journal as dealing with politics. A total of 586 articles were submitted between 2002 and 2005, of which 74 were accepted. The number of articles submitted that the journal identified as focusing on political history during those four years was not large, only 90 of the 586. But 16 of the 90 were accepted for publication. This was roughly 18 percent of all the articles published during those years, a percentage not far below that published (by my aforementioned rough calculations) over the longer, earlier span of years covered by the journal.[17] My own survey of journal articles published between 1990 and 2007 comes up with slightly higher numbers: of the 256 articles published in these years, 52 (roughly 20 percent) can be said to have focused, at least in large part, on political matters, broadly defined.[18]

Should we rely heavily on numbers such as these? Much depends on definitions. Had my survey of published articles between 1990 and 2007 counted only articles resting primarily on archival sources—that is, papers of political figures in the Library of Congress, the National Archives, state archives, and presidential libraries—that many earlier political historians (myself included) had depended on, I would have come up with minuscule numbers. The *Journal of Policy History* was more likely than the *JAH* to receive articles dealing with presidential and congressional activities. Most *JAH* articles concerned with politics, instead, looked at quests for rights from the "bottom up." Many of these focused on the struggles of African Americans for racial justice. Many other articles examined political ideas or political culture, or they traced various conceptions, legal and otherwise, of citizenship.

As Meyerowitz reminded me, there is a "semantic issue" involved in any attempts at categorization. During her tenure as editor, she explained, the journal defined "'political history' in the broadest possible terms." Thus, she added, "submissions on affirmative action in the 1970s, the ideology of nativist candidates in the 1850s, the Yamasee War of 1715, the politics of the civil rights movement of the 1950s, the rejection of the Articles of Confederation, anti-gay policies in the GI Bill, and arguments for woman suffrage in the 1960s (just to name a few submissions) would all be classified as political history."

Any brief itemization of articles in the *JAH* since the early 1990s further reveals the perils involved in placing submissions in hard-and-fast categories. How many of the following, for instance, would we drop in the "political" box? "Republicanism: The Career of a Concept"; "Walt Disney: Art and Politics in the American Century"; "'Closing Ranks' and 'Seeking Honors': W. E. B. DuBois in World War I"; "National Solidarity at the End of the 20th Century: Reflections on the United States and Liberal Nationalism"; "Is the Supreme Court Sometimes Irrelevant? Race and the Jim Crow Justice System in the

1940s"; "Delegitimizing Democracy: 'Civic Slackers,' the Cultural Turn, and the Possibilities of Politics"; "Westbrook Pegler and the Anti-union Movement"; and "'They Are Ancestral Homelands': Race, Place, and Politics in Cold War America, 1945–1961."[19]

My view is that all of the subject areas just mentioned, as well as all the articles I have just listed from journal issues, would pass muster as political history. That is, what Meyerowitz terms the journal's "broadest possible" definition seems to me to be reasonable and one that would not lead to misleading or exaggerated numbers of submissions or articles concerning political history.

In short, the data concerning submissions, articles, and reviews reveal the persistence of a long-range trend: political historians, expanding their definitions of "politics," have regularly been welcome in the pages of the *JAH*. Notwithstanding the great growth of social and cultural history, much of it unrelated to political concerns, there is every reason to believe that this trend will continue.

NOTES

1. Mark Leff, "Revisioning U.S. Political History," *American Historical Review* 100 (June 1995): 829–53. Other useful assessments of writing about American political history include William Leuchtenburg, "The Pertinence of Political History: Reflections on the Significance of the State in America," *Journal of American History* 73 (Dec. 1986): 585–600; Ellen Fitzpatrick, *History's Memory: Writing America's Past, 1880–1980* (Cambridge, MA: Harvard University Press, 2002); Brian Balogh, "The State of the State among Historians," *Social Science History* 27 (Fall 2003): 455–63; and Meg Jacobs et al., *The Democratic Experiment: New Directions in American Political History* (Princeton, NJ: Princeton University Press, 2003). I thank the following for their data and reflections: Ellen Fitzpatrick, John Dittmer, Steven Gillon, David Thelen, Lewis Perry, William Leuchtenburg, Joanne Meyerowitz, David Kennedy, Robert Ferrell, Michael Vorenberg, Richard Kirkendall, Joshua Zeitz, David Thelen, Joan Hoff, and Melissa Beaver.

2. Similar trends may be seen in Bancroft prize awards, with books on politics and foreign affairs dominating between 1948 and 1968 and books on race and gender dominating from the mid-1980s on.

3. Steven Gillon, "The Future of Political History," *Journal of Policy History* 9 (1997): 240–55.

4. Leuchtenburg, "The Pertinence of Political History."

5. Hugh Davis Graham, "The Stunted Career of Policy History: A Critique and Agenda," *The Public Historian* 15 (Spring 1993): 15–38. Quotation: 30.

6. Ibid.

7. The *JAH* featured round-table articles concerning foreign policy history (1990) and military history (2007), but these essays were solicited. Their authors had not voluntarily submitted them.

8. Well-established, prominent political historians who sent in publishable essays between 1990 and 2007 included Daniel Rodgers, Alan Brinkley, Linda Gordon, Mark Leff, and Michael McGerr. Rising young political historians who did so during these

years included Thomas Sugrue, Gareth Davies, Michael Klarman, and Lisa McGirr. The journal solicited many other essays by political historians during these and earlier years, for round-table discussions, review essays, and articles in special issues. Lewis Perry, *JAH* editor from 1978 to 1984, recalls that it was difficult to get senior scholars in *any* specialty to submit articles to the journal (Perry letter to me, Feb. 11, 2007.) A guess is that they were more likely than in the past to skip the article stage or to publish in specialized journals, edited books, and newspapers and magazines, where their work might appear more quickly or reach more targeted or larger audiences.

9. *MVHR* 1 (1914): 116–17.

10. *JAH* 52 (Sept. 1965): 467–68.

11. *JAH* 62 (1975): 514–15.

12. Cohen, *Making a New Deal: Industrial Workers in Chicago, 1919–1939* (New York: Cambridge University Press, 1990); Sugrue, *The Origins of the Urban Crisis: Race and Inequality in Postwar Detroit* (Princeton, NJ: Princeton University Press, 1996).

13. Linda Gordon, *Pitied But Not Entitled: Single Mothers and the History of Welfare, 1890–1935* (New York: Free Press, 1992); Sonya Michel, *Children's Interests/ Mothers' Rights: The Shaping of America's Child Care Policy* (New Haven, CT: Yale University Press, 1999); Alice Kessler-Harris, *In Pursuit of Equity: Women, Men, and the Quest for Economic Citizenship in 20th-Century America* (New York: Oxford University Press, 2001).

14. See Peter Novick, *That Noble Dream: The "Objectivity" Question and the American Historical Profession* (New York: Cambridge University Press, 1988), esp. 572, 627.

15. Letter, Feb. 11, 2007.

16. *JAH* 93 (Sept. 2006): 628–31. Linenthal reported again in September 2007, observing that submissions concerning politics in the previous year were outnumbered only by those concerning African American history. *JAH* 94 (Sept. 2007): 664–67.

17. Letter, Oct. 30, 2006.

18. I excluded from my count all solicited articles—review essays, round table contributions, and essays in special issues.

19. *JAH* examples, 1990–2006.

8

The Continental Empire and the Global Power

Richard S. Kirkendall

Throughout its first century, the MVHA–OAH contributed in major ways to the development of diplomatic history as a field of historical study. The opportunities the organization offered included the publication of articles in its journals, and the story the many articles have told is dominated by two big themes: the development of a continental empire and the rise of a global power, two of the major features of American history.

At its founding in 1914, the *MVHR* gave the field a big push. Two of the three articles in the first issue (June 1914) and two of the four in the second (September 1914) were devoted to international relations. After that, the number dropped off, and for the next twenty-five years, the average was less than three articles each year, less than one each issue.

These articles emphasized the rise of the United States as a continental empire, one that stretched over much of North America from the Atlantic to the Pacific.

The nation was born in an age of empires, competing empires, and rather than reject the idea of empire, the United States joined the game immediately. To succeed, it had to displace not only the Native Americans, but also the European empires—Spain, France, and Great Britain—that competed with one another over many years for positions of control in North America, and each controlled a large space by 1776. In addition to its extensive coverage of the field of Indian History, the *Review*, in its early years, had much to say about the rivalries among the empires. It included articles on Georgia, New Mexico, and Florida, but the coverage, as one might expect, was greater on the competition among these imperialists in the Mississippi Valley, the vast area between the Appalachians and the Rockies that was drained by the Mississippi River and its tributaries.[1]

In its early years, the builders of an American empire focused on that Valley, and in the early years of the *Review*, it published many essays on the rise of the

United States to dominance of that region. Some contributors emphasized the exploits of George Rogers Clark during the American Revolution. "Certainly the winning of the trans-Allegheny wilderness was fundamental in the making of this great nation," one writer asserted, "and if Clark essentially contributed to the winning, his services must be worth study and understanding." Clark's military leadership, his biographer concluded, "made the surrender of the Northwest to the United States inevitable." Had Clark not made the "Northwest Expedition" in 1786–1787 and held the post at Vincennes, another scholar proposed, the British might have "come down the Wabash from Detroit" and Canada "might once again have extended to the Ohio as it had in the days of the Quebec Act."[2]

Contributors also wrote of other actors who worked for U.S. control of the Valley. They examined negotiations with and challenges to Spain, Great Britain, and France by westerners eager to protect and promote their interests, including control of the Mississippi River. "No other man, during the decade, 1775–85, understood so well the ultimate effect on American interests of the Spanish possession of West Florida and the control by Spain of the navigation of the Mississippi River," one historian wrote of Oliver Pollack, praising him for his efforts on behalf of American expansion. Another historian explored the federal government's effort following the revolution to promote development of the "Old Northwest" so as to prevent Britain and Spain, allied with Indians, from gaining control. Others wrote of Spain's efforts to check the westward expansion of the United States during the nation's early years and to control the east bank of the Mississippi below the Ohio River.[3]

The *Review* also offered an outlet for articles on the Louisiana Purchase, some of which explored the French and American background to it. One author wrote of the development over two decades of Thomas Jefferson's great determination to gain for the United States unrestricted use of the great river system. Others explored the consequences of the Purchase, including the enlarged flow of grain on the Mississippi River from the midlands to New Orleans and then to markets beyond the United States. France, the Purchase indicated and a contributor pointed out, was one of the losers in the battle for control of the Valley.[4]

The War of 1812 attracted much attention. Here, one of the most controversial stories concerned the reason many "westerners," meaning residents of the Upper Mississippi Valley, were inclined toward war. One argument was that they hoped to conquer Canada. A hunger for land, Canadian land, was the driving force, one historian maintained. A challenger insisted that this argument underestimated "the British-Indian menace" and exaggerated "land-hunger" but admitted that it was American expansion into Indian lands that explained the behavior of the natives. Another historian proposed that the War of 1812 ended the threat by the British and the Indians to American control of the Valley and paved the way "for the normal westward sweep of the American agricultural frontier, unhampered by foreign influence or Indian hostilities."[5]

Not limited by the *Review*'s name, historians in these early years published articles about expansion beyond the Valley. Some focused on American challenges to Spain from Florida to the Santa Fe Road. One wrote of the 1795 treaty with Spain that "yielded to the Americans in the controversy over the southern boundary and the navigation of the Mississippi River," calling it a treaty of great importance "in relation to the westward expansion of the United States and the development of its foreign policy."[6]

A number of articles focused on Texas. They explored the Louisiana-Texas frontier as an area of importance early in U.S. diplomatic history. They also traced the move by Americans into that Mexican territory, challenged the argument that a commitment to the cause of slavery motivated that move and the subsequent Texas Revolution, and examined American aid to the revolutionaries and U.S.-Mexican relations during the revolution.[7]

A few articles examined the Mexican War. One denied that an "Aggressive Slavocracy" brought on that war. A contributor also wrote of the demand for all of Mexico that arose in the United States late in the war, while another sought to understand Nicholas Trist, the anti-imperialist diplomat who negotiated the settlement of the war and prevented American seizure of practically all of northern Mexico.[8]

In these years before World War II, the writers about U.S. continental "empire building" always portrayed it positively. "The empire we purchased from France," one historian noted in 1928, "was coursed by great rivers . . . and they soon lent themselves to the establishment of adventurous commercial enterprises that were to win the wilderness to civilization."[9]

Territorial expansion within the North American continent was a big story but not the only one told by the historians of international relations. The *Review* and its contributors also demonstrated interest in the Genet Mission, American opinion of the French Revolution, European views of the United States, official responses to the Latin American revolutions, and diplomacy regarding the Isthmus of Tehuantepec.[10]

During the 1930s, a new theme emerged in the pages of the *MVHR*: the rise of the United States as a global power, a nation capable of exerting influence and controlling territories well beyond the limits of the North American continent. A 1932 article explored "The 'Large Policy' of 1898." More critical of imperialism than other contributors, the author maintained that the promoters of the turn to expansion beyond the continent, most notably Senator Henry Cabot Lodge, Theodore Roosevelt, the Assistant Secretary of the Navy, and Captain Alfred Thayer Mahan of the U.S. Navy, sought to make the United States "the indisputably dominant power in the western hemisphere." Three years later, another author explored the rise and fall of the anti-imperialist movement from 1898 to 1900, and in 1937, a contributor challenged historians who "assumed that imperialism was the 'paramount' issue in the campaign of 1900 and that McKinley's triumphant reelection was a generous endorsement of his policy of expansion." These historians wrote during a decade in which most Americans were reluctant to have the United States employ power beyond the North American continent.[11]

Two other essays in the 1930s moved the *MVHR*'s study of international relations into the twentieth century. One dealt with the Reciprocity Agreement of 1911, a highly controversial trade agreement between Canada and the United States. The other explored the large but unsuccessful effort by German-Americans in 1914–1915 to stop the export of war materiel, most of which was headed toward the enemies of the German Empire.[12]

In March of 1940, the *MVHR* devoted all three of its articles to international relations, and for the next quarter century, the journal gave more space to this subject than before, averaging more than three articles per year, almost one per issue.

After 1940, the United States clearly became a global power, consistently employing its now great power well beyond the national boundaries, and this big theme influenced the *MVHR*'s handling of international relations. The building of the continental empire had given the United States many of the resources needed for it to play large roles on the world stage. A few contributors continued to discuss the competition in the eighteenth century among the European empires, but more dealt with the rise of America's empire, beginning with George Rogers Clark and including British support in the 1790s for Indian resistance to U.S. efforts to expand into the area north and west of the Ohio River. Both the European and the American stories were summarized in a 1949 essay on "The Significance of the Mississippi Valley in American Diplomatic History, 1686–1890."[13]

Writing when the United States and Great Britain had become strong allies, contributors did not neglect the War of 1812. They noted that war between the two countries had erupted even though pro-British sentiment in the United States was strong. As one historian pointed out, Americans in the 1790s, influenced by Washington's Farewell Address, scrapped the French alliance and pursued a pro-British policy. Another scholar noted that when President Madison decided for war, Federalists were close to the British, closer than the administration was to the French.[14]

Contributors continued to debate the reasons for the war. One examined the role of the British before the war in generating Indian discontent with the American presence in the Upper Mississippi Valley, but he concluded that the "fundamental cause of this conflict was the Indian realization that the advance of the American frontier was depriving them of their way of life." Another scholar concluded that although early writers had overestimated the importance of maritime matters in bringing on that war, more recent ones might be "committing a serious error in the opposite direction." And on the peace negotiations that ended the war, a scholar concluded that the "American expansionists" won: They did not get Canada, but they did get "a promise of security to the frontiersmen by the assertion of full jurisdiction, as against foreign nations at least, over Indians inhabiting lands lying within the national boundaries of the United States."[15]

Other historians wrote of mid-nineteenth-century matters that earlier had received little attention. One was the Monroe Doctrine that one historian saw as "an illustration of the realism" of the early shapers of American foreign policy. Not isolationists, they were dedicated to American security and "prepared for close cooperation with Great Britain." Other articles dealt with military preparations for war and with the idea that railroad builders should be subsidized, because railroads could be a major element in national defense.[16]

Texas received less attention than before, but the Oregon Country enjoyed more. There had been only one article on the latter published before World War II, and it had dealt with the establishment of British control, represented by the Hudson Bay Company at Fort Vancouver. In the 1940s and 1950s, the *MVHR* carried articles on the "competition for empire" in Oregon Country and the consequent threat of war between Britain and the United States. Relevant articles discussed the British desire for peace, the Webster-Ashburton negotiations, and Daniel Webster's large role in "the abatement of the martial spirit in the United States and the avoidance of war with Great Britain in 1842." Other authors explored Oregon's role in American politics during the mid-1840s and the compromise on the dividing line between American and British territory that avoided war.[17]

During the mid-twentieth century, when one of the prominent features of American foreign policy was the "special relationship" between the United States and Great Britain, several contributors focused directly on the background to that relationship during the second half of the nineteenth century. This tale included friction and crises but also the avoidance of more wars between the two nations. Two authors explored the diplomacy of the Civil War and the avoidance, then, by the United States and Great Britain, of a third war with one another. Another writer focused on British America between the Rockies and Lake Superior in 1869–1870 and "one of the most vigorous and best organized annexation movements in our history." The movement failed, but, the author proposed, it demonstrated that "the frontier continued to foster the expansionist spirit." Still other scholars wrote of legislative restrictions on British investment in the American West, the U.S. government's removal of a British diplomat who had intruded clumsily into the presidential election of 1888, and the handling of an Anglo-American crisis over fur seals in the Bering Sea in 1890–1891 that "turned the corner to an eventual settlement" and removed the issue as a threat to friendship between the two countries. Another wrote of the Venzuela Crisis of 1896 and the successful efforts to prevent it from bringing on a war.[18]

Other historians writing in the *Review* dealt more explicitly with the rise of the United States as a global power. Some carried forward the work begun in the 1930s on the Spanish-American War. Exploring the background to that event, one historian proposed that the chief importance of the 1880s in the international relations of the United States "centers on the fact that it was a period of gradual preparation for the expansionism of the 1890's," but the preparation was not without a break for, as another contributor noted, Secretary of State James G. Blaine's ambitious Latin American policies were reversed in 1882. Focused more sharply on the Spanish-American War, a writer explored opinions of it that had been published in Midwest newspapers, and he called for similar studies in all sections. Another suggested that if the United States had not taken over the Philippine Islands, Russia, fearful that England might seize them, might have done so.[19]

A 1962 article on Mahan introduced the provocative "Open Door Thesis" to the *MVHR*'s article list. Recognizing the 1890s as "a crucial period in American diplomatic history," the author proposed that a "key to the understanding" of it could be found in the naval officer's writings that "discarded older colonial concepts and advocated an open door commercial empire secured by naval bases and a battleship fleet." To Mahan, "mercantilist methods several centuries old had but slight utility in a supposedly frontierless world which was coming under the control of massive financial and industrial corporations."[20]

Contributors to the *MVHR* also carried the story of the rising power into the early twentieth century. One challenged the contention that Progressives opposed imperialism and maintained that they, "with few exceptions, ardently supported the imperialist surge or, at the very least, proved agreeably acquiescent." Another explored the establishment of the American Colonial Office as a means of managing the emerging overseas empire, and yet another outlined the efforts by the rival European alliances during Theodore Roosevelt's presidency to gain American support and described the drift by the United States toward the side of England and France.[21]

Two other authors dealt with the United States in the Philippine Islands. One focused on the establishment of the naval base there, seeing it as an illustration of the expansion of the American empire and the mounting concern about the rise of Japan, while the other concluded that the Wilson administration "brought the Philippines a long step forward on the way to eventual independence, and presidential policy had been an effective guide."[22]

Writing of the early twentieth century, some historians called attention to economic components of foreign relations during those years. Two scholars focused on the wheat trade between the United States and Great Britain.

Others examined Secretary of State Elihu Root's reorganization of the consular service, the use of "Dollar Diplomacy" to gain access to the markets of Turkey, and the impact of Turkish treatment of Armenians on commercial relations between the Turks and the Americans. Another contributor maintained that the concept of the Open Door expanded between 1899 and 1910. It became "the basis for future policy," distanced the United States from the "power diplomacy" of other nations, and "seemed to possess all the elements of good policy—all except the one indispensable component: a reasonable chance of succeeding."[23]

Beginning in 1945, World War I attracted much attention in the *MVHR*. One article focused on the National Security League, the largest of the pressure groups for military preparedness during the war; another challenged the idea, prominent during the 1930s, that American business had pressured the nation into the war.[24]

Scholars writing on Wilson and the war attempted to define his way of interpreting world affairs and that of his top advisers. Were they realists or were they idealists? One contributor argued that the president and Secretary of State William Jennings Bryan "were moved more by a sentimental attachment for China than by a reasoned appraisal of power conditions" in dealing with Japan's entry into the war, while another portrayed Robert Lansing, Bryan's successor, as a realist, favorable to the Allied Powers, and "one of the principal architects of the 1914–1917 neutrality structures." A biographer wrote of the president's "ardent desire to avoid war" and insisted that he "accepted belligerency only after much anguish of heart and mind, prayerfully and soberly," whereas another scholar wrote that his "astute and eminently practical" peace program in early 1918 was partly responsible for the failure of the German Socialists "to touch off the revolutionary chain reaction for which Lenin hoped."[25]

Contributors dealt, also, with foreign relations between the wars, two decades of uncertainty about how large the American role should be. One wrote of two "Irreconcilable" foes of Wilson's proposed League of Nations, another wrote about the Wilson administration's efforts to improve relations with Latin America. One focused on naval disarmament in the 1920s; another on Secretary of State Henry Stimson and the Japanese 1931 invasion of Manchuria.[26]

Much of the discussion of interwar foreign relations focused on Franklin Roosevelt's policies. A contributor concluded that, early in his presidency, Roosevelt had not yet "become a firm believer in collective security," while another portrayed Mexican anticlericalism in the mid-1930s as an issue that plagued Mexican-American relations and tested the president's Good Neighbor Policy. An author surveyed the writing on the influence of one section of the country, the Mississippi Valley, on foreign policy from 1890 to 1941, and in a closely related article, a historian explored the struggle between "internationalists" and "isolationists" over neutrality policies between 1933 and 1940.²⁷

During the last two decades of the *MVHR*, contributors paid little attention to foreign relations during World War II, the event that clearly established the United States as a power with global range. One wrote in 1946 of a "revolutionary change" in American foreign policy that had begun with the Spanish-American War and continued to the present, concluding that the war had killed isolationism and left the form "participation" would take as the only surviving question. This, however, was only a survey of a big story that included the war, and the more specialized articles that focused on it were limited to the failure of German intelligence in the United States before and during the war, the historiography of the American entry, and Roosevelt's commitment to Prime Minister Winston Churchill to provide Britain with armed support if Japan attacked British or Dutch territory or Thailand.²⁸

The Mississippi Valley Historical Review became *The Journal of American History* (*JAH*) in June 1964, the year before the great escalation of the Vietnam War. That war quickly generated widespread criticism throughout the United States and abroad. The criticism was not limited to the war but extended to the whole history of American foreign policy. The new mood exerted some influence on coverage of U.S. foreign relations in the *JAH*, but this "revisionism" did not rise to dominance there.

During the first two decades of the *Journal*, the contributors said little about the eighteenth century competition among the European empires or the building by the United States of a continental empire; it emphasized instead the rise and performance of the United States as a global power.²⁹ Only six articles dealt with episodes in the building of the U.S. empire on the North American continent. One focused on the unsuccessful American policy of trade restriction during the War of 1812, an effort to "coerce" Great Britain and "prevent her from receiving vital supplies from the United States." Another concluded that while "American policy toward France in the war reveals serious deficiencies in statecraft, it also suggests justification for America's faith in its ability to profit from Europe's troubles." Another reassessed Andrew Jackson's Indian policy, challenging the idea that he hated Indians and arguing instead that he was hostile to the British and believed they tried to use Indians against white Americans. The Webster-Ashburton Treaty appeared once again in the OAH publication, doing so in an article challenging the idea that iron in Minnesota influenced the treaty and pointing out that the iron had not yet been discovered. Interested in Texas and the Mexican War, historians wrote of a committee in Massachusetts that opposed annexation, basing its stand on hostility toward slavery, and the historians revisited the Wilmot Proviso.³⁰

Other articles explored the beginnings of American large-scale expansion beyond the continental limits. Topics covered included late-nineteenth-century efforts to reduce tariffs so as to make American manufactured goods more competitive in foreign markets, and American "moods" on the eve of the Spanish-American War. Another article pointed to an element of continuity between the building of the continental empire and the rise of the global power, arguing that the annexation of the Philippines was not a "new departure" but "the last episode of a nineteenth-century pattern of territorial acquisition and direct political rule of subject peoples."[31]

Most of the articles on foreign relations published in the first two decades of the *Journal* dealt with twentieth-century developments. These included efforts before World War I to find peaceful means of settling international disputes, namely, President Taft's promotion of arbitration treaties and the Panama Canals tolls controversy.[32]

World War I continued to attract attention. Authors dealt with interactions among the United States, Britain, and France before American intervention, the failure of ambassadorial diplomacy, and the expansion during the war of trade with Latin America. Others wrote of divisions among progressive publicists and among Irish-Americans, dealt with Wilson's frame of mind when he decided for war, the great influence of Secretary of State Lansing on the president, and General Pershing's disagreement with his chief concerning armistice terms.[33]

Contributors also wrote of the years immediately after the war. They discussed the new situation that American international bankers faced in 1919 and the large contribution of Irish-Americans to the rejection of the Versailles treaty. They also called attention to two actions by Senator Henry Cabot Lodge and other Republicans, one calling for a treaty that would establish a military alliance to check a German resurgence and guarantee French security, the other pressuring Wilson to employ some of the recently demonstrated power of the United States to overthrow the Mexican government and convert Mexico into an American protectorate.[34]

Articles on the years between the world wars indicated that the United States did not ignore the rest of the world during that period. One on the Washington Conference of 1921–1922 illustrated the benefits China received from American friendship. Others looked at America's Soviet policies: an anti-Bolshevik policy in 1920, recognition of the USSR in 1933. Others focused on opposition to fascism among Italian Americans, a division within the State Department on the Theodore Roosevelt Corollary to the Monroe Doctrine, and the development of a narcotic foreign policy.[35]

Several articles on foreign relations between the wars explored economic issues. Two dealt with war debts: one concerned with inadequacies on both sides in the handling of the French debt and the other on shortcomings in the "Open Door Interpretation" as a means of explaining Republican war debt policy. Another focused on the establishment in 1929–1930 of a Bank for

International Settlements, an institution promoted by a group of New York bankers who hoped it would do for the world what the Federal Reserve System was designed to accomplish for the American economy. Two others dealt with President Hoover's defective leadership on the tariff issue and the "international dimension" in early New Deal economic policy.[36]

One contributor challenged the practice among historians of foreign relations of focusing on the American state. This contribution emphasized instead the Rockefeller Foundation and its efforts before World War II to promote "cultural change" in China. The essay offered, the author proposed, an example "of how an important aspect of United States foreign relations can be understood 'less from the study of diplomatic correspondence in government archives than from an examination of extra-governmental forces.'"[37]

The background to American entry into World War II attracted much attention. An article on the Canadian-American Trade Agreement of 1935 argued that it not only ended a trade war but it was also a prelude to close military and political cooperation between the two countries during the war. Another article dealt with Cordell Hull's hope that the Anglo-American Trade Agreement would enable the United States to "effectively exert a pacific influence on the course of world events." Other contributors wrote on the complex pattern of opinion within the United States on the Spanish Civil War, the American commitment late in 1938 to strengthen China in the face of Japanese aggression, and American appeasement of Germany from 1933 to 1940.[38]

A number of articles dealt with the period after the war began and before the United States entered the fighting. One dealt with the intense debate in 1940 between the advocates "of all aid 'short-of-war' and the interventionists who desired to send not only material assistance to Europe but American troops as well." Another defended Sumner Welles' mission to Europe in early 1940 as "a shrewd realistic maneuver . . . designed . . . to give Europe and France additional time to secure war material in the United States" A critique of "backdoor diplomacy" in 1941 claimed that these unofficial interventions "continually disrupted the delicate diplomatic maneuvering through which Japan and the United States hoped to prevent the outbreak of war in the Pacific." Another essay claimed that during 1940–1941, the president focused on raising public morale by suggesting "that while the Nazis posed a threat, the nation had the strength and leadership to meet the challenge," and the mass media cooperated with him.[39]

This outpouring of articles—ten articles in twenty years—on the background to American involvement in World War testified to the American historical profession's recognition of the enormous importance for American history of World War II. Explaining U.S. involvement in that war may have been the most significant challenge that historians of American foreign relations ever faced. I say this because the war impacted powerfully on American life during the war and in so many different ways and explained so much about American history for many years after the war, beginning with U.S. participation in a Cold War with the Soviet Union.

These historians had somewhat less to say about foreign relations during the years of American military participation in the war. They contributed seven articles, all of them between 1973 and 1982. One discussed support in 1942 for a negotiated settlement of the war with Germany. A critic of "Open Door Expansionism" concluded that "the revival of multilateralism during World War II was not a diplomatic tragedy, as revisionists had intimated, but a triumph for the logic of economic internationalism," while other authors challenged the claim that, under the pressures of war, the U.S. government stopped supporting American oil companies in Mexico and focused on prospects for American business in the Middle East. Others debated the issue of civilians as targets for American bombers and explored the Army's insistence upon unconditional surrender.[40]

The *Journal* began to discuss the Cold War in 1969, doing so with two articles on political economy written from divergent points of view. One dealt with America's refusal soon after World War II to grant a loan to the Soviet Union, suggesting that it "perhaps contributed to a continuation of a low standard of living for the Russian people with detrimental international effects. . . ." The other challenged the "revisionist" critique of Truman's decision to halt Lend-Lease to the Soviet Union, concluding that the "question was an irritant in Soviet-American relations during 1945, but not a decisive issue in the origins of the Cold War."[41]

Following this introduction to a large topic, the *Journal* presented a number of articles on the early Cold War, most of them dealing with Truman's presidency. One explored the implications for foreign policy, among other matters, of the change from Roosevelt to Truman; another maintained that U.S. policy in Eastern Europe was a "search for stable spheres of a kind concordant with the principal victors of World War II." Others challenged a prominent book on "Atomic Diplomacy," dismissing it as "Creative Writing" and deserving of more criticism than historians had given it, and criticized the United States and the USSR for failing to bring atomic energy under international control, suggesting that their failure "was both a cause and a consequence of the Cold War." Writing of the atomic bomb tests of 1946, a contributor pointed out that they were "not planned for diplomatic reasons or scheduled with diplomatic motives in mind" but they "appeared to have diplomatic ramifications, for in 1946, nothing to do with atomic weapons could seem innocent."[42]

The *JAH* published still more articles on the United States in the early Cold War. Some offered a complex interpretation of the origins of the European Recovery Program and discussed the critique of American diplomacy by the "old progressives" and the large influence of this new war on the 1948 presidential election. Others detailed the transformation under Truman of the National Security Council from a "mechanism dominated by the defense establishment" into "a presidential instrument" and explored his decisions to build the hydrogen bomb and cross the thirty-eighth parallel during the Korean War. Another article, this one on American policy toward Turkey after World War II, highlighted "the role of strategic imperatives both in the expansion of United States' global interests and in the formation of the nation's alliance system."[43]

The dominant thrust of these Truman-era articles was that the United States was now using its power much more widely and boldly than it had before World War II.

Before the end of the 1970s, some contributors moved beyond Truman in the Cold War. One focused on the U.S. role in the multinational competition for oil in the 1950s. Another examined the decline of American influence in Latin America as the United States became so very active in Europe and Asia, and a third explored the establishment by Eisenhower and Dulles of a policy opposing the use of force in the Taiwan Strait. Two writers on nuclear weapons maintained that the "spirited and acrimonious" politics of the Cuban issue in the fall of 1962 had no more than "limited impact" on either the president's or the voters' decisions and that, soon thereafter, the American people moved from activism to apathy regarding such weapons.[44]

As early as 1972 and again in 1982 and 1984, contributors explored the background to American participation in war in Vietnam. One wrote of Roosevelt's desire during World War II to prevent the French from retaking control of Indochina by establishing an international trusteeship that would lead to independence. The second reported that by the late 1940s, major elements of the American government, convinced that Japan must resume its once-large role in Southeast Asia, "supported the joint assumption by Washington and Tokyo of the mantle of empire Americans had wrested from the Japanese at the close of World War II." Two other authors concluded that the decision not to go to war in 1954 "merely postponed for a decade large-scale United States military involvement in Vietnam" and the decisions may well have been "less important than the commitments made after the fall of Dienbienphu."[45]

Although fields such as the "new social history" were challenging "old histories" for historians' attention during these two decades (1964–1986), the *Journal* did not neglect foreign relations. In fact, there had been a great upsurge in articles in that field during the first eight years of the period, when the average reached nearly six articles per year. A fall off did begin in 1973; the annual average dropped to two, but this low period lasted for only four years. During the following decade, *JAH* articles on foreign relations averaged well over three a year.

During the last two decades of the OAH's first century, the number of articles in the *Journal* devoted to foreign relations fell to well below two per year.

The editors, however, compensated somewhat with new ways of discussing the field: they were multi-author "Round Tables," "Special Issues," and "Interchanges."

For the historian of foreign relations, one of the Round Tables was especially important. Published in 1990, it was written by ten senior scholars, each focused on a topic: culture, ideology, gender, world systems, dependency, national security, corporatism, bureaucratic politics, psychology. These authors, the introduction pointed out, revealed "the field's transformation, diversity, vitality, and connections with other subfields in American history" and demonstrated that "historians of American foreign relations are much more than 'diplomatic' historians and . . . are conversing with larger and more diverse audiences both inside and outside the craft."[46]

Some of the other new features also contributed to the field. A Round Table on "Interpreting the Declaration of Independence by Translation" consisted mainly of essays on the translation and reception of the revolutionary document in several countries, written by historians from those countries. A Special Issue on "Rethinking History and the Nation State" compared Mexico and the United States. Another issue, this one on the "The Nation and Beyond: Transnational Perspectives on United States History," included essays on foreign relations, as did the Round Table on "Empires and Intimacies: Lessons from (Post) Colonial Studies." In September of 2002, the *Journal* devoted nearly 150 pages to the newly defined field, beginning with a Round Table—"History and September 11"—and including discussions of "Anti-Americanism in the Arab World" and "Rethinking American History in a Global Age." Four years later, the *JAH* published a Round Table on "Contemporary Anti-Americanism" in which six scholars from the United States, South Africa, Hungary, and France discussed perceptions of the United States around the world. In the same issue, eight participants in an "Interchange" talked about "Legacies of the Vietnam War."[47]

Turning to the traditional articles published in the *Journal* during the final decades of the Organization's first century, only a small number dealt with foreign relations before 1898. Two dealt with the competition among the European empires in the eighteenth century. One of these maintained that "combatants in America's wars of empire" discussed and waged "biological warfare with the smallpox virus." The other proposed that to explain the movement of people to the Virginia frontier, one must employ "a new perspective that connects the concerns of settlers and the interests of speculators with the geopolitical and imperial forces that defined frontiers and made their settlement both possible and expedient." Other articles looked at the social history of filibustering between the Mexican War and the Civil War, the importance of an American export, baseball, in Cuba in the late nineteenth century, and a cooperative venture in 1892 between the United States and Canada to save the Great Lakes fishery.[48]

Other contributions dealt with America's emergence as a global power, beginning in the late nineteenth century. Writing of a pivotal year, 1898, a contributor defined it as a time "of both liberation and domination" for Puerto Rico, looked at "the positive and negative aspects" of U.S. "imperialism," and denied that the people of this island were "a helpless victim of material and military superiority and imperial discursive constructions." Others looked at longer stretches of time. Two writers examined connections between two empires, the British and the American, from 1880 to 1910 and discussed the "international system of hierarchically ordered states" and the changes from 1898 to 1930 in "the manner in which hegemonic relationships were constructed, conceptualized, and legitimated." Another described a turn in American thinking between 1890 and 1920 "from Madison's sensitivity for the delicate balance between power and liberty" to the "assumption that foreign policy ends justify the means."[49]

Four other articles carried the story to the end of World War II. Two dealt with the importance of East Asia for the rising power. One of them focused on Chinese exclusion, studying U.S. relations with Mexico and Canada as well as China. The other explored the great impact on the United States and Germany of the rise of Japan as a Pacific power between 1904 and 1917. The *JAH* also carried two articles—only two—on World War II and the background to it. One explored the connections between war on humans and war on insects from 1914 to 1945. The other, written by a contributor interested in culture and power, focused on film, chiefly the wartime movie *Mission to Moscow*, in a study of Soviet-American relations.[50]

Contributors on foreign relations during these years from 1987 to 2007 devoted about as much attention to America's participation in the Cold War, an event of less than half a century, as they did to foreign relations during the preceding two centuries. The behavior of the United States as a global power was the greatest draw. One contributor looked at the foreign-service officer, policy planner, and architect of containment, George Kennan, in a new way. "The pervasiveness of emotion, sensuality and personal aspiration in shaping Kennan's attitudes toward the Soviet Union" encouraged this historian to suggest "that historians need to deepen the debate about the origins of the Cold War and to widen diplomatic history by exploring the connections between the personal and public lives of foreign policy makers." Another author focused on gender in analyzing American relations with China and India. A contributor examined U.S. "psychological warfare" during 1948 to 1955; it involved "covert and unofficial intervention" in Italian politics and was designed to "prevent a Communist takeover." Writing of the development from 1947 to 1954 of a military commitment to Pakistan, a contributor concluded that the principal reason for this "lay in Washington's conception of its own interests, interests that were defined almost exclusively, if imprecisely, in strategic terms."[51]

Contributors also focused on race. One wrote about Josephine Baker, an African American entertainer working in self-imposed exile in Paris who "found herself at the center of a critical cultural and ideological weak point in American Cold War diplomacy: the intersection of race and Cold War foreign relations." A contributor on African diplomats in the United States during the early 1960s also explored this intersection, as did a writer interested in how experiences in Africa affected black volunteers during the Peace Corps' first decade.[52]

Historians publishing in the *Journal* offered divergent appraisals of President Kennedy's foreign policies. Focusing on his policy toward Nasser's Egypt, one author suggested in 1988 that JFK "came as close as any president during the past forty years to solving the riddle of American relations with the Arab World." A critic, on the other hand, writing of a "Crisis in American Masculinity" from 1949 to 1960, defined the rise of a frame of mind that gave the United States the Bay of Pigs and Vietnam, among other ventures, and may have rendered them "a seeming masculine imperative." Two scholars, writing about a conversation between Eisenhower and Kennedy, concluded that the forks in the road to intervention in the Vietnam War "were taken by fallible, flesh-and-blood human beings who faced real choices and who cannot be dismissed as mere chips in the tide of history." Another author argued that the president, in his quest for a nuclear test ban in 1963, "not only seriously discussed but also actively pursued the possibility of taking military action *with the Soviet Union* against China's nuclear installations. . . ."[53]

Two other articles carried the *Journal*'s coverage of U.S. foreign relations into the Johnson-Nixon years. One contributor, writing of the overthrow of President Sukarno of Indonesia in the mid-1960s, maintained that "developments of essentially Indonesian origins," not "American machinations," were responsible. In another article, this one on the Nixon-Kissinger China policy, the author regarded the "normalization" of relations with the Peoples' Republic as "laudable" but the means as "deeply flawed." They "fundamentally undermined U.S. credibility and sowed seeds of continuing distrust in United States-Taiwan and United States-China relations."[54]

The Round Tables and other new features carried the story of American foreign relations even closer to the present, and the combination of these new features and the more traditional articles continued the *Review*'s and the *Journal*'s work as important contributors to the development of this highly important field of historical study. Furthermore, nearly all of the many contributions on foreign relations gave readers insights into the development of a continental empire that became a global power. Although no individual scholar could tell this whole tale in the pages of the *JAH*, each contributor who wrote about American foreign relations could offer a piece of it. Most did, and the many pieces supported the themes about empire and power, two of the main features of the history of the United States.

NOTES

1. *MVHR* (June 1925); (Dec. 1915); (Dec. 1917); (June 1928); (Sept. 1926); (Sept. 1917); (Mar. 1923); (Dec. 1929); (Mar., Sept. 1930); (Sept., Dec. 1934).
2. *MVHR* (June 1929); (Sept. 1924): 166; (June 1930): 115; (Dec. 1938): 334.
3. *MVHR* (Dec. 1924); (Sept. 1925); (Dec. 1926); (Mar., June, Dec. 1935); (Dec. 1932): 331, 347; (Sept. 1928), (June 1932), (Mar. 1938).
4. *MVHR* (June 1914); (Dec. 1930); (Sept. 1935); (Mar. 1928); (June 1931).
5. *MVHR* (Dec. 1915); (June 1920); (Mar. 1924); (June 1925); (Mar. 1933): 508.
6. *MVHR* (Dec. 1925); (Mar. 1915); (Mar. 1929): 435.
7. *MVHR* (Dec. 1923); (June 1918); (Sept. 1923); (June 1924); (Mar. 1932); (June 1914).
8. *MVHR* (June, Sept. 1921); (June 1934); (June 1924).
9. *MVHR* (Dec. 1914); (June 1928): 34; see also an 1866 plan to unite the United States with British North America (Mar. 1918).
10. *MVHR* (Mar. 1920); (Sept. 1939); (Mar., Sept. 1915).
11. *MVHR* (Sept. 1932): 223; (Sept. 1935); (June 1937): 43.
12. *MVHR* (June 1939); (Dec. 1938).
13. *MVHR* (Mar. 1946); (Dec. 1947); (Mar., June 1950); (Mar. 1951); (Sept. 1962); (Sept. 1949).
14. *MVHR* (Mar. 1957); (Mar. 1964); on international trade before the war, see Sept. 1955.
15. *MVHR* (June 1958): 66; (Sept. 1941): 171; (Mar. 1940): 510; on Spain's reluctant withdrawal from the Lower Mississippi Valley after the war, see June 1940.
16. *MVHR* (Sept. 1951): 233, 249–50; (Dec. 1940); (Mar. 1948).
17. *MVHR* (Dec. 1962); (June 1934); (June 1943); (Mar. 1950); (Dec. 1953); (Dec. 1956); (Sept. 1947): 187; (June 1960).
18. *MVHR* (Mar. 1940); (June 1958); (Mar. 1953): 693, 711; (Sept. 1955); (Mar. 1958); (Dec. 1961): 393; (Sept. 1963).
19. *MVHR* (Dec. 1953): 491; (Mar. 1956); (Mar. 1940); (Mar. 1942).
20. *MVHR* (Mar. 1962): 685.
21. *MVHR* (Dec. 1952): 483; (Mar. 1944); (Sept. 1955).
22. *MVHR* (June 1954); (Sept. 1954): 452.
23. *MVHR* (Dec. 1958); (Dec. 1960); (Dec. 1942); (Mar., Sept. 1959); (Dec. 1959): 453–54.
24. *MVHR* (June 1960); (Sept. 1945).
25. *MVHR* (Sept. 1953): 290; (June 1956): 59; (June 1985): 17; (Sept. 1951): 187.
26. *MVHR* (Dec., June 1963); (Dec. 1958); (Sept. 1948).
27. *MVHR* (June, 1961): 59; (Sept. 1958); (Mar. 1951); (Mar. 1960).
28. *MVHR* (Dec. 1946); (June 1955); (Mar. 1957); (Mar. 1963).
29. On the competition, see *JAH* (Dec. 1977; for foreign relations articles that did not focus on empires, European or American, see *JAH* (Mar. 1966); (Dec. 1976); and (Sept. 1978).
30. *JAH* (Dec. 1981): 537; (June 1970): 47; (Dec. 1969); (Dec., Sept. 1964); (Sept. 1969).
31. *JAH* (Dec. 1969); (June 1968); (Mar. 1980): 831.
32. *JAH* (Sept. 1966); (Dec. 1968).
33. *JAH* (Sept. 1968); (Dec. 1970); (Sept. 1971); (June 1967); (June 1965); (Dec. 1967); (Dec. 1969); (Sept. 1968).

34. *JAH* (Dec. 1969); (Dec. 1968); (Sept. 1972); (June 1971).
35. *JAH* (June 1977); (Dec. 1965); (Dec. 1966); (Dec. 1967); (Mar. 1965); (Mar. 1986).
36. *JAH* (Mar. 1969); Dec. 1972); (Sept. 1975); (Dec. 1974).
37. *JAH* (Mar. 1984): 799.
38. *JAH* (Sept. 1965); (June 1970): 85; (June, Sept. 1967); (June 1971); (Sept. 1977).
39. *JAH* (Mar. 1970): 840; (June 1971): 94; (June 1972): 72; (June 1984): 92.
40. *JAH* (Dec. 1978); (Mar. 1973); (June 1982); (Mar. 1977); (Sept. 1980); (June 1981); (June 1976).
41. *JAH* (June 1969): 70, 114.
42. *JAH* (Mar. 1970); (Sept. 1981): 314; (Mar. 1973); (Mar. 1974): 1044; (Mar. 1986): 906.
43. *JAH* (Mar.); (Sept. 1979); (June 1972); (Sept. 1985): 361, 378; (June, Sept. 1979); (Mar. 1985): 825.
44. *JAH* (Mar. 1977); (Dec. 1981); (Dec. 1985); (June 1986); (Mar. 1984).
45. *JAH* (Sept. 1972); (Sept. 1982): 393; (Sept. 1984): 363.
46. *JAH* (June 1990): 93, 98.
47. *JAH* (Mar., Sept., Dec. 1999); (Dec. 2001); (Sept. 2006).
48. *JAH* (Mar. 2000): 1553; (Mar. 1998): 1284; (Dec. 1991); (Sept. 1994); (Mar. 1993).
49. *JAH* (June 2000): 64; (Mar. 2002); (June, Dec. 1987): 82, 696.
50. *JAH* (June 2002); (Mar. 1996); (Sept. 2001).
51. *JAH* (Mar. 1997): 1337; (Sept. 1994); (June 1995); (Mar. 2001): 1304–5; (Dec. 1988): 840.
52. *JAH* (Sept. 1994): 543; (Sept. 2000); (Dec. 1995).
53. *JAH* (Sept. 1988): 527; (Sept. 2000): 545; (Sept. 1992): 587; (Mar. 1988): 1287.
54. *JAH* (Dec. 1989): 787; (June 2005): 110.

9

Economic History and American Historians

From Integration to Segregation in One Century

Gavin Wright

Economic history has been largely segregated from the mainstream of American history for some time now—even more so than political history. It has not always been so. Over the past three decades or so, one may search the volumes of the *Journal of American History* almost in vain for studies that might reasonably be counted as contributions to economic history. A search for articles with the word "economic" in the title turned up only one since 1985.[1] This contrasts with the pattern in the prior decade (1975–1985), when there were seven "economic"-titled articles, most of them squarely in the economic-history category, dealing with such issues as American economic growth, slaves as fixed capital, New Deal economic policy, and the commercialization of agriculture. The questions before us today are: What accounts for this estrangement, and does it have to be this way?

In making a diagnosis, there is no need to exaggerate the degree of separation. Obviously many *JAH* articles touch on economic matters to some degree—it can hardly be avoided in studies focused on race, class, gender, ideology, or politics—but almost always in an indirect or secondary manner, with no attempt at or intention of *explaining* some economic trend or development. These incidental intrusions into economics-space actually confirm the diagnosis of segregation better than more quantitative measures might do. Possibly a more serious conceptual bias would be to *define* economic history in terms of studies that make direct use of concepts from the discipline of economics, since to do so might confuse disagreement with exclusion. But even historians who reject what they take to be the received analysis of economics typically do so in a gingerly, arm's-length fashion. In my experience, they are usually the first to say that they are "not really doing economic history," and in this self-diagnosis they are doubtless correct.

I do not mean to suggest that the separation between economic history and "straight" history is becoming steadily more complete and impermeable. On the contrary, a number of *JAH* articles have crossed the line in recent years, and the 2007 meeting included—no doubt thanks to Naomi Lamoreaux's role on the program committee—at least two "hard-core" economic history sessions, plus a handful of "soft-core" varieties. These hopeful signs of progress do not belie my segregation thesis, however. They are happening only because of the concerted efforts of OAH presidents and program committees, who have perceived that the segregation of economic history is unhealthy and that something should be done about it. My aim is to diagnose the situation and ask what value the two disciplines can bring to each other as we move towards rapprochement if not reunification.

Rereading the early issues of the *Mississippi Valley Historical Review*, one encounters little reluctance to engage economic history or even to practice economic history. Consider, for example, this list of subject headings under "The History of the West" in a topical guide to the *MVHR*, published by the MVHA in 1934: Discovery and Exploration, Struggle for Possession, Land, Settlement, Trade, Transportation and Communication, Mining, and The Range. Although the articles published under these headings range across social, political, and military history as well, economic phenomena were prominent and perhaps the primary objects of historical attention.

These founding fathers clearly had many faults from a modern perspective. They were predominantly white males, and (worse than that) their lack of demographic diversity was reflected in their choice and treatment of topics. Referring to the pre–World War I generation, Peter Novick writes that American historians were "serene and untroubled in their celebration of traditional pieties; an island of orthodoxy in a sea of heterodoxy."[2] Even when historians' sympathies began to move in a more progressive direction during the interwar period, the range of their thinking and perception on social issues, with rare exceptions, was distinctly limited.

Despite these limitations, many of the early studies display fine scholarship and insightful historical interpretations. The best of them repay reading even today. Among my favorites are the ones by Archer Butler Hulbert, Wayne E. Stevens, Louis B. Schmidt, and James E. Winston, listed at the end of this essay. Even when the research lacked enduring value, the studies could be clearly argued and informative, as in Howard Copeland Hill on Chicago and the meat packing industry, *MVHR* 10 (1923): 253–73. In those days, many American historians were trying to document and interpret processes of economic change, and no one thought this was out of place.

The next three decades, roughly from the 1930s through the 1950s, were something of a golden age for economic history within American history. This was the age of the great monographs, many of which set such a high standard for encyclopedic coverage that they still stand as basic reference works today: Bidwell and Falconer on northern agriculture (1925); Lewis C. Gray on southern agriculture (1931); Victor S. Clark on U.S. manufactures (1929); Caroline Ware's *Early New England Cotton Manufactures* (1931); Robert Albion's *The Rise of the New York Port* (1939). In the postwar era we can add: Louis C. Hunter, *Steamboats on the Western Rivers* (1949); Louis Hartz, *Economic Policy and Democratic Thought* (1948); Warren Scoville, *Revolution in Glassmaking* (1948); and two classic works by Gibb and Navin on the textile machinery industry (1950). This stream of work culminated in the Rinehart series of commissioned monographs, "The Economic History of the United States," edited by Henry David, which appeared between 1945 and 1962.

These books were eclectic in their methodology and theoretical frameworks and encyclopedic in their scholarship, albeit within narrowly defined subject areas. Whether they had or developed a unifying theme is more difficult to say, since for the most part the writing took a narrative form, and the field had not yet been overtaken by the imperatives of explicitly formulated hypotheses. The implicit theme was economic progress and its roots in American technology, culture, institutions, and policies. Perhaps this focus on progress helps to account for the demise of this type of work in later years. But it would not be correct to assign these monographic writers a predominantly conservative political position; their sympathies generally adhered to the "progressive" view widely prevalent in academic circles at the time—to be sure, a variation on the theme of national progress.

What happened to this Golden Age? Within the economic history camp, the older approaches were challenged in the late 1950s and early 1960s by a new generation of economists, unhappy with the absence of formalized theory and quantitative hypotheses in the "old economic history." In truth, the older school may have been running out of steam anyway, as witnessed most tellingly by the absence of distinguished works interpreting twentieth-century economic history. The best and most enduring monographs dealt with the antebellum era of accelerated growth and development; the closer they got to the present, the more the treatments seemed mediocre—or did not appear at all, like the promised ninth volume of the Rinehart series for the decades 1940–1960. The cliometric insurgents, despite their methodological roots in the notoriously presentist discipline of economics, did not address contemporary concerns but instead returned to nineteenth-century issues such as railroads and slavery, with a new toolkit of models and methods. After a decade or so of coexistence, matters blew sky-high during the 1970s over the controversy ignited by Fogel and Engerman's *Time on the Cross: The Economics of American Negro Slavery* (1974), a quantitative challenge to much that historians had written about that institution. When the dust settled, economic history was almost exclusively in the hands of economics PhDs with appointments in departments of economics.

But it would be a mistake to tell the whole story, or even the major part of it, in terms of the internal dynamics within the small hybrid field of economic history. The historical profession's rejection of economic history was part of a much broader redirection of attention toward cultural history and relativism, and the casualties went well beyond economics to include such once-promising quantitatively oriented specialties as the "new social history" and the "new political history."[3] Today there are many welcome signs of moderation in prevailing attitudes. What historians may not be aware of is that during the decades of estrangement, there have been many signs of moderation on the economics side of the economic history divide as well.

In recent decades, economic history has become steadily more diverse and expansive in both its methods and its subject matter. Some of these tendencies reflect growing diversity in the composition of the economic history intellectual community, which now includes many more women and scholars of differing nationalities than was true in the 1960s and 1970s. Once almost exclusively an American phenomenon, cliometrics is now also pursued by small but thriving groups in Europe, Latin America, Canada, and elsewhere. Another force for diversification is the expanding range of topics now covered within economics itself, including ecology, law, family, gender, and race, all of which have strong historical dimensions. Perhaps the leading hallmark of change within economic history is the new prominence of "institutions" as an object of study.

In the heyday of the New Economic History, "institutional" was a term of dismissal if not contempt, referring to old-fashioned descriptive work that lacked theoretical foundations. As the field has evolved, institutional economic history has again become respectable, although in new and more analytical clothing. Indeed, many argue that the study of institutions is at the heart of the case for historical economics. Whereas the parent discipline of economics specializes in the functioning of markets, the domain of the economic historian is the institutional foundations that allow markets to function as they do. In its beginnings, the so-called New Institutional Economics identified institutions with property rights, rules, and regulations defined and enforced by the state. Subsequent research has found it essential to broaden the concept, to include not only explicit and state-enforced rules but also informal and uncodified constraints on behavior—another name for which might be "culture." Thus in many ways economic history has returned to the roots of economic history as a dissenting force within the discipline of economics, in its renewed appreciation for institutions and culture.

As for the bugbear of accessibility to general historical readers, allow me to quote from a recent survey by a British historian. Supporting Richard Sutch's injunction to economic historians that their next priority should be to get historians to read economic history again, the reviewer writes:

This really should be encouraged. The *Journal [of Economic History]*'s editors have made a successful effort to require contributors to write clearly and to explain themselves. There is a wealth of readable, novel work on, for example, invention during the nineteenth century industrial revolution, labor market behavior in the late nineteenth and early twentieth centuries, racial and other discrimination in urban-industrial labor markets, and the economics of depression and recovery in the 1930s and 1940s, to which other industrial historians and even regular historians should pay attention.[4]

Accessible or not, it cannot be denied that most economic history today takes its orientation—its cues, points of reference, sense of direction—more from economics than from history. The resulting communication difficulties pose a real problem for the reintegration program, and they are not easily remedied. An orientation toward economics is now well entrenched within economic history— made easier ironically by enhanced diversity within economics—and it is reinforced by the incentives related to career paths within economics departments.

Does it have to be this way? My position is no, it does not, and I believe the historical record supports this view. Difficult as the communications problems may be, we may take some comfort from the thought that they are not new. As long ago as 1910, Frederick Jackson Turner made the following statement in his presidential address to the American Historical Association:

> The economic historian is in danger of making his analysis and his statement of a law on the basis of present conditions and then passing to history for justificatory appendixes to his conclusions. . . . In fact the pathway of history is strewn with the wrecks of the "known and acknowledged truths" of economic law, due not only to defective analysis and imperfect statistics, but also to the lack of critical historical methods, of insufficient historical-mindedness on the part of the economist, to the failure to give due attention to the relativity and transiency of the conditions from which his laws were deduced.[5]

Given this persistent danger, economics *needs* historical practitioners, persistent internal critics committed to elaborating the role of historical context in economic analysis.

But there are potential gains to be realized in the other direction as well, from economics to history—and not just because economic life is too important a part of history to be neglected. Perhaps the most fundamental insight from economics is the notion that interactions of purposeful individuals can generate outcomes very different from what any one of them actually wants. In a sense this is *the* basic proposition of the discipline, dating at least as far back as Adam Smith, though Smith's optimistic "invisible hand" formulation is only one of many possible formulations.[6] As a working presumption, it is very different from the emphasis in historical literature on "agency," which I understand as the idea that some class, interest group or individual drives the historical narrative.

If this conception is debatable, or if it applies better to some historical processes and phases than to others, then let's have the debate—in language everyone can use and understand, and with an eye not toward ideological conquest but rather the hope of delineating the best ways of blending economic and historical perspectives.

To imagine that either discipline will convert wholesale to the worldview of the other seems unrealistic, even undesirable. But breaking down the walls of segregation for interested parties is an achievable goal, especially in particular subject specialties where both sides have something to gain. In an effort to develop a constructive agenda towards this end, here are three possibilities (among many) that seem promising.

POPULAR PARTICIPATION IN FINANCE AND INNOVATION

In the September 2006 *JAH*, David Hochfelder presents a fascinating account of explosion in stock trading by small-scale investors after 1880, making use of innovations (the "ticker" and the "quadruplex") that enabled Western Union to expand its capacity and "exploit the growing demand for real-time financial information."[7] Although not a quantitative work, Hochfelder's article draws on the work of economic historians such as Alexander Field, who argued that the advent of the telegraph allowed commodities and securities trading to attain "performance standards we associate with the twentieth century."[8] Hochfelder tells not a dry statistical story but a dramatic tale of the concerted campaign to stamp out illicit trading in so-called bucket shops, intertwined with the tortuous effort to define a legal-philosophical distinction between "speculation" and "gambling." It is a context rich with the elements of class-biased institutional hegemony that fascinate historians, in a setting in which economic historians have an integral part to play. Parallels to contemporary Internet trading are difficult to miss, as are earlier innovations that broadened the potential range of individual behavior, such as the automobile or the camera. Yes, one can pursue historical research on such topics without a prior commitment to the efficiency of the market or the oppressiveness of capitalism.

ALTERNATIVE INSTITUTIONAL FORMS

Economists tend to take a relatively narrow view of the institutional arrangements most conducive to economic growth, emphasizing secure property rights, rule of law, freedom of contract, education, and support for technological innovation. But history serves up a great variety of specific institutional forms, and it is not clear that *convergence* toward a unique best choice is the dominant tendency, even among successful modern economies. A key role for history in these discussions is to guard against the powerful tendency to assume that the forms that emerged and became entrenched must have been superior.

Here is a subject area in which historical perspective, and detailed historical studies, have much to offer economics—and it is a growth area within economic history.

A case in point is the emergence of the American corporation in the nineteenth century. Research by Naomi Lamoreaux and collaborators challenges the idea that the contracting environment in the United States was either freer or more flexible than in other countries, as well as the broader claim that the Anglo-American corporation was a globally superior form of business organization.[9]

Corporate history may be a specialized taste, but on reflection, the study of "paths not taken," alternative forms that did not survive, is a favorite theme for historians old and new. Examples come readily to mind from social, political, and technological as well as economic history—utopian communities, worker-owned enterprise, steam-powered or electric automobiles, plus less nostalgic forms such as polygamy, indentured servitude, and even slavery. The analysis of *why* these forms did not survive should interest historians as well as economists, and both have something to bring to the research agenda. We not agree on the answers going in or coming out, but let the debate begin.

BUSINESS HISTORY

My vision of constructive interaction between two disparate and sometimes incongruent disciplines may seem utopian. But to some degree it is actually being played out in the subfield of business history. Different from economic history, business history emerged in the 1970s in response to what was perceived as the dominance (perhaps takeover) of economic history by economists. Although originally focused largely on the histories of business firms, today's issues of *Enterprise and Society* (a journal founded in 2000) contain articles on a wide range of topics in social, cultural, and political history, side by side with articles that would be perfectly at home in the *Journal of Economic History*. The programs of the Business History Conference generally feature the names of many card-carrying economists, yet the featured speakers at the annual meetings include such distinguished historians as Lizabeth Cohen and Richard White, to name two who do not shy from economic topics (and interactions with economic history) in their research.[10]

More than a decade ago, I wrote:

> As one of a relatively few half-breed economist-historians, I can testify to the rigidity of the prevailing cultural and intellectual segregation between [the] two camps. I often feel like an emissary between hostile tribes, trying to develop a kind of cross-cultural pidgin language through which to inform each one that the other guys are not as bad as they think, and in fact they might actually learn something useful from hearing (or even reading) what they have to say. Although these attempts are often politely applauded, the truth is that neither side really takes them to heart, and one begins to feel that deeper historical and/or economic forces must be working against me.[11]

In this essay, I have tried once again to argue the value of intermarriage between economics and history. This time, the situation seems more hopeful than it was back in the late twentieth century.

NOTES

1. Richard P. Adelstein, "The Nation as an Economic Unit": Keynes, Roosevelt, and the Managerial Ideal," *JAH* 78 (June 1991): 160–87.

2. Peter Novick, *That Noble Dream: The "Objectivity Problem" and the American Historical Profession* (New York: Cambridge University Press, 1988), 70.

3. See the highly autobiographical essay by William H. Sewell Jr., "Whatever Happened to the 'Social' in Social History?" in *Schools of Thought*, ed. Joan W. Scott and Debra Keates, 209–26 (Princeton, NJ: Princeton University Press, 2001).

4. Howell John Harris, "Industrial History: The State of the Art," in *The State of U.S. History*, ed. Melvin Stokes, 179–98 (New York: Berg, 2002).

5. "Social Forces in American History," *American Historical Review* 16 (1911): 231–22. The presidential address was delivered on December 28, 1910.

6. A good collection of examples may be found in Thomas C. Schelling, *Micromotives and Macrobehavior* (New York: W. W. Norton, 1978). A formalized extension to political preferences is Timur Kuran, "Preference Falsification, Policy Continuity, and Collective Conservatism," *Economic Journal* 97 (1987): 642–65.

7. "'Where the Common People Could Speculate': The Ticker, Bucket Shops, and the Origins of Popular Participations in Financial Markets, 1880–1920," *JAH* 93 (Sept. 2006): 335–58.

8. "The Telegraphic Transmission of Financial Asset Prices and Orders to Trade," *Research in Economic History* 18 (1998): 167.

9. Naomi R. Lamoreaux and Jean-Laurent Rosenthal, "Legal Regime and Contractual Flexibility: A Comparison of Business's Organizational Choices in France and the United States during the Era of Industrialization," *American Law and Economics Review* 7 (Spring 2005): 28–61; Timothy Guinnane, Ron Harris, Naomi R. Lamoreaux, and Jean-Laurent Rosenthal, "Putting the Corporation in Its Place," National Bureau of Economic Research Working Paper 13109 (2007).

10. See particularly Richard White, "Information, Markets and Corruption: Transcontinental Railroads in the Gilded Age," *JAH* 90 (June 2003): 19–43.

11. "Economic History as a Cure for Economics," in Scott and Keates, *Schools of Thought*. The conference on which this volume was based was held in 1997.

ECONOMIC HISTORY ARTICLES IN THE MVHR, 1914–1930 (SELECTED LIST)

Archer Butler Hulbert, "The Methods and Operations of the Scioto Group of Speculators," *MVHR* 1 (1915): 502–15.

Wayne E. Stevens, "The Organization of the British Fur Trade, 1760–1800," *MVHR* 3 (1916): 172–202.

Vernon W. Crane, "The Tennessee River as the Road to Carolina: The Beginnings of Exploration and Trade," *MVHR* 3 (1916): 3–18.

Louis B. Schmidt, "The Economic History of American Agriculture as a Field of Study," *MVHR* 3 (1916): 39–49.

B. H. Schockel, "Settlement and Development of the Lead and Zinc Mining Region," *MVHR* 4 (1917): 169–92.

Lester B. Shippee, "The First Railroad between the Mississippi and Lake Superior," *MVHR* 5 (1918): 121–42.

Lester B. Shippee, "Steamboating on the Upper Mississippi after the Civil War," *MVHR* 6 (1920): 470–502.

Howard Copeland Hill, "The Development of Chicago as a Center of the Meat Packing Industry," *MVHR* 10 (1923): 253–73.

James E. Winston, "Notes on the Economic History of New Orleans, 1803–1836," *MVHR* 11 (1924): 200–26.

Hallie Farmer, "Economic Background of Frontier Populism," *MVHR* 10 (1924): 406–27.

Hallie Farmer, "The Railroads and Frontier Populism," *MVHR* 13 (1926): 387–97.

Thomas P. Abernethy, "The Early Development of Commerce and Finance in Tennessee," *MVHR* 14 (1927): 311–25.

James B. Hedges, "Promotion of Immigration to the Pacific Northwest by the Railroads," *MVHR* 15 (1928): 183–203.

Joseph Ellison, "The Currency Question on the Pacific Coast During the Civil War," *MVHR* 16 (1929): 50–66.

Joseph Schouler, "The End of the Open Range in Eastern Montana," *MVHR* 16 (1929): 212–22.

10

The Battle for Military History
Success or Failure?

Edward M. Coffman

In the early years of the twentieth century, academic historians struggled to develop an accurate portrait of the past rather than the nostalgic, heroic, and romantic celebrations of leaders and events. The popularity of the glorification of battles and commanders, "drums and trumpets," as this approach was termed, became an anathema to many of the academics.

Disturbed by this suppression of one of the more significant aspects of history, a member of the Harvard faculty, Robert M. Johnston, attempted to secure a place for that subject in academe by organizing a conference at the American Historical Association's (AHA's) annual meeting in 1912. Johnston, who taught intermittently a course on that subject, which he believed was the only such course in academe, persuaded Albert Bushnell Hart, a colleague and former president of AHA, to chair the gathering, which included not only historians but three Army officers who taught military history at Army schools.[1]

In his opening remarks, Hart pointed out that "it is to the advantage of the American people that there should be a more intelligent understanding of military history." Johnston followed by acknowledging that this field was currently "under a cloud" as it is considered that studying war is "putting back the clock of civilization." He then called for scholars to work with trained soldiers for seminars in the subject, for formation of a military history society and a journal "in which military history could obtain recognition." Although Captain Arthur L. Conger, a Harvard graduate who taught at the Staff College at Fort Leavenworth, recognized that "much can be done by the American Historical Association, by our universities, and by establishment of a magazine devoted to military history," he also called for a historical section consisting of trained soldier-scholars on the War Department General Staff. One of the other officers, Major James W. McAndrew, emphasized that accurate military history would inform the populace of the need for military preparedness. The

AHA president, Theodore Roosevelt, concluded the session by agreeing with McAndrew and pointing out, however, that he did not believe it was "possible to treat military history as something entirely apart from the general national history" and that it should include "the disasters and shortcomings just as well as the triumphs, because we shall have to learn from those disasters as much as from our triumphs."[2] The high hopes for universities' acceptance of military history, however, came to naught, although Johnston and Conger did team teach a military history seminar for undergraduates, gave a series of well-received lectures at Harvard in the summer of 1915, and established a short-lived journal, *Military Historian and Economist*.[3]

Although Johnston took the lead in arguing the case for military history in academe, Conger published an article making that point in volume three of the *Mississippi Valley Historical Review (MVHR)*. It was one of only five military history articles among the fifty-one published in the first four volumes of *MVHR*. The others were one about filibustering in Cuba and three on the Civil War.

In his introduction, Conger described three obstacles to writing history, which reproduced, "as nearly as the evidence will permit, the events," thus leaving interpretation up to the readers. The first was the nation's glorification of its wars and military heroes that had developed over the years. Next was the government's suppression of records that discredit the actions of the military. Finally, he cited the "quite natural demand" of pacifists who want to suppress all military history since they consider wars "blots upon civilization." Then he explained that military history should deal with the causes of war and the nature of war, which was not just one army fighting another army but the total effort of "one people fighting another people." Finally, there were the consequences of war. In other words he accepted Theodore Roosevelt's advice to connect it to the general history of a nation by expanding the study of war to include the political, diplomatic, economic, and social aspects as well as the conduct of war.[4]

Within a year the United States was fighting in World War I, and historians rallied to support the high-minded goals that Woodrow Wilson so eloquently articulated. While some academics contributed by writing articles supporting intervention, Johnston served as a major in the Army's Historical Section. Conger became a colonel and was an intelligence officer and brigade commander in the American Expeditionary Force.

After the war, the negotiations at the Versailles conference and increasing disillusionment with the war brought about a corresponding low period for military history. During the 1920s and 1930s, textbooks tended to ignore the experience of World War I but dealt instead with the causes and results. Popular histories, in the meantime, turned to debunking people and events of the past generally and, as Dixon Ryan Fox, a leader in social history at the time, commented, the emphasis had shifted from drum and trumpet to "bum and strumpet" history.[5]

Throughout the interwar period, any university student interested in military history would be hard put to find outside of Reserve Officer Training Corps classes any courses on the subject. A study of the catalogues from thirty leading universities catalogues in 1935–1936 found virtually no courses in the subject. Indeed, as Colonel Conger said, it was a "sadly neglected field." In 1933, a small group of professional soldiers, active and retired, joined with a few academically trained historians in Washington, DC, to organize the American Military History Foundation. Three years later, it had 199 members and, in 1937, the organization began publication of its quarterly, *The Journal of the American Military History Foundation* because, as explained in the Foreword of the initial issue: "Thus far, our efforts to secure publication through the medium of other organizations have met with no success." Over the years, the organization's name would change to the American Military Institute then the Society for Military History, while the journal became *Military Affairs* and eventually *The Journal of Military History*. By 1941, the subscription list included 590 members and institutions.[6]

In those early years, this organization reached out to the MVHA and the AHA. In 1935, at the AHA's annual meeting, it placed a session that included papers by the German military attaché, an Adelphi College professor, and a National Guard officer, and there were also sessions at the 1938 through 1941 meetings. In 1940, the MVHA accepted an offer from the military historians to jointly publish a volume of documents about the Army's role in the development of the West; however, war disrupted this plan.[7]

In order to gauge MVHA and OAH support for military history, I surveyed titles of articles in the *MVHR* and *JAH*. Yet as past editor David Thelen pointed out, the selection of manuscripts to publish is dependent on submissions, hence subjects of articles are not based entirely on editorial decisions.[8] Nevertheless, a writer who wants to publish on a particular topic is likely to be deterred from submitting his work to a journal by the relatively small number of articles on that subject. Although notes and documents (which appeared in nearly every issue in the early years) often were about military history and the reviews regularly included books on that subject, I did not include them in this survey. Other qualifications are that the *MVHR* listed annual reports under articles, so they are included in the number of articles, and JSTOR, the journal storage and archiving venue, omitted a few issues in their listing. My interpretation of military history is the broad one advocated by Roosevelt and Conger and thus includes the political, diplomatic, economic, and social aspects of war as well as the organization, mobilization, training, planning, and the conduct of campaigns. Indeed, because many historians have a narrow view of the dimensions of military history, I assume that many of the authors whose articles I selected would not consider their work military history.[9]

From 1914 to 1930 in Volumes 1 through 16, there were thirty-one military history articles among the 221 published, or 14 percent. Not surprisingly, the Civil War dominated with nineteen, followed by four about the War of 1812 and three about the Revolutionary War. Others included Conger's article on the general topic of military history, one each on filibustering, the Mexican War, an Indian War, and World War I. Undoubtedly Conger and Fred A. Shannon, who wrote "The Life of the Common Soldier in the Union Army, 1861–1865," knew they were writing military history, although Shannon may have correctly assumed that he was writing about social history as well. But would E. Merton Coulter have thought of his "Commercial Intercourse with the Confederacy in the Mississippi Valley, 1861–1865" as military history or, for that matter, Louis M. Sears, his "Nicholas Trist, A Diplomat of Ideals," or Wilson P. Shortridge, his "Kentucky Neutrality in 1861"? Of course, Coulter's focus was on an economic issue, while Sears dealt with diplomatic history and Shortridge on politics. Yet, weren't Trist's diplomatic efforts crucial in ending the Mexican War? Wasn't the commercial activity Coulter studied an influence on military logistics in the Civil War? Didn't the political situation that Shortridge wrote about impact not only the election but also recruitment for both the Union and the Confederacy? More than half (sixteen) of the articles, however, concentrated on the traditional military aspects of war, whereas seven dealt with political, six with economic, and one each with social and diplomatic issues.[10]

Titles in the *MVHR* during the 1930s indicate a slight slump in interest in military history. There were 153 articles in volumes 17 (June 1930) through 26 (March 1940), and only eighteen (slightly less than 12 percent) were about that subject. The Revolutionary War and Civil War dominated with six articles each, followed by the Spanish-American War (three), and one each about the War of 1812, a colonial war, and World War I. Eight of these probably would have been generally considered military history. The others were about political (seven), diplomatic (two), and economic (one) aspects of war.

In the 1940s and 1950s, two *MVHR* articles traced the momentous development of military history as an academic field. At the 1946 meeting of the MVHA, William C. Binkley's presidential address, "Two World Wars and American Historical Scholarship," traced not only the contributions of historians in those two wars but also the evolution of historical scholarship generally since the turn of the century. During World War II, the government's use of historians was much more widespread than in the earlier war for wartime agencies such as the Office of Production Management and the military services had history offices. Binkley estimated that half of the professional historians between the ages of twenty-five and forty were involved in these programs. Many of these younger historians, among them Forrest C. Pogue and Martin Blumenson, served as combat historians with Army units. The famed Harvard historian Samuel Eliot Morison was commissioned in the Navy and headed a team of researchers who helped him prepare the fifteen-volume *History of the United States Naval Operations in World War II*, and Wesley Frank Caraven and James Lea Cate brought out the five-volume *The Army Air Forces in World War II*. The most comprehensive of these histories is the seventy-eight-volume *United States Army in World War II*. A Chief Historian of the Army, Maurice Matloff, termed this "the largest cooperative historical enterprise ever undertaken in the United States." Although trained in various fields of history, those who served during the war and others who worked on these volumes after the war learned to be military historians on the job. In effect, as Matloff pointed out, the official military history program served as a "school of military history."[11]

A colonial historian who became a prominent military historian, Louis Morton, left the Army's history program in 1960 to accept an appointment as professor at Dartmouth. Two years later, his article in the *MVHR* "The Historian and the Study of War," described the beginnings of military history in academe. Contrasting the virtual absence of any courses in military history in higher education during the 1930s (except those the ROTC offered), he noted a 1954 study made by Richard C. Brown that surveyed 493 colleges and universities and found that thirty-seven offered military-history courses. Most of these dealt with the American Civil War and the French Revolution and Napoleonic Wars, and the military content might be only a third or less in those courses. Princeton, Yale, Dartmouth, and the University of Georgia, however, did have civilian instructors teaching military courses that the ROTC offered. In 1960, the Army offered to turn over their ROTC courses to history departments but, initially, few universities took up that challenge. There was the basic question of who would teach such a course because there were only ten schools in the nation that offered graduate courses in the field. Furthermore, as Morton indicated, the relatively small numbers they trained were far from sufficient to keep pace with increasing student interest. He believed this to be the result of curiosity about World War II and the Cold War, which already had caused the undeclared war in Korea, as well as the perennial general interest in the Civil War.

Morton echoed Theodore Roosevelt and Arthur Conger's assertions fifty years earlier that the study of war included not only military campaigns but also diplomatic, political, social, and economic aspects. He acknowledged that too many professional historians regarded war as "an aberration" that should be avoided "as a subject unworthy of study, if not downright dangerous." Indeed, it seemed to him that its opponents "hoped that by ignoring war they might eliminate it altogether."[12]

Neither World War II nor the increase in military history courses in academe affected the number of articles in the *Review* During the 1940s, of the 142 articles published, eighteen were on military or military related topics (12.5 percent). In the next decade, although there was a general increase in articles, the percentage of military-related topics remained the same (12.6 percent). The Civil War still led in wars covered but with a significant decrease (nine titles in the 1940s and only five in the 1950s), whereas articles about peacetime military developments sharply increased (three in the earlier decade and seven in the latter). The War of 1812 rated only one in each decade. Two articles in the 1940s and four in the 1950s focused on World War I, Binkley's article in 1946 dealt with both World Wars, and there were two articles on World War II in both decades. The Colonial Era attracted four articles and the Revolutionary War two in the 1950s, and one article traced the Anglo-American methods of fighting Indians from 1676 to 1794. Twenty of the articles during these decades emphasized the military, and other emphases trailed behind: political (twelve), diplomatic (seven, all in the 1960s), social (five) and economic and medical (two of each).

Military history flourished along with other fields in history throughout academe during the 1960s and 1970s, even though the Vietnam War wracked the campuses during the last years of the former decade and the early years of the latter. Wisconsin, Michigan, Temple, Indiana, and North Carolina were among the universities that added military historians to their faculties in the 1960s. In 1967, Macmillan published Russell F. Weigley's *History of the United States Army*, the first in a series, edited by Louis Morton, on the wars of the United States. Although not all of the planned volumes appeared over the next sixteen years, those that did were impressive scholarly works. At Duke, during these two decades, Theodore Ropp, with the assistance of I. B. Holley, mentored thirty-nine PhDs.[13] Those military historians already in the classroom soon found that the Vietnam War encouraged greater interest among undergraduates in their classes. At one of the epicenters of protest, the University of Wisconsin, students in the American Military History course increased from fewer than a hundred in 1961 to more than two hundred during the war. Somewhat surprisingly, protesters never targeted this course.

During these two decades, there was little change in the percentage of military-related articles in the *MVHR/JAH* with twenty-six among the 218 articles (11.9 percent) in the 1960s and twenty-one of the 190 (11 percent) in the 1970s. In the earlier decade, seven each were about World War I and the peacetime military, followed by the Civil War (five), two each on World War II and the Cold War, and one each on the Colonial period, the War of 1812, and the Spanish-American War. Eight of these were about military matters; seven about economic aspects; three each about social, political, and diplomatic subjects; and one each on legal and scientific topics.

In the 1970s, for the first time in the publication's history, there were no articles about the Civil War. Seven were on World War II; three each on the Revolutionary War and the peacetime military; two on World War I; and one each on the Colonial Period, the War of 1812, an Indian War, the Spanish

American War, the Cold War, and the Korean War, the only article the *JAH* has published about it. There was a notable shift of approach, indicated by eight articles with an emphasis on social history. The same number of articles emphasized military matters whereas only three dealt with diplomacy and two with politics.

From the 1970s, when there were courses offered in 110 institutions, on into the first years of the new millennium, military history suffered along with history departments generally as universities' budgets tightened and the number of graduate students declined. Ohio State, with the aid of a relatively large endowment and under the leadership of Allan R. Millett, developed the largest military history program in the nation. Yale, Kansas State, and Texas A & M were among other universities that built programs in this field, and Duke and North Carolina's combined efforts remained impressive. In keeping with the evolution of military history from 1960 to the present, the professional organization specializing in the field grew, and its annual meeting, which in 1961 had only drawn some twenty Washington, DC, members for an after-dinner business meeting, expanded into regular multisession affairs attended by three hundred people and held in sites other than the nation's capital. By 2002, 3,022 members and institutions received the quarterly journal. The AHA's 2003–2004 *Directory of History Departments, Historical Organizations, and Historians* reported that 703 faculty members listed military, Civil War, World Wars I and II, and the Vietnam War as interests, and another seventy-eight combined military and diplomatic fields as an interest. Although this is certainly a large increase over the handful of academics who taught in those areas prior to 1950, it represents only 5.5 percent of the 14,050 historians on faculties.[14]

During the period since 1960, with the exception of the 1990s, there was little change in the percentage of military-related articles published in the MVHR/JAH, but scholars who did not consider themselves military historians authored most of the articles that were published. Military history specialists have tended to think that the OAH, with its membership reaching close to 10,000, had virtually no interest in their scholarship. Besides, they had outlets for their articles in their own organization's quarterly as well as *Military History Quarterly*, *Naval History*, and other popular journals in their field. They could point to what seemed to be only a small number of sessions at OAH meetings, which in recent years has an average attendance of 2,200. Recently, OAH presidents have indicated greater interest in the field and, at the 2000 and 2002 annual meetings, there were George C. Marshall Lectures on military history. Nevertheless, no military history scholar has held office in the organization since Francis Paul Prucha served on the Executive Board from 1980 to 1983.[15]

In the 1980s, the *JAH* published 175 articles of which twenty-two (12.5 percent) were about war related matters, including five about the Civil War.

The decade saw the publication of the first Vietnam War article. The Cold War, however, led in articles with six, while World War II had four, the Revolutionary War and the peacetime military contributed two each, and the Colonial Period and War of 1812 as well as the Vietnam War contributed one each. Subject emphasis was on the military in nine titles followed by social history (six), two each on constitutional, diplomatic, and economic history, and one on political history.

From 1990 through 2006, there was a great expansion of titles in the *JAH* as Round Tables on specific topics and Oral History offered articles of shorter length. There has also been a sizable increase in the number of social-history articles, while, in the 1990s, the *Journal* offered a lower percentage of war-related articles than ever before. During that decade, the *JAH* published 340 articles with twenty-nine (8.5 percent) on aspects of military history. None dealt with the Civil War or diplomatic history. Most were on World War II (eighteen), followed by six on World War I, two each on the Colonial Period and the Revolutionary War, and one on the peacetime military. The social-history approach with sixteen titles dominated, followed by the nine with a military emphasis and four on political aspects of war.

During the first six years of this millennium, the twenty-six issues ending in December 2006 published 240 articles, including thirty-one (12.9 percent) on military related topics. An issue devoted to the disaster of September 11, 2001 offered nine articles on the War on Terror, and there were also nine articles about World War II, five on World War I, and two each about the Civil War and the Vietnam War, as well as one each on the Colonial Period, Spanish-American War, and oral history of the military services in World War II and wartime journalism. Seventeen emphasized social history, twelve focused on military aspects, one on diplomacy, another on political history.

Among general readers in the United States, there is now widespread interest in wars and the experiences of people who fight them, as evidenced not only by the best seller lists, but also by the distinctions that military historians have earned. From 1980 to 2000, 40 percent of the History Book Club's selections were in military history, and the high quality of scholarly books in the field was evidenced by two recent Pulitzer Prizes: Rick Atkinson's *An Army at Dawn: The War in North Africa, 1942–1943* (2003) and David Hackett Fischer's *Washington's Crossing* (2005). In 1999, John Whiteclay Chambers II brought out *The Oxford Companion to American Military History*, which showcased the broad approach to military history that current scholars have taken. In a review of that work in *The London Times Literary Supplement,* Hew Strachan, now the Chichele Professor of the History of War at All Souls College, Oxford, was effusive about the state of the field: "In the United States . . . the study of military history is today deeper, broader, and richer (in both senses) than anywhere else in the world. American military historians may moan that their subject matter is the victim of political correctness or of the latest fads of post modernism, but in practice the clash of competing approaches to history has proved remarkably creative."[16]

Military historians, however, as Strachan pointed out, do worry about the state of their specialty. In 2001, thirty-four established military historians in academe responded to a questionnaire in a despondent manner. Several said that colleagues considered them old-fashioned, hence insignificant, and, despite interest among undergraduates who filled their courses, they would likely not be replaced when they retired. Jon Sumida of the University of Maryland worried about the result of such marginalization of the field: "My concern is that history is losing the capacity to teach serious military and political history to such a degree that general undergraduate comprehension of the real world, past, present, and future will be significantly degraded."[17]

Two OAH surveys in 2003 demonstrated that the status of military history may not be as bad as some who practice it think. The *Journal*'s Recent Scholarship Online showed that political history led social history decisively in published articles and books and dissertations. Military history came in seventh in the list of twenty-three fields, ahead of such specialties as Women and Femininity, Urban and Suburban, Indians, and Labor and Working Class history. An OAH survey of the interests of members (each member could list five) showed that interests did not match scholarship in those areas. Among twenty-nine fields, military history ranked fourteenth, far behind the four leaders—social, cultural, political and women—as well as labor and urban history, yet ahead of Indian history, sexuality/gender, and the environment.[18]

Given the fascination of a large audience for military history outside of colleges and universities and of many undergraduates on campus, military history seems likely to stay in academe. My analysis shows that in each decade, except the 1990s, a tenth or more of the articles in the *MVHA/JAH* are war related. The surveys cited here and a Round Table on American Military History in the March 2007 issue of the *JAH* are even more heartening. The future appears to be brighter than some military historians think.

NOTES

1. *Annual Report of the American Historical Association for the Year 1912* (Washington, DC, 1914), 161.

2. Ibid., 159, 162, 169, 179–81, 190, 191, 197. Carol Reardon discusses the development of military history in the Army schools and the interaction with academics in chapters 9 and 10 in *Soldiers and Scholars: The U. S. Army and the Uses of Military History, 1865–1920* (Lawrence: University Press of Kansas, 1990).

3. Ibid., 175–76.

4. Arthur L. Conger, "The Function of Military History," *Mississippi Valley Historical Review* 3 (Sept. 1916): 161, 162, 164.

5. Reardon, 181; William C. Binkley, "Two World Wars and American Historical Scholarship," *MVHR* 33 (June 1946): 7, 10, 11; Louis Morton, "The Historian and the Study of War," *MVHR* 48 (Mar. 1962): 605.

6. Morton, 600; Jesse S. Douglas, "Let History Arm the Mind," *Military Affairs* 8 (Spring 1944): 17, 19, 21; "Foreword," *Journal of the American Military History Foundation* 1 (Spring 1937).

7. Douglas, 20, 23–24.

8. David Thelen, "The Journal of American History and Its Readers," *JAH* 4 (March 1997): 1279.

9. Another qualification is that JSTOR omitted ten issues. These are Volume 8 (June and Sept. 1921), Volume 52 (Sept. 1965), Volume 56 (Sept. 1969), Volume 63 (June 1976), Volume 72 (Mar. 1986), Volume 73 (Sept. 1986), Volume 75 (Mar. 1989), and Volume 76 (June 1989 and Sept. 1989).

10. The articles mentioned, other than Conger who is cited earlier, appeared in the following issues: Shannon, Volume 13 (March 1927); Coulter, Volume 5 (Mar. 1919), and Shortridge, Volume 9 (Mar. 1923).

11. Binkley, 18–25; Maurice Matloff, "The Nature and Scope of Military History," in *New Dimensions in Military History: An Anthology*, ed. Russell F. Weigley, 403, 404–5 (San Rafael, CA: Presidio Press, 1975).

12. Morton, 601, 605, 608–9, 612. One of the early universities to take advantage of the Army's offer to have History Departments take over the teaching of military history was the University of Wisconsin in 1961.

13. Names, subjects of dissertations, and years appear in Theodore Ropp, *History and War* (Augusta, GA: The Hamburg Press, 1984), 77–80. There was also one PhD in 1956, then eight in 1980 through 1982, the year of Ropp's retirement.

14. Matloff, 407; Edward M. Coffman, "The Course of Military History in the Untied States Since World War II," *Journal of Military History* 61: 769–75; and Larry I. Bland (Managing Editor, *JMH*) letter, October 7, 2002. Ian Watson, Ryan Green, David McGarvey, and Magnus Nordenman, graduate students in the Patterson School of Diplomacy and International Commerce at the University of Kentucky, searched and tabulated their findings for me in the American Historical Association *Directory*. I am grateful also to George C. Herring of the History Department and Michael Desch, then of the Patterson School, now at Notre Dame, for their assistance.

15. Ginger L. Foutz (Membership Director, OAH) e-mail March 12, 2007. Although the author of two excellent books in American Military History and an invaluable guide to military posts from 1789 to 1895, Paul Prucha does not consider himself to be a military historian, and certainly he has published major works on Indian affairs. Prucha telephone interview, March 3, 2007.

16. Nancy Whitin (then president of History Book Club) e-mail, December 1, 2000; Strachan's quotation is from *London Times Literary Supplement*, February 16, 2001.

17. Questionnaires and letters sent to the author. The quotation is from Jon Sumida letter, February 19, 2001.

18. *OAH Newsletter* 31 (Nov. 2003): 18, 19.

11

The Challenges to Traditional Histories

Joan Hoff

I headed the Organization of American Historians (OAH) during the decade when some of the changes in the status of the four fields represented by chapters 7 to 10 occurred. The authors tend to define political, economic, military, and diplomatic history[1] in very broad, almost cross-disciplinary terms. All also directly or indirectly single out what could be considered golden ages for their specialties. With the exception of Edward Coffman (and now Richard Kirkendall), all also came to tentative, to say the least, conclusions about the future of their fields. Apparently, military history is more alive and well than the others. But the tentativeness of the other three is both interesting and important, because these four fields are still considered the traditional disciplines of U.S. history. For that very reason they all have been disdained, dismissed, discounted, or generally not considered on the cutting edge of the discipline since the advent of social, cultural, and women's history, especially once these new fields began to employ postmodern theories and deconstructionist methodologies.

Yet I am struck by the fact that the general reading public still gravitates toward these four traditional fields, with the possible exception of economic history. That is, political, military, and even diplomatic history are still popular among consumers of books in the general public as long as they are intelligibly written as traditional narratives. The same is true of biographies.

What do the lamentations about the decline in classes taught in history departments on these fields signify if, indeed, three of them still have a timeless appeal to the reading public? In the long run, I think it may mean that such traditional narratives with broad readership are less likely to be written by academic historians because (1) we are training fewer graduate students exclusively in most of these four fields; and (2) the complicated methodologies we are teaching graduate students almost guarantee that their books will not be as readable as those written by so-called amateur or independent historians outside the academy, particularly those written by journalists and political scientists.

These essays are very valuable for showing the rise, fall, and, in some cases, partial resurrection of these four traditional fields since the founding of the Mississippi Valley Historical Association (MVHA) in 1907. They give us statistical information and perspectives about where their respective specialties have been and where they appear to be going. However, by design, they do not address the profession as a whole since the founding of the MVHA, which I will do, in part because I first talked about a systemic crisis in the profession back in April 1980. In the 1980s, as executive officer of the OAH, I focused on promoting tactical solutions to the crisis as it was then perceived. In retrospect, it occurs to me that some of those solutions may have helped to exacerbate the problems faced by the four fields discussed in these papers. Let me explain.

I gave the 1980 paper "Is the Historical Profession an Endangered Species?" about a year before I became executive secretary. The paper expressed my concern over the precipitous 38 percent drop in membership in the American Historical Association (AHA) between 1970 and 1980 and the projected surplus of PhDs during the decade of the 1980s, for whom there would be very few academic jobs. (OAH membership held steady in that same decade.) I was highly critical of the academy for producing what the Woodrow Wilson Foundation called back then a "generation of lost scholars" and for not addressing the reasons for the gradual decline in the social and intellectual significance of the humanities in general and history in particular since the 1920s. I also excoriated the profession for having abandoned the "rank and file amateur or independent scholars who made up the majority of the membership of the AHA until the Second World War." Until that time, these so-called laymen brought much wealth and prestige to both the AHA and the MVHA.[2] Beginning in the 1950s, academics began to dominate both organizations, and by the 1980s, both were in financial trouble, pointing to the need for less spendthrift organizational activities and more external fund-raising.

Beginning in 1981, as executive secretary, and after consulting with Gerda Lerner, the new president, I came up with "three major ways . . . [for] the OAH . . . [to] better serve the specific needs of the various types of historians who . . . [then made] up its individual membership and [to] address the general crisis in the profession." Number one was to reform the training of undergraduate and graduate history majors so that "they would be better able to find employment outside academe." Number two was to more actively lobby in Washington for expanding humanities funding and for access to, and preservation of, historical documents. Number three was to construct outreach programs "to promote the image of history among the public at large" and in government policy-making positions. To fulfill part of this last goal, I later established a *Magazine of History* for high school history teachers, which can be found today in thousands of secondary schools across the country.

The first two goals resulted in the promotion of public history. This meant the training and promotion of jobs for PhDs in the Park Service, in local oral-history endeavors, in banks and businesses requiring corporate histories or archival advice about preserving their documents, in libraries, in museums, in community history projects, in governmental positions involving policy analysis, in historic preservation, in editing positions at publishing houses, and, in general, wherever young postdoc historians could find meaningful employment outside of academe.

As executive secretary, I did not hit the ground promoting the traditional fields discussed in the previous chapters because I thought they were largely responsible for the glut on the market of PhDs. Instead, I promoted the fledgling fields of public history and social and cultural history to the degree that socio-cultural studies were associated with the rapidly rising field of women's history. The OAH had obtained, under my predecessor, a large NEH grant to produce materials in women's history for integration in both U.S. and European history classes. Often working with Robert Ferrell and other colleagues at Indiana University, I contributed to the implementation of that grant throughout most of the 1980s.

By the end of that decade I had become concerned about a development that Patterson, Coffman, and Wright pointed out in their essays, namely, that the traditional history journals could not or would not publish enough of the high-quality articles being produced by political, diplomatic, military, and economic historians, so such scholars sought out more specialized serial publications like *Diplomatic History*, *Studies in American Political Development*, the *Journal of Policy History*, the *Journal of Military History*, the *Journal of Economic History*, and the *Business History Review*. The same was true of historians of women. For example, the ranks of these historians and of women's history programs had grown exponentially, as evidenced by the 1988 Conference on Graduate Training in U.S. Women's History. Despite the existence of *Signs*, *Feminist Studies*, and the *Women's International Forum*—journals that published articles in many fields besides history—fewer than 10 percent of articles in the *American Historical Review*, the *Journal of American History*, and *Revue Historique* were on women's social and cultural history. Therefore, in 1989 I helped Christie Farnham launch the *Journal of Women's History* (*JWH*) at Indiana University to accommodate the growing numbers of articles in the field.

It should also be remembered that, by the end of the decade of the 1980s, the employment crisis within the profession had abated, as had the financial problems facing the OAH. The organization had consistently taken up the cause of public history and had obtained adequate representation for lobbying purposes in Washington, DC. However, the profession had not broadened its image among the general public and in government circles. By that time, I had begun to question whether the training of graduate students in newer methodologies and subjects, at the expense of traditional fields, had not gone too far. Most important, I began to recognize a new crisis in the profession.

This centennial history, focused, as much of it is, on specific specialties, does not deal with a theoretical debate that is still going on about whether the discipline of history as a whole is in a state of crisis. Yet, historian Robert Berkhofer, in his 1996 book *Beyond the Great Story: History as Text and Discourse*, and many other scholars, including myself, writing in the mid-1990s, believed that the history profession in the United States had not only been seriously challenged but also damaged by the postmodern theories and deconstructionist methodologies that had been largely imported from abroad since the 1960s.

Little wonder that poststructuralism put many traditional historians on the defensive with its denial of experience outside of the ways that language constructs it; its denial of historical agency, that is, real people having an impact on real events; and its denial of linear change over time based on causality. The traditionalists also were not necessarily made more comfortable by Berkhofer's suggestion that perhaps history was the discipline that could mediate between the extremes of poststructural and traditional historical views of context; between textualism and contextualism when interpreting context; and between poetics and politics as determinants of social reality. By the mid-1990s, this mediating role had not been clearly defined, and almost no historians had produced monographs demonstrating its practicality; at best, a few theorized about the possibility.[3]

Interestingly, diplomatic historians on the cutting edge of their field, rather than women historians who became enamored of poststructuralism, became unlikely candidates for this most difficult of mediating roles advocated by Berkhofer. Changes in historical scholarship in the study of U.S. foreign relations since the 1970s have not received as much attention in the profession as those occurring in the new social, cultural, and women's history subfields. My own review of developments in the writing of diplomatic history reveal that, even this most traditional area of historical study has been affected by postmodernism, but in a much more constructive fashion than I think has taken place the field of women's and gender studies.

Poststructuralism is very much alive and well in the twenty-first century in women's and gender studies, despite the fact that, from the beginning, it was evident that poststructuralist philosophy (as opposed to the methodology of deconstructionism for textual analysis) posed serious political problems for feminist activists who happened also to be historians of women. As early as 1988, Mary Poovey pointed out one obvious danger: if "'woman' is *only* a social construct that has no basis in nature . . . this renders the experience women have of themselves and the meaning of their social relations problematic." Poovey wanted to find a way "to think of both women and 'woman'" and predicted that "feminists practicing deconstructive and other poststructuralist techniques from an explicitly political position will so completely rewrite deconstruction as to leave it behind for all intents and purposes."[4] Yet any cursory examination of articles published about women in the *JAH*, the *AHA*, and the *JWH* since the 1980s does not indicate that this happened.

First in 2003 and later in a 2004 article, Gerda Lerner confirmed this, based on her analysis of the books, dissertations, and articles cited in the eight issues of the *JAH* from 1998 through 2000 in its "Current Scholarship" bibliography. Lerner found that of the 290 articles, 150 books, and 280 completed dissertations for that three-year period, the subject matter primarily focused on the twentieth century after 1920 and concentrated on "biographical [figures] and literary subject matter, [and] the study of representation of gender and identity definition." Although there were a number of articles on gender and sexuality, she reported "almost no work on class, and only a smattering of titles on work, suffrage, women's organizations and labor," except for those works about African American women. Moreover, only 6 percent of the books and dissertations she surveyed covered the colonial period. Also neglected were women's struggles for equal rights and political subjects in general. According to Lerner,

> it seems obvious that scholars in Women's History have taken the many discussions on "differences" among women to heart and are producing work that recognizes race, ethnicity, gender, and sexuality as important categories of analysis. What is equally clear is that the subject of "class" is being massively ignored. In fact, it does not figure at all among the fifteen most popular topics. Interest in the economic realities of women's lives in the past seems generally to be fading.

When she published her findings in the *JWH* later in 2004, her conclusions had not changed, and she asked:

> Is it really the case that for history of women what matters most is the study of representations, images, and gender and identify definitions? . . . Are we losing sight of the agency of women, the collective struggles of women seeking to improve their situations? If women's agency in community work, organized activities, or political struggles of the past is no longer of interest to most Women's History specialists, then how will we write a full and complex history of women? And how will we ground our knowledge for present and future social struggles?"[5]

I wholeheartedly agree with Lerner that the past should inform the present more than she found. In my opinion, this shortcoming is largely because of the impact of poststructuralism on the field of women's and gender history.

Poststructuralism has focused on diversity and difference, obscuring the ways in which women's lives are interdependent, and has downplayed feminism, claiming that it represents a set of confounding paradoxes, thus designating feminists unimportant as real people and as nothing more than delusional political agents. My own work on American women's legal status has indicated that second-wave feminists failed to obtain full citizenship for American women not because they were caught in futile paradoxical exercises, as many postmodern women scholars maintain, but because they pursued equal rights with men rather than equitable treatment based on the fact that they are not men. Although the achievements of second-wave feminists cannot be denied in the area of legal rights, much of it has represented change without transformation, to use Judith M. Bennett's term.[6]

In contrast to this dramatic change in the writing of women's and gender history, none of the men in this book's discussion of the traditional fields of U.S. history indicated that poststructuralism had had any significant impact on their specialties. Yet I think it has had at least an indirect influence, because postmodern theories and deconstructionist methodologies have fueled the expansion of social, cultural, and gender studies, which, in turn, has limited the number of classes taught and publications in these traditional fields, with the possible exception of military history. The theories and methodologies have also contributed, I believe, to the expansive definitions now used to describe these specialties. Regardless, this debate over whether a crisis in confidence and credibility continues to exist within certain other subfields and has carried over into the twenty-first century is quite different from the primarily financial and employment crises that the profession faced in 1980.[7]

As a historian who continues to write and teach diplomatic and political history, as well as women's history (largely the legal status of American women), I am saddened by the weakened status of at least three of these four traditional fields within history departments and within the organizational structure of both the OAH and AHA, and in mainstream history publications. Like the authors of these papers, I would prefer to see an intelligent blending of economic and historical perspectives, as well as more encouragement of a broader approach to military history, and I would appreciate more readable narratives based on a mix of social and political history so that more books by academic historians could be sold to nonacademic readers. In particular, I am convinced that since the end of the Cold War, historians have not concentrated enough on the importance of producing interpretative studies of U.S. diplomatic history that would appeal to the general public. I am not convinced we are training history graduate students to write books with such broad general appeal in these traditional fields. Instead, such books are being produced by such outsiders as David McCullough, Doris Kearns Goodwin, Robert Caro, Edmund Morris, David Maraniss, Naomi Klein, James Risen, Kevin Phillips, Gore Vidal, Stephen Kinzer, Thomas E. Ricks, James Bamford, Max Boot, David Rothkopf, Norman Solomon, Bob Woodward, and a whole host of other journalists, along with some political scientists.

The Challenges to Traditional Histories

Let me underscore this one example from the field of women's history. Here is a recent call for papers about feminist biographies issued by the *Journal of Women's History*:

> The return of the embodied subject as a site generative of analytical force and explanatory power in fields of inquiry throughout the humanities and social sciences, including postcolonial theory and even global studies, calls for reassessing the work of feminist biography as a form of historical knowledge. We seek papers that engage the dynamics of feminist biography as a critical mode of historical thinking and especially as an articulation of translocal history. We use the term translocal in dynamic tension with the transnational, in part to re-appropriate the geographical specificities entailed by critical biography as a feminist practice, and in part to insist on the capacity of feminist biography to illuminate geopolitics beyond the boundaries of the nation.

I don't think that this call for papers has the potential to produce work that will be read outside the scholarly subdiscipline, let alone be recognized as prize-winning for the OAH or AHA. However, I am quite hopeful that the sophisticated internationalist school of diplomatic history offers a way to break out of the realist versus revisionist debate, and I completely agree with those who speak about the dramatic decline since the 1970s in the number of history departments offering courses in U.S. foreign relations. If anything, I mistakenly anticipated that the end of the Cold War, when the United States emerged triumphant as the sole global superpower, and the wars in Afghanistan and Iraq, after the terrorists attack on September 11, 2001, would increase departmental offerings and students' interest in diplomatic history, but my impression is that this has not happened.

These are the trends I perceive as having taken place within the field of U.S. foreign policy in the last century.[8] The first generation of the diplomatic historians who began to write in the 1920s were reacting to the way in which the United States became involved in World War I, and they largely ignored ideological, organizational, cultural, and economic interpretations and, of course, all considerations of gender. The early giants in the field, such as Samuel Eliot Morison, Julius Pratt, Dexter Perkins, and Samuel Flagg Bemis, expressed a distinctly ethnocentric and nationalistic approach. They defined foreign relations between nations primarily in terms of formal state-to-state communiqués, interspersed with biographical material about presidents, secretaries of state, and highly placed foreign-service personnel. This interpretation generally ignored domestic influences on American foreign policy and emphasized, primarily, the Western, the European, context in which the United States operated. Occasionally, these early nationalists also placed some emphasis on the presumed impact of public opinion on U.S. foreign policy but seldom with compelling statistical or theoretical analysis. By and large this nationalistic approach assumed that the United States exhibited diplomatic continuity based largely on certain celebrated late-eighteenth- and nineteenth-century principles.[9]

Following World War II this nationalist legacy was significantly modified by the "realists," whose intellectual origins went back to a group of European historians and social scientists writing during the interwar years, such as E. H. Carr, Nicholas Spykman, and Hans J. Morgenthau.[10] In the United States during the early postwar decades, the writings of diplomat George Kennan, journalist Walter Lippmann, theologian Reinhold Niebuhr, economist Herbert Feis, sociologist Lewis Mumford, and assorted foreign policy scholars, such as Morison, Bemis, Perkins, Thomas Bailey, Richard B. Morris, and Arnold Wolfers, gave rise to the realist school. Most of them wrote under the influence of the lesson of Munich. For them, according to Gerald Combs, "the sacrifice of Czechoslovakia . . . by Chamberlain and Daladier, egged on by Roosevelt, was a tragic and stupid move."[11]

Later on, Arthur M. Schlesinger Jr., Norman A. Graebner, Robert Ferrell, and Ernest R. May joined the ranks of these early realists. They all continued, as their nationalist predecessors had, to focus on archival documents to determine how state policy was formulated by an elite group of men, and they usually assumed such leaders were rational actors making decisions on the basis of national self-interest and geopolitical forces after assessing facts prepared by expert advisers. When presidents or secretaries of state became driven by adherence to moralism, idealism, liberal internationalism, and, worse yet, isolationism in the 1950s and 1960s, these realist scholars of U.S. foreign relations judged them harshly. In a basic sense, the early nationalists and later the realists carried on the Rankean tradition of historical research, using official sources for the syntax and context of their writings and generally downplaying the role economic considerations may have played in decision making. Additionally, as they became more methodologically sophisticated in the 1960s and 1970s, they began to incorporate strategic studies, bureaucratic politics, various forms of individual and group psychology, and other political science, sociological, and international relations models for explaining decision making among diplomatic elites in the United States and abroad.[12]

Although these new disciplinary methodologies broadened the perspectives of the realists, they remained committed to the following assumptions: (1) official documents of diplomacy are more important than any other sources for explaining U.S. foreign relations; (2) the international "system" of any time period (inevitably based on "structural anarchy" as nations vied with one another to maintain national security) offers the best explanation for international crises and their temporary resolutions; (3) conflict, therefore, is natural and to be expected in foreign affairs; (4) because all states are guided by national self-interest, a "rational foreign policy minimizes risks and maximizes benefits"; and (5) state behavior is rational and primarily determined by external rather than internal political conditions, although sometimes domestic politics or public opinion can cause an irrational foreign policy to develop. Finally, the realists expressed a status quo mentality, rather than a critical evaluation of policy. This was especially obvious with respect to U.S. participation in the Cold War and the ethical questions that fighting it raised as it adopted the tactics of the enemy in order to win that conflict. In particular, realists tended to ignore the connection between political economies at home and abroad on the formulation of foreign policy because their definition of policy was so narrowly tied to official government sources. They also seldom questioned the myth about the exceptional role that the United States was destined to play in the world since its inception and the country's virtuous intentions or the naive assumption about the ease with which liberty (i.e., American democracy and capitalism) could be transferred anywhere in the world.[13]

A second school of interpretation developed almost simultaneously with the nationalist one following World War I, but it never achieved the dominance in professional circles that the nationalist/realist approach acquired after World War II. It took its name "progressive" from turn-of-the-century historians led by Charles Beard, and it stressed domestic influences on foreign policy, especially economic ones, rather than state-to-state relations. In doing so, these progressive historians emphasized the irrational nature of decision making and, hence, discontinuity in U.S. foreign relations—not a rational continuum or consensus. Thus, the progressive school of interpretation focused on regional influence on national interests, individual personalities, and public or private forces affecting the development of American foreign policy, ignoring European and other areas of the world. In particular, they stressed the domestic economic foundations of U.S. diplomacy and, unlike the realists, often criticized the elite group of government and corporate decision makers who structured American foreign policy to suit the country's economic needs at the expense of its domestic ideals of democracy and justice. Consequently, they did not feel obliged to do research in foreign archives. Sometimes these early progressive critics of U.S. diplomacy, such as Beard, Charles C. Tansill, and Harry Elmer Barnes, also adopted conspiracy theories about the intentions of American leaders, and their works quickly succumbed after World War II to attacks from realists who questioned their expertise, politics, patriotism, and logic. Ultimately, the best of the progressive economic critics of U.S. foreign policy experienced a renaissance in the 1960s under the influence of William Appleman Williams and the "Wisconsin School" of revisionist, new left scholars.[14]

This revisionist, anticapitalist approach immediately locked horns with the procapitalist predilections of the realists over everything from American exceptionalism and expansionism in the late nineteenth century to the origins of the Cold War. Although this debate reached a point of diminishing historiographical returns over the war in Vietnam, it gave rise to greater diversity and methodological sophistication among the radical revisionists for whom American destabilization of Indochina became a major influence as they interpreted U.S. diplomacy. Never as influential within the historical profession or as unified in their interpretations as the realists, despite their materialist orientation, the revisionists began, during the 1970s, to split into three groups in response to severe criticism from, not only the realists, but also Marxists and business historians.

One set of revisionists continued to emphasize economics but expanded their horizons beyond systemic economic questions to look at (and begin utilizing) modernization-, dependency-, and world-system models. Another group began to look more carefully at the cultural forces and gendered links between the state and society in the formulation of foreign policy. This broad perspective about the meaning of foreign policy led them to study the basis for expansionist views, by borrowing ideas from sociologists and political scientists to understand the complicated process whereby elites arrive at decisions, and to attempt quantitative prosopographical studies of decision makers in the private and public sector.

Still a third faction of revisionists, known as "corporatists," began to examine the complex intermingling of ideological and economic factors as they affected the structural relationships and role playing within government agencies and business organizations. In particular, corporatists have drawn from interdisciplinary socioeconomic, psycho-organizational theories first developed by such post-World War II business historians and structural functionalists as Allan Nevins, Fritz Redlich, Thomas C. Cochran, and Edward Chase Kirkland, as well as sociologists like C. Wright Mills, Arnold Rose, and G. William Domhoff. These theories were later refined by work conducted at the Research Seminar on Bureaucracy, Politics, and Policy of the Institute of Government in the John F. Kennedy School of Government at Harvard. Studying the collaboration that takes place among recognized functional groups in government and the public and private sectors in determining foreign policy, corporatists began explaining the interaction between domestic and international politics.[15]

Early corporatist revisionists, such as Charles Vevier, Ellis W. Hawley, Lloyd C. Gardner, Walter LaFeber, Thomas J. McCormick, Carl Parrini, Burton Kaufman, Michael Hogan, Melvyn Leffler, Frank Costigliola, and myself, first wrote about the 1890s and the interwar years, and political scientists using corporatist theories analyzed decisions made during certain Cold War crises. Instead of relying on pluralist explanations so characteristic of the more liberal realists, or simplistic Marxist-statist interpretation typical of the early radical revisionists of the 1960s, corporatists explained the ideological, organizational, and economic aspects of American foreign relations by demonstrating how public and private leaders, bureaucrats, technocrats, and organized economic interest groups such as banks, labor unions, export-import associations, and farm groups all vied with one another to influence U.S. foreign policy. In this process, a corporate ideology based on controlled economic growth and stability emerged in which the state and these economic interests cooperated to both formulate and execute foreign policy. Corporatists argued that for most of the twentieth century government and economic elites in all industrialized western nations have built a multinational system of power sharing and bureaucratic control based on informal collaboration with each other. Although a corporatist analysis can provide insight into long-term interaction among key functional groups in the public and private sectors, it has been criticized for not paying enough attention to the impact individuals have had on U.S. foreign policy, especially in times of crises, such as the Great Depression.

Corporatism and the two other strains of revisionism that developed in the 1970s—the world systems approach and the more culturally and biographically oriented approach to decision making—all offered a much more complex view of the formulation of diplomacy devoid of demons and monolithic economic interests. The result has been to legitimize the interconnectedness of internal and external issues in major foreign policy disputes such as the origins of the Cold War and to blend both dependency and modernization theories, especially in studying the complex hierarchial relationships among periphery (Third World) and semiperiphery (Second World) nations and core countries (First World).[16]

In general, therefore, revisionists were energized by criticism from realists to branch out in three productive directions in their study of U.S. foreign policy from the 1970s to the 1990s. Their own divisions and largely critical approach to American foreign relations continued to relegate revisionists to a marginal, rather than dominant, position within the professional circles of diplomatic scholars in the United States.

To varying degrees, these diplomatic schools of thought have all continued to analyze state-to-state relations because, for government decision makers, the bottom line in U.S. foreign relations remains the issues of national power and security, regardless of the sophisticated ways in which diplomatic scholars advise them or interpret their policies.

Since the original generation of nationalists and progressives, with their post–World War II realist and revisionist offshoots, one other major interpretative school has emerged. Known as the internationalist school, it has only begun to influence the study of U.S. foreign relations. It is the most eclectic approach to the study of diplomacy, delving into all aspects of the international environment, including the pros and cons of globalization, comparative international relations, cultural systems, social structure orientations, and deconstructionist analysis. Many realists and revisionists have joined ranks with the internationalists because the latter also often study relationships among nations and the interaction of elites in different countries. However, this intrasystemic approach has its limitations because there is a tendency among some internationalists to study primarily hegemonic or dominant beliefs of a society or region rather than the many subcultures that exist as well. So those internationalists on the cutting edge of the field advocate nontraditional sources and the study of cross national images and perceptions that go far beyond the traditional power relationships of nation states and approach the mediating role between poststructuralism and traditionalism recommended by Berkhofer. In particular, they question the uniqueness of national ideologies, traditions, political systems, and cultures, stressing the extrasystemic influence of one on the other. For example, American pop culture and supposed dominance of the U.S. media abroad began to be changed by foreign influences even as it transformed the values and fashions of youth all over the world.

Internationalists using a world systems approach also offer hope for increased investigation of one of the most neglected areas of foreign relations to date: women. American women have been studied in more traditional ways, showing how marginal they remain in diplomatic circles and the importance of their roles as missionaries or as members of peace movements. Less has been done to deconstruct the gendered overtones of the socioeconomic and cultural assumptions underpinning the foreign policies of nations.[17]

In the final analysis, I continue to be bothered by some of the subject and methodological innovations that I recommended to the profession for the training of undergraduate and graduate students in the 1980s. I am not exactly sure of the impact this has had, but a College Board examination of survey classes in U.S. history published recently in the *OAH Newsletter* indicated that, as of 2003, 43 percent of topical coverage consisted of social and cultural themes compared to 30 percent for political ones and 15 percent each for diplomatic and economic ones.[18] These results seem to imply the possibility that U.S. survey courses suffer from too little factual chronology and basic political, economic, military, and diplomatic information about American history. When I suggested this in critiquing the 1996 revised *National History Standards*, I was taken to task in the *Journal of Women's History*.[19]

While I have not quite come full circle from 1980, I now defend teaching the four traditional fields at both the graduate and undergraduate levels more than I did back then. I also call for more traditional, rather than poststructural, analysis of the domestic- and foreign-policy problems facing the United States because of the end of the Cold War and the events of September 11, which have thrown the country into an endless war on terrorism.

NOTES

1. Editor's note: At the 2007 meeting, Robert H. Ferrell delivered informal remarks on diplomatic history, but later he was unable to prepare them for publication. That

persuaded me to write chapter 8, which became available after the completion of this chapter (11).

2. Joan Hoff Wilson, "Is the Historical Profession an 'Endangered Species'?" paper delivered at the OAH annual meeting, April 11, 1980.

3. Joan Hoff, "Clio at the Crossroads: Historiographical and Methodological Developments within the Discipline of History," unpublished 2004 paper.

4. Mary Poovey, "Feminism and Deconstruction," *Feminist Studies* 14 (1988): 51–65; quotations at 52, 62.

5. Gerda Lerner, "The Future of Women History: Considering the State of Women History," *Journal of Women's History* 15 (Spring 2003): 145–82 (Lerner's remarks at 146–47, 160–61); Gerda Lerner, "U.S. Women's History: Past, Present, and Future" *JWH* 16 (Winter 2004): 10–27 (quotations at 21–23).

6. Bonnie Smith, "Feminist Webs, Feminist Magma: New Histories of Women's Activism," *JWH* 13 (Autumn 2001): 208–13; Joan Hoff, *Law, Gender and Injustice; A Legal History of U.S. Women* (New York: New York University Press, 1991; rev. ed., 1994); and Judith M. Bennett, "Theoretical Issues: Confronting Continuity," *JWH* 9 (Autumn 1997): 73–94.

7. Joan Hoff, "The Pernicious Effects of Poststructuralism on Women's History," *Chronicle of Higher Education*, October 20, 1993; Hoff, "The Pernicious Effects of Poststructuralism on Women's History," in *Radically Speaking: Feminism Reclaimed*, ed. Diane Bell and Renate Klein, 393–412 (Melbourne: Spinfex Press, 1996); and Hoff, "Agency and Collective Action versus Diversity and Differences," *JWH* 20, no. 1 (Spring 2008).

8. Joan Hoff, "Historiography of U.S. Foreign Policy at the End of the Cold War," unpublished 2003 paper.

9. Jerald A. Combs, *American Diplomatic History: Two Centuries of Changing Interpretations* (Berkeley: University of California Press, 1983), 113–98.

10. Ole R. Holsti, "International Relations Models," and Stephen Pelz, "Balance of Power," in *Explaining the History of American Foreign Relations*, ed. Michael J. Hogan and Thomas G. Paterson, 58 (New York: Cambridge University Press, 1991); and Combs, American *Diplomatic History*, 198–204.

11. Combs, *American Diplomatic History*, 205.

12. Holsti, "International Relations Models," and Stephen Pelz, "Balance of Power," in *American Foreign Relations*, ed. Hogan and Paterson, 57–61, 111; Combs, *American Diplomatic History*, 199–219; and Michael H. Hunt, "The Long Crisis in U.S. Diplomatic History," *Diplomatic History* 16 (Winter 1992): 117–19.

13. Holsti, "International Relations Models," 59–60; and Hunt, "Long Crisis," 118–21; and Joan Hoff, *A Faustian Foreign Policy from Woodrow Wilson to George W. Bush: Dreams of Perfectibility* (New York: Cambridge University Press, 2007), 2–5, 14–21, 113–14, 199–203.

14. Combs, *American Diplomatic History*, 256–57, 347–83; and Hunt, "Long Crisis," 124–25.

15. Michael Hogan, "Corporatism," in *American Foreign Relations*, ed. Hogan and Patterson, 226–36; Joan Hoff-Wilson, "Economic Issues and Foreign Policy," in *Guide to American Foreign Relations Since 1700*, ed. Richard Dean Burns, 1143–45 (Santa Barbara, CA: ABC-CLIO, 1982); and Hunt, "Long Crisis," 125–26.

16. Thomas J. McCormick, "World Systems," in *American Foreign Relations*, ed. Hogan and Patterson, 90; and McCormick, *America's Half-Century: United States*

Foreign Policy in the Cold War and After (Baltimore: Johns Hopkins University Press, 1995), 1–17. Core or First World Countries "monopolize high-tech, high profit enterprises"; periphery or Third World countries specialize "in primary production of agricultural commodities and raw materials"; and semiperiphery or Second World countries perform "intermediate function of transport, local capital mobilization, and less complex less profitable forms of manufacturing."

17. Rhodri Jeffreys-Jones, *Changing Differences: Women and the Shaping of American Foreign Policy, 1917–1994* (New Brunswick, NJ: Rutgers University Press, 1995); Dorothy G. McGuigan, *The Role of Women in Conflict and Peace* (Ann Arbor: University of Michigan Center for Continuing Education of Women, 1977); Ole R. Holsti and James N. Rosenau, "The Foreign Policy Beliefs of Women in Leadership Positions," in *Women Power and Policy*, ed. Ellen Boneparth, 238–65 (New York: Pergamon Press, 1988); Edward P. Crapol, ed., *Women and American Foreign Policy: Lobbyists, Critics, and Insiders* (Westport, CT: Greenwood Press, 1987; reprinted by Scholarly Resources, 1992); Emily S. Rosenberg, "Gender," *JAH* 77 (June 1990): 116–24.

18. Robert B. Townsend, "College Board Examines Survey Course," *OAH Newsletter*, August 2005.

19. Joan Hoff, "The National History Standards: Let's Go," and Joan W. Scott, Comment on "Women's History and the National History Standards, both in *JWH* 9, no. 4 (1997): 164–71, 172–76.

12

Social History and Intellectual History

James T. Kloppenberg

This part of our centennial history brings together various fields of social history and intellectual history. That combination might strike some readers as odd. Others will know that, for much of the last century, these fields were routinely combined. When I was an undergraduate at Dartmouth College in the late 1960s and early 1970s, for example, the History Department still offered a very popular course entitled "American Social and Intellectual History." Similar courses were offered at many colleges and universities around the nation, as had been true for half a century at least. At Harvard, the largest enrollments in the History Department were typically in the course entitled "American Social and Intellectual History" that Arthur Schlesinger Sr. taught from 1924, when he joined the Harvard faculty, until 1947. In that year he renamed the course American Social and Cultural History so that his son, Arthur Schlesinger Jr., could begin offering his own course in American intellectual history, a practice that has continued at Harvard ever since.

As David Hollinger notes, there have been gains as well as losses in the development of American intellectual history as a separate field. But the rigorous analysis of difficult ideas need not be, indeed should not be, pursued in isolation from the rigorous study of social history; Hollinger's own work on race and ethnicity shows how fruitfully they can be combined. All of us, whether we identify ourselves as intellectual or social historians, will do our work better if we remain aware of the work being done by specialists in the fields other than our own. That is the purpose of this part of this book. As the recent rise of a field entitled cultural history suggests, all forms of human behavior are meaningful, and, as historians, we should attend both to social activity and to the meanings individuals attach to their behavior.

The more rigid separation of the fields of social and intellectual history dates from the emergence in the 1960s of what was then called "the new social history," or "history from the bottom up." The combination of new methods of quantitative analysis; new emphases on understanding the everyday life of understudied people, including women, African Americans, and other ethnic and racial groups; and new theoretical perspectives shifted the focus of many historians away from the relation between thought and culture to other topics of concern. Until that time it was not uncommon for scholars, such as Merle Curti and John Higham, to publish in both fields of social and intellectual history that our profession now tends to distinguish. The fact that the Organization of American Historians awards two prizes bearing the name of Merle Curti, one in intellectual history and one in social history, reflects the once-common practice of an earlier generation of historians who joined together what our profession now too often splits apart.

So instead of bringing together strange bedfellows, this book hearkens back to a long and distinguished tradition, the common practice of American historians in the first six decades of this organization who examined—and taught—social and intellectual history in relation to one another. These pioneering historians, as Ellen Fitzpatrick has made clear in *History's Memory: Writing America's Past, 1880–1980*, from the outset studied immigration along with political thought, or African American history together with changing ideas of freedom and equality. They treated all these fields as they should be treated, simply as different dimensions of the shared history of the American people. The more recent division between these fields is a function of our sometimes hyperspecialized profession. Here, we return to the older, and wiser, tradition of joining together thought and practice, ideas and behavior, as aspects of the single, albeit multifaceted, reality that all of us American historians study.

13

The Long and Influential Life of Social History in the *MVHR* and the *JAH*

Stephanie J. Shaw

In a chapter entitled "Sociology, Meet History," Charles Tilly included a subsection, "The Historical Zoo," in which he wrote:

> I hope my description does not make the historical profession seem smoothly organized, neatly hierarchical, or deeply coherent. In reality, the practice of history resembles a zoo more than a herbarium, and a herbarium more than a cyclotron.

His zoo was one in which species occasionally escaped their cages and wandered into the domain of other animals, and sometimes they became something altogether different from what they originally were.[1]

Tilly's metaphor is a useful one for this effort to trace the development of social history in the *Mississippi Valley Historical Review (MVHR)* and the *Journal of American History (JAH)*. This essay suggests that, by now, at least in part, as a consequence of the influence of social history, the "inmates" (disciplines, fields, and subfields) are not simply occasionally escaping their cages, mingling, co-mingling, and morphing into different species, but that some of the cages have come down, and the genus itself (history) has been transformed in some important ways.

Born of a rightly perceived need to complicate (or complete) the picture of the past, largely defined up to the start of the twentieth century by the study of elites, events, and governments (nations), social historians sought to invigorate historical interrogations by encouraging the humanization of history. Over time, this process would include three strategies. First was attention to ordinary people and everyday life. Second was the inclusion of interdisciplinary methods. And third was study from the bottom up.[2] In their own time, each of these was a fairly radical proposition, and incorporating them indeed *seemed* to make a mess of American history. But the end result yielded narratives that were often complex and sophisticated. Moreover, they were often perfectly coherent. Indeed, all those fragments that some scholars worried about during the early 1960s have begun to yield the kind of syntheses that early social historians envisioned and subsequent scholars explicitly encouraged. These were syntheses that would not have been possible without all of what, early on, appeared to be a bit of a mess.[3]

An examination of social history in the journal allows us to see how it changed in its appearance over the generations. While there are clear parallels between what appears in the journal and developments in the larger field, there are, nevertheless, some differences. Obviously, research findings often appear in print as articles before being published in book form; some discussions only appear in article form; and some discussions, important though they may be, never make it into the journals. But this kind of survey yields other benefits as well. It allows us to consider generalizations and conclusions about the larger field in the context of this very specific venue.

Social history appeared in the journal almost from the beginning of its publication, and one does not have to stretch, modify, or blur definitions and distinctions in order to make these works fit the label. Much of this early work focused on the west and on agriculture, and it considered how people lived, worked, and otherwise participated in developing and transforming regions, cultures, and communities. If this work is not particularly focused on "the bottom" of the social-cultural hierarchies that existed, it is likely to be because the subjects of these early studies made it difficult to see where the bottom was and who was there.

This is not to ignore American Indians, who were ever present in the early history of the Mississippi Valley. However, few of the early articles provided much detail about them. Most focused on the experience of government officials, missionary efforts, and Americanization projects. There were, however, two early exceptions to this generalization, and they could not have been more different. The first, George Pare's article, "The St. Joseph Mission," provided great detail on the everyday lives of Sauk, Huron, and Potawatomi Indians. Grace Lee Nute's 1926 study, "The American Fur Company's Fishing Enterprises on Lake Superior," although a better example of the economic/business history focus of American history at the time, paid close attention to the Indians who inhabited much of the British, French, and American territory, and detailed the roles of these Indians in the development of this major business enterprise.[4] Still, the manner in which American Indians appeared (and, more generally, did not appear) in these early studies represents the big, glaring gap in these early examinations of the West. That gap simply would not be filled until the mandates of "the new social history" that called for attention to the previously neglected groups and subgroups came to fruition.

Until that attention to more subgroups materialized, one useful characterization of the early articles appearing in the journal was that they provided more social content than social history. In "Early Negro Deportation Projects," appearing in 1916, for example, it is clear that it was not particularly the people being removed from the colonies who were the subjects of this article. The article was about colonial laws and government interests in maintaining order. And clearly one way to achieve that order was to remove people who had been judged criminal. But in elucidating this process, the author surveyed the laws, which revealed not only the removal of criminals but processes of individual emancipations, and various church and state sponsored colonization schemes, as well, dating back to 1714. Examining the actual removal of these individuals reached into business history—the business of the New England slavers, the ship owners whose livelihood derived, in part, from this removal process. In addition to some business history, legal history, church history, and, African American history, there was also the antislavery response to it all. The point here is that social history is, in some of these early articles, hidden in plain view.[5]

Although we do not learn as much as we would like about the individuals being deported—the snippets of their lives amounted to social content—the whole article does suggest the way social history is written in the early years: it typically focused broadly on a town, legal traditions, a business, or some other political, economic, or geographic entity. Some of the early town studies utilized quantitative methods, and some even began to address what we now characterize as "borderlands" constructions—hybrid, fluid cultures on the margins of overlapping traditions—where, in one case, "northern, southern, and western interests clearly overlap[,] and class, any fiction of a homogeneous or united economic and social group coincident with state boundaries, breaks down." These studies did not generally employ the disciplines of philosophy or psychology, so terms like *identity* and *consciousness* did not appear consistently in them, but even where such terms were not used, inferences may, nevertheless, easily be drawn.[6]

The social groups who appeared in detail in the early articles are fairly predictable—Puritans, immigrants, farmers—and they, more often than not, are elites. Among this group of early articles were a few noteworthy examples. In one immigrant study, Carl Russell Fish traced a small "group of simple, perhaps stodgy peasants," who moved from Scrooby and Auserfeld in England to the Low Countries and then to America, and who, by the time "they settled Plymouth . . . were no longer English peasants." They had already begun the process of "becoming a new people." Although Fish's Puritans were somewhat exceptional people, more important is the fact that the process he described evoked more recent discussions of social and cultural transformations—creolization—that regularly took place in steps, on both sides of the Atlantic, before and after immigration. Similarly, a 1920 essay looked at Jane Grey Swisshelm's life in marriage and outside of it: as a single woman, a wife, and divorcee; as an antislavery agitator and a woman's rights advocate; and, altogether, as a woman who battled the institutions of law, marriage, family, and politics, as a decidedly self-possessed woman. This kind of exploration would not be duplicated for decades.

There was even among these early articles at least one study from the perspective of the lower rungs. A study of Coxey's Army reconstructed the larger economic and political environment that spawned this movement, looked at the rank and file along with the leadership, and traced the movement from its Midwestern foundation to its arrival in Washington, DC. The author looked at the diverse reasons for people's participation in the movement and the march, internal political organization, and the government of the groups, along with business/industry response. In short, this article provided as complete a portrait of this group as one could expect.[7]

The articles just singled out suggest the occasional zoo inmate that escaped its cage and ultimately mutated into something different from most of those of its species still behind their bars. In the early decades of the journal's publication, they were the exceptions to the rule. But this *is* the MVHR, and studies of the region enjoyed early advantages, and, therefore, developed more quickly than others. Thus, one can see the confluence of social-cultural processes with larger political and economic structures more consistently when the focus is on farmers, ranchers, and less lawful characters of the newly developing West. Because these studies of western settlement were often "tests" of one of the early major paradigm shifts in American history (Turner's "frontier thesis") even before 1930, they begin to distinguish between and among the groups settling the frontier, making it clear that this was not "free" land; that Anglo-American settlement cost other people dearly; and that the settlers themselves were different enough from one another that various, sometimes violent, contests developed between and among them (between sheep herders and cattle ranchers, cattle ranchers and farmers, between these new settlers and Indians, and between all of them and squatters and homesteaders, for example).[8] Some of these early articles diversified "the frontier" itself, underscoring that no single distinction, especially, perhaps, geography, adequately characterized it or its inhabitants. In other essays, the frontier was as much an ideology as a place, and in one case, the words *interests* and *self-consciousness* explicitly replace *section* and *sectionalism*. Merchants and artisans in the Northeast, who were themselves making decisions about whether to "go west," joined the (stereo)typical western subjects (farmers, ranchers, merchants, and adventurers) in tests of the frontier thesis. Throughout these articles, it becomes clearer precisely who made their way to this frontier, how they got there, how they fared once there, how they related to one another, and why some decided not to go.[9]

Chronology shows that the American historians were not entirely derivative or uniformly lagging behind the call of the first generation of *Annales* historians to look beyond the traditional study of the politics and diplomacy of the state. The attention to social and economic processes and structures was evident early on. Moreover, articles addressed early social history interests in language and language use.[10]

Still, the 1940s appear to be a turning point in the articles in terms of approach and subjects. There are undoubtedly many explanations for these changes. One has to do with the increasing influence of other disciplinary fields. Cultural anthropology, for example, along with the already existing attention to structural issues, begins to yield a better picture of everyday life. Dancing; newspaper writing; humor; theater; sports; reading and publishing; violence; aspects of social, and often public, culture were among the topics explored in articles that also considered the people engaged in those activities and the various conditions of their lives and the places where they lived.[11]

The decline in articles that tested big theories—forces—suggests another source of change, as American historians during and after World War II became more interested in human motivations (mentalité, perhaps) and the social aspects of American history. Edward Pessen's study, "The Workingmen's Movement of the Jacksonian Era," looked closely at the activities of the working men's associations, their leaders, and their members, in order to determine who, actually, directed them, the workers or the politicians. John E. Bauer looked at westward migration in an entirely new way, focusing, not on the farmers, ranchers, gold seekers, and adventurers, but on invalids, and not on the lure of land and the potential for a more democratic lifestyle but the western climate and its apparent health benefits. The efforts of veterans of the Mexican War to organize themselves were the focus of another study. A study that paid particular attention to Mormons who worked at Sutter's Fort *before* gold was discovered there not only expanded the traditional view of the West and the "49ers" but also considered a not-so-traditional religious group outside the context of religion. The prairie "cattle kings," got an entirely new look in these pre-1960s articles, situating them in a social (class) hierarchy that might have excluded or ignored them before. Almost in anticipation of the later turn to race, and particularly to whiteness, a study of white people—orphans, apprentices, vagrants, convicts, and others—pushed the concept of bondage in the slave South beyond its traditional boundaries.

Although the minority groups who appeared in the studies of this period remained primarily ancillary subjects, they, at least, finally showed up. And even in an area as traditional as military history, new views, if not yet a new species, started to emerge during this period in which veterans, soldier relief, public health, and protest replaced more traditional focus on battles, strategies, tactics, weaponry, and officers. The loyalists were no longer Revolutionary War, but Civil War, veterans, and Southern Claims Commission Records replaced voting records for sources of evidence of loyalism.[12]

One can also detect the impact of World War II on the expansion in social history articles during the 1940s and '50s. The rapid technological changes wrought by the war, the government's use of psychologists in the prosecution of the war, and the maturation of advertising as a profession during the war also helped to shape the direction of social history articles.[13] War-era heightened sensitivity to past social prejudices and inequalities influenced some historians to pay more attention to neglected groups and even to consider the historical roots of contemporary ideologies.[14]

Finally, one can also see the development of quantitative methods during this period, as they reach beyond demonstrations of the relationship between wealth and political party or religious denomination to reveal the *movement* of wealth (across Revolutionary Era Virginia, in one case) and to provide more complete analyses of farm economies, even allowing domestic and international comparisons. Some studies distinguished further between types of farmers (wage laborers, tenant farmers, and sharecroppers) and landowners (owner-planters, absentee owners, and landlords), whether they were on the frontier or not; and they reexamine many old subjects, including traditional elites, in much greater detail than ever before.[15]

When, during the 1960s, social historians called for more studies from the bottom up, the process was already well under way. The attention in the articles, however, does not consistently focus, this early, on the interior lives of the people in any of the particular groups. Rather, the early attention is more on social and political (often, protest) movements (throughout history), whose (re-)examination no doubt received some inspiration from the extensive public activism taking place at the time.[16]

Collectively viewing this particular body of scholarship as about protest rather than, or in addition to, about groups helps to blunt at least one aspect of the contemporary concern with fragmentation. What these articles accomplished beyond the attention to the groups is very important. Challenging public/private sphere dichotomies, social/political dichotomies, and work/community dichotomies, among others, helped to break down some of the barriers, the cages, between disparate areas. Thus, New Deal scholars, for example, would continue to consider government policy, administrative debates, and program development, but they would also scour presidential papers for evidence of the influence of ordinary people on these political processes. The workers in the New Deal programs became as important as the programs. And farmers whose lives and lifestyles came into view here included those who not only owned no land, but also many—sharecroppers—who owned nothing.[17]

Despite all the evidence of shifting scholarly directions, the mandates of "the new social history" would not be completely fulfilled until well into the 1980s, and we should not minimize the consequences. Interdisciplinary methods expanded and appeared in a much more diverse array of studies than before;[18] more articles paid systematic attention to the everyday life of ordinary people;[19] and bottom-up approaches became commonplace.[20] Many of these articles put power, community, and social consciousness at the center of the discussions.[21]

Equally important, this detailed attention to the complexity of social interaction helped to create entirely new paradigms. For example, whereas most of the studies involving black people appearing in the journal between the 1940s and early 1980s were largely studies of race leaders, race organizations, and, especially, race relations, the new attention to broader conditions of black life centralized race, itself; made race, even whiteness, the subject of study; and eventually came to study race as ideology.[22] Studies of women similarly evolved, later but more quickly between the 1980s and today, from studies of leading ladies, prescriptive literature, policy developments, and women's movements to studies of women as women, framed by feminism and feminist theory, and, finally, gender. Through gender analyses, scholars finally made the connection between men and masculinity.[23] Thus, the study of social groups evolved from treating people almost as "others," to recognizing social identities that centered the subjects as social, cultural, and political beings, and finally to considering ideological constructs that linked those subjects to larger social, political, intellectual, economic, and cultural phenomena.

But the 1980s call for a new synthesis concerned more than social groups. Ideally, this synthesis would not only center human subjects, eliminate their isolation from one another, and eliminate the boundaries between them and the larger society in which they lived, but it would also eliminate more disciplinary divisions, geographical boundaries, and temporal limitations as well. Of course, no article can accomplish all that a book can, and so the articles in the journal rarely accomplished all these things. But there is a way in which the *JAH* articles reflected other very useful syntheses, often like those Thomas Bender proposed and, perhaps, are hinted at in the thinking of various authors about race and gender rather than color and sex.[24]

One type of synthesis is evident in transformations within specific subfields of American history. The study of the city, once largely political, demographic, or economic in its orientation, now focused more broadly on the process of urbanization. By this process, obviously time is important, but so are diverse social groups, their coming and going, and their interaction with one another and with the other institutions of the city. The people on the bottom are as important to this process as those on the top or in the middle. Their family, community, and organizational life are all as important as their encounters with social reformers, police, workplace supervisors, and machine politicians. In this context, politics concerns much more than voting, and processes of urbanization go beyond the city.[25]

Articles in political history reflected similar synthetic tendencies. Authors continued to consider voters, parties, and policies, but now the politics were often local; they included groups whose exclusion earlier seemed logical because their members could not or did not vote or otherwise seemed unimportant; and, because of that inclusion, political processes involved much more than elections.[26] In both of these areas, and in all the others, these works bore the marked influence of multidisciplinary perspectives.

Other developments within, and the creation of, new subfields, also reflected synthesis. Articles on consumer culture, first of all, exposed a fourth transformation within economic history (after the studies of business, then unions, then workers). Although the articles appearing to this point on consumer culture were few, some movement toward crossing all the traditional boundaries of discipline, social group, time, technology, and geography was evident.[27] Discussions of public or mass culture, which were not as numerous to this point as work in consumer culture in the journal, moved even further toward synthesis. Discussions of the ways large groups of people used public space to advance social, cultural, and political interests simultaneously connected them to the structures and processes of the larger society.[28] Environmental history combined science and technology, race and place, class and power, and culture in ways that easily represented synthesis.[29] Finally, it is important to remember that social historians began this move toward syntheses before the official call came. It occurred first in a context related to an old, traditional area of study, namely, slavery.[30]

There were, however, topics that did not yet appear in the detail that one might expect in these journals. First, it was the Vietnam War, rather than the Civil War, that social historians seemed (still) to be losing to the military historians.[31] American Indians, first appearing in the journal articles as objects of missionary work, military campaigns, and government projects, became subjects in their own right during the 1970s, but quickly disappeared again until around 2000.[32] Articles on sex and sexuality, appearing early on in the context of cultural values and traditions, yielded to studies of sexual identity, but the latter are now just beginning to make their way into the journal.[33] Both Asian Americans and Latinos remain barely represented in the *Journal*.[34] And the study of immigrants and immigration after the turn of the twentieth century and outside the North and Midwest is virtually nonexistent.[35]

There are other kinds of gaps as well. Given the centrality of family to social-cultural traditions, family history in the *JAH* does not go significantly beyond studies of family size, household structures, and the distribution of wealth. Examples of the important life-course studies that began to appear during the 1970s are barely evident in the articles.[36] Although within the studies of various social groups, traditions, and institutions, articles reveal much about the quality and conditions of everyday life, the study of everyday life itself lag far behind. Within the subfields, the most consistent site of considerations of everyday life is the study of work culture.[37] Otherwise, there is only scant attention to leisure, recreation, death, disease, education, food, and even material culture, in general.³⁸ Comparative studies are not well represented in the journal.³⁹ Very few studies consider change in inter- or transnational contexts.⁴⁰ Although individual social groups and phenomena are no longer isolated from the state, the larger culture, and other social groups, very few works examine any group or phenomena in the context of change over long periods of time, an important interest of the early social historians.⁴¹

Despite these caveats, most of which can be explained, at least in part, by the proliferation of other specialty journals and the shifting of some articles to them, social history conceptualizations have indeed transformed both the disparate subfields and American history generally. Much of this change was a direct result of our borrowing from other disciplines. But recent studies of history and memory suggest that we have moved beyond simply borrowing from other disciplines in order to complete the pictures of the past that we are trying to construct. The study of historical memory, although certainly reflecting the influence of philosophy, psychology, and anthropology, provides an altogether new way of looking for history, a new source of history, and a new way of thinking about knowledge in general, all of which the old and the new social historians encouraged.⁴²

In short, social history, though it will continue to change, has undoubtedly come of age. The individual species are no longer just occasionally escaping their cages and becoming something different from others of their kind. The species (the fields and subfields) are now different from what they were before. The genus (history) is now different from what it was as well. And the zoo itself, with many of the cages eliminated, has indeed been transformed.

NOTES

1. Charles Tilly, *As Sociology Meets History* (New York, and other cities: Academic Press, 1981), 15.

2. *Annales* founders Lucien Febvre and Marc Bloch, through their own work and through the journal, encouraged history that paid more attention to people (as opposed to events and institutions) and that incorporated ideas and methods from natural, social, and behavioral sciences. Fernand Braudel, a second generation *Annales* historian, added considerable emphasis on studies over long spans of time (*la longue durée*). There were also British, German, and American counterparts to the French scholars and scholarship.

3. Although the initial conceptualization of synthesis was broad based, it was probably the push to include the histories of minority groups that raised some of the first fears of fragmentation among American historians. One article that expresses explicit concerns in this way was C. Vann Woodward, "Clio with Soul," *JAH* 56 (June 1969): 5–29. Subsequent presidential addresses worked to soften these criticisms. See Carl N. Degler, "Remaking American History," *JAH* 67 (June 1980): 7–25; and Edmund Morgan, "Slavery and Freedom: The American Paradox," *JAH* 59 (June 1972): 5–29. Although synthesis was the aim of early social historians, a more recent discussion came

from Thomas Bender in "Wholes and Parts: The Need for Synthesis in American History," *JAH* 73 (June 1986): 120–36.

4. See William E. Connelley, "Religious Conceptions of the Modern Hurons," *MVHR* 9 (Sept. 1922): 110–25; Marie J. Kohnova, "The Moravians and Their Missionaries: A Problem in Americanization," *MVHR* 19 (Dec. 1932): 348–61; George Pare, "The St. Joseph Mission," *MVHR* 17 (June 1930): 24–54; and Grace Lee Nute, "The American Fur Company's Fishing Enterprises on Lake Superior," *MVHR* 12 (Mar. 1926): 483–503.

5. See H. N. Sherwood, "Early Negro Deportation Projects," *MVHR* 2 (Mar. 1916): 484–508. The Grace Lee Nute article, cited in note 4, also fits this characterization, though it is essentially business history. This broad-based study of the American Fur Company traces its development to its becoming a monopoly. In addition to detailing the processes of vertical and horizontal integration, the article considers changes in territorial possession, town site development, the development of subsidiary industries (coopers, fishermen, boating), and the struggle of and wages of workers.

6. Charles R. Wilson, "Cincinnati: A Southern Outpost in 1860–61?" *MVHR* 24 (Mar. 1938): 473–82 and Jonas Viles, "Sections and Sectionalism in a Border State," *MVHR* 21 (June 1934): 3–22; quotation at 3. Viles ultimately eschews the terms *section* and *sectionalism* because of their connection to rather rigid geography rather than more fluid social phenomena. A detailed quantitative study related to public health issues is Gerald M. Capers Jr., "Yellow Fever in Memphis in the 1870s," *MVHR* 24 (Mar. 1938): 483–502.

7. Carl Russell Fish, "The Pilgrim and the Melting Pot," *MVHR* 3 (Dec. 1920): 187–205; Lester Burrell Shippee, "Jane Grey Swisshelm: Agitator," *MVHR* 7 (Dec. 1920): 206–27; and Donald McMurry, "The Industrial Armies and the Commonweal," *MVHR* 10 (Dec. 1923): 215–52. Also see Theodore C. Blegen, "Cleng Peerson and Norwegian Immigration," *MVHR* 7 (Mar. 1921): 303–31, which captures the complexity of social and economic networks facilitating immigration and the chain migration that took place as well.

8. Although there are additional studies on these topics, these more clearly reflect characteristics of social history and, in general, provide more than social content, even though it is also generally the case that these articles do not yet look closely at the interior lives of the members of the groups. See John D. Hicks, "The Origin and Early History of the Farmers' Alliance in Minnesota," *MVHR* 9 (Dec. 1922): 201–26; Robert S. Fletcher, "The End of the Open Range in Eastern Montana," *MVHR* 16 (June 1929): 188–211; Thomas Perkins Abernethy, "Social Relations and Political Control in the Old Southwest," *MVHR* 16 (Mar. 1930): 529–37; C. C. Rister, "Outlaws and Vigilantes of the Southern Plains, 1856–1885," *MVHR* 19 (Mar. 1933): 537–54; Edward Everett Dale, "The Cow Country in Transition," *MVHR* 24 (June 1937): 3–20; and Benton H. Wilcox, "An Historical Definition of Northwestern Radicalism," *MVHR* 26 (Dec. 1939): 377–94.

9. Hicks, "The Farmers' Alliance in Minnesota"; Fletcher, "The Open Range in Eastern Montana," *MVHR* 16 (June 1929): 188–211; Abernethy, "Social Relations and Political Control in the Old Southwest"; Viles, "Sections and Sectionalism in a Border State"; Murray Kane, "Some Considerations of the Safety Valve Doctrine," *MVHR* 23 (Sept. 1936): 169–88. This theme of overlapping "border life" and "border culture" is

the subject of Carl Coke Rister, "The Oilman's Frontier," *MVHR* 37 (June 1950): 3–16, in which the subject is an industrial (oil producing) frontier.

10. See F. H. Hodder, "Propaganda as a Source of American History," *MVHR* 9 (June 1922): 3–18. R. Carlyle Buley, "Glimpses of Pioneer Mid-west Social and Cultural History," *MVHR* 23 (Mar. 1937): 481–510 pays particular attention to language as does Philip D. Jordan, "Humor in the Backwoods, 1820–1840," *MVHR* 25 (June 1938): 25–38.

11. Philip D. Jordan, "Humor in the Backwoods," Cole, "The Puritan and Fair Terpischore," and Frank Luther Mott, "Facetious News Writing, 1833–1883,"*MVHR* 29 (June 1942): 3–34, 35–54; W. S. Tryon, "Ticknor and Fields' Publications in the Old Northwest, 1840–1860," *MVHR* 34 (Mar. 1948): 589–610; Harold E. Briggs and Ernestine Bennett Briggs, "The Early Theater on the Northern Plains," *MVHR* 37 (Sept. 1950): 231–64; Clement Eaton, "Mob Violence in the Old South," *MVHR* 29 (Dec. 1942): 351–70; John Richards Betts, "The Technological Revolution and the Rise of Sport, 1850–1900," *MVHR* 40 (Sept. 1953): 231–56. And see Lewis E. Atherton, "Mercantile Education in the Ante-bellum South," *MVHR* 29 (Mar. 1953): 623–40, on the self-education of members of the merchant class.

12. Edward Pessen, "The Workingmen's Movement of the Jacksonian Era," *MVHR* 43 (Dec. 1956): 428–43; Wallace E. Davies, "Mexican War Veterans as an Organized Group," *MVHR* 35 (Sept. 1948): 221–38; John E. Baur, "The Health Seeker in the Westward Movement, 1830–1900," *MVHR* 46 (June 1959): 91–110; Ralph P. Bieber, "California Gold Mania," *MVHR* 35 (June 1948): 3–28; Paul Wallace Gates, "Cattle Kings in the Prairies," *MVHR* 35 (Dec. 1948): 379–412; Richard B. Morris, "The Measure of Bondage in the Slave States," *MVHR* 41 (Sept. 1954): 219–40; Bennett H. Wall, "Medical Care of Ebenezer Pettigrew's Slaves," *MVHR* 37 (Dec. 1950): 451–70, focused on the planters and physicians, and Julius Yanuck's "The Garner Fugitive Slave Case," *MVHR* 40 (June 1953): 47–66, focused on legal issues. Among these articles was one on American Indians that did provide more than social context. Stanley Clark, "Ponca Publicity," *MVHR* 29 (Mar. 1943): 495–516, focused on efforts to remove Ponca Indians from reserve land and organized efforts (often very public and performance-oriented among diverse factions, including Indian families) to resist. And, finally, see Frank Wysor Klingbert, "The Southern Claims Commission: A Postwar Agency in Operation," *MVHR* 32 (June 1945): 195–214; Howard D. Kramer, "Effect of the Civil War on the Public Health Movement," *MVHR* 35 (Dec. 1948): 449–62; Edwin B. Coddington, "Soldiers' Relief in the Seaboard States of the Southern Confederacy," *MVHR* 37 (June 1950): 17–38.

13. See Merle Curti and Kendall Birr, "The Immigrant and the American Image in Europe," *MVHR* 37 (Sept. 1950): 203–30. While looking at the traditional aspects of immigration studies including social networks and migration patters, this article also considered the use of image in American business and government promotion of European immigration between the Civil War and World War I. Hugo A. Meier's "Technology and Democracy, 1800–1860," *MVHR* 43 (Mar. 1957): 618–40, was a clear forerunner to recent discussions of "imagined communities," in its examination of the relationship between technological changes and the development and promotion of social and political ideas in the decades before the Civil War. But also see Oscar Osburn Winther, "The Use of Climate as a Means of Promoting Migration to Southern California," *MVHR* 33 (Dec. 1946): 411–24. Advertising and propaganda were also the subject

of Robert K. Murray, "Communism and the Great Steel Strike of 1919," *MHVR* 38 (Dec. 1951): 445–66.

14. See John Higham, "Anti-Semitism in the Gilded Age: A Reinterpretation," *MVHR* 43 (Mar. 1957): 559–78. On the increase in attention to African American and American Indian history, see Leslie H. Fishel Jr., "The Negro in Northern Politics, 1870–1900," *MVHR* 42 (Dec. 1955): 466–89; Emma Lou Thornbrough, "The Brownsville Episode and the Negro Vote," *MVHR* 44 (Dec. 1957): 469–93; and Mary E. Young's "The Creek Frauds: A Study in Conscience and Corruption," *MVHR* 42 (Dec. 1955): 411–37. (See additional examples in note 12.) Exceptions to the preceding generalization include Stanley Clark's "Ponca Publicity," which, as already noted, did start to pay attention to Indians as subjects and, in fact, almost described a "movement," and Benjamin Quarles's "Sources of Abolitionist Income," *MVHR* 32 (June 1945): 63–94, which provided a level of detail about the contributors, their activities, and networks, that would eventually become standard among social historians. Still, one sees the broadening of the topics (to include minority groups) before one sees African Americans and American Indians as real subjects.

15. Richard P. McCormick, "Suffrage Classes and Party Alignments: A Study in Voter Behavior," *MVHR* 46 (Nov. 1959): 397–410; Jackson Turner Main, "The Distribution of Property in Post-Revolutionary Virginia," *MVHR* 41 (Sept. 1945): 241–58; Fred A. Shannon, "The Status of the Midwestern Farmer in 1900," *MVHR* 37 (Dec. 1950): 491–510; Gates, "Cattle Kings in the Prairies." Subsequent quantitative studies, including those that re-examined traditional questions and topics, included Robert Emmet Wall Jr., "A New Look at Cambridge," *JAH* 52 (Dec. 1965): 599–605; Carl E. Prince, "The Passing of the Aristocracy: Jefferson's Removal of the Federalists, 1801–1805," *JAH* 57 (Dec. 1970): 563–75; Herbert Ershkowitz and William G. Shade, "Consensus or Conflict? Political Behavior in the State Legislatures During the Jacksonian Era," *JAH* 58 (Dec. 1971): 591–621; Robert Emmet Wall Jr., "The Decline of the Massachusetts Franchise: 1647–1666," *JAH* 59 (Sept. 1972): 303–10.

16. On women, for example, see Robert E. Riegel, "The Split of the Feminist Movement in 1869," *MVHR* 49 (Dec. 1962): 485–96, and Sharon Hartman Strom, "Leadership and Tactics in the American Woman Suffrage Movement: A New Perspective from Massachusetts," *JAH* 62 (Sept. 1974): 296–315. For more about political than social processes, see J. Stanley Lemons, "The Sheppard-Towner Act: Progressivism in the 1920s," *JAH* 55 (Mar. 1969): 776–86. On African Americans, see August Meier and Elliott Rudwick, "The Boycott Movement against Jim Crow Streetcars in the South, 1900–1906," *JAH* 55 (Mar. 1969): 756–75; Louis Cantor, "A Prologue to the Protest Movement"; James M. McPherson, "Abolitionists and the Civil Rights Act of 1875," *JAH* 52 (Sept. 1965): 493–510; R. Alton Lee, "The Army 'Mutiny' of 1946," *JAH* 53 (Dec. 1966): 555–71; William B. Hixson Jr., "Moorfield Storey and the Struggle for Equality," *JAH* 55 (Dec. 1968): 533–54; Richard M. Dalfiume, "The 'Forgotten Years' of the Negro Revolution," *JAH* 55 (June 1968): 90–106; Jane H. Pease and William H. Pease, "Confrontation and Abolition in the 1850s," *JAH* 58 (Mar. 1972): 923–37; Lee Finkle, "The Conservative Aims of Militant Rhetoric: Black Protest during World War II," *JAH* 60 (Dec. 1973): 692–713. Articles on blacks not in this protest tradition are few, but important. See Gilbert Osofsky's "The Enduring Ghetto," *JAH* 55 (Sept. 1968): 243–55 and Walter Ehrlich's "Was the Dred Scott Case Valid?" *JAH* 55 (Sept. 1968): 256–65, which is more concerned with legal issues than African American history. On

labor, see Robert H. Wiebe, "The Anthracite Strike of 1902: A Record of Confusion," *MVHR* 47 (Sept. 1961): 229–51; John L. Shover, "The Communist Party and the Midwest Farm Crisis of 1933," *JAH* 50 (June 1964): 248–66; Edward M. Steel, "Mother Jones in the Fairmont Field, 1902," *JAH* 57 (Sept. 1970): 290–307; Lowell K. Dyson, "The Red Peasant International in America," *JAH* 58 (Mar. 1972): 958–73; Allan M. Winkler, "The Philadelphia Transit Strike of 1944," *JAH* 59 (June 1972): 73–89; Robert H. Zieger, "The Limits of Militancy: Organizing Paper Workers, 1933–1935," *JAH* 63 (Dec. 1976): 638–57. The studies in labor and agricultural history began this study of protest during the 1950s. See Frank L. Klement, "Middle Western Copperheadism and the Genesis of the Granger Movement," *MVHR* 38 (Mar. 1951): 679–94; Pessen, "The Workingmen's Movement of the Jacksonian Era"; and Sidney Fine, "The Eight-Hour Day Movement in the United States, 1888–1891," *MVHR* 40 (Dec. 1953): 441–62.

17. Gilbert C. Fite, "Farmer Opinion and the Agricultural Adjustment Act, 1933," *MVHR* 48 (Mar. 1962): 656–73; John A. Salmond, "The Civilian Conservation Corps and the Negro," *JAH* 52, June 1965, 75–88; Louis Cantor, "A Prologue to the Protest Movement." Other changes in the approach to study of the New Deal were evident in Rite Werner Gordon, "The Change in the Political Alignment of Chicago's Negroes during the New Deal," *JAH* 56 (Dec. 1969): 584–603, which used black voting patterns to determine whether the New Deal was simply a continuation of Progressive Era reforms or something entirely new.

18. Until about the 1960s, the appearance of interdisciplinary traditions tended to be limited to the incorporation of quantitative methods and sociological and anthropological questions. And the studies reflecting these methods concentrated in political, agricultural, urban, and family studies. After that time, these methods reached all areas of historical study and included methods and concerns from physical, biological, and environmental sciences as well as from an expanding social science foundation. James Harvey Young, "American Medical Quackery in the Age of the Common Man," *MVHR* 47 (Mar. 1961): 579–93; Howard P. Chudacoff, "A New Look at Ethnic Neighborhoods: Residential Dispersion and the Concept of Visibility in a Medium-Sized City," *JAH* 60 (June 1973): 76–93; Carroll Smith-Rosenberg and Charles Rosenberg, "The Female Animal: Medical and Biological Views of Woman and Her Role in Nineteenth-Century America," *JAH* 60 (Sept. 1973): 332–56; Ralph V. Anderson and Robert E. Gallman, "Slaves as Fixed Capital: Slave Labor and Southern Economic Development," *JAH* 64 (June 1977): 24–46; Joan Jacobs Brumberg, "Zenanas and Girlless Villages: The Ethnology of American Evangelical Women, 1870–1910," *JAH* 60 (Sept. 1982): 347–71; Flores, "Bison Ecology and Bison Diplomacy"; and Elizabeth A. Perkins, "The Consumer Frontier: Household Consumption in Early Kentucky," *JAH* 78 (Sept. 1991): 465–85 and 486–510, respectively; Susan E. Klepp, "Revolutionary Bodies: Women and the Fertility Transition in the Mid-Atlantic Region, 1760–1820," *JAH* 85 (Dec. 1998): 910–45; Erik R. Seeman, "Reading Indians' Deathbed Scenes: Ethnohistorical and Representational Approaches," *JAH* 88 (June 2001): 17–47. But one should also note that even in the use of quantitative methods for political analyses, there was no longer an assumption that a single factor (party, denomination, wealth) would determine any outcomes. See Wall Jr., "A New Look at Cambridge"; J. M. Bumstead, "Religion, Finance, and Democracy in Massachusetts: The Town of Norton as a Case Study," *JAH* 57 (Mar. 1970): 817–31; Prince, "The Passing of the Aristocracy."

19. See Paton Yoder, "Private Hospitality in the South, 1775–1850," *MVHR* 47 (Dec. 1960): 419–33; Christopher G. Wye, "The New Deal and the Negro Community: Toward a Broader Conceptualization," *JAH* 59 (Dec. 1972): 621–39; Richard A. Easterlin, "Factors in the Decline of Farm Family Fertility in the United States: Some Preliminary Research Results," *JAH* 63 (Dec. 1976): 600–14; Winifred D. Wandersee Bolin, "The Economics of Middle-Income Family Life: Working Women during the Great Depression," *JAH* 65 (June 1978): 60–74; Karen Ordahl Kupperman, "Apathy and Death in Early Jamestown," *JAH* 66 (June 1979): 24–40; William F. Holmes, "Moonshining and Collective Violence: Georgia, 1889–1895," *JAH* 67 (Dec. 1980): 589–611; Judith Walzer Leavitt, "'Science' Enters the Birthing Room: Obstetrics in America since the Eighteenth Century," *JAH* 70 (Sept. 1983): 281–304; Michael J. Doucet and John C. Weaver, "Material Culture and the North American House: The Era of the Common Man, 1870–1920," *JAH* 72 (Dec. 1985): 560–87; Jo Ann Manfra and Robert R. Dykstra, "Serial Marriage and the Origins of the Black Stepfamily: The Rowanty Evidence," *JAH* 72 (June 1985): 18–44; Mark Peel, "On the Margins: Lodgers and Boarders in Boston, 1860–1900," *JAH* 72 (Mar. 1986): 813–34; Nancy Schrom Dye and Daniel Blake Smith, "Mother Love and Infant Death, 1750–1920," *JAH* 73 (Sept. 1986): 329–53; Klepp, "Revolutionary Bodies"; Simone Cinotto, "Leonard Covello, the Covello Papers, and the History of Eating Habits among Italian Immigrants in New York," *JAH* 91 (Sept. 2004): 497–521; and Laura McEnaney, "Nightmares on Elm Street: Demobilization in Chicago, 1945–53," *JAH* 92 (Mar. 2006): 1265–91.

20. See Pete Daniel, "Up from Slavery and Down to Peonage: The Alonzo Bailey Case," *JAH* 57 (Dec. 1970): 654–70; Zieger, "The Limits of Militancy"; Gary B. Nash, "The Transformation of Urban Politics, 1700–65," *JAH* 60 (Dec. 1973): 605–32; Karen Tucker Anderson, "Last Hired, First Fired: Black Women Workers during World War II," *JAH* 69 (June 1982): 82–97; Shane White, "'We Dwell in Safety and Pursue Our Honest Callings': Free Blacks in New York City, 1787–1810," *JAH* 75 (Sept. 1988): 445–70; Jonathan Prude, "To Look upon the 'Lower Sort': Runaway Ads and the Appearance of Unfree Laborers in America, 1750–1800," *JAH* 78 (June 1991): 124–59; Michael Kazin and Steven J. Ross, "America's Labor Day: The Dilemma of a Workers' Celebration," *JAH* 78 (Mar. 1992): 1294–1323; James R. Barrett, "Americanization from the Bottom Up: Immigration and the Remaking of the Working Class in the United States, 1880–1930," *JAH* 79 (Dec. 1992): 996–1020; Peter Way, "Evil Humors and Ardent Spirits: The Rough Culture of Canal Construction Laborers," *JAH* 79 (Mar. 1993): 1397–1428; Robin D. G. Kelley, "'We Are Not What We Seem': Rethinking Black Working-Class Opposition in the Jim Crow South," *JAH* 80 (June 1993): 75–112; Shane White, "'It Was a Proud Day': African Americans, Festivals, and Parades in the North, 1741–1834," *JAH* 81 (June 1994): 13–50; Dylan Penningroth, "Slavery, Freedom, and Social Claims to Property among African Americans in Liberty County, Georgia, 1850–1880," *JAH* 84 (Sept. 1997): 405–35.

21. See Daniel H. Usner Jr., "American Indians on the Cotton Frontier: Changing Economic Relations with Citizens and Slaves in the Mississippi Territory," *JAH* 72 (Sept. 1985): 297–317; Prude, "To Look upon the 'Lower Sort'"; Peel, "On the Margins"; Gerald Zahavi, "Passionate Commitments: Race, Sex and Communism at Schenectady General Electric, 1932–1954," *JAH* 83 (Sept. 1996): 514–48; Mary Lether Wingerd, "Rethinking Paternalism: Power and Parochialism in a Southern Mill Village," *JAH* (Dec. 1996): 872–902; Michael A. McDonnell, "Popular Mobilization and

Political Culture in Revolutionary Virginia: The Failure of the Minutemen and the Revolution from Below," *JAH* (Dec. 1998): 946–81. In these and other examples appearing earlier, labor history probably leads in fully contextualizing the workers under study in the most complete ways. See also Cantor, "A Prologue to the Protest Movement"; Barrett, "Americanization from the Bottom Up"; Way, "Evil Humors and Ardent Spirits"; Kelley "'We Are Not What We Seem'"; Dylan Penningroth, "Slavery, Freedom, and Social Claims to Property among African Americans in Liberty County, Georgia"; and Timothy B. Tyson, "Robert F. Williams, 'Black Power,' and the Roots of the African American Freedom Struggle," *JAH* 82 (Sept. 1998): 540–70.

22. An early article about slavery in which the slave is a true subject of the study was John Hebron Moore, "Simon Gray, Riverman: A Slave Who Was Almost Free," *MVHR* 49 (Mar. 1962): 656–73. On black life seen in more recent articles, see Shane White, "'We Dwell in Safety and Pursue Our Honest Callings': Free Blacks in New York City, 1787–1810," *JAH* 75 (Sept. 1988): 445–70; W. Jeffrey Bolster, "'To Feel Like a Man': Black Seamen in the Northern States, 1800–1860," *JAH* 76 (Mar. 1990): 1173–1200; Kelley, "'We Are Not What We Seem'"; Shane White, "'It was a Proud Day'"; and Darlene Clark Hine, "Black Professionals and Race Consciousness: Origins of the Civil Rights Movement, 1890–1950," *JAH* 89 (Mar. 2003): 1279–94. On race as ideology and identity, see James C. Kotter, "The Black South and White Appalachia," *JAH* 66 (Mar. 1980): 832–49; Zahavi, "Passionate Commitments"; Andrew Wiese, "The Other Suburbanites: African American Suburbanization in the North before 1950," *JAH* 85 (Mar. 1999): 1495–1525; Peggy Pascoe, "Miscegenation Law, Court Cases, and Ideologies of 'Race' in Twentieth-Century America," *JAH* 83 (June 1996): 44–69; Thomas J. Sugrue, "Crabgrass-Roots Politics: Race, Rights, and the Reaction against Liberalism in the Urban North, 1940–1964," *JAH* 82 (Sept. 1995): 551–78; Paul A. Kramer, "Empires, Exceptions, and Anglo-Saxons: Race and Rule between the British and United States Empires, 1880–1910," *JAH* 88 (Mar. 2002): 1315–53. An examination of race studies was Peter Kolchin, "Whiteness Studies: The New History of Race in America," *JAH* 89 (June 2002): 154–73.

23. Policy related studies included, Lemons, "The Sheppard-Towner Act"; Cynthia E. Harrison, "A 'New Frontier' for Women: The Public Policy of the Kennedy Administration," *JAH* 67 (Dec. 1980): 630–46. Studies of women's leadership included Edward M. Steel, "Mother Jones in the Fairmont Field, 1902"; Srom, "Leadership and Tactics in the American Woman Suffrage Movement"; and Anne Firor Scott, "What, Then, Is the American: This New Woman?" *JAH* 65 (Dec. 1978): 679–703. On prescriptive roles, see James R. McGovern, "The American Woman's Pre-World War I Freedom in Manners and Morals," *JAH* 55 (Sept. 1968): 315–33, and a large body of work related to medicine including Rosenberg and Rosenberg, "The Female Animal." After 1980, studies that focus on women as women often from feminist perspectives include Cindy S. Aron, "'To Barter their Souls for Gold': Female Clerks in the Federal Government Offices, 1862–1890," *JAH* 67 (Mar. 1981): 835–53; Susan Levine, "Labor's True Woman: Domesticity and Equal Rights in the Knights of Labor," *JAH* 70 (Sept. 1983): 323–39; Nancy F. Cott, "Feminist Politics In the 1920s: The National Woman's Party," *JAH* 71 (June 1984): 43–68; Jacquelyn Dowd Hall, "Disorderly Women: Gender and Labor Militancy in the Appalachian South," *JAH* 73 (Sept. 1986): 354–82; Drew Gilpin Faust, "Altars of Sacrifice: Confederate Women and the Narratives of War," *JAH* 76 (Mar. 1990): 1200–28; Klepp, "Revolutionary Bodies"; Regina

Markell Morantz and Sue Zschoche compare medical care directed by males and females in "Professionalism, Feminism, and Gender Roles: A Comparative Study of Nineteenth-Century Medical Therapeutics," *JAH* 67 (Dec. 1980): 568–87. And see Maurine Weiner Greenwald, "Working-Class Feminism and the Family Wage Ideal: The Seattle Debate on Married Women's Right to Work, 1914–1920," *JAH* (June 1989): 118–49.

24. Thomas Bender, "Wholes and Parts." This topic was addressed again in the journal in the June 1987 issue. And see John Higham, "The Future of American History," *JAH* 80 (Mar. 1994): 1289–1309, which continued the discussion of "synthesis" and some of its implications.

25. The city as a subject captured the attention of historians during the early 1940s. See Authur M. Schlesinger, "The City in American History," *MVHR* 27 (June 1940): 43–66 and Bayrd Still, "Patterns of Mid-Nineteenth Century Urbanization in the Middle West," *MVHR* 28 (Sept. 1941): 187–206. Recent articles paying much more attention to socio-cultural traditions and processes in political and economic contexts include: Stanley K. Schultz and Clay McShane, "To Engineer the Metropolis: Sewers, Sanitation, and City Planning in Late-Nineteenth Century America," *JAH* 65 (Sept. 1978): 389–411; Daniel Czitrom, "Underworlds and Underdogs: Big Tim Sullivan and Metropolitan Politics in New York, 1889–1913," *JAH* 78 (Sept. 1991): 536–58; Gary B. Nash, "The Transformation of Urban Politics, 1700–1765," *JAH* 60 (Dec. 1973): 605–32; Richard Carwardine, "The Second Great Awakening in the Urban Centers: An Examination of Methodism and the 'New Measures,'" *JAH* 59 (Sept. 1972): 327–40; Richard D. Brown, "The Emergence of Urban Society in Rural Massachusetts, 1760–1820," *JAH* 61 (June 1974): 29–51; Timothy R. Mahoney, "Urban History in a Regional Context: River Towns on the Upper Mississippi, 1840–1860," *JAH* 72 (Sept. 1985): 318–19; and Dennis C. Rousey, "Aliens in the WASP Nest: Ethnocultural Diversity in the Antebellum Urban South," *JAH* 79 (June 1992): 152–64. Peel, "On the Margins"; Edward J. Escobar, "The Dialectics of Repression: The Los Angeles Police Department and the Chicano Movement, 1968–1971," *JAH* 79 (Mar. 1993): 1483–1514; and Kenneth L. Kusmer, "The Functions of Organized Charity in the Progressive Era: Chicago as a Case Study," *JAH* 60 (Dec. 1973): 657–78. Also see Raymond A. Mohl, "Humanitarianism in the Preindustrial City: The New York Society for the Prevention of Pauperism, 1817–1823," *JAH* 57 (Dec. 1970): 576–99; and Eugene J. Watts, "Police Response to Crime and Disorder in Twentieth-Century St. Louis," *JAH* 70 (Sept. 1983): 340–58; John Bodnar, Michael Weber, and Roger Simon, "Migration, Kinship, and Urban Adjustment: Blacks and Poles in Pittsburgh, 1900–1930," *JAH* 66 (Dec. 1979) 548–66; Wiese, "The Other Suburbanites."

26. See Richael Rogin, "Progressivism and the California Electorate," *JAH* 55 (Sept. 1968): 297–314; Dyson, "The Red Peasant International in America"; Cott, "Feminist Politics in the 1920s"; Kathleen Smith Kutolowski, "Antimasonry Reexamined: Social Bases of the Grass-Roots Party," *JAH* 71 (Sept. 1984): 269–94; Czitrom, "Underworlds and Underdogs"; Sugrue, "Crabgrass-Roots Politics"; Elizabeth R. Varon, "'Tippecanoe and the Ladies, Too': White Women and Party Politics in Antebellum Virginia," *JAH* 82 (Sept. 1995): 494–521; Zahavi, "Passionate Commitments"; Sarah Barringer Gordon, "'The Liberty of Self-Degradation': Polygamy, Woman Suffrage, and Consent in Nineteenth-Century America," *JAH* 83 (Dec. 1996): 815–47; and Flores, "Bison Ecology and Bison Diplomacy."

27. See William R. Leach, "Transformations in a Culture of Consumption: Women and Department Stores, 1890–1925," *JAH* 71 (Sept. 1984): 319–24; Perkins, "The Consumer Frontier"; David Jaffee, "Peddler of Progress and the Transformation of the Rural North, 1760–1860," *JAH* 78 (Sept. 1991): 511–35; Nancy Tomes, "Merchants of Health: Medicine and Consumer Culture in the United Sates, 1900–1940," *JAH* 88 (Sept. 2001): 519–47; Lawrence B. Glickman, "The Strike in the Temple of Consumption: Consumer Activism and Twentieth Century American Political Culture," *JAH* 88 (June 2001): 99–128.

28. Kazin and Ross, "America's Labor Day"; White, "'It Was a Proud Day'"; Adam Rome, "'Give Earth a Chance': The Environmental Movement and the Sixties," *JAH* 90 (Sept. 2003): 525–54; Ruth Feldstein, "'I Don't Trust You Anymore': Nina Simone, Culture, and Black Activism in the 1960s," *JAH* 91 (Mar. 2005): 1349–79.

29. Flores, "Bison Ecology and Bison Diplomacy"; Mansel G. Blackford, "Environmental Justice, Native Rights, Tourism and Opposition to Military Control: The Case of Kaho'olawe," *JAH* (Sept. 2004): 544–71.

30. See especially, Morgan, "Slavery and Freedom," *JAH* 59 (June 1972): 5–29. Eric Foner, "The Meaning of Freedom in the Age of Emancipation," *JAH* 81 (Sept. 1994): 435–60, also reflects this more synthetic view and speaks directly to Bender's article.

31. Maris Vinovskis's article, "Have Social Historians Lost the Civil War? Some Preliminary Demographic Speculations," *JAH* 76 (June 1989) 34–58, was seemingly answered by Faust, "Altars of Sacrifice." But also see Megan J. McClintock, "Civil War Pensions and the Reconstruction of Union Families," *JAH* 83 (Sept. 1996): 456–24, which replies explicitly to Vinovskis. Even before Vinovskis, several important articles on the Civil War incorporated important social history methods and topics. See Eugene C. Murdock, "New York's Civil War Bounty Brokers," *JAH* 53 (Sept. 1966): 259–78; and Peter Levine, "Draft Evasion in the North during the Civil War, 1863–65," *JAH* 67 (Mar. 1981): 816–34.

Next to the Civil War, the social aspects of the Revolutionary War have received the most attention. See McDonnell, "Popular Mobilization and Political Culture in Revolutionary Virginia." On the Mexican War, see Davies, "Mexican War Veterans as an Organized Group." On the Spanish Civil War, see Robert A. Rosenstone, "The Men of the Abraham Lincoln Battalion," *JAH* 54 (Sept. 1967): 327–38. On World War I, see Daniel J. Kevles, "Testing the Army's Intelligence: Psychologists and the Military in World War I," *JAH* 55 (Dec. 1968): 565–81, and Steven A. Reich, "Soldiers of Democracy: Black Texans and the Fight for Citizenship, 1917–1921," *JAH* 82 (Mar. 1996): 1478–1504. On World War II, see Lee, "The Army 'Mutiny' of 1946"; and Dalfiume, "The 'Forgotten Years' of the Negro Revolution."

32. The earliest study of American Indians that puts Indians at the center and blends political and social history is P. Richard Metcalf, "Who Should Rule at Home? Native American Politics and Indian-White Relations," *JAH* 61 (Dec. 1974): 651–65. A close demographic study of the Cherokee in North Carolina is William G. McLoughlin and Walter H. Conser Jr., "The Cherokees in Transition: A Statistical Analysis of the Federal Cherokee Census of 1835," *JAH* 64 (Dec. 1977): 678–703. Richard White, "The Winning of the West: The Expansion of the Western Sioux in the Eighteenth and Nineteenth Centuries," *JAH* 65 (Sept. 1978): 319–43, focused not on the wars between Indians and whites but also on the struggles among Indians. A clear study of the way life was changing for Indians during the nineteenth century is Daniel H. Usner Jr., "American

Indians on the Cotton Frontier." Also see Flores, "Bison Ecology and Bison Diplomacy"; Seeman, "Reading Indians' Deathbed Scenes"; Pekka Hämäläinen, "The Rise and Fall of Plains Indian Horse Cultures," *JAH* 90 (Dec. 2003): 833–62; William L. Ramsey, "'Something Cloudy in Their Looks': The Origins of the Yamasee War Reconsidered," *JAH* 90 (June 2003): 44–75; Alexandra Harmon, "American Indians and Land Monopolies in the Gilded Age," *JAH* 90 (June 2003): 106–33; Paul C. Rosier, "'They are Ancestral Homelands': Race, Place, and Politics in Cold War Native America, 1945–1961," *JAH* (Mar. 2006): 1300–26.

33. Early examples of discussions of sex/sexuality in terms of socio-cultural values and traditions included John C. Burnham, "The Progressive Era Revolution in American Attitudes toward Sex," *JAH* 59 (Mar. 1973): 885–908 and James R. McGovern, "The American Woman's Pre-World War I Freedom in Manners and Morals," *JAH* (Sept. 1968): 315–33. Subsequent studies on sexuality and identity include Jodi Vandenberg-Daves, "The Manly Pursuit of a Partnership between the Sexes: The Debate over YMCA Programs for Women and Girls, 1914–1933," *JAH* 78 (Mar. 1992): 1324–46; Margot Canady, "Building a Straight State: Sexuality and Social Citizenship under the 1944 G. I. Bill," *JAH* (Dec. 2003): 935–57; Elizabeth Reis, "Impossible Hermaphrodites: Intersex in America, 1620–1960," *JAH* 90 (Sept. 2005): 411–41.

34. Escobar, "The Dialectics of Repression." Although there are a few more articles in the journal on Asian Americans, they tend to be intellectual, political, and diplomatic in their orientation, and where there is more attention to the group as a subject, the studies, like those in earlier African American history, tend to focus on race relations. See Rodman W. Paul's "The Origin of the Chinese Issue in California," *MVHR* 25 (June 1938): 181–96, and Fred H. Matthews, "White Community and 'Yellow Peril,'" *MVHR* 50 (Mar. 1964): 612–33, both of which provide social content.

35. Broadening the scope of traditional studies of immigrants and immigration is Rousey, "Aliens in the WASP Nest." Also see the earlier related study, Robert L. Brandfon, "The End of Immigration to the Cotton Fields," *MVRH* 50 (Mar. 1964): 591–611. Most studies related to immigrants are in labor history traditions and are still structural in their approaches, but the structures are much broader than simply, for example, class formation from the narrow perspective of work alone and incorporate the larger social and cultural environment of the workers. See Barrett, "Americanization from the Bottom Up"; Way, "Evil Humors and Ardent Spirits"; Gunther Peck, "Reinventing Free Labor: Immigrant Padrones and Contract Laborers in North America, 1885–1925," *JAH* 83 (Dec. 1996): 848–71; and Cinotto, "Leonard Covello, the Covello Papers, and the History of Eating Habits among Italian Immigrants."

36. Paying particular attention to life-course issues are Bolin, "The Economics of Middle-Income Family Life during the Great Depression," and Klepp, "Revolutionary Bodies." Also see Richard A. Easterlin, "Factors in the Decline of Farm Family Fertility in the United States"; Bodnar, Weber, and Simon, "Migration, Kinship, and Urban Adjustment"; Manfra and Dykstra, "Serial Marriage and the Origins of the Black Stepfamily"; and Thomas Dublin, "Rural-Urban Migrants in Industrial New England: The Case of Lynn, Massachusetts in Mid-Nineteenth Century," *JAH* (Dec. 1986): 623–44.

37. See, for example, Nelson Lichtenstein, "Auto Worker Militancy and the Structure of Factory Life, 1937–1955," *JAH* 67 (Sept. 1980): 335–53; Jacqueline Dowd Hall, "Disorderly Women"; Peter Way, "Evil Humors and Ardent Spirits"; and Wingerd, "Rethinking Paternalism."

38. Although one can include the previously mentioned articles on consumer culture and public culture for some evidence of aspects of everyday life, few articles focused on this historical aspect. See Kupperman, "Apathy and Death in Early Jamestown"; Holmes, "Moonshining and Collective Violence"; Doucet and Weaver, "Material Culture and the North American House"; Dye and Smith, "Mother Love and Infant Death, 1750–1920"; Cinotto, "Leonard Covello, the Covello Papers, and the History of Eating Habits among Italian Immigrants in New York"; Weaver, "Material Culture and the North American House: The Era of the Common Man, 1870–1920," *JAH* (Dec. 1985): 560–87; Peel, "On the Margins"; and on the struggle for rental housing after World War II, see McEnaney, "Nightmares on Elm Street." Surprisingly little study pertaining to everyday life addressed education. See Atherton, "Mercantile Education in the Antebellum South"; Joel Perlmann, "Who Stayed in School? Social Structure and Academic Achievement in the Determination of Enrollment Patterns, Providence, Rhode Island, 1880–1925," *JAH* 72 (Dec. 1985): 588–614; Jonathan Zimmerman, "Ethnics against Ethnicity: European Immigrants and Foreign-Language Instruction, 1890–1940," *JAH* 88 (Mar. 2002): 1383–1404; Christopher P. Loss, "'The Most Wonderful Thing Has Happened to Me in the Army': Psychology, Citizenship, and American Higher Education in WW II," *JAH* 92 (Dec. 2005): 864–91.

39. Bodnar, Weber, and Simon, "Migration, Kinship, and Urban Adjustment"; Paul A. Kramer, "Empires, Exceptions, and Anglo-Saxons: Race and Rule between the British and United States Empires, 1880–1910," *JAH* (Mar. 2002): 1315–53.

40. Dyson, "The Red Peasant International in America"; Kevin Kenny, "Diaspora and Comparison: The Global Irish as a Case Study," *JAH* 90 (June 2003): 134–62; Kevin Dawson, "Enslaved Swimmers and Divers in the Atlantic World," *JAH* 92 (Mar. 2006): 1327–55.

41. Examples taking this approach in the journal include, Leavitt, "'Science' Enters the Birthing Room"; Dye and Smith, "Mother Love and Infant Death"; Reis, "Impossible Hermaphrodites"; Kenny, "Diaspora and Comparison"; Patricia Kelly Hall and Steven Ruggles, "'Restless in the Midst of their Prosperity': New Evidence in the Internal Migration of Americans, 1850–2000," *JAH* 91 (Dec. 2004): 829–46.

42. Scott A. Sandage, "A Marble House Divided: The Lincoln Memorial, the Civil Rights Movement, and the Politics of Memory, 1939–1963," *JAH* (June 1993): 135–67; W. Fitzhugh Brundage, "Meta Warrick's 1907 'Negro Tableaux' and (Re)Presenting African-American Historical Memory," *JAH* (Mar. 2003): 1368–1400; Ira Berlin, "American Slavery in History and Memory and the Search for Social Justice," *JAH* (Mar. 2004): 1251–68.

14

The *MVHR*, the *JAH*, and Intellectual History
From Margin to Mainstream

David A. Hollinger

"America for the Americans; Europe for the Europeans," wrote John C. Greene mockingly in 1957 in the *Mississippi Valley Historical Review* (*MVHR*). Greene, writing conveniently at the exact midpoint of the one-hundred-year span I have been asked to address, condemned the Monroe Doctrine in relation to intellectual history.[1] Greene's important article, "Objectives and Methods in Intellectual History," stands after half a century as a vivid marker of the integration in the 1950s of the subfield of intellectual history into the mainstream of the profession of historians studying the United States. Greene's article was the first sustained discussion of intellectual history in the pages of the *MVHR*. It was the generational equivalent of the spate of essays on social history, women's history, African American history, and cultural history that accompanied the emergence of these other subfields shortly thereafter.

But Greene's essay is more than a convenient chronological marker. Greene's principled denunciation of nationalist parochialism in scholarship tells us much about the dynamics of the emergence of American intellectual history as a subfield of U.S. history and about the relationship of this subfield to other subfields during the half-century that followed Greene's manifesto. That relationship has included, on the one hand, a concern on the part of advocates of "history from the bottom up" that intellectual historians were paying too much attention to Americans who were educated enough to know what was doing in Germany and France, and, on the other hand, a robust appreciation for the striking leadership that intellectual historians have offered in the larger effort, now so widely celebrated, to conceptualize the history of the United States in transnational perspective.

Greene's wisecrack about the Monroe Doctrine carried a weight in 1957 measured only when we remind ourselves that the major organization sustaining the entire field of U.S. history was still called by the name of *Mississippi Valley*, conveying the implications, however anachronistic even for 1957, that the middle section of the country was more American than the parts of the country east of the Appalachians and west of the Rockies and that the study of things American was more appropriate for people from Cincinnati and Chicago and Nashville and New Orleans and Minneapolis and Madison than it was for those living in New York or Boston or Philadelphia or San Francisco. Greene articulated a trans-Atlantic perspective on the history of the United States that eventually took firm hold. This perspective has defined much of the work done by American intellectual history specialists, including their work in the pages of the *Journal of American History (JAH)*, during the last thirty years.

Greene's quip is rendered all the more charming by the fact that the first mention of "the history of ideas" in the pages of the *MVHR* was a 1934 book review of Dexter Perkins's *History of the Monroe Doctrine*.[2] And thanks to the wonders of JSTOR, we can see that after a scattering of references to intellectual history and history of ideas in the late 1930s, both terms come up increasingly in book reviews and articles of the 1940s, but that these terms did not become common until the early 1950s. A clear pattern in the references to "intellectual history" and "the history of ideas" during this period from the late 1930s through the early 1950s is the frequency with which the books being reviewed and the books and articles being cited in *MVHR* articles were written by scholars who were not trained historians teaching in departments of history. Rather, the authors were professors of English, like Perry Miller and Henry Nash Smith, or professors of political science, like Louis Hartz and Charles Merriam, or professors of philosophy, like Morton White, Adrienne Koch, and Philip Wiener. This is consistent with the fact that, during that era, the *MVHR* published relatively few articles that we today would recognize as intellectual history. Intellectual history entered the journal largely through reviews of books by nonhistorians.

To be sure, bona fide historians Merle Curti and Henry Steele Commager were major figures in the pages of the *MVHR* by the early 1950s, but we miss a vital part of the story unless we consider the role of nonhistorians. That role, in turn, is best understood in the context of a fairly sharp division of labor that had been in place during the first half of the twentieth century between the history profession and these other academic professions.

It was left to historically oriented literary scholars, philosophers, and political scientists, by and large, to deal with *thinking* as a human activity like voting, fighting, farming, manufacturing, exploring, taxing, and litigating. All these other activities historians dealt with comfortably, but thinking was taken to be different. Historians had studied ideas in America, but usually in strict relation to politics. George Bancroft, Francis Parkman, and Henry Adams, to cite three great nineteenth-century historians, attended to some of the ideas held by the presidents and generals who dominated their grand narratives. Yet for these historians and their successors, down through the generation of Charles A. Beard, the central subject was most often the state, political movements, the economy, diplomacy, and warfare.

Prior to the 1940s, one of the few widely noted books by a leading professional historian written in the mode of what would later be called intellectual history was Carl Becker's study of the Declaration of Independence, published in 1922.[3] Another, a bit earlier, was Albert Bushnell Hart's *National Ideals Historically Traced, 1607–1907*,[4] which appeared in 1907. The study of United States history during Hart's generation was heavily influenced by the deeply anti-intellectual "Frontier Thesis" of Frederick Jackson Turner, according to which ideas were epiphenomenal to material conditions, especially free land and population density. The leading intellectual historian in the United States during the 1920s was Vernon Louis Parrington, a professor of English.[5] Parrington's stature among guild historians was recognized in 1952 when the MVHR published a survey organized by historian John Caughey in which Parrington's *Main Currents of American Thought* was rated one of the most important of all works addressing the history of the United States.[6]

Philosophers and literary scholars helped historians of Greene's generation to see the importance of ideas in history. The very concept of "the history of ideas" was popularized by philosopher Arthur O. Lovejoy in the 1930s, especially through his 1936 book, *The Great Chain of Being*.[7] This study traced the development over many centuries of the metaphysical idea of a hierarchy of life forms. Lovejoy's rigorous approach flowered in *The Journal of the History of Ideas*, an important interdisciplinary journal founded in 1940 by Lovejoy and a group of philosophers and literary scholars he recruited. During the 1940s and early 1950s, the journal published a series of dazzling analyses of renaissance Europe and Mediterranean antiquity, many written by European émigrés whose work commanded instant and rapt attention from the learned world. These scholars included Hans Baron, Ernst Cassirer, Alexander Koyre, Paul Oskar Kristeller, and Leo Spitzer. American thought was marginal to the specific engagements of *The Journal of the History of Ideas*, but in 1949 one of that journal's early contributors, philosopher Morton White, published *Social Thought in America: The Revolt Against Formalism*, a book that won immediate and lasting attention from historians interested in the philosophical underpinnings of liberal politics in the Progressive Era and after.[8]

The methodological impact of White's book in particular and of *The Journal of the History of Ideas* in general increased in the mid-1950s in the context of a series of historically focused books of breathtaking ambition and erudition written by literary scholars and political theorists. Chief among these landmark books, which, along with White's, long defined what "intellectual history" meant for professional historians, were *The Liberal Tradition in America*, by political theorist Louis Hartz, and a series of books about Puritanism by the literary scholar, Perry Miller. Hartz's sweeping study of how a set of liberal ideas had controlled much of American political history appeared in 1955, two years after Miller's most influential book, *The New England Mind: From Colony to Province*. Miller analyzed the changes in theology and political doctrine of New England intellectuals in the late seventeenth and early eighteenth centuries,[9] which the *MVHR* review lauded for its quality of once-in-a-decade distinction.[10] Indeed, after historians started attending to Miller, who was a writer of exceptional intensity and muscle, they found themselves caught up in his earlier works: *The New England Mind: The Seventeenth Century* (1939), which had not been reviewed in the *MVHR*; *Jonathan Edwards* (1949); and, soon thereafter, his most accessible book, a collection of essays published in 1956, *Errand into the Wilderness*.

If it was the philosopher Lovejoy who more than any other single scholar popularized "the history of ideas," it was the literary scholar Miller who did more than anyone else to make historians of the United States aware of how ideas could be studied in their social context. Miller focused not on ideas in their disembodied state, as Lovejoy and his followers often did. Rather, he studied how leading intellectuals did their thinking in a series of specific historical settings, especially the changing economic and political circumstances of British North America. Historians were quick to see the promise of this more contextual approach to ideas when practiced compellingly. Although some work on American thought followed the classical Lovejoyan model of studying ideas as passed from one thinker to another, regardless of the historical setting, most of the scholars who came to be known as "American intellectual historians" in the 1950s and after were concerned with the dialectical relation between thought and its immediate social environment.

This was true, for example, of Merle Curti, who, as early as 1943 in the first edition of his textbook, *The Growth of American Thought*, linked intellectual history closely with social history.[11] The same link preoccupied John Higham, Curti's most prominent student. Higham's *Strangers in the Land* (1955) explained the ebb and flow of ethnic and racial prejudice in terms of the social and political settings of successive generations of Anglo-Protestants.[12] But Miller, Hartz, and White differed from Curti and Higham in the technical detail with which they analyzed ideas and in the attention they devoted to the most highly developed of philosophical, theological, and political theoretical discourses. Curti and Higham studied general ideas that had broad popular appeal, but Miller, Hartz, and White were willing to address the most sophisticated writings of Americans who were full participants in the intellectual life of the Europe-centered North Atlantic West. Miller, Hartz, and White showed that theoretical discussion in the United States invited, and indeed vindicated, the same kind of rigorous analysis being devoted to European thinkers by an increasing number of historians trained in the field of modern European history, including H. Stuart Hughes, Leonard Krieger, and Carl Schorske.

It was in this precise context that John C. Greene invoked Miller. "Most writers on American intellectual history have been content to describe the surface" of thought, said Greene. He named only one exception—Perry Miller[13]— and then launched into a defense of the closer and deeper analyses of texts, a kind of analysis he said was rarely done by historians studying American thought. There is no reason to doubt that when Greene referred to merely "surface description," he was talking above all about Merle Curti. To be sure, Curti's name is listed first among the fifteen people whose critical readings of a draft Greene acknowledges in a footnote.[14] And Curti himself was always generous to Miller. Yet the feeling was not reciprocal. Miller was widely quoted as telling two generations of Harvard graduate students that Curti's textbook, *The Growth of American Thought*, was basically a "seed catalogue."

Miller's arrogance cannot be defended, nor can the decision of a faithful student of Miller's, Kenneth Lynn, to quote this slander in a 1980 *Journal of American History* review of Curti's last book.[15] But the distinction between the kind of history Miller wrote and the kind that Curti wrote is genuine and important. Greene was trying to get specialists in U.S. history to write more in the mode of contemporary Europeanists. Nearly all of Greene's references in his 1957 *MVHR* article were to works of European intellectual history, especially history of science and history of religious ideas. Miller was the crucial stepping stone to making the subfield of American intellectual history look more like the subfield of European intellectual history. Miller was also more international than Curti, analyzing his Puritan subjects in relation to the intellectual issues of renaissance and reformation Europe. Hence Miller's capacity as a transnationalist as well as his capacity as a rigorous analyst of argumentation was at issue in the turn Greene urged away from Curti toward Miller.

And so it played out in the next several decades, when Miller decisively eclipsed Curti as the paradigmatic American intellectual historian. An emblem for this fact is a state-of-the-art book entitled *New Directions in American Intellectual History* published in 1979.[16] This book was dedicated to Curti and edited by two scholars, John Higham and Paul Conkin, who tried to steer in Curti's direction the conference of 1977 on which the volume was based. Yet Miller was, by far, the most cited scholar, more often mentioned even than those goliaths of 1970s footnotes, Clifford Geertz and Thomas Kuhn. Curti's name was invoked respectfully, if mostly in passing, by five of this volume's thirteen contributors, but when it came to actually engaging the practice of intellectual history, nine of the thirteen discussed Miller's work, sometimes in considerable detail.

Returning for a moment to the era of John C. Greene's article, I want to call attention to the appearance, within the pages of the *MVHR*, of the intellectual historian Henry F. May. In 1956, May published the essay "Shifting Perspectives on the 1920s," which became the foundation for his influential 1959 book, *The End of American Innocence*.[17] This book surveyed the entire panorama of public discourse about politics, religion, and literature in the United States during the five-year period, 1912 to 1917. Whereas Hartz, Miller, and White focused on a relatively small number of obviously important texts, May analyzed a host of ideas of middle-brow thinkers and demonstrated that these journalists and popular writers participated in the same large conversation that engaged major thinkers like William James, Mark Twain, and Charles Beard. May's work, although capacious in scope, was thus more specialized than most previous work in the field; by concentrating on a short time span May offered a virtual ethnography of the educated classes of the United States in a sharply defined era.

May's work was thus both an emblem for and agent of the drift toward the more specialized work characteristic of American intellectual historians during the second half of the century. Many of May's contemporaries in English departments, like Henry Nash Smith and R. W. B. Lewis, and in history departments, like Daniel J. Boorstin and Henry Steele Commager, worked on grand themes, as in such works as *Virgin Land*, *The American Adam*, *The Genius of American Politics*, and *The American Mind*, all classics of the field of American Studies.[18] Meanwhile, May showed the way to the more specialized kinds of intellectual history that the old *MVHR* published in its last few years of operation, such as the 1963 essay "The Academic Mind of Woodrow Wilson" by his student, Laurence R. Veysey,[19] and that appeared much more frequently in the new *JAH*, especially in the 1980s and 1990s, during the editorships of Lewis Perry (himself a distinguished intellectual historian), David Thelen, and Joanne Meyerowitz.

Under the leadership of Perry, Thelen, and Meyerowitz, the frequency of articles in the field of intellectual history increased considerably. These articles were often devoted to individual thinkers, such as Daniel Walker Howe's article on Horace Bushnell and Howard Brick's article on Talcott Parsons, or to specific intellectual movements, such as James T. Kloppenberg's article on Pragmatism and Charles Capper's article on Transcendentalism, or to intellectual institutions, such as Joan Shelley Rubin's article on the Book-of-the-Month Club, or to key concepts in the study of the United States, such as Daniel T. Rodgers's essay on Republicanism and Philip Gleason's article on identity, or to specific episodes, such as John T. McGreevy's article on Catholicism and the freedom of thought issue in the 1940s and Kenneth Cmiel's article on the acceleration of human rights consciousness in the 1970s.[20]

As this formidable list of widely cited articles from the *JAH* in the last quarter century instantly reminds us, the *JAH* has become a major venue for the publication of research in American intellectual history. This continues to be the case, right down to the present. In recent issues, editor Edward Linenthal published Jennifer Ratner-Rosenhagen's analysis of Nietzsche's role in American thought and Joanne Meyerowitz's study of social scientific engagements with sexual and racial categories,[21] topics that the editors of the old *MVHR* would almost certainly have sniffed at as "not history" but philosophy, in the first case, and science, in the second.

The 2006 essay on Nietzsche is representative of the internationalist perspective now more dominant than ever among the intellectual historians who write for the *JAH*. It is ironic, perhaps, that one of the most popular works in the field in recent years was highly anomalous in the terms on which it engaged the Atlantic. I refer to Louis Menand's *The Metaphysical Club*, which won several prizes when published in 2001. Menand offered an unreconstructed American exceptionalist 1950s-style interpretation of the pragmatist intellectuals of the late nineteenth and early twentieth centuries.[22] By contrast, James T. Kloppenberg's book fifteen years earlier, *Uncertain Victory*, had demonstrated commandingly that the deeply Protestant culture of post–Civil War New England was but one of several sites in the industrialized world for the simultaneous development of a historicist sensitivity to uncertainty and of a recognition of the instrumental character of concepts.[23] The literary scholar Menand's book was a terrific read, much praised even by intellectual history specialists, but many of the latter felt, with some justice, that Menand had harvested a generation of intellectual history scholarship while ignoring its profoundly transnationalist and indeed anti-exceptionalist message. Nowadays, most historians concerned with the intellectual history of the United States in any period are more likely than ever to begin their work with an understanding that their subject matter is comparable to that of historians of British or German or Russian thought in relation to the larger history of the North Atlantic West: each national culture has its own intellectual history, but that history is extensively the product of a set of dialectical exchanges with the work of thinkers in other national cultures with overlapping traditions and circumstances. This perspective was enunciated in the most recent methodological commentary on intellectual history to appear in the *JAH*, in the course of an interchange involving nine senior historians published in September 2003.[24]

This frank engagement with the wider world is consistent with the intellectual historian's traditional focus on the use of evidence and reasoning in human behavior. In an era when many educators worry about the dumbing down of the American population, intellectual historians in their teaching and in their scholarly writings continue to explore and to reinforce the most critically minded aspects of the United States. Intellectual historians have demonstrated that the use of evidence and reasoning are not exotic arts suitable only for Vienna and Paris; rather, these arts are also practiced throughout the Mississippi Valley and elsewhere. Serious thinking, intellectual historians have proven, is as American as the frontier. The editors of the *MVHR* eventually came to recognize this truth, and the editors of the *JAH* have never forgotten it.[25]

NOTES

For helpful suggestions about this paper, I wish to thank Ira Berlin, Charles Capper, Bruce Kuklick, and Lewis Perry.

1. John C. Greene, "Objectives and Methods in Intellectual History," *MVHR* 44 (June 1957): 68.
2. Isaac J. Cox, review of Dexter Perkins, *The Monroe Doctrine, 1826–1867*, *MVHR* 20 (Mar. 1934): 576–77.
3. Carl Becker, *The Declaration of Independence* (New York: Harcourt, Brace, 1922).
4. Albert Bushnell Hart, *National Ideals Historically Traced, 1607–1907* (New York: Harper, 1907).
5. Parrington's historic role in bringing intellectual history to specialists in U.S. history has long been recognized; see, e.g., John Higham's classic account of the history profession, *History* (Englewood Cliffs, NJ: Prentice Hall, 1965), 195–97; and Richard Hofstadter's similarly classic work, *The Progressive Historians: Turner, Beard, Parrington* (New York: Knopf, 1968).
6. John Walton Caughey, "Historian's Choice: Results of a Poll on Recently Published American History and Biography," *MVHR* 39 (Sept. 1952): 289–302, esp. 299.
7. Arthur O. Lovejoy, *The Great Chain of Being* (Cambridge, MA: Harvard University Press, 1936).
8. Morton White, *Social Thought in America: The Revolt Against Formalism* (Boston: Viking Press, 1949).
9. Louis Hartz, *The Liberal Tradition in America: An Interpretation of American Political Thought since the Revolution* (New York: Harcourt, Brace, 1955); Perry Miller, *The New England Mind: From Colony to Province* (Cambridge, MA: Harvard University Press, 1953).
10. John E. Pomfret, review of Perry Miller, *The New England Mind: From Colony to Province*, *MVHR* 41 (June 1954): 114–16.
11. Merle Curti, *The Growth of American Thought* (New York: Harper & Brothers, 1943). This textbook was reissued in revised editions in 1951 and 1964.
12. John Higham, *Strangers in the Land* (New Brunswick, NJ: Rutgers University Press, 1955).
13. Greene, "Objectives and Methods," 72.
14. Greene, "Objectives and Methods," 59.
15. Kenneth Lynn, review of Merle Curti, *Human Nature in American Thought: A History*, *JAH* 67 (Sept. 1980): 375–76.
16. John Higham and Paul Conkin, eds., *New Directions in American Intellectual History* (Baltimore: Johns Hopkins University Press, 1979).
17. Henry F. May, "Shifting Perspectives on the 1920s," *MVHR* 43 (Dec. 1956): 405–27; Henry F. May, *The End of American Innocence* (New York: Knopf, 1959).

18. Henry Nash Smith, *Virgin Land: The American West as Symbol and Myth* (Cambridge, MA: Harvard University Press, 1950); R. W. B. Lewis, *The American Adam: Innocence, Tragedy, and Tradition in the Nineteenth Century* (Chicago: University of Chicago Press, 1955); Daniel J. Boorstin, *The Genius of American Politics* (Chicago: University of Chicago Press, 1953); Henry Steele Commager, *The American Mind: An Interpretation of American Thought and Character since the 1880's* (New Haven, CT: Yale University Press, 1950).

19. Laurence R. Veysey, "The Academic Mind of Woodrow Wilson," *MVHR* 49 (Mar. 1963): 613–34.

20. Daniel Walker Howe, "The Social Science of Horace Bushnell," *JAH* 70 (Sept. 1983); Howard Brick, "Talcott Parsons's 'Shift Away from Economics,' 1937–1946," *JAH* 87 (Sept. 2000), 490–514; James T. Kloppenberg, "Pragmatism: An Old Name for Some New Ways of Thinking?" *JAH* 83 (June 1996): 100–138; Charles Capper, "'A Little Beyond': The Problem of the Transcendentalist Movement in American History," *JAH* 85 (Sept. 1998): 502–39; Joan Shelley Rubin, "Self, Culture, and Self-Culture in Modern America: The Early History of the Book-of-the-Month Club," *JAH* 71 (Mar. 1985): 782–806; Daniel T. Rodgers, "Republicanism: The Career of a Concept," *JAH* 79 (June 1992): 11–38; Philip Gleason, "Identifying Identity: A Semantic History," *JAH* 69 (Mar. 1983): 910–31; John T. McGreevy, "Thinking on One's Own: Catholicism in the American Intellectual Imagination, 1928–1960," *JAH* 84 (June 1997): 97–131; Kenneth Cmiel, "The Emergence of Human Rights Politics in the United States," *JAH* 86 (Dec. 1999): 1231–50.

21. Jennifer Ratner-Rosenhagen, "Conventional Iconoclasm: The Cultural Work of the Nietzsche Image in Twentieth-Century America," *JAH* 93 (Dec. 2006): 728–54; Joanne Meyerowitz, "'How Common Culture Shapes the Separate Lives': Sexuality, Race, and Mid-Twentieth Century Social Constructionist Thought," *JAH* 96 (Mar. 2010), 1057–84.

22. Louis Menand, *The Metaphysical Club* (New York: Farrar, Straus, and Giroux, 2001).

23. James T. Kloppenberg, *Uncertain Victory: Social Democracy and Progressivism in European and American Thought, 1870–1920* (New York: Oxford University Press, 1986).

24. See my own contributions to "Interchange," *JAH* (Sept. 2003): 576–611, especially 580–82 and 588–91.

25. This paragraph and several others in this essay draw upon my "American Intellectual History, 1907–2007," *OAH Magazine of History* (Apr. 2007): 14–17; republished in *A Century of American Historiography*, ed. James M. Banner, Jr. (New York: Bedford/St. Martin's, 2009).

15

Immigration and the Tattered Narrative of Progressive History

John Bodnar

In the middle of World War II, Theodore C. Blegen of the University of Minnesota delivered his presidential address to the annual meeting of the Mississippi Valley Historical Association (MVHA) in St. Louis. Blegen, a pioneer in American immigration history, focused his remarks on the growth and development of the association since its founding in 1907. The title of his talk, "Our Widening Province," referred both to his belief that historians needed constantly to expand the range of topics they addressed and to his conviction that, despite its location in the "valley" between the Appalachian and the Rocky Mountains, the association should support scholarship intimately tied to a larger project of nation building. He reminded his listeners that the MVHA was founded, in part, to move scholarship away from an older and narrower focus on military and political affairs. In this regard, Blegen, a scholar who made calls for "grass roots history" and "history from the bottom up" during his career, insisted on more studies of "the people," including immigrants who settled in the "valley," the transition these newcomers made into a new culture, and even what he called rather vaguely the "minority group problem." He also made a special appeal for more studies of what he called "cooperative activity" or the "fundamental subject of how people work together." In his call for more historical subjects, however, Blegen was no pedant. He made it very clear that what he ultimately wanted was a wider set of specialized studies of groups and places that could all be folded into a more pluralistic story of the development of the United States. For that reason, he declared in his talk that he felt the bonds between the "valley" and the nation were "insoluble." The importance he attributed to his task of broadening the set of specialized studies was clear in his concluding remarks where he made a point that I suspect few historians would make at the OAH today when he exclaimed that the thoughts and actions of the American "people" were profoundly significant to "the present and future of mankind."[1]

Fifty-four years later, in another presidential address to the OAH, George M. Fredrickson of Stanford University again took up the subject of America's immigrant and minority groups in the nation's history. By this time, Fredrickson did not have to make special appeals to study cultural groups or ordinary people. That project had already been fully under way for several decades. And he certainly did not assume that the histories of different cultural and social groups would inevitably be melded easily into a seamless national history along the lines Blegen imagined. Fredrickson's remarks were dominated, not by an ideal of national history, but by the weight of ethnic and racial conflict that had moved to the center of the historian's enterprise in his lifetime. He stressed, not the transition of immigrant groups into Americans, but the divisions that had existed between "Old Stock Americans of British or northern European extraction" in our history and people of different ethnic and racial backgrounds. He claimed that, over time, the "Old Stock" had taken turns seeing some people as worthy of citizenship and assimilation and others as worthy of only being consigned to a "lower caste" or excluded completely. Fredrickson was struck not so much by the ability of the United States to absorb people of varying backgrounds as he was by the considerable level of "ethnic cleavage" he found in our history and the rise of a more contested culture in which minority groups were claiming their rights. He did not take for granted the growth of national unity in the way Blegen did, but he did hold out some hope. In comparing America to other nations, he suggested that at least it had a relatively stronger tradition of accepting immigrants than many other nations and a strain of liberal values that sometimes helped it to overcome its equally powerful impulses toward intolerance and racism. He noted especially the existence in America of a political system in which all kinds of groups could trade votes for influence to some degree. Fredrickson's awareness of racial intolerance and the centrality he granted to racial and cultural divisions in American history put him squarely in the camp of most scholars working on these subjects today. His brief nod to a strain of American exceptionalism, however, made him stand out from many contemporary students and suggested that he retained traces of faith in the myth of a liberal future in America the way Blegen did.[2]

A full analysis of the changes that have permeated the study of topics such as national history, immigration, assimilation, and racism is not possible here. In a more tentative way, however, this chapter will attempt to at least suggest some of the broad transformations that have taken place in the way historians approached these topics in the organization's major journal. Blegen and his contemporaries, for instance, worked before the 1950s within a broad paradigm called Progressive history. Indeed, Blegen and colleagues like Marcus Lee Hansen and Carl Wittke constituted the first wave of professional historians in America that undertook the study of immigrant and ethnic groups. These men were raised in "Old Stock" immigrant communities in the Midwest where they directed much of their path-breaking scholarship and derived the sensitivity they had to the "bottom" layers of society. Like other Progressives, they held to the belief that what they did was meaningful because it not only contributed to the larger story of national history but because they were tied to some extent to a mythical idea that America itself represented a new opportunity for all men and women who came to it to leave behind the corruption and oppression of old-order Europe. This was why Blegen ended his addresses by linking the story of America to a larger ideal of human progress. It is also why Hansen ended his pioneering study of *The Atlantic Migration, 1607–1860* by expressing the hope that all newcomers and natives would someday evolve into "one people." In the work of scholars like Blegen and Hansen we can detect traces of an older, more sentimental vision of America—what, in another context, Michael Denning has referred to as the "Lincoln Republic"—which looked forward to the realization of a dream of material progress and equality for "the people." In many ways, this legacy of Lincoln and this faith in the future of a liberal nation to create a just society still permeated much of the political life of the "valley" that gave birth to this organization in 1907—a legacy that I suspect might be more fully explored in historical research.[3]

Progressives were not unaware of conflict. One of their leading spokesmen, Charles Beard (who came from the "valley" as well), stirred considerable public debate with his claims about the centrality of economic strife in American history. In fact, in looking harder at those with less, Progressives were able to move more naturally into histories of farmers, pioneers, and immigrants. Many of them were keenly aware of the divisions in American society between the privileged and the underprivileged and desired and dreamed of the eventual "emancipation of the masses" as well as the assimilation of the foreign-born into a nation that was, at its core, democratic. That is the version of the nation and the story that Blegen felt was actually indispensable for all of mankind. We know now that the Progressives failed miserably to see the full extent of racial strife and oppression in America, and their faith in the nation as a unifying force that would bring more justice and progress was almost mystical. To many today, it would also seem naïve. But Progressives were radicals in their time, rebelling against conservative forms of history that sought to mythologize the nation completely, turn most of its leaders into heroes, and deny the saliency of any claims from the lower orders. Their desire for a more diverse history still informs what we do. Clearly, historians in the "valley," like Blegen, were driven as well by a felt need to oppose the elite scholars of the Northeast who were located at prestigious universities and less appreciative as a group of the history of various social groups and of a national story where myth was disrupted by conflict. When one considers, also, that much of the academic job market for historians early in the twentieth century was grounded in regional ties, the rebellion against what Ian Tyrell called the "Eastern establishment" made quite a bit of sense.[4]

The Progressive paradigm certainly shaped much of the immigration history that was published in the organization's journal prior to the 1950s. Written by professional historians who were concerned at the time not only with challenging more "conservative" scholars but filiopietists in their region, these individuals crafted a body of work that explained the movement of Northern Europeans into the region where most of them now lived. Their work was, in fact, a blend of local, regional, and national concerns. They were very much interested in the question of how newcomers learned of America, which, for them, was an important discovery usually made through "grass-roots" exchanges, such as letters written to the old country or messages carried by people who had left Europe and returned. Their focus on a largely rural region also allowed them to take up questions formulated by Fredrick Jackson Turner on the settlement of the land, which they always saw as a crucial step in nation building. And they made numerous attempts to place their topics and subjects into a larger national narrative of moving to America, which began before the American Revolution itself.

Immigration as an important part of national development was certainly central to an essay published by Carl Russell Fish of the University of Wisconsin in 1920. Writing around the time of the tercentenary of the "Pilgrim voyage," Fish wrote one the earliest essays on immigration by focusing on the departure of the Pilgrims from England. He admitted that, by the twentieth century, these "sturdy English folks" had been thoroughly devoured by the "melting-pot" and their identity had been lost over time. But his main point was that, for him, they represented the essence of what immigration to America was about. That is to say they came, like many after them, not from the top or bottom of European society but from the middle layers where people were not locked into a social position and were inclined to imagine new possibilities for their lives. It was this willingness to improve upon the past and reject the status quo, especially the fixed hierarchies of the old world, that Fish believed tied the Pilgrims to the many who later made similar moves. The Wisconsin historian certainly saw that there were exceptions to this view. He remarked that the "enforced migration of the Negroes" deprived them of seeking improvement in their condition and that there were variations in the experience of different ethnic groups. But transcending all of this, he thought, was a process of "natural selection" whereby the "dreamers and the activists" were separated from those tied to old ways. And it was this dream of making things better for all that had been and would continue to be the glue that would unite people of "differing races" in America. In settlements all over the nation, Fish saw the "conquest of the wilderness" and the "slow advance of civilization" moving toward the formation of a new society in which "Americanism" was growing and "democracy" was bringing everyone together.[5]

Fish's portrayal of immigration as a form of uplift and improvement was also suggested by Blegen in an essay on Norwegians moving to the Midwest, published the following year. In studying "America letters" that were read in the old country, he noted how such correspondence explained where migrants could improve their social and economic condition in the new world. Even when noted historian Arthur Schlesinger published his famous essay on "The City in American History" in 1940, which, in reality, constituted a critique on the effort to focus on frontier and rural areas, he still showed a faith in the nation's progressive possibilities when he argued that both rural and urban realms were important, for it was their "interplay" that had helped America to "realize her promise."[6]

The earliest work on immigration history not only upheld a faith in assimilation and the progressive potential of the nation but also took pains to explain some of the ways such transformations took place. An essay published in 1937 probed how the Swedish American press helped to link immigrant voters to national political parties. Most Swedes had been swept into the Republican Party by their staunch support for Abraham Lincoln and the crusade to save the union. But this essay showed that the political views of the Swedish American press could also be shaped by cash contributions from various parties. And in the 1890s, some staunch Republicans could suddenly be moved by economic issues to support agrarian Populism. Whatever stand they took, however, the point was clear that the dynamics of party politics were fostering a fairly rapid pace of integration into American life. Carl Wittke's 1952 essay furthered the project to explain assimilation by looking at American mass culture. In an article entitled "The Immigrant Theme on the American Stage" he looked at theater productions in the nineteenth and twentieth centuries and how many of them were based on stories and stereotypes of immigrant newcomers. Some of the "immigrant caricatures" were, to be sure, humorous and others were demeaning, such as the many Irish figures of the nineteenth century who were prone to drinking too much whiskey. Wittke actually saw some similarities in such figures and the stereotypes of African Americans that also moved across the American stage in the nineteenth and twentieth centuries. He did not pick up, however, on the interpretations of blackface in minstrel shows the way modern scholars have. That is to say, he did not see that many of the white performers who donned blackface were actually trying to demonstrate their acceptance of racist outlooks as a way to perform new American identities. For Wittke, curiously, the presentation of these stereotypes actually familiarized American audiences with different groups in the nation and, more importantly for him, caused each ethnic group to take steps in the real world to refute the negative images and "clean up the caricature" as a way of becoming American.[7]

World War II brought significant transformations to American politics and culture. Registering the sense of victory and unity that came from the war, many historians viewed the nation as even more virtuous and mythical than before. By the early 1950s, progressive tendencies to see regional or ethnic differences (even if they might go away), as well as class and regional divisions, were scorned. Peter Novick has described the dominant tendency of historical writing in this postwar era as essentially "counterprogressive." There was, in fact, much talk in American culture at this time of the blending of many European groups in America into the major religious denominations of Protestant, Catholic, and Jew. The emergence of this more celebratory view of the nation and its assimilative forces is well known. Less appreciated, however, is the fact that, in the pages of the organization's journal, a reaction to the consensual and antiprogressive views of leading historians was brewing. This challenge would be driven in part by the lessons from Nazi Germany about how harmful prejudice and hatred could be, but it would also emanate from scholars working in the field of immigration whose studies had made them sensitive to the vast experience with prejudice and intolerance that had taken place in America as well.[8]

The charge was led by John Higham. In his 1957 article "Anti-Semitism in the Gilded Age" he made it quite clear that he was intent on questioning the "present mood" toward the American past, which he characterized as "warm, almost nostalgic." Higham felt that anti-Semitism in the United States was a longstanding and pervasive problem that emerged from the intense competition for resources and standing that marked American society and the resentment many had toward Jews (and others) who were successful in this competitive process. He particularly noted that many old-stock "patrician intellectuals" hated Jews because they felt they were losing their elevated status to them and other newcomers. In fact, Higham claimed the deep-seated nature of intolerance in America and the fears of decline on the part of the "old stock" explained the emergence of a "racist immigration policy" in the United States in the 1920s. In his insistence that intolerance was fundamental to the nation, Higham revealed what he meant in other writings at the time when he complained of the moral timidity of the historical profession.[9]

Higham had not only kept alive some of the sensibilities of Progressives like Beard to conflict and of immigrant historians to ethnic difference, he had anticipated a major change in the study of immigration and ethnicity in the profession by linking it to the problem of bigotry, which was something older Progressives had failed to do. It was not long before other articles on the subject of intolerance appeared. In the early sixties Paul L. Murphy authored the essay "Sources and the Nature of Intolerance in the 1920s" and Fred H. Matthews wrote a piece entitled the "White Community and the 'Yellow Peril.'" Murphy described his work as one that approached "the seamy side of the national character which periodically displayed broad-scale intolerance, prejudice, nativism, and xenophobia." He noted how the 1920s was marked by what he called "waves of public intolerance" and "antipathy between Catholics, Jews, Negroes, and Orientals." Murphy was particularly surprised by the fact that so much of this intolerance was sanctioned by national leaders who referred to the era as one of "normalcy" after World War I. Matthews helped to open up the field to the problem of racism toward newcomers from Asia that had plagued the West Coast. His article extended the connection Higham made between economic, ethnic, and racial competition and the rising tide of immigration-restriction measures in the 1920s. In fact, it is possible to see the seminal 1964 essay by Rudolph Vecoli on Italian Americans, which challenged Oscar Handlin's view of immigration history as a tale of assimilation (no matter how difficult) and affirmed the lasting effects of premigration folkways, as part of a larger effort in the profession to upset the simple faith many older Progressives and postwar scholars had in the integrative power of the liberal nation to bring people of all kinds together.[10]

In the past three decades, historians in the organization have remolded the idea of assimilation and moved scholarship on immigration away from the European focus that had dominated it through much of the twentieth century to look more closely at newcomers from Asia and Latin America. Easy assumptions that liberal ideals could fuse people of varying backgrounds into a common mass were thrown out. The path of immigrants into American society was now riddled with structures and tensions based especially on race and class. The new attention that historians paid to matters of racial violence and conflict in the American past that followed the Civil Rights era not only had a significant impact on the study of immigration but, in many ways, reshaped it totally. It must be stressed that, even before this era, the study of the European immigrant experience was already moving in a direction that emphasized the intolerance and divisiveness of the United States. With racial sensibilities aroused, however, some historians contended that the very incorporation of European immigrants into American society was based, not on the liberalism of that society, but on its illiberalism or its powerful impulse to turn many into second-class citizens. Scholars now argued that the assimilation of southern and eastern Europeans into America was best explained by their "whiteness" or the fact that, in the twentieth century, people of different ethnic and religious backgrounds could come together reasonably well if their skin was relatively light. This argument inferred that immigrants and their children readily accepted the racial hierarchies that permeated American life in exchange for jobs and life in neighborhoods and suburbs that held few people of color.[11]

The key essay that acknowledged the altered understanding of immigrant assimilation and the necessity of looking at the experience of European newcomers in conjunction with matters of race was Gary Gerstle's article "Liberty, Coercion and the Making of Americans," published in 1997. Gerstle acknowledged the import of a vast body of scholarship to assert that liberalism could no longer explain what assimilation had been in American history. A liberal view had contended that people moved with eagerness into a new culture and nation in common pursuit of new opportunities for improvement and freedom. From many peoples came a new race of prosperous and cooperative Americans, an outlook at the center of much of the old Progressive view. Gerstle did not discard the liberal dream entirely, but clearly the weight of his evidence suggested that the integration of the foreign-born was more often the result of what he called "coercion." It was imposed by pre-existing structures of thought and power in America that were brought to bear on immigrants, such as mass culture, government-sponsored Americanization campaigns, job structures, and racial preferences and outlooks. In his view, becoming American was contingent less on the attractions of equality and progress and more on the acceptance of powerful ideologies of patriotism and racism.[12]

The connection between immigration and racial issues was furthered by historians who came to the study of immigration through labor history. This was quite evident in the presidential address to the organization delivered by David Montgomery in 2000 in St. Louis, the site of Blegen's address in 1944. An eminent historian of the American working class, Montgomery could not but help take note of racial issues at that year's convention. Prior to the beginning of the meeting, the OAH learned that the hotel chain scheduled to host the convention had been involved with a number of cases involving racial discrimination. In moving the convention location, it affirmed just how far it had come as a professional group on the subject of racism. In the 1950s, the matter of whether the MVHA should discontinue holding its annual meetings in cities that still tolerated segregated convention facilities prompted not a ringing denunciation of racism but merely a debate over whether to accept the continuation of such backward practices.[13]

In his talk, Montgomery argued for the centrality of race in American history and cast the story of immigration into this larger template. He argued that historians could no longer even begin the study of immigration with the model of millions of Europeans deciding to come here after 1820, as the pioneer immigrant historians had done. For him the focus on European migrations constituted a gross injustice to the harsh experience of African Americans whose involuntary immigrant experience and arduous labor had produced profits for their masters long before, as he said, "Irish immigrants dug canals" in the early nineteenth century. In linking European immigrants to the exploitation of blacks, Montgomery moved far away from the type of connections that Carl Fish made in the 1920s between immigrants and Pilgrim ancestors who shared a desire for change and improvement in their lives. His larger dream (and the value of focusing on racism) was about the constant need to challenge oppression and inequality. His democratic future would be realized not by the mere existence of liberal ideals or institutions but by the active agency of the working masses of many colors.[14]

Montgomery's refusal to consider immigration history outside the critical frames of race and class is at the center of how most scholars treat the subject today. Immigrants are generally placed not so much into ethnic but racial categories that run a spectrum of colors, from black to white and nearly everything in between. Mostly they are seen, not as adherents to some idea of progress, but as victims who need to be ready to mobilize and fight for their rights at a moment's notice, or, at times, they are seen as beneficiaries (if they are white) of America's sordid racist past. The Progressive idea of "the people," always masking more divisions than it connoted, has been taken apart, on the one hand, but surprisingly narrowed, on the other, to a focus on the bottom level of society and now mostly to people of color. Trace amounts of the promise of the liberal nation survive in this work, for it implies the value of struggling for equality and justice. However, no one who reads it could come away with the faith Blegen and Higham had that meaningful progress on this front will take place. Such uncertainty makes sense in the light of the discovery of so much violence and oppression in the nation's past. Indeed, the rise of this more sordid history is seen as grounds by some, not only to temper the hope of the Progressives, but to abandon the framework of national history completely for new perspectives centered on global flows of migrants and capital or in the creation of transnational diasporas. Illiberalism is now as much a part of the American narrative as liberalism used to be.[15]

Immigration as a constant struggle against oppression is seen in a number of recent essays. James Barrett published an argument that Americanization took place largely from the "bottom up." His goal was to link Americanization to the process of "working-class formation" that took place in urban America between 1880 and 1930. For Barrett it was not coercion or the impact of corporate and governmental programs designed to foster 100 percent Americanism that truly explained assimilation but the constant agitation and negotiations that took place in unions and labor alliances that forced immigrant workers to seek ways to find a place in the structure of industrial cities in the Untied States. Out of this crucible came, what he called, "labor's version of Americanism," which emphasized, not a benign acceptance of all things American, but a particular demand for civil liberties and rights that were beneficial to people who toiled hard for a living. The theme is repeated in a recent article by Thomas Guglielmo on Mexican American activism in Texas during World War II. He explained how wartime pressures for unity allowed Mexican American activists to gain some headway in their ongoing efforts to dismantle discriminatory practices aimed against them and other minorities. In 1943, these activists, with support from the Mexican government, were actually able to get the Texas legislature to pass a resolution entitled "Caucasian Race—Equal Privileges" that declared that all Caucasians, which in this instance included Mexican-Americans, would have equal access to "places of public business or amusement" in the state. These activists quickly learned, however, that there were still racial boundaries that were difficult to cross, even in the atmosphere of wartime patriotism in Texas, when they subsequently tried to get the same rights ensured by the passage of a law that had the legal standing that a resolution did not. This "Racial Equality Bill" never made it out of the Texas house. The struggles of ethnic minorities are also seen as racial issues in Mae Ngai's essay in 1999. She insightfully shows how Americans continually invented various racial categories as a way to view immigrants and at times exclude them. She noted how this was particularly true in the 1920s with the invention of the idea of "National Origins" and the term "Asiatic" as a way to restrict the inflow of some people completely.[16]

In a recent presidential address to the organization in 2006, Vicki Ruiz continued to invoke the contemporary focus on racial and ethnic differences that inform contemporary scholarship and to raise questions about the democratic spirit of the nation that many Progressives presumed would shape the future. Ruiz entitled her talk "Nuestra America" in an acknowledgement of Jose Marti's 1891 essay that had articulated a hope not of progress toward equality in America but of the realization of equality on a transnational or hemispheric basis where American imperialism and racism would be replaced by relations of mutual respect between Americans and the many peoples that lived south of its borders. Ruiz, interestingly, claimed that the subjects of her historical interest were not immigrants to America but what she termed "Spanish-speaking" individuals who made history within and beyond national boundaries. And she did leave open the door to movement beyond a history of group struggle to raise awareness of how individuals—at the micro level of history—all have to negotiate the realities of their local lives and the larger structures that impinge upon them. This was an embryonic idea that could point the way to a common history for people of all kinds of color and backgrounds.[17]

In matters of immigration and ethnic diversity, scholars in the organization have made decisive shifts. In the first half of the twentieth century, Progressive historians were responsible for initiating the professional study of America's immigrant history and helping to raise an awareness of the plural nature of American society. They did this while retaining a deep faith in the national project itself and its ability to deliver material improvement and democracy for people of all backgrounds. In retrospect, their shortcomings appear evident. Their conception of Americanization was much too blurry; their sensitivity to racial and ethnic conflict was much too underdeveloped. As they moved down the path of scientific history, they proved unwilling to relinquish some of their impossible dreams.

Successive generations of historians in the organization took turns dismantling this earlier framework on immigration. In the immediate postwar era of the 1950s and early 1960s, scholars peeled back some of the innocence about

America by exposing the long-term problem of intolerance and ethnic differences that surrounded the movement of newcomers to America throughout its history. Eventually a new generation would insist that racism, not assimilation and progress, was not only at the heart of American history but immigrant history as well. Under this new paradigm, scholars were more likely to link the study of immigration to the struggles of people of color, especially workers, and their need to constantly claim their rights and expose the harsh tendencies of assimilative forces to separate and control newcomers more than open doors for them. In all of this change, the very idea of the nation itself was challenged. No longer was it possible to write about it as an exceptional place where reasonableness trumped unreasonableness. It was at this point that the older faith of liberal nationalists like Blegen and Higham began to give way to the perspectives that were multicultural and transnational—frameworks that were marked by their distance from a faith in nationalist history. The protagonists of immigrant history were now more likely to be racial minorities fighting for their rights and tied to imagined communities outside America as well as inside.

It is not surprising in our times to note the eclipse of a progressive framework of national history and the erosion of confidence that both citizens and historians have in it. Scholars, however, have thought less about the implications of this transformation. To a certain extent, it has led to what political theorist Wendy Brown has called "political disorientation." That is to say, following Brown's arguments, that the emergence of stories of class, and racial and gender victimization have led not only to a weakening of faith in both the idea of the nation and its ability to shape historical accounts but to an overall impasse in narrative direction. No reasonable person can deny the irrational and violent aspects of the nation's past or claim any longer that newcomers could become Americans with ease—if they, in fact, could get through the door. But with larger visions of national history shredded, Brown wondered about future directions. In place of progressive visions, she argued, we are now more likely to get endless rounds of "righteous moralizing" from the Left, the Center, and the Right. Peter Kolchin suggests as much in a recent review of the scholarship on "whiteness" when he says that this literature has been "highly didactic" and has emerged at a time when there is less optimism about any kind of progressive future. Few today could dismiss the long legacy of racial and ethnic division in the American past and, therefore, it is reasonable to conclude that some "disorientation" and "moralizing" is inevitable and necessary. But the question of how to sustain some longer-term progressive vision remains. Scholars of modern nationalism have often remarked that the narrative form furthest removed from the story of the virtuous nation is to be found in the modern novel. Here, people struggle with emotional turmoil and fractured identities more than they move through history. Mythical histories tend to efface turmoil; modern fiction tends to get bogged down in it.[18]

A number of scholars have addressed the issue of how broader visions of hope for a more just future can be saved. James Kloppenberg and David Hollinger, for instance, have written of a legacy of a cosmopolitan nationalism in America and the need for a "postethnic" sensibility that is grounded neither in high principles nor fixed notions of color and blood but is tolerant of multiple identities and a history that is both progressive and violent.[19] Gerstle would say that such plans are a bit optimistic and that "coercion" will not go away. However, in reality, what scholars in this organization have done best for nearly a century is to find a way to examine history in an intellectual valley of their own that has always been positioned somewhere between the myth of exceptionalism and the grimness of victimization. No one who has read their work can fail to see that they worked endlessly with the contradictions of American life, which are grounded in myth and turmoil, hope and anger, reason and hate, and consensus and conflict. They have told us that at least when it comes to questions of immigration and ethnicity no version of our past was ever settled. I cannot imagine why we would want it any other way.

NOTES

1. Theodore C. Blegen, "Our Widening Province," *MVHR* 31 (June 1944): 3–20. On Blegen's background, see Jon Gjerde, "New Growth on Old Vines—The State of the Field: The Social History of Immigration and Ethnicity in the United States," *Journal of American Ethnic History* 18 (Summer 1999): 41–46.

2. George M. Fredrickson, "America's Diversity in Comparative Perspective," *Journal of American History (JAH)* 85 (Dec. 1988): 859–75.

3. John Higham, "From Process to Structure: Formulations of American Immigration History," in *American Immigrants and Their Generations: Studies and Commentaries on the Hansen Thesis after Fifty Years*, ed. Peter Kivisto and Dag Blanck, 11–41 (Urbana: University of Illinois Press, 1990). Higham discusses the "myth of American newness" in "The Future of American History," *JAH* 80 (Mar. 1990): 1292. Michael Denning, *The Cultural Front: The Laboring of American Culture in the Twentieth Century* (London: Verso, 1996), 124–52, discusses the idea of the "Lincoln Republic." Marcus Lee Hansen, *The Atlantic Migration, 1607–1860* (Cambridge, MA: Harvard University Press, 1940).

4. John Higham, *History: Professional Scholarship in America* (Baltimore: Johns Hopkins University Press, 1965), 176–93; Ian Tyrell, *Historians in Public: The Practice of American History, 1890–1970* (Chicago: University of Chicago Press, 2005), 29; Peter Novick, *That Noble Dream: The 'Objectivity Question' and the American Historical Profession* (Cambridge: Cambridge University Press, 1988), 183.

5. Carl Russell Fish, "The Pilgrim and the Melting Pot," *MVHR* 7 (Dec. 1920): 187–205.

6. Ibid.; Theodore C. Blegen, "Cleng Peerson and Norwegian Immigration," *MVHR* 7 (Mar. 1921): 303–31. Also see James B. Hedges, "Promotion of Immigration to the Pacific Northwest by the Railroads," *MVHR* 15 (Sept. 1928): 183–203. Arthur

Schlesinger, "The City in American History," *MVHR* 27 (June 1940): 43–66. Also see Catherine S. Crary, "The Humble Immigrant and the American Dream: Some Case Histories, 1746–76," *MVHR* 46 (June 1959): 46–66.

7. O. Fritiof Ander, "The Swedish-American Press and the Election of 1892," *MVHR* 23 (Mar. 1937): 533–54; Carl Wittke, "The Immigrant Theme on the American Stage," *MVHR* 39 (Sept. 1952): 211–32. Michael Rogin, *Blackface, White Noise: Jewish Immigrants in the Hollywood Melting Pot* (Berkeley: University of California Press, 1998), 17.

8. Novick, *That Noble Dream*, 332–33.

9. John Higham, "Anti-Semitism in the Gilded Age: A Reinterpretation," *MVHR* 43 (Mar. 1957): 559–78. See especially Kenneth Cmiel, "John Higham: the Contrarian as Optimist," *Intellectual History Newsletter* 24 (2002): 134–38.

10. Paul L. Murphy, "Sources and the Nature of Intolerance in the 1920s," *JAH* 51 (June 1964): 60–76; Fred H. Matthews, "White Community and 'Yellow Peril,'" *MVHR* 50 (Mar. 1964): 612–33; Rudolph J. Vecoli, "Contadini in Chicago: A Critique of the Uprooted," *JAH* 51 (Dec. 1964): 404–17; John Higham, *Strangers in the Land: Patterns of American Nativism, 1860–1920* (New Brunswick, NJ: Rutgers University Press, 1955).

11. On the study of "whiteness," see David R. Roediger, *Working Toward Whiteness: How America's Immigrants Became White* (New York: Basic Books, 2005). On racial preferences in hiring practices that favored "new immigrants" over blacks, see John Bodnar, Roger Simon, and Michael Weber, "Migration, Kinship, and Urban Adjustment: Blacks and Poles in Pittsburgh, 1900–1930," *JAH* 66 (Dec. 1979): 548–65.

12. Gary Gerstle, "Liberty, Coercion, and the Making of Americans," *JAH* 84 (Sept. 1997): 524–58.

13. David Montgomery, "Racism, Immigrants, and Political Reform," *JAH* 87 (Mar. 2001); Novick, *That Noble Dream*, 225, 349, discusses racism in the Mississippi Valley Historical Association.

14. Montgomery, "Racism, Immigration, and Political Reform."

15. On the narrowing of the Progressive idea of "the people" see Ernst A. Breisach, *American Progressive History: An Experiment in Modernization* (Chicago: University of Chicago Press, 1993), 207.

16. James R. Barrett, "Americanization from the Bottom Up: Immigration and the Remaking of the Working Class in the United States," *JAH* 79 (Dec. 1992): 996–1020; Thomas A. Guglielmo, "Fighting for Caucasian Rights: Mexicans, Mexican-Americans and the Transnational Struggle for Civil Rights in World War II Texas," *JAH* 92 (Mar. 2006): 1212–37; Mae M. Ngai, "The Architecture of Race in American Immigration Law: A Reexamination of the Immigration Act of 1924," *JAH* 86 (June 1999): 67–92. On transnational history and immigrant history see Donna R. Gabaccia, "Is Everywhere Nowhere? Nomads, Nations, and the Immigrant Paradigm in United States History," *JAH* 86 (Dec. 1999): 1115–34, who argues for more transnational approaches as a way to counter the "tyranny" of a nation-centered history.

17. Vicki L. Ruiz, "Nuestra America: Latino History as United States History," *JAH* 93 (Dec. 2006): 655–72.

18. Wendy Brown, *Politics Out of History* (Princeton, NJ: Princeton University Press, 2001), 3–25, 140, 170–73; Peter Kolchin, "Whiteness Studies: The New History of Race in America," *JAH* 89 (June 2002): 154–73. On the ambiguity of writing the nation and

the relationship between narratives of nationhood and the novel see Simon During, "Literature—Nationalism's Other—The Case for Revision," in *Nation and Narration*, ed. Homi K. Bhabha (London: Routledge, 1990), 138–53.

19. James Kloppenberg, "Aspirational Nationalism in America," *Intellectual History Newsletter* 24 (2002): 60–71; David A. Hollinger, *Postethnic America: Beyond Multiculturalism* (New York: Basic Books, 1995), 14.

16

The Slow Rise to Prominence of African American History

Arvarh E. Strickland and Richard S. Kirkendall

The secretaries of the state historical societies who met in Lincoln, Nebraska, in October 1907 did not envision African Americans as members of their new organization, and they could not conceive of a field of historical study and research called Negro history. This remained true of the men who met later to refine the plans and to launch the new Mississippi Valley Historical Association. These men came from states where either *de jure* or *de facto* segregation was practiced, and most of them were adherents of William A. Dunning's "tragic era" interpretation of Reconstruction history. Several of the leaders completed studies of southern states during Reconstruction as doctoral dissertations under Dunning's supervision. It took over a half century for new generations to complete a gradual process of reform that brought changes in attitudes that welcomed African American participation and recognized African American history as an integral part of American history. Then, during the 1960s, the field and its practitioners achieved prominence within the historical profession and the OAH, and for the next half century, African American history maintained and built upon its lofty position.

For a moment in time, during the World War I era, the *MVHR*, under the direction of the founding managing editor, Clarence W. Alvord of the University of Illinois, reviewed a few books by African American authors and invited a small number of African Americans to review books. The first review of a book by an African American author appeared in March 1916. Carter G. Woodson's *The Education of the Negro Prior to 1861* was declared a definitive treatment by a white reviewer who was a member of the Dunning school. It is interesting to note that, unique to this review, the school granting Woodson's doctorate, Harvard, appeared in parentheses. The acceptance Woodson received probably was out of respect for his Harvard degree and the fact that his work was characterized by thorough research and meticulous documentation. In June 1916, another member of the Dunning school reviewed favorably *The Facts of Reconstruction*, written by John R. Lynch, an African American politician of the Reconstruction period.[1]

Woodson was called upon periodically to review books on African American topics written by both white and African American authors. It was somewhat surprising, however, to find that he was invited to review Ulrich B. Phillip's *American Negro Slavery*, a positive portrayal of the institution. Woodson's review, though critical, was scholarly in tone; still, it seems likely that the overwhelming majority of the Association's members were more in agreement with Phillip's interpretation of the institution of slavery than with Woodson's criticisms.[2]

The white reviewer who reviewed the volume by Woodson's protégé, Alrutheus A. Taylor, on Reconstruction in South Carolina did not extend to him the respect that Woodson received. In what was his Harvard M.A. thesis, Taylor was sharply critical of the works of the members of the Dunning school. The reviewer, Philip M. Hamer of the University of Tennessee, pronounced Taylor's book to be "so great a degree confused patchworks of inaccuracies and of unassimilated portions of the writings of others, that the work as a whole can not be accepted as a trustworthy presentation of the subject with which it deals."[3] (Later reviewers gave Taylor's subsequent works the same objective analysis that Woodson's works received.) An editorial comment in the same issue of the *MVHR* containing the review of Taylor's book cited his work as an example of the propaganda that the Association for the Study of Negro Life and History was trying to pass off as scholarly work.[4]

Throughout the 1920s and 1930s, books by Woodson continued to be reviewed and given rather objective treatment. Moreover, books by both white and African American authors published by Woodson's enterprise, the Association for the Study of Negro History and the Associated Publishers, regularly appeared. In addition, reviews of books in the field, mainly by white authors and published by mainstream presses, began to show up in the pages of the *MVHR* devoted to reviews.[5]

By the 1940s, slight breezes if not winds of change on racial matters were beginning to blow. On April 24, 1943, the Teacher's Section of the Association met jointly with the National Council of the Social Studies and the Iowa Council for the Social Studies, and one of the papers scheduled for presentation was by Charles H. Wesley, African American historian and president of Wilberforce University. It was entitled "Teaching the Role of the Negro in American History."[6] In 1945, Benjamin Quarles's "Sources of Abolitionist Income" was the first article by an African American historian to appear in the *Review*. Fourteen years later, in 1959, the second article by an African American, "The Colonial Militia and Negro Manpower," was also by Quarles.[7]

Worthy of note, the editors of the *Review* turned over John Hope Franklin's *From Slavery to Freedom: A History of American Negroes* to the distinguished, but not totally "reconstructed," professor at the University of Illinois, James G. Randall, for review. Surprisingly, at least for us, Randall found the book to be "a work of impressive industry, effective presentation, and undoubted value."[8]

The 1950s brought challenges to the comfortable status of the "old order," but supporters of the status quo did not yield without a struggle. One issue concerned the Association's name, whether it should be changed to reflect the fact that the organization was no longer regional in character. Two positions were outlined in the September 1951 issue of the *Review*, and the members were called upon to vote. Paul W. Gates of Cornell presented the argument in favor of change, and John D. Barnhart of Indiana University argued for the status quo. He probably drew a responsive chord from a majority of the members with the argument that changes that encouraged growth could make the association a "large unwieldy group, destroy its present character and defeat its purpose." They would not be able to meet in small Midwestern cities, and the "intimacy and friendly character of the annual meetings" would be lost.[9] At a meeting of the executive committee in December, the proponents of change learned that that the membership had overwhelmingly rejected the name-change proposal.

At the annual meeting held in Cincinnati earlier that year, members had glimpses of the future that probably disturbed many of them. For the first time, an African American historian was on the program. John Hope Franklin chaired a session in which three white scholars, one of whom was a woman, Betty Fladeland, presented papers. The report on the session noted that more than 100 persons attended the session but only "approximately one fourth of them commented favorably on the program."[10]

The issue of racial discrimination came to the forefront even more explicitly at this Cincinnati meeting. The immediate cause of the acrimony was an invitation to hold the 1952 meeting in New Orleans, where African Americans would be totally excluded from the headquarters hotel. Incoming president Merle Curti announced that he would not deliver his presidential address where African American members could not at least attend the sessions. Curti hoped to find a compromise that would not lead to a split in the Association. A committee to study discrimination, chaired by Carl Wittke, was established. It soon submitted a report that stated all members "are entitled to participate in the annual convention and other meetings and activities of the Association." The committee called upon the Executive Committee to recommend that the association select "as a meeting place for its annual spring convention, only such localities or institutions where all members of the Association will be permitted to participate in all official sessions, including luncheon and dinner meetings which are part of the official program." Even though the recommendation avoided the volatile issue of desegregated housing, the Executive Committee procrastinated and resolved to have another committee study the subject further and make recommendations no later than the 1953 annual meeting. A new committee, chaired by Thomas D. Clark, was charged with this responsibility.[11]

Clark and his committee promoted change. At the next meeting of the Executive Committee, he and A. D. Kirwan, both of them from the University of Kentucky, invited the Association to hold the 1953 meeting in Lexington and "assured the executive committee of the absence of discrimination in that city."[12] Finally, in 1954 the Executive Committee accepted the recommendation of the Clark committee on discrimination that the Association refuse to accept invitations unless sponsors guaranteed there would be no discrimination in meals and housing.[13]

The Lexington meeting broke the ice on scheduling Negro history sessions. The program committee scheduled what can be considered the first real Negro history session. The papers explored African American attitudes and thought in the nineteenth and twentieth century, but only one African American, Elsie M. Lewis, presented a paper. At the 1954 meeting in Madison, Wisconsin, the program included a session on the Negro in politics. The token African American presenter, Rayford W. Logan, was unable to attend, however, and his paper was read by a substitute.

The St. Louis meeting in 1955 did not have a session devoted to Negro history, but this was the first meeting at which the new policy of non-discrimination was followed. The only hint that anything unusual had taken place contained in Joe B. Frantz's report of the meeting was this statement: "A new generation of historians had arisen since the Mississippi Valley Historical Association had last met in St. Louis, but it will likely take more than one succeeding generation to erase the memory . . . of the forty-eighth annual meeting. . . ."[14]

The Negro history session reappeared in 1956 with a panel chaired by C. Vann Woodward, papers delivered by Kenneth M. Stampp and Guion G. Johnson, and comments by Fletcher M. Green and John Hope Franklin. Franklin was also elected to the executive committee in 1958 and named to the program committee in 1960.[15]

And then came the 1960s! The pace of change accelerated during that decade. From beginning to end of the sixties, change was a major theme in the life of the nation; the organization felt the pressures and, illustrative of that fact, changed its name. One of the big national themes was the demand for reform in race relations; the field of African American history benefited from that.

The organization contributed to the field's development in several ways. The *MVHR-JAH* published more articles on Negro history than ever before: one in 1961, a second in 1963, four in 1965, and ten more during the second half of the decade. After a slow start in 1961, the Program Committee sponsored eight sessions on the field from 1962 to 1965 and then thirteen in the next five years. Also, the book-review sections in each issue of the *Review* and the *Journal* testified to the rapid development of the field and the recognition of it by the OAH. While the *MVHR* reviewed only fifteen of these books in its last three years, the *JAH* reviewed nearly twenty in one year (1965) and nearly forty in the next five.

During the 1960s, the field as presented in the MVHA-OAH had two major parts. One focused on whites who had significant relations with blacks, both negative and positive. There were studies of racism, including racism outside the South, the slave trade, slaveholders, slavery, fears of slave uprisings, and plans to colonize blacks in Africa. Other work focused on and opposition to the abolitionists and to Reconstruction's challenge to the race system. The Ku Klux Klan, race riots, the Scottsboro case, and resistance to the mid-twentieth-century attack on Jim Crow (the post–Civil War racial order) also attracted attention. In addition, the OAH gave much space to studies of white abolitionists, including those who ended slavery in the North, while other work focused on missionaries who served slaves, Radical and other Republicans who battled for black rights from the 1860s to the 1890s, and white critics of Jim Crow during the twentieth century.

The other part of the field focused directly on African Americans and their actions. Benjamin Quarles did work of this kind in the 1965 OAH meeting and in books that the *MVHR* and the *JAH* reviewed: *The Negro in the American Revolution* (1961), *Negroes and Lincoln* (1962), and *Black Abolitionists* (1969). Some white historians also contributed, including August Meier. His book *Negro Thought in America, 1880–1915: Racial Ideologies in the Age of Booker T. Washington* (1963) portrayed African Americans as actors, not only acted upon. The *Journal* reviewed it favorably, and he drew upon it in a presentation at the 1964 meeting. The *JAH* also reviewed another of his books, *From Plantation to Ghetto: An Interpretive History of American Negroes* (1966), written with Elliott Rudwick, and, in 1969, published their article "The Boycott Movement Against Jim Crow Streetcars in the South, 1900–1906." A year earlier, Richard M. Dalfiume, in another *JAH* article, had emphasized the importance of World War II in the history of black activism, calling the war years the forgotten years of the Negro Revolution and the watershed in recent Negro history.[16]

At the same time, other historians who received attention and opportunities in the OAH portrayed Negroes as active participants in American history. They wrote of slaves and other black people in various southern places, including cities. They discussed the slaves' religion, black nationalism, Negro contributions to the Confederacy, Negroes in Reconstruction, black ghettos in northern cities, and challenges by blacks to their economic status after slavery. They wrote and spoke of Negro participation in politics and the federal government, including the military, and also explored the National Association for the Advancement of Colored People (NAACP), the mind and mood of blacks in the twentieth century, a protest by sharecroppers, and "the Second Reconstruction."

Who were the appropriate people to write "Black history," some asked, as that name increasingly became the term of choice for the field.

By 1970, the OAH recognized the field as an established and highly important component of what the American historical profession had to offer. Would the Organization continue to contribute to the development of the field? The most important test would be the articles published in the *Journal*, for that depended on two sets of decision makers: authors and editors. For the OAH to pass the test, the historians in the field needed to continue to regard the *JAH* as a good place for their work and one that was receptive to what they had to say, and the editors had to continue to be receptive to good work in the field.

Martin Ridge, who served as editor from 1966 to 1977, had already demonstrated during his first five years that he accepted the rising field, and he continued to publish work in it—fifteen articles—to the end of his term. Some of them dealt with whites who impacted negatively on African Americans. Michael S. Hindus showed that the legal system in South Carolina from 1740 to 1865 supported white dominance, not black justice, while Robert E. Gallman and Ralph V. Anderson maintained that slaveholders developed a diversified agricultural system so as to keep their slaves busy all of the time. John M. McFaul argued that most politicians of the Jacksonian era tried to keep slavery out of politics so as to preserve the union of slaveholders and non-slaveholders.[17]

Other articles portrayed white-black relations from other angles. A. E. Keir Nash wrote of a remarkable antebellum tradition of fair treatment of blacks by the Texas Supreme Court, an all-white institution. Focusing on a mostly white group, Jane and William Pease and Michael Fellman argued that during the 1850s, abolitionists, influenced by passage and enforcement of the Fugitive Slave Law, among other events, became more radical—more confrontational and more willing to use violence. Radical Republicans continued to be portrayed quite positively, a trend that had begun before the 1970s, but Louis S. Gerteis argued that their success had been exaggerated. They had failed, for example, in their efforts to distribute land to the freedmen. One obstacle they faced, Michael Les Benedict maintained, was the constitutional conservatism of most Republicans. By 1890, these Republicans as well as southern Redeemers and even southern blacks had, Howard N. Rabinowitz concluded, given the South a system of *de facto* racial segregation.[18]

During Ridge's last years as editor, most of the articles on twentieth-century race relations focused on black activism. There was one exception: Christopher G. Wye's essay on two sets of New Deal agencies, those focused on housing and on jobs. While alleviating problems that many blacks had, the programs contributed to the preservation of racial segregation and a racial occupational pattern.[19]

Four other articles emphasized challenges by African Americans to the race system. Meier and Rudwick studied the lawyers with whom the NAACP worked and found that in the early years this force for change relied on white lawyers but before the end of the 1930s switched to blacks at the top and in the local communities. Turning to black activism during World War II, Harvard Sitkoff found that the war stimulated racial militancy; militancy led to increased racial violence, and violence persuaded Negro leaders to retreat to a moderation that enabled them to form alliances with white liberals. Basing his essay on the black press, Lee Finkle maintained that the leaders adopted a new rhetoric capable of both gaining concessions from a reluctant administration and restraining the militants. Alan Winkler used the Philadelphia transit strike of 1944 to illustrate how the war stimulated demands for change. In that city, black transit workers pressed for better jobs, whites resisted, but the city avoided violence.[20]

In the year-long interim between Ridge and Lewis Perry, the *Journal* published only one article in the field. Written by William M. Wiecek, it focused on slavery and abolition before the U.S. Supreme Court between 1820 and 1860 and criticized the tendency of the Taney Court, unlike earlier ones, to get involved in slavery cases.[21]

During Perry's time as editor (from late in 1978 to the middle of 1984), the *JAH* averaged fewer than two black history articles per year, mainly because competition for space had become greater than ever. The field now had to compete not only against the long-established fields but also against the other rising ones. Nevertheless, specialists in Black history continued to find opportunities in the *Journal*'s pages.

The opportunities included two review essays, a new feature in which the editor, as in regular book reviews, solicited the contributors. In one of them, August Meier reviewed two surveys of Black history by black scholars and used them to discuss the direction in which such scholars were moving the field. The other reviewer, Jan S. Hogendorn, discussed three books on the economics of the African slave trade that testified to a recent widening of slave-trade investigations.[22]

Two articles of the traditional type, ones voluntarily submitted by authors, discussed both enslaved and free blacks. Peter Kolchin applauded recent work on the slave community that demolished the view of slaves as depersonalized victims but suggested that some scholars had gone too far, replacing the Sambo myth with the myth of the idyllic slave community. He called for reevaluations, some of them by comparisons with slavery outside the United States. Looking at free Negroes in antebellum Alabama, Gary B. Mills challenged more negative views with evidence that they were tolerated and not regarded as threats to society or the slave system.[23]

Other articles took the story from Reconstruction to the end of the century. While Armstead L. Robinson emphasized black activism during Reconstruction, Pete Daniel concluded that by 1900, slavery had truly ended for some blacks but for others it had metamorphosed into peonage, a subtle form of control. James C. Klotter reported that many late nineteenth century reformers saw conditions among whites in Appalachia as similar to those among southern blacks and shifted their attention away from blacks to the mountain whites.[24]

Two other articles, both dealing with black social history, emphasized the limits on black progress during the years between 1900 and 1945. Studying blacks and Poles in Pittsburgh from 1900 to 1930, John Bodnar, Michael Weber, and Roger Simon maintained that although black migrants to this industrial city experienced some upward mobility, they encountered racism in the plants from both employers who preferred immigrants and immigrants who resisted blacks, and they failed to find the occupational security obtained by the Poles. Karen Tucker Anderson's article on black women workers during World War II challenged the emphasis of earlier studies on wartime improvement in opportunities for blacks, seeing it as ignoring the persistence of discrimination and the unequal distribution of the benefits of a full employment economy. For black women, she concluded, what was most significant was the extent to which barriers remained in place.[25]

Following a lull from September 1984 to the end of the following year, the number of articles in the field moved up again. They rose to three in 1986 and again in 1988, five in 1989, six in 1990, and then averaged nearly four per year from 1993 to 1998. The new editor, David Thelen, who served from 1985 to 1999, dealt with the problem of increased competition for space by enlarging the space the *Journal* offered. It had slightly more than 1,300 pages in his first year, 1985–1986, expanded to more than 1,500 two years later, and averaged nearly 1,800 pages per year from 1991 to 1999.

Some of the articles dealt with the slave system and its ideology. Christopher Morris drew upon the now rich literature on slavery to offer a theory of the master-slave relationship that emphasized its structure and concluded that slavery may have been both more humane that we sometimes think and more insidiously oppressive. Looking at a Kentucky county during the two decades before the Civil War, Keith C. Barton reported that the hiring of slaves for domestic labor was a common practice that enabled owners to profit from their excess labor and small and middling farmers and craftsmen to relieve their women of household drudgery. And Michael Wayne maintained that by the 1830s, white southerners ceased to tolerate debates over slavery, saw perpetuation of it as necessary to preserve their own liberty and equality, and believed blacks were innately suited to be slaves and largely accepting of their fate.[26]

Historians continued to pay attention to the anti-slavery movement. Elizabeth B. Clark noted that, beginning in the 1830s, it made the cruel treatment of the slaves a major theme. Nell Irvin Painter explored how Sojourner Truth, a black woman who had been freed from slavery in the North, used speech, writing, and photography as a preacher and an abolitionist. Seymour Drescher's article, "Servile Insurrection and John Brown's Body in Europe," included a discussion of the abolitionists' use of the European reaction to Brown, and Robert E. McGlone offered a study of the effort by the Brown family to come to a satisfactory understanding of the big event in its history: Brown's effort to promote a violent slave uprising and the consequent deaths of family members.[27]

The beneficiaries of abolition in the North attracted much attention. In two articles, one on African American festivals and parades in the North, the other on free blacks in New York City from 1783 to 1810, Shane White proposed that the parades were attempts to foster unity among freedmen and to proclaim to whites that blacks were no longer slaves but were citizens with a right to the street, and the New Yorkers were not passive ciphers but exceptional men and women. Robert E. Desrochers Jr. wrote of an eighteenth-century African American who had experienced Africa, the slave trade, slavery in the North, freedom, and prosperity and proudly told his life story. Daniel R. Mandell, covering a long period after the American Revolution, explored Indian-Black intermarriage in southern New England, demonstrated that the history of race relations in America involves more than white-black relations, and proposed that the issues of American race relations first emerged among these New England Indians. At the beginning of the nineteenth century, W. Jeffrey Bolster reported, seafaring was one of the few jobs readily available to blacks; the maritime culture made them feel like men, and thus this way of life had great appeal, but the good conditions eroded before the Civil War. In one of his articles, Shane White noted that the positive situation he described would change soon after 1810, and in another piece, Rowland Berthoff explained how white males by mid-century justified barring free blacks (and also married women) from the equal rights and protection the Constitution assured all persons.[28]

Several contributors carried the story of freed men and women into the Reconstruction era. Two focused on battles for control between whites and blacks. In a county study, Christopher Waldrep explored efforts by Mississippi whites during Reconstruction to use the law as defined by the Black Codes and administered by the courts to control the freedmen. Not fully satisfied, these whites felt compelled to employ violent means as well. Focused on Alabama soon after the war, Michael W. Fitzgerald explained the emergence of a decentralized system of tenant farming, emphasizing the political mobilization of freedmen who challenged efforts by landowners to tightly control the labor force.[29]

The *JAH* during Thelen's years also offered essays on the race system that emerged before the end of the nineteenth century. An article by David W. Bright focused on Frederick Douglass, the freedman who had championed abolition before and during the war and, troubled by the forces at work in his late years, upheld his memory of the war as a struggle for both union and liberty. Robert J. Norell, looking at "Jim Crow Careers" in the South's leading industrial city, Birmingham, reported that blacks were limited to the lower level industrial jobs, giving white workers a stake in a system that lasted until the 1960s. Robin D. G. Kelley, challenging the idea that black working people during the days of Jim Crow did not protest, called attention to daily, unorganized, evasive, seemingly spontaneous actions at work and in public spaces and saw them as undermining the divisions between political history and social history.[30]

Four articles dealt with an early critic of the system, W.E.B. Du Bois. Richard Cullen Rath argued that at the turn of the twentieth century, Du Bois created an Afrocentric philosophy of history that rejected power being located and fixed in white folk and that projected a world in which the longings of black folk would have respect. Writing of this black intellectual during World War I, Mark Ellis sought to explain his "close ranks" editorial of 1918 and concluded that it was highly probable that he wrote it to secure a position in military intelligence and that it crucially influenced the War Department's decision to offer him one. In response, William Jordan maintained that "accommodation" was a sensible choice in 1918 and that Du Bois was guided by an understanding of the dangers of militancy amid wartime frenzy and encouraged by the government's wartime racial strategies—only one of which was the offer of a commission. Returning to the discussion, Ellis suggested that Jordan emphasized the wider response to the war by equal rights champions while he, Ellis, traced the day-to-day events surrounding Du Bois in the summer of 1918 and these suggested that the editorial and the captaincy were linked.[31]

The *JAH* during these years carried one more article on the impact of World War I on African Americans. Written by Steven A. Reich, the article argued that during and right after the war, southern blacks, stimulated by wartime rhetoric, mobilized in opposition to white supremacy. Using Texas as a case study, Reich reported that in the Lone Star State a wide range of blacks participated, alarmed the elites, and were put down by the coercive resources of both state and federal governments.[32]

World War II continued to attract the attention of historians of Black history. Dominic J. Capeci contributed an article on a lynching in 1942 that drew the U.S. Department of Justice into the era of civil rights for the first time and brought the federal government more directly into the protection of blacks and the struggle for racial equality than at any time since Reconstruction. Clayton R. Koppes and Gregory D. Black wrote of the Roosevelt administration's concern about the loyalty of black Americans and the Office of War Information's efforts to mobilize black support and interpret American race relations to the world. To accomplish its goals, the OWI tried to improve Hollywood's portrayal of people of color but accomplished much less than black leaders wanted. Adding a broad survey of the war's impact on the South, Pete Daniel proposed that the changes included a restructuring of agriculture, the rapid growth of cities, and the launching of a civil rights movement.[33]

Two articles enlarged the *Journal*'s discussion of the war, labor, and the civil rights movement. Robert Korstad and Nelson Lichtenstein, arguing that the civil rights era began in the early 1940s when black America became more urban and proletarian, illustrated this with two examples: the predominantly black tobacco workers in Winston-Salem and the biracial United Auto Workers in Detroit. Moving beyond the war period, these authors noted the collapse of the worker-based movement during the early Cold War. Carrying further the question of organized labor and the struggle for black equality, Bruce Nelson maintained that the vast majority of white shipyard workers in Mobile were unwilling to make concessions to demands from their black co-workers. While many whites saw the blacks as threats, others accepted them as necessary, though subordinate participants in the workplace.[34]

Other discussions of the civil rights movement stretched from 1939 to the 1960s and beyond. Promoting a cultural history of the movement, Scott A. Sandage argued that African American struggles from 1939 to 1963 to hold rallies at the Lincoln Memorial in Washington, DC, made use of one conception of Lincoln and contributed to the movement's strategy of nonviolent action. Looking at the consequences of the *Brown* case, Michael J. Klarman maintained that its importance lay not in desegregating the schools but in its step-by-step causal relationship with the civil rights legislation of the mid-1960s. James F. Findlay argued for the great importance of the mainline churches in the passage of the 1964 act, seeing their heavy involvement as a break with their past but only a brief interlude in their history. Writing of federal farm and welfare policies and the civil rights movement in the Mississippi Delta, James C. Cobb stressed their conflicting impacts and the difficulties that accompany attempts to promote reform in a society without altering its traditional power relationships.[35]

Timothy B. Tyson challenged the established chronology of black history that sees reliance on appeals to the Supreme Court as the first stage of the civil rights movement, nonviolent action the second, and Black Power the third. Focusing on the important role of Robert F. Williams in what the author calls the African American Freedom Struggle, he proposed that Williams' story reveals that throughout World War II and the postwar years, independent black political action, black cultural pride, and armed self-reliance operated in the South in tension and in tandem with legal efforts and nonviolent protest. This current of militancy included a willingness to use guns to defend home and community.[36]

The articles of importance for African American history during Thelen's time as editor also included a survey of the ideologies of race by Peggy Pascoe. She focused not on the decline of scientific racism early in the twentieth century but on the emergence of new ideologies and then the winnowing down to one by the 1960s. Although some people still employed racial categories, this powerfully pervasive belief, which she called the modernist racial ideology, maintained that the eradication of racism depended on the deliberate refusal to recognize race.[37]

During these years from the mid-1980s to the late 1990s, the *JAH* not only published many articles on African American history. It also published new features in which the essays, usually short, were solicited, most often by the editor. The authors did not initiate the contact. The new features included the review essay, an innovation created by Perry and continued by Thelen, and the Round Table, the Special Issue, the Research Note, and Perspectives, all of them Thelen's contributions. He also added several special series.

A number of these new features dealt with African American history. A Round Table in September 1987 focused on Martin Luther King Jr. and offered short essays by five established scholars in the field. In a Round Table on World War II, published in September 1990, John Hope Franklin spoke of his negative experiences in that war. In March 1991, a dozen contributors to another Round Table on King dealt with plagiarism and originality. Two other Round Tables, one in September 1995 on Massive Resistance in Chicago in the 1950s and 1960s and related topics, the other in March 1997 on lynching, appeared before the end of Thelen's reign.

The other innovations also contributed discussions of the field. A Special Issue on the Constitution in December 1987 included three essays in Black history. In a Review Essay in June 1988, Franklin commented on the development of the field and two survey of it, one by Meier and Rudwick, the other by Darlene Clark Hine. In September of that year, a special issue on research included an essay by Kim Lacy Rogers on the great importance of oral history for the field, and in December, a section entitled Perspectives consisted of an appraisal by Howard Rabinowitz of a major book in the field, *The Strange Career of Jim Crow*, and a response from the author, C. Vann Woodward. In December 1994, a Special Issue included an essay by John E. Fleming on African American museums and another by Greg Cuthbertson on historiographical alliances between South Africa and the United States. Three Research Notes, one by Richard Lowe, another by John Modell, Marc Goulden, and Sigurdur Magnuson, and a third by James N. Gregory, dealt with the Freedman's Bureau (December 1993), World War II and black Americans (December 1989), and the Southern Diaspora (June 1995), and in another Special Issue, Robin D. G. Kelley contributed an essay on Black history's global vision (December 1999).

After Thelen, the editors—Joanne Meyerowitz and Edward Linenthal[38] and also Edward Paul Nord, who served twice as Acting Editor—continued to be receptive to the field and to make the *JAH* attractive to its historians. From 2000 to 2010, they published an average of four articles per year in Black history and included essays in the field in the new features: one Perspective (June 2000), a Special Issue (December 2007), and eight Round Tables (December

2000, March 2001, March 2003, June 2004, March 2006, September 2008, September 2009). And all of this happened even though the *Journal* was shrinking from 1,962 pages in 2000 to 1,628 in 2006 and to 1,280 in 2010.

The articles covered a long range from the seventeenth century to the present. Several focused on slavery. Wendy Anne Warren drew large meaning from a report in 1638 of a rape in the Massachusetts Bay Colony of a recently arrived African woman by another slave. It was ordered by their master who was eager to promote slave breeding. Kevin Dawson dealt with the large importance of swimming and diving for West Africans and American slaves, skills in which they were clearly superior to whites. Drawing upon a wide scope of evidence, Terri L. Snyder looked at suicide from multiple perspectives, showing that it was a part of the history of slavery.[39]

More articles dealt with the slavery controversy. Kenneth P. Minkema and Harry S. Stout presented an essay with a long time period but a sharp focus. They explored the participation in the debate from 1740 to 1865 by the theologian Jonathan Edwards and his followers, showing that for them it reached its highpoint with his first generation disciples during the revolutionary era. While Edwards criticized the slave trade but owned slaves, these disciples demanded immediate emancipation and racial integration, but later Edwardseans moved to more moderate positions.

Other articles on the great controversy covered somewhat shorter time periods. Nicholas Guyatt wrote that between 1776 and 1840, Americans troubled about slavery often proposed colonization, believing the removal of blacks from land occupied by whites would allow the former to transform themselves into citizens of civilized nations. Lacy Ford focused on the evolving efforts of opinion makers in the South to grapple with the problem of slavery, arguing that by the late 1830s they had discarded the idea that slavery was the root of corruption and hypocrisy in a republican society and acclaimed slavery as the surest foundation of an egalitarian republic crafted for whites only. Looking at one Southerner, Roger B. Taney, and his change over time from a moderately antislavery lawyer into a zealously proslavery judge, Timothy S. Huebner presented him as an illustration of how the terms of the debate shifted. Coming of age during the founding era, he expressed an early nineteenth century brand of antislavery that began to evaporate during the 1830s in response to the rise of radical abolitionists.[40]

These abolitionists continued to draw attention. Marc M. Arkin found continuity between the Federalist Fisher Ames and the abolitionist William Lloyd Garrison. Both believed in New England's exceptionalism, distrusted southern culture, feared southern hegemony, and highlighted a link between power and passion. Daniel Feller challenged the idea that Jacksonian Democracy was essentially proslavery and anti-black and held up Benjamin Tappan, a prominent Jacksonian Democrat and a sincere foe of slavery, as support for his challenge. Joseph Yanielli focused on George Thompson, a missionary and militant abolitionist who moved to Africa in 1848 and carried on his crusade against oppression there, helping to educate the first generation of African anti-colonial activists.[41]

Several contributors carried forward the discussion of the Civil War and emancipation. Kate Masur explored the use by Union officers of the term *contraband* to apply to slaves who fled to Union forces and the widespread adoption of the term throughout the North. Dorothy Ross, writing of Lincoln's moral conflict between liberty and national survival, concluded that the president solved the conflict by linking the two, though the Union remained his top priority. And Gary J. Kornblith, engaging in a counterfactural exercise, concluded that the Mexican-American War was a necessary if not sufficient cause of the Civil War and the latter was a necessary if not sufficient cause of American abolition in the nineteenth century.[42]

Reconstruction and the establishment of the Jim Crow system were but minor themes in the *JAH* during the years of Meyerowitz and Linenthal. Elaine Frantz Parsons contributed an article on costume and performance in the Reconstruction-era Ku Klux Klan that argued that the Klan was intimately intertwined with and completely dependent on popular cultural forms and institutions, and Andrew W. Kahrl, focusing on steamboat excursions and pleasure resorts, told the story of the emergence of segregation on the Potomac River in the late nineteenth-early twentieth century.[43]

As a promoter of African American history, the *Journal*'s emphases during these early years of the twenty-first century were life under Reconstruction and Jim Crow and, above all, the attacks upon that racial system. Stephen Kantrowitz discussed the many free blacks who became Freemasons and, as activists, benefited from it, for it enabled them to develop leadership skills, connect with others outside their localities, gain political experience, and imagine what equal citizenship could be. Sven Beckert wrote of freedom, cotton, and global capitalism, focusing on black Americans from Booker T. Washington's Tuskegee and officials and workers in Germany's African empire. Adam Fairclough, writing of the great importance of black teachers, argued that though they worked under the limitations of the Jim Crow South, they promoted learning and self improvement.[44]

Once again, the *JAH* published an article on W.E.B. Du Bois. In this piece, Axel R. Shafer focused on the influence during the late nineteenth century of the German historical school of economics on his thinking about race and the potential of black people. This posed a difficulty for him, as white progressives found in that same way of thinking a new rationale for discrimination. This quickly persuaded him to distance himself from German scholarship and progressive social thought.[45]

Another article concerned with the intellectual history of race discussed a quite different school. Written by Joanne Meyerowitz, it focused on the culture-personality group of social scientists from the 1920s to the 1950s. They rejected biological theories of race, investigated how different cultures produce diverse patterns of human behavior, and, among other results, influenced the civil rights movement.[46]

Three articles on the 1920s and 1930s dealt with black business and music, the Scopes Trial, and the civil rights lawyer. David Suisman focused on Black Swan Records and its owner, Harry Pace, who saw his company as a potentially powerful means of responding to the hostile conditions blacks faced, boosting their spirits, encouraging black business and self-sufficiency, and influencing popular opinion. According to Jeffrey P. Moran, secular black elites in northern cities viewed urbanism, secularism, and science as the forces of progress and employed Scopes in their struggles against white supremacy in the South and ministerial dominance throughout African America. And Kenneth W. Mack defined a debate in civil rights circles during the 1930s over the roles of law and mass politics and concluded that the African American takeover of the NAACP litigation program was less a victory of legalism over mass politics than an attempt to fuse the two.[47]

Two articles demonstrated that there was still more to be said about World War II and African Americans. Lauren Rebecca Sklaroff demonstrated that the black boxer Joe Louis was a central part of the American state's efforts to use mass culture to address the troublesome racial issues. Thomas A. Guglielmo showed that the life-saving blood donor program excluded blacks at first, then accepted them but on a segregated basis, became a target of the rising protest movement, and was defended by milder racist assumptions than had been employed in the past, not by claims that whites were the superior race.[48]

Other articles dealt with another war that affected race relations, the Cold War. Manfred Berg challenged critics of the NAACP who charged it missed a great opportunity for civil rights and social reform in postwar America and argued that the group struggled in a difficult situation to keep the cause of civil rights on the agenda. Andrea Friedman, focusing on Annie Lee Moss, a black civilian employee of the Defense Department, and critiquing postwar liberalism, challenged the portrayal of her as an insignificant woman, victimized by Senator Joseph McCarthy and dependent on protection from white Democrats.[49]

Other contributors focused on several other participants in the civil rights contest of the 1950s and after: the U.S. Supreme Court, black teenagers, the Christian churches, and Dr. King. Michael J. Klarman suggested that while the Court had little impact on southern criminal justice, it did contribute to the civil rights movement by attacking the white primary and segregation in higher education and helping to mobilize civil rights consciousness and to educate white northerners and judges about the evils of the Jim Crow system. Jane Dailey demonstrated that religion played a central role on both sides of the controversy, with segregationists and integrationists making competing claims to Christian orthodoxy. Victoria W. Wolcott used a small event at a Buffalo amusement park in 1956 to illustrate the importance in the civil rights movement of black teenagers and recreation sites, the contrasting white and black visions of integrated recreation, and the death of the parks. And Joseph Kip Kosek introduced Richard Gregg, America's first major theorist of nonviolent action. This historian portrayed Greg as one of the major influences on King and the latter as the person who came closest to fulfilling Gregg's goal of revitalizing democratic politics.[50]

Yet another cluster of articles focused on black universities, Africa, black voters, and John Kennedy. Jason C. Parker spotlighted the roles America's black universities in the civil rights victories in the United States and the creation of nation-states in Africa, two parts of the decolonization of the Black Atlantic. James H. Meriwether emphasized Kennedy's attention to Africa, more than to civil rights and to King, in his successful effort to appeal to black voters in 1960 without pushing away white southerners, while Renee Romano focused on African diplomats in the United States, Kennedy's State Department, and the international pressures that contributed to the successes of the civil rights movement.[51]

Another cluster focused on the radicalization of black activism during the 1960s. One article, by Ruth Feldstein, focused on Nina Simone, an African American singer/songwriter who became an activist in the 1960s, offered in her music visions of black cultural nationalism and female power, and had connections with many cultural producers and activists. Daniel Martin opposed the dominant understanding of Le Roi Jones/Amiri Baraka as a relentless champion of black macho, questioned the utility of that term as a characterization of the black power ideal, and presented Baraka as one who reformulated the long-standing ideals of social and moral uplift in ways that preserved the notion of a socially responsible patriarchy. In addition, Peniel E. Joseph examined black power historiography, its changing meaning within civil rights scholarship and its recent growth as a distinct subfield within U.S. history. He ended with a plea to the profession to come to terms with the black power movement's complexity in order to rethink postwar American history.[52]

Thomas J. Sugrue wrote of another effort at reorientation, doing so in an essay on the politics of racial equality in the urban north from 1945 to 1969. He discussed the struggle over employment discrimination from its origins in World War II through the racial liberalism of the postwar years to the militant protests and counter-protests of the 1960s. The key actors included white construction unionists who opposed affirmative action, fought to maintain the status quo, and fundamentally reoriented the civil rights debate.[53]

In the midst of this flourishing of the field of African American history in the pages of the *JAH*, Lew Formwalt, the executive director of the OAH, reported in 2006 that minorities constituted only 7 percent of the membership.[54] This was so even though, as this essay demonstrates, the *JAH* had, for nearly half a century, recognized African American history as a major part of American history. It was true also even though the members over the same time period had testified for nearly as long to their sense of the large importance of the field in their choices for the presidency of the Organization. John Hope Franklin, who served in 1974–1975), was the first African American president. Since then, four other African Americans have followed him in that office: Mary Frances Berry (1990–1991), Darlene Clark Hine (2001–2002), James O. Horton (2004–2005), and Nell Irvin Painter (2007–2008). Furthermore, more than a dozen white contributors to the field, beginning with C. Vann Woodward in 1968–1969, have also served as president. In short, more than a third of the presidents since the MVHA became the OAH have contributed in large ways to the development of African American history. Still further, since 1984 the OAH has had a standing and active Committee on the Status of Minority Historians and Minority History.[55]

African American history's rise to prominence has been a major part of the democratization of the Organization of American historians. That change involves much more than recognition of the writing of some black historians. The rise means that the OAH now recognizes that all black Americans are important in the American story. For many years, the study of their history was but a small part of the American historical profession's activities, and during those years, the Mississippi Valley Historical Association paid little attention to that history. The change came in the 1960s and thereafter, and the field became a prominent part of the work of the historical profession and of one of its major representatives, the OAH.

NOTES

1. Walter F. Fleming, review of *The Education of the Negro Prior to 1861*, by Carter G. Woodson, in *MVHR* 2 (Mar. 1916): 586–89; J. W. Garner, Review of *The Facts of Reconstruction*, by John R. Lynch, in *MVHR* 3 (June 1916): 112–13.

2. Carter G. Woodson, review of *American Negro Slavery*, by Ulrich Bonnell Phillips, in *MVHR* 5 (Mar. 1919): 480–82.

3. Philip M. Hamer, review of *The Negro in South Carolina During Reconstruction*, by Alrutheus Ambush Taylor, in the *Mississippi Valley Historical Review* (*MVHR*) 12 (Mar. 1926): 606–8, quotation on 608.

4. "Editorial Comment," *MVHR* 12 (Mar. 1926): 628–29.

5. See, for example, Arthur C. Cole, review of *Anti-Slavery Sentiment in American Literature Prior to 1865*, by Lorenzo Dow Turner, in *MVHR* 17 (Mar. 1931): 624–25; Percy Scott Flippin, review of *George Washington and the Negro*, by Walter H. Mazyck, in *MVHR* 19 (Sept. 1932): 305; Paul Lewinson, review of *The Negro in American National Politics*, by William F. Nowlin, in *MVHR* 19 (June 1932): 125–26; and N. N. Puckett, review of *The Negro in the Slaughtering and Meat-Packing Industry in Chicago*, by Alma Herbst, in *MVHR* 20 (June 1933): 164. See also Puckett's review of *The*

Education of the Negro in the American Social Order, by Horace Mann Bond, in *MVHR* 21 (Dec. 1934): 418–20.

6. "Historical News and Comments," *MVHR* 29 (Mar. 1943): 649.

7. Benjamin Quarles, "Sources of Abolitionist Income," *MVHR* 32 (June 1945): 63–76; Benjamin Quarles, "The Colonial Militia and Negro Manpower," *MVHR* 45 (Mar. 1959): 643–52.

8. J. G. Randall, review of *From Slavery to Freedom: A History of American Negroes*, by John Hope Franklin, *MVHR* 35 (Sept. 1948): 288–90.

9. "Historical News and Comments," *MVHR* 38 (Sept. 1951): 350–52.

10. George L. Anderson, "The Forty-Fourth Annual Meeting of the Mississippi Valley Historical Association," *MVHR* 38 (Sept. 1951): 262.

11. "Report of the Secretary-Treasurer for the Year 1951–1952," *MVHR* 39 (Sept. 1952): 393–94; Ray Allen Billington, "From Association to Organization: The OAH in the 'Bad Old Days,'" *Journal of American History* (*JAH*) 65 (June 1978): 78–80; August Meier and Elliott Rudwick, *Black History and the Historical Profession, 1915–1980* (Urbana: University of Illinois Press, 1986), 155.

12. Meier and Rudwick, 155; Billington, 82; George E. Mowry, "The Forty-Sixth Annual Meeting of the Mississippi Valley Historical Association," *MVHR* 40 (Sept. 1953): 310.

13. Paul W. Gates, "The Forty-seventh Annual Meeting of the Mississippi Valley Historical Association," *MVHR* 41 (Sept. 1954): 292; Billington, 82.

14. Joe B. Frantz, "The Forty-eighth Annual Meeting of the Mississippi Valley Historical Association," *MVHR* 42 (Sept. 1955): 288.

15. Richard W. Leopold, "The Forty-ninth Annual Meeting of the Mississippi Valley Historical Association," *MVHR* 43 (Sept. 1956): 277; William D. Aeschbacher, "Report of the Secretary-Treasurer for the Year 1957–1958," *MVHR* 45 (Sept. 1958): 382; "Historical News and Comments," *MVHR* 47 (June 1960): 182.

16. Editor's note: For me, one event more than any other symbolized the rise to prominence of African American history at the time. It was the appointment in 1969 of Arvarh Strickland as professor of history at the University of Missouri, Columbia. I chaired the history department at the time; he was the first African American appointed to the faculty of the Columbia campus, and he established courses in the field as a major part of the department's offerings.

17. Dec. 1976; June 1977; June 1975.

18. Dec. 1971; Mar. 1972; Dec. 1974; June 1973; June 1974; Sept. 1976.

19. Dec. 1972.

20. Mar. 1976; Dec. 1971; Dec. 1973; June 1972.

21. June 1978.

22. June 1983; Mar. 1984.

23. Dec. 1983; June 1981.

24. Sept. 1981; June 1979; Mar. 1980.

25. Dec. 1979; June 1982.

26. Dec. 1998; Sept. 1997; Dec. 1990.

27. Sept. 1995; Sept. 1994; Sept. 1993; Mar. 1989.

28. June 1994; Sept. 1988; June 1997; Sept. 1998; Mar. 1990; Dec. 1989.

29. Mar. 1996; Sept. 1989. See also articles by Dylan Penningroth (Sept. 1997) and Amy Dru Stanley (Sept. 1988).

30. Mar. 1989; Dec. 1986; June 1993.
31. Sept. 1997; June 1992; Mar. 1995.
32. Mar. 1996.
33. Mar. 1986; Sept. 1986; Dec. 1990.
34. Dec. 1988; Dec. 1993. See also the articles on Josephine Baker, the Communist Party, and African American suburbanization by Mary L. Dudziak, Gerald Zihavi, and Andrew Wiese (Sept. 1994; Sept. 1996; Mar. 1999).
35. June 1993; June 1994; June 1990; Dec. 1990.
36. Sept. 1998. See also the article by Jonathan Zimmerman (Dec. 1995) on the impact on African Americans of their service in Africa as Peace Corps volunteers.
37. June 1996.
38. Edward Paul Nord served three times as Acting/Interim Editor during the years from 1997 to 2005.
39. Mar. 2006; Mar. 2007; June 2010.
40. June 2005; Mar. 2009; June 2008; June 2010.
41. June 2001; Mar. 2010. In an essay on the politics of the 1850s (Sept. 2001), Bruce Levine includes a discussion of the importance of the slavery issue.
42. Mar. 2007; Sept. 2009; June 2003.
43. Dec. 2005; Mar. 2008.
44. Mar. 2010; Sept. 2005; June 2000.
45. Dec. 2001.
46. Mar. 2010.
47. Mar. 2004; Dec. 2003; June 2006.
48. Dec. 2002; June 2010. Patricia Kelly Hall and Steven Ruggles dealt with a force of large importance during the war, before it, and after it: migration from the South to the North during the twentieth century (Dec. 2004).
49. June 2007; Sept. 2007.
50. June 2002; June 2004; June 2006; Mar. 2005.
51. Dec. 2009; Dec. 2008; Sept. 2000.
52. Mar. 2005; June 2006; Dec. 2009.
53. June 2004. See also the article by Michael B. Katz, Mark J. Stern, and Jamie J. Fades, "The New African American Inequality" (June 2005).
54. "Centennial Reflections," *OAH Newsletter* 34 (Nov. 2006): 2.
55. OAH, "Guide to Service, Award & Prize Committee Structure 1998–1999," 18 and 51n20; Arvarh E. Strickland to Estelle B. Freedman and Thomas Dublin, July 28, 1997; William H. Chafe to Paul Boyer, April 14, 1998; Strickland, "Report of the Committee on the Status of Minority Historians and Minority History," 1997, Strickland files.

17

Women's History
From Neglect to Prominence and to Integration

Alice Kessler-Harris

It is embarrassingly easy to summarize the relationship of the MVHA and the OAH to the history of women and gender in a few sentences: from 1907 to 1971, the organization paid little if any attention to women, and none to anything that now remotely resembles women's history. Beginning in 1971, as women's history entered the consciousness of the historical community, the OAH and the *Journal of American History* (*JAH*) slowly turned a corner. By 1980, women's history had found a somewhat precarious place in the pages of the journal and in the programs of the annual meeting. Ten years later, that place was well established. Finally, in the last decade of the last century, not only do we witness a dramatic integration of women's history and the history of gender into the historical vocabulary, but we can identify some of the ways that the new field had begun to alter the shape of American History.

If there are no surprises in the general trajectory of the field within the OAH, I confess that I was both horrified and gratified, by turns, at how much of its intellectual history affirmed the mythology of an emerging field. When I took on this task, I expected it to be relatively small. Indeed, as a veteran of the struggle to legitimize the history of women (I completed my degree, and started my first real job in 1968) and to claim women's place in the academy, I thought I already knew everything that there was to know. This was, after all, *our* history. As I suppose I should have known by now, a search in the archives revealed not only how poor my memory was in many instances, but how completely wishful thinking had colored my vision of the past. The successes I thought were there came much later than I imagined, and the full integration of the history of women into American history has been the product of just this past decade.

Having been so chagrined by the discovery of my mis-memories, I have based the comments that follow on a careful survey of the tables of contents of the *MVHR* and the *JAH*, as well as on a perusal of many of the articles themselves.

They are also based on the reports of the annual meetings, which appeared in the *MVHR* and then the *JAH*. These, however, seemed to disappear after 1980, perhaps as the conventions became too unwieldy for the session-by-session summaries that characterized the reports in their early years. I do not pretend to scientific accuracy, but I have tried here to think about the meaning of the data. I have also tried to separate the history of women as a field from that of women historians, but this separation sometimes became so difficult that I frequently conflate the two.

By some measures, the picture is not as bleak as I imagined it would be. The MVHA functioned in the early years more like a social club than a professional society, and as such it did not so much exclude women as it assigned them to what were then imagined as appropriate places. Annual reports reassured members that what counted was "the spirit of the meeting," a spirit that, in the words of one early president, was engendered by "the contact of minds made congenial by a background of common experiences and common interests."[1] The 840 members of the organization in 1923, when that comment was made, were female as well as male. The women seemed to be mostly nonacademic librarians, archivists, and employees of the state historical societies that had been the MVHA's founders.

With a single exception, all of the officers between the MVHA's founding in 1907 until 1930 were male. Officers served on the Association's Executive Committee until they tired of the role, and then they were replaced. The exception is instructive. In 1916, Clara Paine (known to members throughout her years as Mrs. Clarence S. Paine) succeeded her husband, Clarence Paine, as the MVHA's secretary-treasurer. Clara was re-elected annually to the post for thirty-six years until she died in 1952. By all accounts she deserves the credit for "maintaining the association as an active, going organization."

In 1930, the MVHA elected its first female president. She was Louise Phelps Kellogg, a researcher at the Wisconsin Historical Society, and the author of several distinguished volumes on the history of the early West and the Great Lakes region. She would remain the Association's only female president until 1981.

Early meetings (which, through the 1920s, accommodated around 100 members) tended to emphasize the social as much as the academic: the wives of university administrators often hosted events; wives of historians were invited to tea. Women attended as guests and to serve the men. "We are especially grateful to the Women's Auxiliary of the . . . American Legion" the report of the April 1946 meeting avowed, "who have voluntarily served the luncheons and dinners of this meeting of the Association."[2] Down to the early 1960s, members were routinely described as men. Thus, in 1962, Charles Grier Sellers noted that "members and their wives" had been hosted at a pleasant reception.[3]

The generally undemocratic temper of the association is embodied in the gender of members of the Program Committee, and in the programs they produced.

Like the officers, Program Committees consisted almost entirely of men: the 1952 meeting boasted Martha E. Layman as the lone female member. Women did occasionally appear on the program, generally in a peripheral capacity, and never speaking on the subject of women. The annual report of the 1922 meeting for example informed its readers that "Miss Eunice G. Anderson, state historian of Wyoming" had delivered a paper on "The Promotion of Helpful Relations between State Historical Societies and other Organizations." The report's author then went on to inform his readers that Miss Anderson's work had been supported by the DAR, the State Federation of Women's Clubs, and the American Legion.[4] In 1923, women fared better: Miss Grace Lee Nute gave a paper on James Dickson's expedition to Texas; Miss Harriet Smithers read a paper entitled "The English Abolition Movement and the Annexation of Texas," and Miss Lucy Simmons spoke about "The Relations of Sterling Price with Jefferson Davis." The recorder of this information could not resist relating that Miss Simmons "unfortunately lost her manuscript" so when she stood up to read her paper, she had to reproduce it from memory.[5] Still the presence of women offering commentaries on mainstream subjects suggests that their presence was taken seriously.

The subject of women was less visible than the presence of women participants. We glimpse females occasionally in the work of men like Daniel Becker whose exploration of the life of the Comanche chief, Quannah Parker, revealed that his white mother was captured at the age of nine by Comanches and repatriated only after her marriage to an Indian chief and the birth of a son. Not even the Saturday morning sessions, which, as Ray Allen Billington put it, "were designed to appeal to the local schoolmarms" harbored a hint of what we would now call the history of women or family life.[6]

By the late 1930s, and especially during World War II, women began to appear on the program with greater frequency, though still on isolated occasions. Their papers spoke to mainline subjects, such as foreign policy and diplomacy.[7] The bottom line is that, as far as I can tell, from 1907 to 1971, not a single session on the program, nor a single paper in any of those sessions, was devoted to the history of women.

The *MVHR* boasts a similarly dismal record. From its inception in June 1914, it included pieces *by* women though not *about* women, and generally in the form of notes or book reviews. Until 1920, the subject of women did not appear in its pages. Then, in 1920, the *MVHR* published a piece by Lester Burrell Shippee on Jane Grey Swisshelm, an early-nineteenth-century advocate of abolition and women's property rights.[8] Eleven years later, Bertha-Monica Stearns authored a study of midwestern ladies' magazines.[9] A professor of English at Wellesley, she may have been the first woman to write on women's issues. Thirty-one years of silence with respect to women's issues followed. In the early and middle 1960s, even as the *Journal of American History* opened its pages to the young historians of an emerging new left, its pages remained silent about women.

In the early years, no women appeared among the members of the *MVHR* or *JAH* boards of editors, and, as best I can tell, no women participated in the article refereeing process. Yet women are not entirely absent from the pages of these publications. Louise Phelps Kellogg wrote two notes in the journal's second issue in September of 1914 and followed these with frequent reviews of books in western history. Susan Martha Reed published a piece on British cartography in 1915—the first article by a woman.[10] By my count, such pieces average one every two to three years. And when the journal began to offer its readers biographical notes about its contributors, the women who wrote articles in these years did not always appear as full partners. Mildred Stahl Fletcher, whose piece on Louisiana as a factor in French diplomacy appeared in 1931, is identified as a "reference assistant in the Washington University Library at St. Louis." The note on contributors continues: "Her husband, Ralph Fletcher, who is an assistant professor in economics and statistics at the same institution, collaborated with Mrs. Fletcher in the writing of this article."[11] And Leota Driver, who co-authored the summary of the organization's twenty-ninth annual meeting with William Binkley in the September 1936 issue, is identified only as "the widow of the late Carl S. Driver of Vanderbilt University."[12]

In the 1950s, the journal published an increasing number of pieces by women, amounting to about one article per year. The distinguished scholars included economic historian Irene Neu, Indian historian Mary Young, and agricultural historian Gertrude Slichter. In the same decade, Laura Wood Roper published a piece on Frederick Law Olmsted, LaWanda Cox on freedmen, and Catherine Crary on immigrants.[13] At the end of the decade, Ruth Miller Elson published what, because of the attention it paid to women teachers, might be called a transitional piece on education and schoolteachers.[14] Despite the increase in their numbers, most female historians dealt with a consistently limited range of subjects that included diplomatic history, the history of Indian policy and the West, the history of education, and state and local history. Even as articles on labor history and immigration began to appear in the pages of the journal in the early 1960s, little suggests excitement generated by an emerging generation of women historians.[15]

If there is an exception to this, it lies in the pages of the book-review sections. There one finds the undercurrent of activity that demonstrates that women lived and breathed as part of the profession and that the editor recognized their presence there and in history. Women appear as the occasional subjects of books reviewed; Ann Hutchinson gets her due, as do Mary Baker Eddy, Sacajawea, and the women of the South. Significant female authors like Julia Spruill, Alice Morse Earle, Mary Beard, and Eleanor Flexner draw attention in the book-review pages. Alice Baldwin, Ruth Higgins, Karen Larsen, and Louise

Phelps Kellogg were frequent reviewers. By the late 1960s, reviews of books on American feminism occasionally appeared; names like Aileen Kraditor, Alice Felt Tyler, William O'Neill, and Robert Riegel dot the book-review section.

Finally, in 1968 and 1969, two pieces, both written by men (James McGovern and J. Stanley Lemons) heralded the beginning of a new moment in the organization.[16] Perhaps it was inevitable that the OAH and the *JAH* would pay attention to the history of women. A rising number of women were earning doctorates in history in the 1960s (up to 15 percent by the end of the decade). The 1965 creation of the Equal Employment Opportunities Commission (EEOC) and the 1966 National Organization of Women (NOW) both spoke to an emerging sensitivity to discrimination against women. Among historians, the 1969 creation of the Coordinating Committee on Women in the Historical Profession (CCWHP) signaled a new assertiveness on the part of female historians. In addition, a few leaders, Gerda Lerner, Anne Firor Scott, and Bernice Carroll among them, had begun to make the connection between women in the profession and the field of women's history. Classes in women's history began to dot the curricula of colleges and universities; articles about something called "women's history" began to appear in newsletters and in smaller journals.[17]

The change within the Organization of American Historians first became palpable in its structure. Until March 1970, the OAH still included no women among its officers or on its executive board; the *JAH* had no women on its board of editors, and only one on its staff. In March, Willie Lee Rose assumed a position on the executive board along with Carl Degler and David Cronon. The same year, Suellen Hoy became the first female editorial assistant at the *JAH*; Elizabeth Pleck participated in a major session on social mobility; Willie Lee Rose delivered a paper on the black family; Joseph Kett offered a piece on the child study movement, which focused on female school teachers; and David Kennedy read a paper on late-nineteenth-century sexual roles. In September, the *JAH* published a piece by Edward Steel, "Mother Jones in the Fairmont Field, 1902."[18]

After that, the changes came more quickly. Anne Firor Scott joined Willie Lee Rose on the executive board in 1972; Emma Lou Thornbrough followed in 1973, and Mary Frances Berry in 1974. The names are worth recording because each was both an advocate of equality for women within the profession and a scholar with a reputation in the history of women. They set both an intellectual tone that legitimized the work of a generation of historians of women now entering graduate school, and they expanded the space for them and for the field. After 1974 there were generally two and sometimes three female elected members on the OAH executive board. It was to be five more years (1979) before a woman (Gerda Lerner) would be nominated to the organization's presidency, and by then it was only marginally surprising that a female who was a historian of women could assume that post.

The annual meeting programs changed even more rapidly than the gender composition of the officers. In 1971, sixty-four years after the founding of the organization, a number of papers and two entire sessions were devoted to women: one to women in the profession and the second, chaired by Blanche Wiesen Cook, to "New Perspectives on Women in History." The audience for each exceeded two hundred people. By 1973, the convention included five panels devoted to various aspects of women's history, one of them archival.

But the most dramatic change came at the April 1974 meeting (Denver). The program committee for that meeting, intent on exploring new fields in history, took social history as its focus, and within that rubric (which included cliometricians and urban historians) incorporated a goodly number of practitioners of the new women's history. With Anne Firor Scott playing an active role, the program committee invited many of the names that would soon become well known to historians. Linda Kerber, Carroll Smith-Rosenberg, and Alice Kessler-Harris delivered papers; Karen Lystra and Barbara Welter commented. A few sessions were devoted in their entirety to women (including one to working women), and women also constituted the subject matter of many papers sprinkled in and about other sessions. The panels that focused on political, intellectual, and diplomatic issues rarely incorporated women either as paper-givers or as subjects for discussion.[19]

By 1976, women were feeling excluded from the mainstream panels in which a few had participated earlier. That year, Gerda Lerner stood up from the audience during a 1976 bicentennial session on revolutionary ideology to remind the panelists that "women, as well as men, took part in the revolutionary turmoil and that they deserve more attention and more research" than they had yet received.[20]

By 1978 and 1979, large crowds attended sessions concerned with subtle intellectual issues around the separation of spheres, sexuality, and interdisciplinarity. Other sessions on prostitution, childhood, and old age included females as the subjects of research. "Women's history" had clearly arrived.

The *Journal of American History* changed more slowly. The years 1971–1972 and the first part of 1973 offered little in the way of women's history. Journal referees remained almost exclusively male. The articles, still primarily written by men, focused on political history, narrowly construed, with some attention to the new social history, as it was represented in the work of such historians as Gary Nash and Ken Kusmer, as well as to institutional social work, which then seemed largely to be a function of the male initiative. In 1972, the *JAH* appointed Mary Young of Ohio State University to its editorial board. Young was not a historian of women, but she was followed in 1973 by Anne Scott, then perhaps the best-known feminist historian. Scott's appointment both reflected the change in the profession and precipitated a transformation in the journal. It also captured the prevailing intellectual climate, which had now begun to produce too much scholarship on women to ignore. In September of 1973, the *JAH* published Carroll Smith-Rosenberg and Charles Rosenberg's jointly authored "The Female Animal."[21] Anne Scott's essay, "Women's Perspective on the Patriarchy in the 1850s," appeared in 1974.[22] The September 1975 issue included four major articles written by women, though only one, Sharon Hartman Strom's discussion of "Leadership and Tactics in the American Women Suffrage Movement" fell into the category of women's history.[23] Still things did not move as quickly as they might have. During the rest of 1975 only one article by a woman appeared. By Barbara Sicherman, it was not specifically about women.

The slow dribble reflects the sluggish nature of change within the Organization. At first Anne Firor Scott's name seemed to be virtually alone, punctuating the elected boards, the editorial boards, and the Program Committee. As she was joined by other women in all these venues, the Organization became a different place, and in 1980, it elected its second female president, Gerda Lerner, to be followed three years later by Anne Scott. Both women were pioneers in, and scholars of, the history of women. By 1983, the profile of the OAH looked startlingly different. Gerda Lerner and Anne Scott were on the Executive Board; the elected officers of the Organization included five women among the nine members; and the *Journal's* editorial board included two well-known and well-respected female historians of women.

A glance at the *Journal* in the 1980s leaves no doubt that something had changed in the profession. Under the leadership of Louis Perry and then of David Thelen, the pages began to reflect the intellectual directions of a new constituency. Between 1983 and 1990, the *JAH* settled into a random pattern that generally included one article per issue about women and written by a woman; occasionally an issue skipped the subject; occasionally there were two such pieces; and every once in a while a related piece—as, for example, on infant nurture or family demography—included the perspectives of women as subjects. The pieces spanned the subjects that had been opened by a new, more analytic, women's history, ranging from birthing (Leavitt, 1983) to sexuality and abortion (Freedman, 1987; Reagan, 1991). They spoke to issues of wage-earning women (Levine (1983) and home-work (Boris, June 1984) as well as to women in the labor movement (Hall, June 1986; Greenwald, 1989) and social policy (Zimmerman). They contemplated new theoretical approaches to race and gender (Painter, Stanley) and to women and gender (Kerber, 1988; Cott, 1989). By 1990, the inclusion of women in history as well as of women's history had provoked an exciting new dimension to social history, its subject matter now encompassing domesticity, political power, literary and mass culture and consumption, the environment, and war.[24]

And still the transformation continued. In 1990, articles on women gave way to ones on gender and to pieces that explored the implications of the new history. With Thelen as editor of the *JAH*, the subject of women wound its way into the general subject matter of history and reached out into fields that had never concerned themselves with gender in any form. In this transformation, gender became the vehicle for moving the history of women into the mainstream. Perhaps the best example of this phenomenon is the piece by Emily Rosenberg in June of 1990. In it, Rosenberg asked how the field of foreign relations could encompass and use the insights of women's history. Not, she suggested, by focusing on important women or on atypical women but by emphasizing "ideologies related to gender and their social and political implications."[25] Such a focus would, she argued, illuminate the "transhistorical myths" or core values on which a nation constructed and rationalized its foreign policies.

Rosenberg's piece was the first of several in the journal to articulate a growing sense among historians that feminist scholarship could illuminate basic notions of power and knowledge. It was followed by articles by Linda Gordon, Mary Berry, Nancy MacLean, Stephanie McCurry, Amy Dru Stanley, Joanne Meyerowitz, and many others. These pieces spanned a huge variety of subject matter, but each used a particular moment in time, (rotating around men acting as men or women acting as women) to expose a gendered mechanism that fostered institutional (or behavioral) change or reaction. At the same time, gender, as a social system and a way of organizing thought, necessarily incorporated masculinity within its framework, leading to a series of articles that examined the meaning of manliness and the uses of masculinity as they were deployed to organize the labor force, to construct visions of nation, and to embolden ideologies of race. Race was intrinsically woven into many of these pieces, sometimes as a subject of comparison between and among various groups of women (Gordon), sometimes as the vehicle for looking at how particular groups of men or women understood and responded to their own historical circumstances (McCurry, Berry, Stanley, MacLean). Soon it became apparent that gender could foster a range of new insights around issues that extended from mass culture to consumption, to race and religion, and to politics and the Constitution.[26] The *Journal of American History* was now at the cutting edge of historical interpretation.

We used to talk about main-streaming as the potential goal of a woman's history, which would one day no longer be necessary because other arenas would learn to incorporate women and deal with their presence, but the language of main-streaming is no longer sufficient to capture the influence of women's history. Like labor history, which burst its boundaries to encompass the history of family, of community, of the daily lives of ordinary folk, so women's history has now nudged and pushed until it has fulfilled its promise of fostering a history of all the people. The pages of the *JAH* and the programs of the OAH have fully participated in this process. The development and expansion of the field of women's history would have been possible without them, but the transformation of U.S. history would surely not have been. The role of the *JAH* in creating a conversation among historians in which historians of women and of gender have fully participated and the legitimizing authority of the Organization's annual meetings have, at least in this instance, served the profession well, helping to turn women's history into a vehicle for understanding the uses of gender and sexuality in the construction of borderlands, nations, and global cultures.

NOTES

1. Benjamin F. Shambaugh, "The Sixteenth Annual Meeting of the Mississippi Valley Historical Association," *MVHR* 10 (Sept. 1923) 111. The previous year, Louis Pelzer reassured members that they had "a definite field of work" which was "being carried on better every year." *MVHR* 9 (Sept. 1922): 103.

2. "Transactions at the Annual Meeting, April 18, 19, 20, 1946," *MVHR* 33 (Sept. 1946): 276.

3. Charles Grier Sellers, "The Fifty-fifth Annual Meeting of the Mississippi Valley Historical Association," *MVHR* 49 (Sept. 1962): 1.

4. Louis Pelzer, "The Fifteenth Annual Meeting of the Mississippi Valley Historical Association," *MVHR* 9 (Dec. 1922): 103.

5. This was duly reported by Benjamin F. Shumbaugh, "The Sixteenth Annual Meeting," *MVHR* 10 (Sept. 1923): 115, 121.

6. Ray Allen Billington, "From Association to Organization: The OAH in the Bad Old Days," *JAH* 65 (June 1978): 76.

7. Jeannette Nichols's work on Midwest isolationism provides a good example. See Thomas Le Duc, "The 45th Annual Meeting of the Mississippi Valley Historical Association," *MVHR* 7 (Dec. 1920): 277.

8. Lester Burrell Shippee, "Jane Grey Swisshelm: Agitator," *MVHR* 7 (Dec. 1920): 206–27.

9. Bertha-Monica Stearns, "Early Western Magazines for Ladies," *MVHR* 18 (Dec. 1931): 319–30. Opportunities to deal with women abounded in this early period: the failure to take them up suggests an absence of consciousness with respect to women's history. For example, pieces on the history of immigration (Mar. 1921), on religion (June 1928), and on the English Common law (Dec. 1929) did not deal with women.

10. Susan Martha Reed, "British Cartography of the Mississippi Valley in the Eighteenth Century," *MVHR* 2 (Sept. 1914): 213–24.

11. *MVHR* 17 (Dec. 1930): 342.

12. *MVHR* 23 (Sept. 1936): 213.

13. Laura Wood Roper, "Frederick Law Olmsted in the "Literary Republic," *MVHR* 39 (Dec. 1952): 459–82, the first piece by a woman in more than a decade; Irene D. Neu, "The Building of the Sault Canal: 1852–1855," *MVHR* 40 (June 1953): 25–46; Mary E. Young, "The Creek Frauds: A Study in Conscience and Corruption," *MVHR* 42 (Dec. 1955): 411–37; Gertrude Almy Slichter, "Franklin D. Roosevelt and the Farm Problem, 1929–1932," *MVHR* 43 (Sept. 1956): 238–58; LaWanda Cox, "The Promise of Land for the Freedmen," *MVHR* 45 (Dec. 1958): 413–40; Catherine S. Crary, "The Humble Immigrant and the American Dream: Some Case Histories, 1746–1776," *MVHR* 46 (June 1959): 46–66.

14. Ruth Miller Elson, "American Schoolbooks and 'Culture' in the Nineteenth Century," *MVHR* 46 (Dec. 1959): 411–34; this was followed by Paton Yoder "Private Hospitality in the South, 1775–1850," *MVHR* 47 (Dec. 1960): 419–33.

15. These are the years of, for example, Sidney Fine, "The Eight-Hour Day Movement in the United States, 1888–1891," *MVHR* 40 (Dec. 1953): 441–62; Ed Pessen, "The Workingmen's Movement of the Jacksonian Era," *MVHR* 43 (Dec. 1956): 428–43; and John Laslett, "Reflections on the Failure of Socialism in the American Federation of Labor," *MVHR* 50 (Mar. 1964): 634–51.

16. James R. McGovern, "American Women's Pre-World War I Freedom in Manners and Morals," *JAH* 55 (June 1968): 315–33; J. Stanley Lemons, "The Sheppard-Towner Act: Progressivism in the 1920s," *JAH* 55 (Mar. 1969): 776–86.

17. For example, see Gerda Lerner, "New Approaches to the Study of Women in American History," *Journal of American Social History*; Judith P. Zinsser, *History and Feminism: A Glass Half Full* (New York: Twayne, 1993), Ch. 2.

18. *JAH* 57 (Sept. 1970): 290–307.

19. These papers included Carroll Smith-Rosenberg's "The Female World of Love and Ritual," a paper that has since become a classic in women's history and beyond.

20. 69th annual meeting, *JAH* 63 (Mar. 1977): 961.

21. *JAH* 60 (Sept. 1973).

22. *JAH* 61 (June 1974): 52–64.

23. The other authors were Linda Kerber, Jane De Hart Mathews, and Deborah Wing Ray. *JAH* 62 (Sept. 1965).

24. For example, "A Round Table: The Living and Reliving of World War II," *JAH* 77 (Sept. 1990): 535–93; Michael McGerr, "Political Style and Women's Power, 1830–1930" *JAH* 77 (Dec. 1990): 864–85.

25. Emily S. Rosenberg, "Gender," *JAH* 77 (June 1990): 119.

26. Examples include articles by Jacquelyn Dowd Hall, Arnaldo Testi, Mary Dudziak, Elizabeth Reis, Elizabeth Varon, Mary Kelley, Sarah Barringer Gordon, and Nancy Isenberg.

18

The Presence of Native American History

Frederick E. Hoxie

Most people would assume, as I did, that a review of the place of Native American History in the Mississippi Valley Historical Association (MVHA) and Organization of American Historians (OAH) would produce a sad tale of neglect and marginalization. The theme would be absence, rather than presence, and our predecessors' oversights. Like many assumptions that launch our research, these were proven to be incorrect. A century ago, in the organization's first year, Orin G. Libby, who had received his PhD from Wisconsin under Frederick Jackson Turner before moving to North Dakota to become chair of the history department at the state university there, delivered a paper, "The Mandans from the Archaeological and Historical Perspective." Libby had written a dissertation on the ratification of the federal constitution at Wisconsin, but once he relocated to Grand Forks, he turned to local history. Libby reorganized the state historical society (serving as secretary for forty years) and edited its journals. He even won an appropriation from the state legislature for his program. In our second year as an organization, papers on Indian subjects were delivered by Harlow Lindley, head of the history department at the Indiana State Library, and a pair of Smithsonian anthropologists, John R. Swanton and William Henry Holmes.

Clearly, the story of American Indian history's role in the organization is not a simple one. In order to explore it more fully, I compiled a roster of all the papers delivered at annual meetings of the MVHA and OAH over the past century and all the articles in the association's journal that focused on Native American subjects.[1] The article list indicated a steady interest in the field. Fifty-three essays were published between 1917 and 2007. The rate at which these articles appeared accelerated—twelve published in the first twenty-five years versus eighteen in the last twenty-five years—and the topics addressed shifted focus. Eight of the first ten articles to appear in the association journal addressed frontier topics: government policies affecting Indians and public land, western missions and Indian agencies, and incidents of border conflict.

Only two of the most recent ten articles focused on incidents of conflict—the Pequot and Yamasee wars—and only two (Pekka Hamalinen's article, "The Rise and Fall of Plains Horse Cultures," and Juliana Barr's on borderland slave trading) could be considered frontier essays.[2] The impression from the roster of journal articles is of a steady production of scholarship that has gradually shifted direction and focus. The common format of the essays, together with their measured, scholarly tone, communicates continuity in a slowly expanding field.

The list of presentations at our annual meeting is more unruly and more interesting. First, it shows an explosion of interest in Native American topics in recent years, a sharp contrast to the gradual rise in the number of articles in the journal. In the first twenty-five years of the organization, programs were available for twenty meetings. Those twenty programs reveal that during the organization's founding generation, forty papers were delivered on American Indian topics. In the second twenty-five years, that number rose to forty-four (two programs for this period were unavailable). In the third twenty-five years, the number rose to sixty-seven. In the association's first seventy-five years (1907–1982), between one and two papers on Indian subjects were presented at each meeting. But this roster of presentations also revealed significant gaps. Only one meeting between 1938 and 1946 contained a panel on an Indian subject, and, interestingly, seven of the ten meetings from 1960 to 1969 (the "turbulent sixties") heard no papers on Indian history. By contrast, in the last twenty-five years, the meetings since 1982, 336 papers have been given on American Indian topics, a rate of more than ten per meeting. No meeting since 1969 has failed to hear a panel on Native American history. The organization has grown dramatically over the past three decades, and our annual meetings have become more ambitious with roundtables and workshops, so the absolute numbers may be deceptive. Nevertheless, a near tenfold increase in attention paid to this subject among the association's membership is remarkable.

But did the increase in the rate of paper giving and publication reflect an equally dramatic shift in content and personnel? Here the answer is less clear, because the programs reveal an interesting series of continuities. Of the first forty presentations at our annual meetings—the papers given during our first twenty-five years—ten were given by nonacademic historians, twelve by scholars from museums or historical societies (six of those by anthropologists from the Smithsonian Institution), and only eighteen by professors at colleges and universities, most of them in the West. It is clear that Indian history attracted a wide array of practitioners in these early years, but it also appeared to have generated most interest among historians focused on regional history and those engaged with local historical societies and archives. Among those dozen museum and historical society presenters in the first quarter century were Doane Robinson, who, as secretary of the South Dakota State Historical

Society from 1901–1926, built that organization's collections of primary materials on the state's history; Reuben Gold Thwaites and Milo Milton Quaife, both directors of the Wisconsin State Historical Society and widely celebrated documentary editors; Libby from North Dakota; and Melvin Gilmore, a curator at the Nebraska State Historical Society.

Equally interesting, the data from the association's first generation revealed the presence of a great many nonhistorians at the annual meetings. John Swanton and James Mooney, who appeared together at the Iowa City meeting in 1910, were among the first generation of anthropologists in the United States and pioneers of a historical approach that later came to be labeled ethnohistory. Swanton drew on his historical and linguistic studies of southeastern tribes for his presentations, and Mooney, whose research for his classic work on the Ghost Dance had included interviewing Wovoka, the movement's founding prophet, spoke on the history of the Delawares. Arlow Stout, a botanist, gave a paper on effigy mounds in Iowa City in 1910 and Melvin Gilmore was himself defining the new field of ethnobotany when he gave his paper on "The Aboriginal Geography of the Nebraska Country" in Omaha in 1913. Although it is difficult to identify everyone on the programs by discipline, it appears that this impressive presence of anthropologists on annual meeting programs ended before World War I. There does not seem to have been a presentation by an anthropologist between Gilmore's paper in 1913 and a 1951 session entitled "Prehistoric Indians of the Ohio Valley." No cultural anthropologist appears to have presented a paper between Swanton in 1912 and Erminie Wheeler-Voegelin in 1956.

Interestingly, then, the 2007 program with its off-site session at the Minnesota Historical Society, its session on Native history in museums, and its roundtable on Dakota commemorative marches that includes a musician and a filmmaker, was broadly consistent with the approach to Indian history in the organization's early programs. The MVHA and the OAH were open to participation by historians from a variety of backgrounds, as well as to contributions from anthropologists, librarians, archivists, and classroom teachers.

One final continuity before shifting to the evidence of change: the absence of Native American participation in the association's meetings and in the profession. The first Indian presence detected in the organization's meetings came in 1923 when the group met in Oklahoma City and nearby Norman. In addition to a panel chaired by Roy Gittinger, an English professor who wrote extensively on the history of Oklahoma territory, the meeting featured a luncheon in "The Teepee" on the Oklahoma University campus. Stratton Brooks, president of the university, presided, and the program consisted of an Indian feature program by the University of Oklahoma Indian Club. It is not clear what this feature involved, but there is no indication that the club members spoke to the group. The organization returned to Oklahoma in 1950; at that meeting the

Oklahoma Historical Society hosted a reception that featured Spencer Asah, the celebrated Kiowa artist—one of the Kiowa Five—and "his Indian Dancers." Another continuity, then, was the tradition of non-Indian scholars speaking about Native history, with Indian people providing occasional entertainment and apparently remaining officially mute.

This pattern changed in 1970 when W. Roger Buffalohead, then of UCLA, gave a paper at the Los Angeles meeting. His appearance, the first by a Native American scholar, began a new pattern. Anthropologist Bea Medicine delivered a paper on Indian agents and the Dakota in San Francisco the next year, and in 1973 both Vine Deloria Jr. and D'Arcy McNickle commented on papers examining the Indian New Deal. Later in the decade Veronica Tiller, Sam Deloria, and Roxanne Dunbar Ortiz also spoke. The pattern in the *Journal* was similar. It appears that Ned Blackhawk's essay in the April 2007, issue was the first contribution by a Native American scholar to appear.[3]

There is a great deal of evidence of change over the organization's first century. Obviously the level of academic interest in Native history has risen significantly, and the composition and interests of scholars speaking and writing about indigenous issues has changed dramatically. Native American historians have appeared in growing numbers. A wider array of topics are heard and discussed. But even as this broadening scale of participation becomes evident, continuities continue to appear.

In the early years of the organization, most papers at the annual meeting and most of the essays published in the journal were by people from Midwestern or western universities. The first five essays published in the journal came from historians at the universities of Oklahoma, Chicago, and Kansas, as well as Beloit College and Oregon State University. The affiliations of authors of articles in the journal are not always clear, but it appears that Mary Young, a young historian from Cornell, was the first person from the Northeast to publish an article on Native American history when her essay on Creek removal was published in 1955. Aside from the Smithsonian anthropologists, the first easterner to have presented a paper at the annual meeting seems to have been George D. Harrison from Lehigh University who spoke on a panel on the fur trade in 1933. Patrick Malone's paper delivered in 1972 in Washington, D.C., appears to be the first contribution by an Ivy League-affiliated scholar to this field at one of our meetings.[4] The organization began as a regional one, so perhaps this pattern is not so surprising. The 2007 program, with papers presented by historians from Yale, George Washington, Towson, Connecticut, and Villanova (not to mention scholars from Canada and New Zealand), seems to signal that this regional bias had been overturned. As was true of other patterns, the *Journal* was slower to change. Of the last ten articles published in it, beginning with Ronald Dale Karr's essay on the Pequot war published in 1998 and ending with Blackhawk's piece on teaching Indian history in 2007, only Karr from the University of Massachusetts and Erik Seeman from SUNY Buffalo were affiliated with eastern institutions.[5] The pattern of western and Midwestern bias in Indian history presentations was likely not so much a reflection of regional interest alone as it was evidence of a long tradition that equated Indian topics with the West and the frontier.

As someone who came of age in the social-history era, I could not help but begin my analysis of Indian history's presence and absence in our organization counting and categorizing. But, as we have learned elsewhere, counting alone doesn't take you very far. If the changes that have occurred cannot be reduced to a simple story of absence and presence or a dramatic tale of sudden revolutionary change, if there are continuities here as well as important changes, then it might be more useful to turn from the subjects of this inquiry to the scholarly context in which those activities took place.

One kind of context is obvious: despite their failings in the past, the MVHA-OAH and the historical profession generally are more inclusive today than they were a century ago. Women, indigenous scholars, members of other racial minorities, public historians, and high school teachers represent important constituencies and interests. What power exists in a small academic, relatively poor scholarly organization is wielded today by a wide array of people who represent a variety of institutions. One might debate how deeply democratic the OAH has become, but it has clearly changed dramatically over the past ten decades, and democratization has expanded participation, opened new areas of inquiry, and disrupted old patterns of thought. In broad terms, the changes identified here with regard to Native history reflect this democratization process.

But there is something deeper at work here. Reading over the programs of the first annual meetings, one has the impression of a wild grab bag of topics: the Mandans, the Indian agent, the character of Sitting Bull, Chickasaw town names, and the Indian policy of the Spanish empire. In the years before World War I, Native American history lacked an overarching theme or common set of questions. It wasn't really considered a field. Instead, one has the sense of a rising interest in the fur trade and frontier politics, particularly in papers given by Turner's students, such as Orin Libby, but little that would define it as a distinctive arena of scholarly inquiry. Reuben Thwaites, Doane Robinson, and John Swanton were committed to the preservation of archival sources; others were primarily interested in colonial topics or local history or the frontier. We might retrospectively categorize these presentations as Native American, but it is doubtful that anyone at the time would have used that category.

By the 1930s, the topics appear more coherent and more narrow. Frontier topics dominated in papers delivered on the colonial Indian trade, the role of frontier conflict in national development, the behavior of frontier politicians, and the complex histories of Indian Territory and Oklahoma. The dominance of frontier themes continued into the 1950s as Wilbur Jacobs (1950) spoke about "The Indian Frontier of 1763," William T. Hagan (1955) examined "Private Property, the Indian's Door to Civilization," and Robert Athearn (1956) discussed the role of the U.S. Army in the West. This frontier theme seems to have run its course by the end of that decade, however; there were no papers on Indian topics at the meetings of 1958, 1959, or 1960.

Meanwhile, a new focus arose, signaled perhaps by a panel at the 1955 meeting devoted to American Indian Policy. Similar panels in 1956 and 1957 featured young historians who did not seem to fit the Turner profile. They included Francis Paul Prucha, a Jesuit priest who had studied at Harvard, and Reginald Horsman, an Englishman who had come to the states for graduate school. Traditional frontier topics appeared occasionally, but in diminishing numbers. These were outnumbered over the next two decades by panels on policy topics in 1968 ("Early American Indian Policy"), 1970 ("Bureaucracy and the West"), 1973 ("The American Indian and the New Deal"), and 1975 ("Recent Tribal Experience with the Indian Claims Commission"). This trend reflected broad interest at the time in public policy and the history of race relations and the American nation state.

Soon after the policy-focused panels appeared, another group of sessions appeared that explicitly adopted social-science categories and themes to address Indian topics. This group began with a 1962 session entitled "The Acculturation of the American Indian" that featured papers by Robert Berkhofer and anthropologist Fred Voget. In the decade following that session, other panels devoted to the comparison of African American and Native American experiences (1971), the interplay of race and culture (also 1971), and the process of culture change (1972) appeared on the program.

A third theme appeared in 1987 at a session devoted to "Comparative History and Native Peoples." Chaired by a Canadian, the panel included papers on Canada and Australia. It was followed by an inevitable "1492 in World Perspective" panel in 1992, a panel on Indians and the indigenous peoples of northern Scandinavia in 1994, a discussion of a transnational Metis history in 1998, and, fittingly, a broadly comparative panel on indigenous experiences in Canada, the United States, and the Pacific, at the 1999 meeting in Toronto.

Over the past generation, then, policy, culture change, and transnational approaches to Native American history have eclipsed the frontier as the principal organizing concepts in Native American history. They remain major foci for scholarship in the field. They have provided organizing frameworks, but they, too, seem to be running their course. Organization members continue to explore questions related to the sources of policy, the impact of policy in communities, and the relationship between policies in various regions or nations. They continue to explore the nature of culture change in the wake of the European invasion of North America, both among indigenous peoples and among the colonizers. They have also expanded the definition of *Native history* so that indigenous experiences across the globe have come increasingly into the membership's field of vision. And historians remain fascinated by what are now more properly called zones of contact, that is, those many middle grounds that populate the history of North America. These broad themes were evident in many papers at the 2007 centennial meeting—on genocide, Native debates over American values, American Indian political activists, and the teaching of indigenous history in the United States and Canada—as well as in recent essays in the journal. But I think we are ready for more.

Looking back over the roster of speakers at the annual meetings and the authors in the journal, a roster that includes prominent figures like James Mooney, Angie Debo, and Vine Deloria Jr., as well as lesser-known ones like the Minnesota Historical Society's longtime manuscript curator, Grace Lee Nute, one cannot help but see a succession of dedicated scholars with a common passion for understanding the Native past and explaining its significance for broad themes in history. There is continuity in this common bond of research and curiosity—Mooney traveling to Nevada to interview Wovoka, Reuben Gold Thwaites compiling the Jesuit Relations, Erminie Wheeler-Voegelin assembling the Great Lakes Ethnohistory archive at Indiana University. The dramatic shifts in the field came, not with exploding numbers of participants and authors, but with shifting intellectual contexts that inspired new definitions of historical significance.

Reviewing this history of scholarly activity, it is not hard to imagine a large lecture hall with all three hundred or so of the people whose contributions are reviewed here crowded together before us. They all signed up for the same class—Native American History—even though some would have called it public history; others frontier history, local history, or western history; and still others ethnohistory. We can see the women—Grace Lee Nute, Angie Debo, Erminie Wheeler-Voegelin, Helen Tanner, Bea Medicine, and their younger colleagues—scattered through the group, a clear minority. We can also imagine the anthropologists, James Mooney, D'Arcy McNickle, Glen Black, and Waldo Wedel, sitting apart from the historians, perpetually skeptical of what historical scholarship can contribute. In another section of this imaginary lecture hall sit a mixed group of representatives from state historical societies and the National Park Service. One can also imagine the critical gaze of Vine Deloria cast across the room as he sits off to one side chuckling at some private joke.

Who might speak to this diverse group? How could their many interests be combined in a single set of questions or scholarly concerns? The person whose work might be most fitting is someone who never appeared before the MVHA or OAH: Ella Deloria, the Sioux linguist. Deloria studied with Franz Boas and knew Swanton, Mooney, and many of the Smithsonian pioneers from the beginning of the twentieth century, as well as those who would lead the transformation of the field in the 1970s and afterward. (Deloria died in 1971.) Deloria's classic book, *Speaking of Indians*, contains truths that would apply across this entire imaginary lecture hall.[6] They would all grasp the significance of her words; She wrote that Indian people "belong to the great human family, [and] have the same innate power, inborn intelligence and potentialities as the rest of mankind." She would also remind her audience that "Indians have imagination and inventiveness" and that they participate in cultural traditions that affect "all who live within [their] sphere." "What can I do . . . to help you understand the Indians?" she wrote. Her answer: Indian cultures represent "a scheme of life that works." Too many people, she declared, believe Indians should be "supervised and taken care of." It was that presumption and the paternalism that produced it that she hated most. "Let's face it," she declared, "and start correcting it now."

Thanks to the people crowded into this imaginary lecture hall, scholarship on American Indians has reached a unique and exciting moment. A century of activity, both within the OAH and beyond, has produced a scholarly infrastructure for research and inquiry. Sources are available, doors have been pried open; even more difficult, professional minds have been pried open as well. Dozens of graduate students are busily preparing dissertations in the field, supervised by an expanding cadre of mentors, both Indian and non-Indian. Over the past century, historians have explored ways of linking indigenous peoples to each other and to the larger historical processes taking place around them. The themes of the frontier, public policy, culture change, and transnationalism have been illuminated by examinations of Indian peoples' experiences, and these experiences have marked their significance in human history. This scholarship has been valuable as an intellectual enterprise and a public good; and it has served both native and non-native people. In short, these intellectual categories and constructs have managed, too slowly and often quite clumsily, to transport a subject no academic really imagined as a coherent field of study in 1907 into history. It is true, of course, that other people in the general public as well as in Native communities themselves have other ways of thinking about the past that don't always coincide with these scholarly themes; these too have been significant. Still, learning to think about Indian people historically, as historical actors who are connected to universally recognized social and cultural processes and who are figures of global significance in human history, although a narrowly academic achievement, has broad social consequences. Essentially, those consequences can be summarized in Ella Deloria's phrase: people have come to understand that the indigenous peoples of North America were not and are not "deficient" and, therefore, unimportant or irrelevant to the continent's history. Intellectually, no less than politically, it is clear, after a century of scholarship, that Indians do not need to be "supervised and taken care of."

Looking forward, Ella Deloria's injunction suggests that the profession should not be content with the current state of things. Historians in the future will need to be open to the ways in which historical actors enter our imagination, curious about new questions that arise, and willing to entertain new ways of thinking about historical significance. Once they have managed to bring Indian history into the historical arena and to have overcome the conceptual, social, and cultural blinders that prevented earlier generations from viewing Native people historically, historians must face this subject with unblinking courage. New questions arise: To whom are historians responsible? By what authority do historians speak about Native people and communities? Who is the audience for this inquiry? What difference will historical insights make in general understanding of terms such as *culture, nation, indigenous, sovereignty, justice,* and *persistence?* After a century of work, and an almost identical period of reflection and self-criticism, it is almost possible to believe that these questions would animate our imaginary lecture hall of scholars and persuade everyone in it that Indian history has only just begun.

NOTES

1. Brian Ingrassia helped me to prepare this roster of meeting speakers and journal articles. We used a generous definition of Native American history in the compilation, including all items that addressed Indian people in some way, whether it be an article on warfare or on images of tribes. For the journal, we counted only articles. For the annual meetings, we counted only papers delivered, not comments.
2. Pekka Hämäläinen, "The Rise and Fall of the Plains Indian Horse Cultures," *JAH* 90 (Dec. 2003): 833–62; Juliana Barr, "From Captives to Slaves: Commodifying Indian Women in the Borderlands," *JAH* 92 (June 2005): 19–46.
3. Ned Blackhawk, "Recasting the Narrative of America: The Rewards and Challenges of Teaching American Indian History," *JAH* 93 (Mar. 2007): 1165–70.
4. Malone was affiliated then with Penn; he is now a lecturer at Brown and the author of *The Skulking Way of War: Technology and Tactics Among New England Indians* (Lanham, MD: Madison Books, 2000).
5. Ronald Dale Karr, "Why Should You Be So Furious? The Violence of the Pequot War," *JAH* 85 (Dec. 1998): 876–909; Mary Hershberger, "Mobilizing Women, Anticipating Abolition: The Struggle against Indian Removal in the 1830s," *JAH* 86 (June 1999): 15–41; Erik R. Seeman, "Reading Indians' Deathbed Scenes: Ethnohistorical and Representational Approaches," *JAH* 88 (June 2001): 17–48; William L. Ramsey, "'Something Cloudy in Their Looks': The Origins of the Yamasee War Reconsidered," *JAH* 90 (June 2003): 44–75; Alexandra Harmon, "American Indians and Land Monopolies in the Gilded Age," *JAH* 90 (June 2003): 106–33; Pekka Hämäläinen, "The Rise and Fall of Plains Indian Horse Cultures"; Mansel G. Blackford, "Environmental Justice, Native Rights, Tourism, and Opposition to Military Control: The Case of

Kaho'olawe," *JAH* 91 (Sept. 2004): 544–71; Juliana Barr, "From Captives to Slaves: Commodifying Indian Women in the Borderlands"; Claudio Saunt, "Telling Stories: The Political Use of Myth and History in the Cherokee and Creek Nations," *JAH* 93 (Dec. 2006): 673–97; and Ned Blackhawk, "Recasting the Narrative of America: The Rewards and Challenges of Teaching American Indian History," *JAH* 93 (Mar. 2007): 1165–70.

6. Ella Deloria, *Speaking of Indians* (New York: Friendship Press, 1944), 20, 158.

19

The Wild One: Environmental History as Redheaded Stepchild

Karl Brooks

The Organization of American Historians' (OAH) century party in Minneapolis fused back patting with introspection.[1] One hundred years after the Mississippi Valley Historical Association (MVHA) first assembled, OAH convened various panels not only to "celebrate the past one hundred years," but to "consider the contributions of the organization and its members to the historical profession."[2] Instead of providing me with rose petals to toss at the base of OAH's creative legacy, the chair of the Centennial Committee encouraged me to write as an environmental historian, not as a chorister.

My job was to explore how or even whether MVHA and OAH had promoted cutting-edge historical scholarship about the natural world's relationship to American history. I particularly sought to assess how well the editors of the *MVHR* and the *JAH* had selected articles to cultivate my once-new field. Accepting the chair's generous invitation to consider "the amount of attention paid to Environmental History and to the varieties of [its] interpretation," I joined a panel of distinguished pioneers. I strove to emulate their professional examples, especially the courage and curiosity that characterize their scholarship, in accepting the challenge.[3]

My basic conclusion about OAH and environmental history made me appear an honored but ungrateful guest. We all know this breed: They show up promptly at your party, then gripe about its inconvenient time and place. For several hours, well past juvenile bedtimes, they grouse about the difficulties of finding good child care. Plates laden, they dismiss the quality of the food. And such small portions . . . well, don't *even* get me started!

Environmental history might have emerged before the later 1970s as a distinctive field, posing new questions and deploying innovative methods to suggest answers, had OAH and *JAH* nurtured early shoots that sprouted inside *MVHR*'s regionalist hothouse. If later editors had shown the same interest as their predecessors, especially in the two decades after World War II, they might have helped mature interwar scholarship that had tried to take seriously this key methodological insight: place does matter to people. Had older writing about the Mississippi Basin's distinctiveness been subjected to the kind of critical scrutiny that generated the new social history of the 1960s, it may have shed its particularist origins and muted its pugnacious cheerleading about all things "middle American." Environmental history, which revels in the diversity of space, time, and peoples that makes America interesting, might have emerged nearly a generation earlier.

Instead, as the MVHA became the OAH, its leaders seemed eager to distance themselves and their professional body from what they disdained as its provincial origins and celebratory, boosterish approach to the midcontinent. *JAH* promoted historical fields premised on the methodology of reflexive anthropocentrism: the conviction that people came first, last, and always. This stance helped OAH bravely take its place in the vanguard of larger social and political movements seeking liberation, equality, diversity, and reform. OAH's professional commitment to critically examine the American past, often from the bottom up, yielded real gains. Yet what was thereby lost should not be underestimated. Only in the past two decades has *JAH* fully endorsed environmental history's legitimacy.[4]

Environmental historians during the past fifteen years have published their most important articles primarily in *Environmental History*, which largely replaced the older journal *Environment and History* after 1995. Important articles also regularly appear in *Agricultural History*, *Pacific Historical Review*, *Journal of Southern History*, and *Western Historical Quarterly*, as well as in nearly all the journals dedicated to scholarship about distinctive places, such as *Kansas History: A Journal of the Central Plains*, *Oregon Historical Quarterly*, and *Montana: The Magazine of Western History*. For those working in the field of environmental history, attendance at the annual American Society for Environmental History (ASEH) conference is *de rigeur*. Attendance at OAH's annual conference is nice, if one has the funds and time.[5]

This polite but cautious interplay between OAH and *JAH* on the one hand, and ASEH and *Environmental History* on the other, still unnecessarily divides environmental historians from the wider community of American historians. We environmental historians still plead for the wider profession to take us, and our work, more seriously. *Environmental History*'s former editor, Adam Rome, even had to insist, like Mrs. Willy Loman, that "attention must be paid." Rome argued, in 2002, that our field's insights can only strengthen the major interpretive frameworks historians use to explain America to Americans, and to the curious world.[6] By hesitating to embrace environmental history, our colleagues have far too long missed hearing what Aldo Leopold once called "marsh music and prairie song," natural harmonies our field translates, albeit imperfectly, into human prose.[7]

They, also, too often have ignored more discordant notes—the quotidian clatter and thump—made by people running into nonhuman features, forces, and inhabitants everywhere, every day, while trying to secure their very existence.

It was important that OAH hear an environmental historian discuss my field's links to our common organizational past. It was important for *JAH* to start publishing our works. It made sense to ask one of us to the centennial bash. But, as I told my panel colleagues and our audience, including my tolerant host Dick Kirkendall, you sure took your own sweet time!

JAH today now steadily publishes important new environmental-history writing.[8] Both masters and apprentices seek, and find, an outlet in its pages. We benefit from the vigorous scholarly debate generated by the nation's leading journal of top-drawer American-history writing. And the OAH can justly claim these days to be a valuable promoter of environmental-history scholarship. A field leader, Richard White, concluded his OAH presidency by hosting the Minneapolis 2007 centenary.[9] Colleagues and friends, from my own University of Kansas and from institutions all over the continent, came to Minneapolis to share their ongoing work. All of us benefited from the conversation that pumps lifeblood through any professional conference.[10]

My assessment of articles published in *MVHR* and *JAH* during this century impels me to present two main points about environmental history's touchy relationship to OAH. First, it took environmental history a mighty long time— more than fifteen years—to crash the *JAH*'s gates, or pages. During the years that separated our field's emergence in the middle 1970s and the *JAH*'s first sustained interest in 1990, environmental history attained its early maturity. The *Journal*, and, perhaps, by parity of reasoning, the OAH itself, played the deadbeat dad to environmental history's wild redheaded stepchild: following from a distance our difficult teething stage, occasionally alluding to our childish promise, then mostly ignoring the adolescent trials that must accompany any intellectual advance.

A lot of good writing, arguing, and thinking went on—in other places, in front of other professional audiences—before 1990. Only then did the *Journal* notice something interesting was happening out there on the plains and in the forests, down in the sewers of our great cities, and inside Americans' hearts and heads as they strove to survive amidst nature's sovereign contingencies.[11]

My second point is that during environmental history's seedtime, *JAH* exerted little creative influence. Its editors, and by extension the OAH itself, might even have ignored opportunities to stimulate and guide new historical scholarship that related people to their natural environment. In the exciting, consequential years, between 1945 and 1975, while pioneers invented environmental history's methods and defined its purposes, OAH did *not* play the role of nurturing parent to the "wild one" running the streets (or prairies) and staying up late (in the library, of course).

Few of environmental history's progenitors published in *MVHR/JAH*. I found no major articles between World War II's end and the middle 1970s by Vernon Carstensen, Alfred Runte, Robert Swierenga, Richard Petulla, John Opie, Leo Marx, Norris Hundley, Carl Sauer, Richard Lowenthal, or J. Donald Hughes. Of their students and successors, the "shock troops" who composed the first cadre of self-described environmental historians, none published in *JAH* before 1990: Donald Worster, Susan Flader, Roderick Nash, Joel Tarr, Carolyn Merchant, Stephen Pyne, Alfred Crosby, Patricia Nelson Limerick, William Cronon, or Samuel Hays.[12]

By 1972, the field's basic historiographical landscape and methodological directions had attained enough clarity to merit both a retrospective and an article by a leading practitioner about pedagogy.[13] But environmental history was still beyond or below *JAH*'s purview.[14] By 1982, the American Society for Environmental History (ASEH) was up and running, suggestive evidence of field maturity. The incoming president, Worster, had enough historiography spread before him to catalogue the fruits (and failures) of the field's first decade of labor.[15] But still the *Journal*'s editors seemed indifferent. By 1985, environmental history had attained enough breadth and depth to merit Richard White's long, thoughtful study of its birth and adolescence.[16] But, significantly, his essay appeared in *Pacific Historical Review*, not in the *JAH*! Not until the seminal 1990 "Round Table on Environmental History," featuring such heavyweights as White, Worster, Cronon, Crosby, Merchant, and Pyne, did the *JAH*'s editors consider environmental history's emergence as important enough story to cover.

Even after the "Round Table" opened the *Journal*'s front door, environmental history was mostly sharpened and complicated elsewhere during the crucial decade of the 1990s. The list of those who did *not* publish in *JAH* between 1990 and 2000 composes an honor roll of environmental historians: Arthur McEvoy, William Robbins, Stephen Fox, John Reiger, Ted Steinberg, Tom Dunlap, Mark Harvey, Adam Rome, and Nancy Langston.[17] I'd be delighted to quaff a beer or two with any of them. And I usually do when we gather at ASEH conferences, but not yet under OAH's auspices.

Despite *JAH*'s neglect, all these eminent environmental historians went right on doing what historians do: writing books, publishing articles, delivering papers, hustling grants, training students, and imagining themselves rich and famous. But they did these things without OAH's blessing, prodigals in the land of scholarship. I doubt they were exactly desperate for paternal approval, but some quite possibly might have drafted stern speeches they would deliver as soon as *they* held the presidency of OAH. Richard White may have experienced deep satisfaction as he rehearsed his Minneapolis presidential address: the redheaded stepchild had not only come home, but returned wreathed in accolades.

My reading of *MVHR* and *JAH* suggests several reasons that may explain why an unfortunate divide separated *JAH* from environmental history. The preeminent historical journal tackling American problems, *JAH* has always set high standards. Admittedly, during environmental history's earliest years — between, say, 1967 and Roderick Nash's *Wilderness and the American Mind* and 1979 and Worster's *Dust Bowl: The Southern Plains in the 1930s* — the field was striving to invent itself.[18] As late as 1983, when Bill Cronon published his canonical *Changes in the Land: Indians, Colonists, and the Ecology of New England*, environmental history's founders were still trying to figure out just what they were doing that was new and distinctive.[19] Their early work may have felt a little too uncertain to *JAH*'s editors.

Part of the answer may also lie in the legacies bequeathed by *JAH*'s predecessor, the *MVHR*, and OAH's predecessor, the MVHA. The Association's founders were nearly all Midwesterners, by choice if not by birth.[20] The first *MVHR* volumes exude a strong aroma of the Midwest: wheaty, earthy, redolent with more than a trace of self-consciousness and prideful arrogance. Uncorked eighty-five years later, early *MVHRs* fairly breathe a sense of the great hinterland surrounding such metropolitan centers as Minneapolis. The *Review*'s authors wrote a lot about the Midwest, generously defined. They were enmeshed in and fascinated by, and often frustrated with, the uneasy relations among Midwestern public universities, state/local/regional history societies, and the region's first professional history scholars.[21]

Review editors during its first quarter century seemed to share strong convictions: that the Midwest was a distinctive place, different from New England and the South; that this distinctive place did not just mutely witness, but actually produced, distinctive human responses to cross-cultural encounters; and that among the most distinctive encounters shaped by the Midwest were those between its first Euro-Americans and more undisturbed nature than their ancestors imagined even existed.[22]

Articles about nature were thus relatively common in the *Review*'s early volumes. I suspect the editors' preference was (sorry!) "natural" because many of the writers and editors came from rural backgrounds. And if not to the log cabin born, they worked amidst rural enterprises and taught often on campuses founded to serve the goals of agricultural capital and society.

During the early decades of the twentieth century, the *Review*'s interest in nature's influence on human history often reflected or even proclaimed regional pride in the writers' and editors' particular place and chosen mission. Neither New England nor Old South, MVHA's founders and members were not Ivy League. Or, if the universities in that league had been their early training grounds, they had emigrated to settle in the Old Northwest or Great West. The association's leaders seemed proud to be neither old money nor high society. Furthermore, taken as a whole, the Mississippi Valley was not highly urban.

Perhaps, therefore, it became easy, later on, once MVHA had cast off its parochial heritage to become fully "American," to dismiss much early-twentieth-century *MVHR* musing about nature as simple, even simplistic, Midwestern boosterism. One can imagine the embarrassment with which postwar historians read MVHA president Beverley Bond's 1932 presidential address, which proclaimed that "the composite American civilization which these settlers [from New England and the Appalachian backwoods] founded in the Old Northwest was in decided contrast to the distinctively Southern customs and institutions which were established in the Old Southwest, on the opposite bank of the Ohio River."[23]

Environmental history's early development among Western historians, such as Worster and Patricia Nelson Limerick, might have pigeonholed it as "mere local stuff," best handled by regional journals.[24] Earl Pomeroy, one of the deans of Western history, concluded in a 1955 *MVHR* historiographic study that his field "still tends to concentrate on those aspects of the West where the impact of the environment is clearest and sharpest," even though "the old environment-radical theme no longer seems so relevant to the present as it once did."[25] Possibly *JAH* editors, during the 1970s, even sniffed the dread contagion of geographic determinism, long since ousted as one of the embarrassing relics of MVHA's early poltroon period.[26]

By the 1930s, *MVHR* editors were fully invested in Progressive historians' concerns with power and social structures.[27] Articles wrestled time and again with capitalism's influence on democracy. Some authors did use nature as a sort of moral blackboard. Fields, forests, mills, and laboring people functioned as interactive screens on which historians traced patterns of exploitation by unraveling webs of influence. The Progressive historians became so interested in labor and capital that they didn't pursue those early hints from *Review* articles that something exciting could be learned about power by looking at human relationships, over time, with the natural world.[28]

Progressive historians in turn influenced the "new social historians," who began publishing as the *Review* became the *Journal* during the 1960s. Social history's deepening interest in power, rights, and oppression steered *JAH* into the thick of writing about race and class. The new social history argued that much of what had previously passed for political, social, and economic history was distorted by a narrow choice of agents: the rich, the powerful, the white, the male. These historians, passionately dedicated to unearthing untold stories about unsung people, considered they had quite enough to do in recovering lost human histories.[29]

Their deep interests in "the people" might have encouraged *JAH* editors to overlook scholarship that contended "nature" deserved scrutiny, respect, even empathy. Telling about nature would have taken the spotlight off people. It would have been "unnatural" for these socially inclined historians to elevate trees, rivers, bears, and microbes into the pantheon of agency. They defined their mission as finding agency in low human places in order to critique a nation that had, for far too long, consigned the politically marginal to history's margins.

During the postwar years, some *MVHR* articles had spotlighted such now-classic environmental history issues as economic opportunity's challenge to community security.[30] Issues of land and power interested Walter Prescott Webb, Paul Wallace Gates, and James Malin. Heavily involved in the association, Gates and Malin served on the editorial board, and Webb and Gates each had a term as president.

The *Review* did publish several articles about people and animals, transportation and technology, climate and demography, but they turned out to be one-shot efforts rather than trailblazers. They failed to inspire newer scholars seeking to publish in the *JAH* after the name change in 1964.[31] Topics pregnant with possibility got submerged, "outsourced" to specialized historical journals of technology and science. Environmental history's early connection with agricultural and conservation history may also have inclined *JAH* editors to think that specialized journals of agriculture, ecology, and forestry could best handle such "disciplinary" histories.

By the later 1970s, environmental history was emerging as a distinctive discipline, but it still awaited its time in the *Journal*'s sun. *JAH* instead began promoting cutting-edge scholarship that explored gender's influence on our past. So much work had to be done in this area, and still does, that environmental history again missed the bus. As with the new social histories published after the 1950s, gender-inflected history writing interrogated relationships, quite powerful but long obscured or willfully ignored, that surely deserved scholarship's light.

Some historians contend that American society, at its most basic level, has had to enforce gender definitions in order to operate. Certainly, it cannot be denied that society's maintenance fundamentally depends on relationships between and among men and women. With human gender and sexuality so central to the American experience, *Journal* editors might have decided they had plenty to do, after the mid-1970s, in understanding our own species without nonliterate life forms complicating the picture.

Some historians of long experience have noted that specialists in every field of history have, at some time, felt neglected, but I suggest that environmental historians don't nurse grudges for too long and don't question other fields' salience. Instead, we keep demonstrating our own. For, surely, our American past comprehends the Earth and its multitude of inhabitants, people not least among them.

NOTES

1. This revised version of the paper I presented in Minneapolis has benefited greatly from Thomas Bender's perceptive conference commentary and generous reading before publication.

2. Organization of American Historians, *2007 OAH Annual Meeting: Minneapolis*, 10.

3. Richard S. Kirkendall to Karl Brooks, October 18, 2005 [in author's possession]; "The MVHA-OAH and the Fields of History, Part III," *2007 OAH Annual Meeting: Onsite Program*, 25.

4. See, for example, the important articles by William Cronon, "A Place for Stories: Nature, History, and Narrative," *JAH* 78 (Mar. 1992): 1347–76, and Richard White, "Discovering Nature in North America," *JAH* 79 (Dec. 1992): 874–91 [in a special issue dedicated to the Columbian Encounter, "Discovering America"].

5. For a discussion of *Environmental History*'s ambitious objectives, see the collection of articles introduced by Adam Rome, "Anniversary Forum: What's Next for Environmental History?" *Environmental History* 10 (Jan. 2005): 30–109. An example of articles appearing regularly in regional history journals is Karl Brooks, "Review Essay: Kansas History as Environmental History," *Kansas History: A Journal of the Central Plains* 29 (Summer 2006): 116–31.

6. Adam Rome, "What Really Matters in History," *Environmental History* 7 (Apr. 2002): 303–18.

7. Aldo Leopold, *A Sand County Almanac* (New York: Ballentine Books, 1966), especially "Marshland Elegy," "Clandeboye," and "Illinois Bus Ride," 101–7, 168–77, and 124–26.

8. Adam Rome, "'Give Earth a Chance': The Environmental Movement and the Sixties," *JAH* 90 (Sept. 2003): 525–54, offers one example.

9. Richard White, "The Relevance of History, and the Problems with Relevance," *OAH 2007 Onsite Program*, 34.

10. "The Science and Values of Rural Reform in the Early Twentieth Century" and "Switching Currents: Energy Transitions in American History," Minneapolis panel sessions, featured rising environmental historians Kevin Armitage, Mark Hersey, and Karen Merrill. Ibid., 16, 36.

11. "Round Table on Environmental History," *JAH* 76 (Mar. 1990): 1087 et seq.

12. Any list of field pioneers betrays its compiler's limits and displays its author's preferences. This environmental history "founders hall" is no different.

13. Lawrence Rakestraw, "Conservation Historiography," *Pacific Historical Review* 41 (May 1972): 271–88; Roderick Nash, "American Environmental History," *Pacific Historical Review* 41: 362–72.

14. Richard White, "The Winning of the West: The Expansion of the Western Sioux in the Eighteenth and Nineteenth Century, *JAH* 65 (Sept. 1978): 319–43, dealt primarily with Native historical problems, although he considered nature an extremely important agent of change in Indian folkways, social structure, and diplomatic strategies.

15. Donald Worster, "History as Natural History: An Essay on Theory and Method," *Pacific Historical Review* 53 (Feb. 1984): 1–19.

16. Richard White, "American Environmental History: The Development of a New Historical Field," *Pacific Historical Review* 54 (June 1985): 297–335.

17. Dan Flores, "Bison Ecology and Bison Diplomacy: The Southern Plains from 1800 to 1850," *JAH* 78 (Sept. 1991): 464–85; and Edmund Russell, "'Speaking of Annihilation': Mobilizing for War Against Human and Insect Enemies, 1914–1945," *JAH* 82 (Mar. 1996): 1505–29, are conspicuous by their presence.

18. (New Haven, CT: Yale University Press, 1967); (New York: Oxford University Press, 1979).

19. (New York: Hill & Wang, 1983).

20. Thomas D. Clark, "Notes on the History of the Organization: Our Roots Flourished in the Valley," *JAH* 65 (June 1978): 85–107.

21. Examples include Hallie Farmer, "The Economic Background of Frontier Populism," *MVHR* 10 (Mar. 1924): 406–27; James B. Hedges, "Promotion of Immigration to the Pacific Northwest by the Railroads," *MVHR* 15 (Sept. 1928): 183–203; and Beverley W. Bond, "American Civilization Comes to the Old Northwest," *MVHR* 19 (June 1932): 3–29.

22. Clarence Alvord, "Virginia and the West: An Interpretation," *MVHR* 3 (June 1916): 19–38; and Louis Hacker, "Western Land Hunger and the War of 1812: A Conjecture," *MVHR* 10 (Mar. 1924): 365–95, are emblematic.

23. Bond, "American Civilization," 4.

24. The early ties between long-established Western history, even of the "new historical" variety, and the emerging field of environmental history can be discerned in Patricia Nelson Limerick, Clyde A. Milner II, and Charles E. Rankin, eds., *Trails: Toward a New Western History* (Lawrence: University Press of Kansas, 1991); William Cronon, George Miles, and Jay Gitlin, eds., *Under an Open Sky: Rethinking America's Western Past* (New York: Norton, 1992); and Donald Worster, *Under Western Skies: Nature and History in the American West* (New York: Oxford University Press, 1992).

25. Earl Pomeroy, "Toward a Reorientation of Western History: Continuity and Environment," *MVHR* 41 (Mar. 1955): 579–600, at 580–81. Writing nearly 40 years later, Limerick tried to remedy this determinist deficiency in "Disorientation and Reorientation: The American Landscape Discovered from the West," *JAH* 79 (Dec. 1992): 1021–49.

26. Earle D. Ross, "A Generation of Prairie Historiography," *MVHR* 33 (Dec. 1946): 391–410, at 408, contended that the Midwest's "traditional conservatism [was caused by] reasons of origins, locations, and occupational interests."

27. Richard Hofstadter, *The Progressive Historians: Turner, Beard, Parrington* (New York: Alfred A. Knopf, 1969), remains the best synoptic account.

28. Typical of the articles authored by historians who fit the "Progressive" label are Merrill Jensen, "The Cession of the Old Northwest," *MVHR* 23 (June 1936): 27–48; Roy E. Appleman, "Timber Empire from the Public Domain," *MVHR* 26 (Sept. 1939): 139–208; and Dwight L. Agnew, "The Government Land Surveyor as a Pioneer," *MVHR* 23 (Dec. 1941): 369–82.

29. Philip Shaw Paludan's "Prefaces" to the first and second editions of *A People's Contest: The Union & Civil War, 1861–1865* (1986; Lawrence: University Press of Kansas, 1996), ix-xx, eloquently and briefly analyzed the emergence and impact of the "new social history" of the 1960s and 1970s. My teacher and former colleague, sadly, was too ill to attend the OAH centennial conference in Minneapolis and died in Springfield, Illinois, in August 2007.

30. Robert F. Fries, "The Mississippi River Logging Company and the Struggle for the Free Navigation of Logs, 1865–1900," *MVHR* 35 (Dec. 1948): 429–48, and Paul Wallace Gates, "Cattle Kings in the Prairies," *MVHR* 35 (Dec. 1948): 379–412, pursued this theme.

31. Robert Leslie Jones, "The Horse and Mule Industry in Ohio to 1865," *MVHR* 33 (June 1946): 61–88; Oscar Osburn Winther, "The Use of Climate as a Means of Promoting Migration to Southern California," *MVHR* 33 (Dec. 1946): 411–24; Henry Nash Smith, "The Western Farmer in Imaginative Literature, 1818–1891," *MVHR* 36 (Dec. 1949): 479–90; and John A. DeNovo, "Petroleum and the United States Navy before World War I," *MVHR* 41 (March 1955): 641–56.

20

The History That Dare Not Speak Its Name

Kathy Peiss

My task, to survey the development of the history of sexuality in the Organization of American Historians (OAH), seemed an easy one. Sexuality studies has emerged and grown only in the last four decades, a period through which I lived and which indelibly shaped my own work. Still, knowing the oblique ways that sexuality infuses the past, I wondered if, perhaps, there was a hidden history buried in the *Mississippi Valley Historical Review (MVHR)* and the *Journal of American History (JAH)*. Idly searching in JSTOR on such keywords as *prostitution*, *courtship*, and *homosexuality*, I finally typed in *queer*, only to discover a link to Laurence Veysey's 1963 article, "The Academic Mind of Woodrow Wilson." Refuting the idea that Wilson's educational philosophy was forward looking, Veysey quoted a speech Wilson had given in 1902, the year he was appointed president of Princeton. Wilson proclaimed to an appreciative audience: "I don't know what sociology is (laughter); moreover, I am convinced that there isn't a man living who does (laughter and applause); whenever a man is studying anything queer he calls it sociology (laughter)." Wilson employed the term to mean odd or questionable, and Veysey's use of this quotation at first seemed to measure the distance between an earlier period of public decorum in scholarship and sexual life, on the one hand, and our own unruly times on the other. But as I mulled it over, Veysey's usage seemed queer in the contemporary sense of the word. The quotation offered Veysey some vivid language with which to make his point, but then why relegate it to a footnote? Perhaps such a quotation in the text might have betrayed the conventions of professional historical writing. It is just as likely, however, that Veysey chose to create a queer moment in the footnotes, inserted in the same way that the sanitized films of the Production Code era—to quote Cary Grant in *Bringing Up Baby*—"just went gay all of a sudden." After all, later in his life, Vesey came out as a gay man and he had, as one colleague recalled, an "often mischievous penchant for truth-telling."[1]

Such hidden expressions are rare in the *MVHR* and early *JAH*. Sexuality in any guise—as an evolving set of ideas and practices, as an object of reform, as an aspect of marriage and family life, as an integral part of race relations—is virtually absent from the journal for two-thirds of its history. Indeed, it is not until the 1990s that sexuality regularly appeared as a category of analysis. There is a conventional explanation for this, one that, in fact, has appeared on several occasions in the *JAH* itself: The rise of liberation politics and identity-based movements in the 1960s and 1970s challenged and ultimately transformed historical scholarship and the professional organizations that support, evaluate, and reward this work. That narrative seems right in a broad sense, although a closer examination of this chronology raises questions about how long it took the OAH to integrate sexuality into the fields of history it deemed significant. This essay is not a study into the internal workings of the OAH and its relationship to academic, professional, political, and grassroots organizations. Rather, it examines the publishing history of the organization and considers how historians of sexuality fared in the pages of the *JAH*. By asking what subjects could be addressed and when, I hope to suggest a more complex interplay between the political impetus behind the field and the intellectual work that appeared in print.

Addressing how the profession had changed in the late twentieth century, Carl Degler recalled that "in the 1940s and 1950s the history of sexuality, whether homosexual or heterosexual, was not even considered a subject of conversation, much less a field of research and publication." Indeed, prior to the late 1960s, the *MVHR-JAH* rarely mentioned sex; brief discussions appeared in a handful of articles on antebellum utopian thought, nativist movements, and racial purity and miscegenation.[2] Yet it is worth observing that some scholars in the humanities and social sciences had, in fact, been making sexuality the subject of conversation for some decades. From the 1910s into the 1930s, the Chicago School of Sociology investigated prostitution, homosexuality, and interracial sexuality, an "unprecedented effort," historian Chad Heap writes, "to situate sexuality in a social context." American sexuality was a core question for anthropologists, including such pioneering women as Margaret Mead and Ruth Benedict, themselves products of the sexual revolution and feminist impulse of the 1910s. Leslie Fiedler's landmark 1948 essay in *Partisan Review*, "Come Back to the Raft Ag'in, Huck Honey," traced homoerotic themes in nineteenth-century American literature. In the same year Alfred Kinsey published his path-breaking survey, *Sexual Behavior in the Human Male*.[3]

Perhaps there was no sex in the Mississippi Valley, but that is unlikely. Mid-century American historians, like many others in American society, had lived through tumultuous changes in sexual mores and behavior, but they bracketed off these experiences from their inquiries as historians. An essentialist view of sexuality as biological drive, the separation of public acts and private desires, the border patrolling of a profession that did not have a scientific method or guiding theory, the limited presence of women, and the stigma of homosexuality: these all must have occluded the historical imagination when it came to sexual matters. In a 1974 account of the "bad old days" of the MVHA, Ray Allen Billington observed that the earlier generations of historians in the MVHA were marked by a "refusal to dabble in the social problems of the wider world." "Business meetings were unsullied by resolutions on war, women's liberation, or the gay front," he wrote, and racial discrimination was challenged slowly.[4] The organization's acute concern about professional status as a regional or national body may have led to even greater cautiousness about subject matter and approach.

In the 1950s through the late 1960s, historians who seemed most open to the study of sexuality were intellectual and cultural historians, often in dialogue with scholars in other fields. The *Journal of the History of Ideas* published social theorist Philip Rieff on Freud, as well as historian Keith Thomas on the double standard.[5] *American Quarterly*, embracing what was, at the time, a new sense of interdisciplinary possibility, published several pieces in the mid-1950s touching upon sexuality in American literature.[6] The psychological turn of the post–World War II period led some to psychohistory, applying Freudian analysis to an understanding of individual and collective motivation. Psychosexual development seemed an especially promising line of inquiry, for example, to German historians seeking to explain the insanity and calamity of Nazism.[7]

Americanists largely shunned this approach, and Freud's name barely appears in the pages of the *MVHR* or early *JAH*. Nevertheless, there were U.S. historians in the late 1950s and early 1960s who were beginning to identify sexuality as an area of interest, if not a distinct domain. This seems a product of the bracing liberalism of the time, which fostered not only political change but also a personal and cultural opening. For Carl Bode, serving as a witness for the defense in an obscenity case brought against Henry Miller led him to ponder sexually explicit literature in the nineteenth century in the *American Quarterly* in 1963. Roy Lubove and Egal Feldman's work on prostitution, William O'Neill on divorce, and David Kennedy's biography of Margaret Sanger reflected a reassessment of Progressive Era social reform in light of the spirited politics of the 1960s and growing sexual liberalism.[8] As Christopher Lasch later observed, "something in the atmosphere of the late fifties made it seem important to come to terms with the 'woman question.' There was already a lot of sexual experimentation . . ., experimentation with 'open marriages' and other unconventional arrangements." This interest in feminism was focused, notably, on sexual and interpersonal relations. Strikingly, Lasch, writing with William R. Taylor, prefigured the mid-1970s interest in women's romantic friendships in a 1963 study of two antebellum women seeking literary careers and finding each other. "In such a society as nineteenth-century America," Lasch and

Taylor wrote, "the kind of behavior we are concerned with here may have been normal rather than perverse."[9]

Others considered sexuality in the new social history of the family; these included works on white adolescents, premarital pregnancy rates and the timing of the sexual revolution, and, in a different vein, the conditions of sexuality, marriage, and childrearing in slavery.[10] In only one case, however, was an article on sexuality published in the *JAH* in the 1960s, James R. McGovern's 1968 piece, "American Woman's Pre-World War I Freedom in Manners and Morals." McGovern took up where Morton White and Henry May had left off, exploring the 1910s as a moment of cultural revolt against Victorianism and nascent sexual modernity, marked especially by the changing behavior and attitudes of women—a framework that would prove an important one in the history of sexuality in the years that followed.[11]

The advent of the feminist and gay liberation movements in the late 1960s and early 1970s sparked a profusion of research and writing on sexuality, moving beyond these early approaches to transform how we think about the subject. It required a number of conceptual leaps to imagine sexuality as an historical field: the widespread acceptance of the social construction of sexuality; the disentangling of the terms "sex," "gender," and "sexuality"; the assertion that intimate behaviors and practices needed to be understood in terms of politics and power. These and other ideas were largely debated and worked out in places where activism and intellectual work coalesced, far from the professional associations. Grassroots and community history efforts took shape, and feminist, lesbian-feminist, and gay liberationist intellectual circles arose. Women's studies programs, the Berkshire Conference on the History of Women, the Gay Academic Union, and other alternative institutions developed. New journals like *Feminist Studies, Frontiers, Signs,* and *Radical History Review* began publishing the emergent scholarship on sexuality starting in the early 1970s. Most striking of all was the change of voice, as feminists and gay scholars rethought conventional wisdom with a fresh sense of urgency and commitment, in language that was both personal and political. Whatever the subsequent problems were with the authority of experience, at the time it felt like a rush of oxygen.

Where was the OAH in this ferment? Although the archives and individual memories may present a different picture, if we are to judge from the *JAH*, the organization's response was halting. The 1971 meeting seems to have been the first to hold a session on the history of sexuality, with Ben Barker-Benfield's paper, "The Spermatic Economy," and Ron Walters's "Antislavery and Sexuality." In 1972, in a session on changing sex roles in industrial America, Stephen Nissenbaum spoke on "Sex Reform and Social Change" and Sondra Herman on the late-nineteenth-century marriage market. Two years later, Carroll Smith-Rosenberg presented with Judith Colucci-Breault a version of her path-breaking work, "The Female World of Love and Ritual."[12]

Although coverage of these sessions in the *JAH* is thin, some concerns are apparent. One was anxiety about evidence. This was already a source of conflict dividing generations of historians, but it seemed to have been exacerbated by the subject of sexuality. In the 1971 session, for example, Anne Firor Scott "cautioned that the novelty of subjects like sexuality should not lead historians away from a conventional respect for evidence."[13] Also hampering historians was an ongoing confusion over the terminology and conceptualization of sexuality, especially the slippage between such terms as sex, sex roles, sexuality, women, and gender. The stated purpose of the session featuring Nissenbaum and Herman, for example, was "to offer a more balanced insight into American history through an examination of male and female attitudes toward sex and the anxieties resulting from new habits of living and new values which conditioned sex roles."[14] Carl Degler, in a 1980 address, correctly observed that women's history "forced American historians to confront sexuality in the past," and then he slipped into an essentialist explanation: "for sex is to women's history as color is to black history: a prime basis of differentiation and therefore a source of conflict."[15]

Even as women's history and women's historians gained a foothold in the organization, this linkage made it difficult to address the specificity of sexuality and especially constricted thinking about gay history and historians. At the 1976 annual meeting, Dennis Rubini introduced a resolution that the OAH "affirms the right of gay historians and others to engage in the research and teaching of the history of single and gay people as well as members of all other sexual minorities" and condemns the obstruction of such work as a violation of academic freedom. During the debate, a member introduced an amendment that eliminated the word *gay* from "right of gay historians," using the universalistic argument that the OAH should affirm everyone's rights to do such work. It was this version of the motion that passed.[16] However true that point is, the amended resolution reflected an inability to understand why, at that moment, it was gay historians who were most likely to do such research and be harmed by hostility to it.

Even as the OAH opened the door a crack, we can see how constrained its welcome was. None of the papers presented in those early OAH sessions were published as articles in the *JAH*. Without access to the *JAH*'s list of rejected articles, it is unclear whether their authors even submitted them to the journal or whether they had decided, in the first instance, to seek a different audience in journals that were more receptive to radical and interdisciplinary scholarship, such as *Radical History Review* and *American Quarterly*, or in those with an explicitly feminist focus, such as *Feminist Studies* and *Signs*.[17] Only two articles on the history of sexuality were published in the *JAH* in these years, both appearing in 1973: Carroll Smith-Rosenberg and Charles Rosenberg's "The Female Animal: Medical and Biological Views of Woman and Her Role in Nineteenth Century America," and John C. Burnham's "Progressive Era Revolution in American Attitudes Toward Sex."[18] Both fulfilled the evidence test, mining the rich vein of medical, biological, and social hygiene sources for evidence of attitudes toward sexuality.

For the history of sexuality, there was a long dry spell in the *JAH* between the early 1970s and the late 1980s. The *Journal* published several articles in women's history and African American history that made sexual attitudes and practices a crucial aspect of the analysis, including studies of miscegenation and race relations, evangelical women, and union women who linked sexual nonconformity and labor militancy.[19] But it was not until 1987, fourteen years after Burnham's piece, that the *JAH* again published an article whose primary subject was sexuality. This time, however, its author was an historian who approached sexuality from a radical feminist and lesbian-feminist perspective. Estelle Freedman's "Uncontrolled Desires," a study of the legal and medical concept of the sexual psychopath in the mid-twentieth century, was the first article in the *JAH* to examine non-normative sexuality. It still seems fresh, because of its attention to the constructedness of heterosexuality and its analysis of sexuality in terms of mid-century politics and power dynamics. The article provoked two readers to write to the *Journal*, protesting Freedman's scholarship and politics, and decrying the loss of standards in the historical profession. One accused Freedman of poor writing, faulty logic, and moral depravity, asserting that she had tried "to defend pederasty and homosexuality, while she regarded heterosexuality . . . as 'perverted,'" and "expounded immoral conduct under the guise of scholarship." The other letter attacked her simultaneously for too little evidence and too much, commenting on the "massive footnotes," "whose very bulk aroused my suspicions"![20]

Were these readers right to worry? In a *JAH* roundtable in 1989 on "what has changed and not changed in historical practices," John D'Emilio offered a deeply personal and largely pessimistic view. In the roundtable's lead essay, Jonathan Weiner celebrated New Left historians' confrontation with the profession and their success. In contrast, D'Emilio wrote of the cognitive dissonance of being a professional historian and a gay historian-activist. He characterized the sense of wonderment and exhilaration in uncovering the gay past—work that was "transformatory . . . and inherently political"—but observed that he had necessarily "looked outside the academy and the profession for intellectual sustenance and challenge." He pointedly observed, "I would no more have thought of going to a meeting of the American Historical Association or the Organization of American Historians than I would have considered working on Wall Street."[21] D'Emilio said starkly what many graduate students and young faculty in the 1980s generally felt; we, too, would not have considered publishing in the *JAH*, which we viewed as conventional, stodgy, and unwelcoming, a description that characterized, not only the old guard of male historians, but many of the New Left Young Turks as well. Strikingly, this roundtable itself reenacted D'Emilio's critique, with comments by Carl Degler, John Higham, Christopher Lasch, and Herbert Aptheker all engaging Weiner's narrative of the triumph of (white, straight, mainly male) radical historians; D'Emilio's essay, as well as ones by Gerda Lerner and David Levering Lewis, voiced other views of radical history but were effectively sidelined.[22]

D'Emilio saw signs that the 1980s were a "breakthrough" decade for gay and lesbian history, but he also hesitated in that assessment. It was still the case, in 1989, that much of the new scholarship on sexuality was produced by community history groups, activist historians, and graduate students just starting out and still on the margins of the profession. If *breakthrough* means "acceptance and legitimacy within the profession," however, for the history of sexuality that did not come until the 1990s.

From 1990 to 2000, the *JAH* published a number of articles that contribute directly and significantly to the history of sexuality: articles on abortion, birth control, sex censorship, sex education, and the challenges of archival sources in the field.[23] It also featured one or more articles most years that treated sexuality as a category of analysis in studies of race relations, gender, and/or politics. Mary Frances Berry, in her published 1991 presidential address, discussed sexual behavior, morality, and the law in the late-nineteenth-century South; other articles on sex and race addressed Northern labor relations, miscegenation in court rulings, and the Leo Frank case and revival of the Ku Klux Klan.[24] The impact of sexuality on formal politics and political culture was explored in articles on marriage and morals as an issue in the election of 1828, the challenge of Mormon polygamy to women's rights and ideas of consent, and the use of sexualized language in Cold War liberalism.[25] If at times these studies seemed to make a sexual encounter or scandal into an historian's "MacGuffin" (Alfred Hitchcock's term for a plot device that motivates the story but is not central to it), at their best they showed how attention to sexuality can illuminate historical events and broad historical processes.

The intellectual turns of the 1990s toward culture and discourse, as well as historians' belated assimilation of Foucault, decades after European scholarship and many academic disciplines in America had done so, opened greater possibilities for analyzing the relationship between intimate life and sexuality, on the one hand, and politics and the state, on the other. Anthropologist Ann Stoler's "Tense and Tender Ties," published in 2001, was an unusual and welcome piece for the *JAH*, given its strong theoretical analysis, and has been especially inspirational for many historians. In the last few years, articles appeared for the first time in the *JAH* that centered on homosexuality and intersexuality, as well as sexual violence.[26] The *OAH Magazine of History* has also offered much more coverage of the history of sexuality in issues on sex, courtship, and dating in 2004, gender in 2005, and non-normative sexuality in 2006.

What more should be done? Sexuality has certainly become a legitimate area of inquiry in the organization, and in the profession more broadly in the last fifteen years. But the process of legitimation has been an uneven one. It is striking, for example, that in the 1990s the *JAH* published articles on George Kennan and Arthur Schlesinger Jr.'s use of sexual language (specifically metaphors referencing homosexuality, such as perversion and penetration), but nothing on the erotic lives, political experiences, or cultures of homosexuals themselves.[27] This changed in the 2000s, under Joanne Meyerowitz's editorship. Still, the question of what defines historical significance remains. Often sexual subjects, especially those related to sexual minorities, are treated in articles on teaching or in the *Magazine of History*. The only article to appear on the AIDS crisis, arguably one of the most important social and political events of the late twentieth century, concerns how to teach the subject.[28] Nothing has appeared on gay rights and gay liberation as social movements. Although the *JAH* has published at least one work that deals with same-sex "romantic friendship," there has been nothing on modern lesbians.[29] And most of what we read about sexuality in this journal is drained of any erotic and sensory dimension one might associate with sex. One hears murmurs that there is too much emphasis on non-normative sexuality or that the study of sexuality is "over" or passé, yet we've only begun to write a full history of sexuality in the United States.[30]

For the OAH, this is not only an academic matter, in which we debate the scope of scholarly inquiry and assess trends in historiography. Among students and those who aspire to be professional historians, the history of sexuality is vibrant and compelling, personally, politically, and intellectually. Even so, there continues to be a palpable and, I believe, rational fear that, to follow this passion may derail an historian's career. Professional organizations are key players in the process of legitimation and inclusion; articles in the *JAH*, whatever their scholarly contributions, validate their authors for academic jobs, fellowships, and other forms of recognition.[31] This remains an important goal for historians of sexuality.

Still, there is something to be said for being on the margins. When I think of the work that caused my heart to race these past thirty years, it was more often than not writing that appeared in new feminist journals, interdisciplinary anthologies, radical publications, and the like. So much important new work is produced at the border of theory and history, recently, for example, in studies of transsexuality and transgendered experience. Away from the conference hotel and journal's pages, the classroom, the Lesbian, Gay, Bisexual, Transgender, Intersex, Queer, and Questioning (LGBTIQQ) center, and the activist organization have powerfully influenced and continue to shape the research and writing historians of sexuality do. Even as the field has achieved a significant presence within the mainstream of U.S. history, the margins continue to be generative of new ideas and creative approaches. The challenge of a professional organization like the OAH is to encourage both.

NOTES

Note: References to articles from MVHR and the JAH through 2001 have been accessed from JSTOR; those after 2001 from History Cooperative.

1. Laurence Veysey, "The Academic Mind of Woodrow Wilson," *Mississippi Valley Historical Review* 49 (Mar. 1963): 618 [hereafter MVHR]. Jonathan Beecher, "Remembering Laurence Veysey (1933–2004)," *History of Education Quarterly* 45 (Sept. 2005), 407–11 [accessed from Blackwell Synergy]; Dave Ford, "Hut with a Heart," *San Francisco Chronicle*, Sept. 12, 2003, www.sfgate.com/cgi-bin/article.cgi?file=/chronicle/archive/2003/09/12/WBGMO1J65R1.DTL.

2. Carl N. Degler, "Remaking American History," *JAH* 67 (June 1980): 8. See, e.g., Richard H. Shryock, "Sylvester Graham and the Popular Health Movement, 1830–1870," *MVHR* 18 (Sept. 1931): 172–83; David Brion Davis, "Some Themes of Counter-Subversion: An Analysis of Anti-Masonic, Anti-Catholic, and Anti-Mormon Literature," *MVHR* 47 (Sept. 1960): 205–24.

3. Chad Heap, "The City as a Sexual Laboratory: The Queer Heritage of the Chicago School," *Qualitative Sociology* 26 (Winter 2003): 457–87; Lois Banner, *Intertwined Lives: Margaret Mead, Ruth Benedict, and Their Circle* (New York: Knopf, 2003); Leslie Fiedler, "Come Back to the Raft Ag'in, Huck Honey!" *Partisan Review* 15 (June 1948): 664–71.

4. Ray Allen Billington, "From Association to Organization: The OAH in the Bad Old Days," *JAH* 65 (June 1978): 77.

5. Philip Rieff, "The Origins of Freud's Political Psychology," *Journal of the History of Ideas* 17 (Apr. 1956): 235–49; Keith Thomas, "The Double Standard," *Journal of the History of Ideas* 20 (Apr. 1959): 195–216.

6. One of the first was Newton Arvin, "Melville's Mardi," *American Quarterly* 2 (Spring 1950): 71–81. Arvin was later arrested for receiving male physique magazines, coerced into naming gay faculty at Smith College, and forced to resign his professorship there. See Barry Werth, *The Scarlet Professor* (New York: Nan A. Talese, 2001).

7. E.g., Peter Loewenberg, "The Unsuccessful Adolescence of Heinrich Himmler," *American Historical Review* 76 (June 1971): 612–41. In his 1957 presidential address, European diplomatic historian William L. Langer called for the application of psychological insights to historical problems: "The Next Assignment," *American Historical Review* 63 (Jan. 1958): 283–304. For a set of very useful essays on intellectual developments after World War II, see David A. Hollinger, *The Humanities and the Dynamics of Inclusion Since World War II* (Baltimore: Johns Hopkins University Press, 2006).

8. Carl Bode, "Columbia's Carnal Bed," *American Quarterly* 15 (Spring 1963): 52–64; Roy Lubove, "Progressives and Prostitution," *Historian* 24 (1962): 308–30; Egal Feldman, "Prostitution, the Alien Woman and the Progressive Imagination, 1910–1915," *American Quarterly* 19 (1967): 192–206; William O'Neill, "Divorce in the Progressive Era," *American Quarterly* 17 (1965): 203–17; David Kennedy, *Birth Control in America: The Career of Margaret Sanger* (New Haven, CT: Yale University Press, 1970).

9. Casey Blake and Christopher Phelps, "History as Social Criticism: Conversations with Christopher Lasch," *JAH* 80 (Mar 1994): 1326–27; Christopher Lasch and William

R. Taylor, "Two 'Kindred Spirits': Sorority and Family in New England, 1839–1846," *New England Quarterly* 36 (Mar. 1963): 23–41 (quotation on 33).

10. E.g., Daniel Scott Smith and Michael S. Hindus, "Premarital Pregnancy in America, 1640–1971: An Overview and Interpretation," *Journal of Interdisciplinary History* 5 (Spring 1975): 537–70; Herbert G. Gutman, "Review: *The Slave Family, Slave Sexual Behavior, and Slave Sales*," *Journal of Negro History* 60 (Jan. 1975): 138–215.

11. James R. McGovern, "The American Woman's Pre-World War I Freedom in Manners and Morals," *JAH* 55 (Sept. 1968): 315–33.

12. Jack P. Greene, "The Sixty-Fourth Annual meeting of the Organization of American Historians," *JAH* 58 (Dec. 1971): 706; Allen Weinstein, "The Sixty-Fifth Annual Meeting of the Organization of American Historians," *JAH* 60 (Sept. 1973): 378–80; Robert Kelley, "The Sixty-Seventh Annual meeting of the Organization of American Historians," *JAH* 61 (Mar. 1975): 1047.

13. Greene, "Sixty-Fourth Annual Meeting," 706.

14. Weinstein, "Sixty-Fifth Annual Meeting," 379.

15. Degler, "Remaking American History," 8.

16. "Historical News and Comments" *JAH* 62 (Sept. 1975): 518–19.

17. Herman and Walters published their articles in *American Quarterly* in 1973; Barker-Benfield in the inaugural issue of *Feminist Studies* in 1972; Smith-Rosenberg in the inaugural issue of *Signs* in 1975.

18. John C. Burnham, "Progressive Era Revolution in American Attitudes toward Sex," *JAH* 59 (Mar. 1973): 885–908; Carroll Smith-Rosenberg and Charles Rosenberg, "The Female Animal: Medical and Biological Views of Woman and Her Role in Nineteenth-Century America," *JAH* 60 (Sept. 1973): 332–56.

19. Gary B. Mills, "Miscegenation and the Free Negro in Antebellum 'Anglo' Alabama: A Reexamination of Southern Race Relations," *JAH* 68 (June 1981): 16–34; Joan Jacobs Brumberg, "Zenanas and Girlless Villages: The Ethnology of American Evangelical Women, 1870–1910," *JAH* 69 (Sept. 1982): 347–71; Jacquelyn Dowd Hall, "Disorderly Women: Gender and Labor Militancy in the Appalachian South," *JAH* 73 (Sept. 1986): 354–82.

20. Estelle B. Freedman, "'Uncontrolled Desires': The Response to the Sexual Psychopath, 1920–1960," *JAH* 74 (June 1987): 83–106. William Rosenberg, Art Scherr, "Letters to the Editor," *JAH* 76 (Dec. 1989): 1025–29.

21. John D'Emilio, "Not a Simple Matter: Gay History and Gay Historians," *JAH* 76 (Sept. 1989): 435–42 (quotation on 438).

22. This point is trenchantly made in Michael Sherry's Letter to the Editor, *JAH* 77 (June 1990): 388–91.

23. Leslie J. Reagan, "'About to Meet Her Maker': Women, Doctors, Dying Declarations, and the State's Investigation of Abortion, 1867–1940," *JAH* 77 (Mar. 1991): 1240–64; Andrea Tone, "Black Market Birth Control: Contraceptive Entrepreneurship and Criminality in the Gilded Age," *JAH* 87 (Sept. 2000): 435–59; Jeffrey P. Moran, "Modernism Gone Mad: Sex Education Comes to Chicago, 1913," *JAH* 83 (Sept. 1996): 481–513; Helen Lefkowitz Horowitz, "Victoria Woodhull, Anthony Comstock, and Conflicts over Sex in the United States in the 1870s," *JAH* 87 (Sept. 2000): 403–34; John D. Wrathall, "Provenance as Text: Reading the Silences Around Sexuality in Manuscript Collections," *JAH* 79 (June 1992): 165–78.

24. Mary Frances Berry, "Judging Morality: Sexual Behavior and Legal Consequences in the Late Nineteenth Century South," *JAH* 78 (Dec. 1991): 835–56; Gerald Zahavi, "Passionate Commitments: Race, Sex, and Communism at Schenectady General Electric, 1932–1954," *JAH* 83 (Sept. 1996): 514–48; Kevin Boyle, "The Kiss; Racial and Gender Conflict in a 1950s Automobile Factory," *JAH* 84 (Sept. 1997): 496–523; Peggy Pascoe, "Miscegenation Law, Court Cases and Ideologies of 'Race' in Twentieth Century America," *JAH* 83 (June 1996): 44–69; Nancy MacLean, "The Leo Frank Case Reconsidered: Gender and Sexual Politics in the Making of Reactionary Populism," *JAH* 78 (Dec. 1991): 917–48.

25. Norma Basch, "Marriage, Morals and Politics in the Election of 1828," *JAH* 80 (Dec. 1993): 890–918; Sarah Barringer Gordon, "The Liberty of Self-Degradation: Polygamy, Woman Suffrage, and Consent in Nineteenth-Century America," *JAH* 83 (Dec. 1996): 815–47; K. A. Cuordileone, "'Politics in an Age of Anxiety': Cold War Political Culture and the Crisis in American Masculinity, 1949–1960," *JAH* 87 (Sept. 2000): 515–45.

26. Ann Laura Stoler, "Tense and Tender Ties: The Politics of Comparison in North American History and (Post) Colonial Studies," *JAH* 85 (Dec. 2001): 829–65; Margot Canaday, "Building a Straight State: Sexuality and Social Citizenship under the 1944 G.I. Bill," *JAH* 90 (Dec. 2003): 935–57; Elizabeth Reis, "Impossible Hermaphrodites: Intersex in America, 1620–1960," *JAH* 92 (Sept. 2005): 411–41; Danielle L. McGuire, "'It Was like All of Us Had Been Raped': Sexual Violence, Community Mobilization, and the African American Freedom Struggle," *JAH* 91 (Dec. 2004): 906–32; Wendy Anne Warren, "'The Cause of Her Grief': The Rape of a Slave in Early New England," *JAH* 93 (Mar. 2007): 1031–49.

27. Frank Costigliola, "'Unceasing Pressure for Penetration': Gender, Pathology, and Emotion in George Kennan's Formation of the Cold War," *JAH* 83 (Mar. 1997): 1309–39; Cuordileone, "Politics in an Age of Anxiety."

28. Douglas Bailey et al., "AIDS and American History: Four Perspectives on Experiential Learning," *JAH* 86 (Mar. 2000): 1721–33.

29. Helen Lefkowitz Horowitz, "'Nous Autres': Reading, Passion, and the Creation of M. Carey Thomas," *JAH* 79 (June 1992): 68–95.

30. See, e.g., Helen Lefkowitz Horowitz, Letter to the Editor, *OAH Magazine of History*, May 2006, 54.

31. See Marc Stein, "Crossing Borders: Memories, Dreams, Fantasies, and Nightmares of the History Job Market," *Left History* 9 (Spring/Summer 2004): 119–39; Stein, "Post-Tenure Lavender Blues," *History News Network*, January 7, 2006, http://hnn.us/articles/19941.html. My thanks to Bruce Kuklick, for the notion of *JAH* articles as "certification narratives."†

21

How Discipline Change Happens

Thomas Bender

•

The authors of chapters 17–20 on the fields of history all reported that they found the task more difficult or, at least, more time-consuming than they had expected. The result is valuable collective information about who we are as historians of the United States. We are indebted. I expect many things were not a surprise, but it is good to have them documented. But there were surprises, too, and that is particularly good to see. Beyond some comments on individual papers, I want to focus mainly on points of convergence on which I might speculate more generally about the course of the discipline over a century. My comments were stimulated by the preceding four chapters but are relevant to the entire discussion of historical fields.

When I first saw the mélange of fields and developments selected for inclusion, I wondered whether the planners drew them out of a hat. Differences are manifest among the fields, and the most interesting finding perhaps is that, for women's history and the history of sexuality, Alice Kessler-Harris and Kathy Peiss were not surprised by the lateness of the field's arrival in the *Journal of American History* (*JAH*), nor might readers, except that it may have been even later than we anticipated. Fred Hoxie, by contrast, was surprised to learn that publication of studies of American Indians has a longer history than one would have guessed. Most interesting, perhaps, was the finding for environmental history. Karl Brooks found that it fared better in the *Mississippi Valley Historical Review* (*MVHR*) than in the *JAH*, being somewhat visible in the interwar years then disappearing only to re-emerge in the *Journal* very late, not until the 1990s.

I think there is an explanation for this finding and, perhaps, it may suggest, albeit indirectly, the lateness of women's history, gender studies, and the history of sexuality. Admittedly, the data do not perfectly fit my answer, but it seems to at least point in that direction. The first reason is that history's professional charter could more easily accommodate the studies cited by Hoxie. They are state related. The frontier, Indian relations, and Indian policy all impinged on state issues or were impinged upon by the state, and history as a professional discipline was joined at the hip to the modern nation-state. In fact, had we been examining the *American Historical Review* instead of the *MVHR/JAH*, all of those peoples not organized into nation-states a hundred years ago, that is, those peoples who resided on 85 to 90 percent of the Earth's land surface and subject to imperial rule, would be absent. The nation-state and "history as past politics" were central to historical practice. Perhaps for the same reason, a particular version of environmental history found a place early on in the *MVHR*. Women and sexuality were not seen as part of that project.

The second reason is that, at least before World War I, there was a lot of interaction and collaboration between historians and archeologists and anthropologists that may have aided entry of the field, as well as the scholars themselves. One of the issues was, in fact, whether Native Americans were or were not part of American national history, as the natives are in Mexico and New Zealand, for example. As it turns out, their history was deliberately separated out, put into natural history museums, while our national history went into history museums. A century ago, this was still a bit ambiguous, but in recent decades, Native Americans have been incorporated into national historical studies.

The case of women, gender, and sexuality had a different barrier. They were considered a part of the private, not the public, realm. That was changing, but it had not changed enough. Gender and family studies belonged to anthropology, where kinship, not the state, was a major focus. Although there was a blending of interests of anthropology and history (as would later become ethnohistory), with respect to gender studies, the disciplinary difference was substantial. History was still overwhelmingly past politics. Early-twentieth-century studies of women's history or studies of gender were mostly the work of amateur scholars, or scholars in anthropology, most of whom (from Elsie Clews Parsons to Margaret Mead) were on the fringes of academe and not bound by the academic definitions of history's domain. Much to this point, I think, Kessler-Harris notes that studies of women showed up in the book-review section but not as articles. The topic was not ignored but neither was it allowed into the mainstream.

All of these essays share a methodological problem, however. It is most evident in the language used by Brooks in his presentation. Some impute motive and suppose negative decisions on the part of *Journal* editors, presumably because they are more interested in other sorts of history. The problem is that we do not know what came in over the transom. Thus we cannot say anything certain about editorial judgment. Did they reject papers, or did they not have any to reject? Was there a qualitative difference involved? We do not know because we do not know even how many submissions there were in these fields, to say nothing of their quality.

There is reason to be hesitant in pointing the finger at editorial judgment. In passing, Karl Brooks notes that James C. Malin, a pioneering environmental historian at the University of Kansas, Brooks's own institution, served on the editorial board of the *MVHR* after World War II. At that point, he was surely recognized as an environmental historian. Therefore, appointing him was a gesture in the direction of the field, and one hopes that he would have been alert to any prejudice against it. More interesting, in the 1940s and 1950s, when he was publishing a number of characteristically quirky but often brilliant works in the field, none of it was published in the *MVHR*. Rather he published repeatedly in *Agricultural History* and *Scientific Monthly*.[1] This raises the important question of the role of specialized journals and their relation to mainstream disciplinary journals, or journals of record.

Yet for all the chronological difference in the arrival of these fields on the pages of the journal, there is a kind of intellectual arc that all the fields followed. To a greater or lesser extent these fields—gender the greater, perhaps Native American history the lesser—challenged the founding charter of history as a professional discipline. As such, the fields spent a good deal of time developing concepts, themes, fundamental questions, and distinctive methods appropriate to the novel subject matter. Specialized journals may be the place for that sort of work. For example, a great deal of important work in gender studies was done in *Feminist Studies* before it appeared in the *JAH*. In time, scholars in the field had done that work; they gathered in more practitioners, and they began producing substantial amounts of scholarship for both specialized journals and the *MVHR-JAH*.

The issues of specialization and special-topic journals are important to this larger story of incorporation of new fields and methodological innovations. Moreover, during the past quarter century or so, all the new fields underwent a similar intellectual revolution, analogous but not identical. Still, despite the different issues in each field, I see a convergence or a very important and revealing family resemblance. If it is not already obvious, I should note at this point that I have always been a lumper, not a splitter. The degree of commonality I see may not be apparent at all.

The historical study of women moved from women's history, as a largely compensatory study that included those formerly excluded from history, to gender as a category of analysis. Although this move was formally articulated by Joan Scott in a notable article, one could see it coming.[2] It was a remarkable collective project. The success of this project also established the platform for the emergence of the history of sexuality.

There was an analogous shift in the study of Native Americans, enriched by ethno-history, which got historians closer to everyday experience. The model for study became interactive, with a pluralization of agency. Richard White provided the most compelling formulation with his concept of the "middle ground," which has now been adapted to the study of the interaction of settler societies and indigenous societies on every continent.[3] But that, too, was a collective project, anticipated before its crystallization in his brilliant book.

Environmental history moved in the same direction at about the same time and it, too was a collective project. Early environmental history had focused on environmental policies and attitudes, but gradually the environment came to be understood as a shaper of history, as an actor. This revolution in historiography was most graphically illustrated and effectively theorized in William Cronon's book on Chicago, *Nature's Metropolis: Chicago and the Great West*.[4]

There is more to the resemblance I propose than a similar morphology of development in each field. All these examples explore power and agency as a pattern of relations. Defining power and agency in relational terms is not a new notion; Marx understood it. But in these conceptual innovations, it is more agile, open to more forms of power and sorts of agency, including, in the case of Cronon's book, the nonhuman as well as the human.[5]

There are two more things that the fields all share. I quote from Hoxie, but what he says about Native American history applies to all of these: Not only have the number of participants in history been increased by these changes, as has the diversity of writers and teachers of history, but the real revolution has been the emergence of "new definitions of historical significance." The second point is implicit in all these essays, but it deserves emphasis, for it is the payoff, the whole point of bringing new themes and methods into the discipline. These fields have matured and aspire to reshape the larger interpretation of American history, the "mainstream" narrative, to use Kathy Peiss's term. That is difficult to achieve; disciplines are by nature conservative. In fact, I am puzzled by the relative lack of impact this work, given its quantity and quality, has had on public understanding of the basic or default narrative of United States history. Too often this work is "bracketed," acknowledged but not integrated and not allowed to reshape. There is a second potential for change within each of these fields that has not been realized. They all operate both inside the nation framework and outside of it or beyond it. Yet even as transnational approaches have been developing rapidly in the past decade or so, these specific fields have not been particularly central to that reorientation of scholarship and teaching. Commodities and wars seem to be leading the way.

I come away from these essays intensely aware of the degree to which important developments within the discipline have been interdisciplinary and have depended upon publications in interdisciplinary journals or journals outside of history. In fact, much of the new scholarship we have been discussing has drawn heavily from the social sciences and from poststructuralist literary theories. Much has been gained by these routes. Yet the particular thread of social and cultural theory that has drawn our attention and expanded the domain of our analysis has also narrowed our vision of history in other respects. It has cut us off from social theories of institutional power. As someone trained as an intellectual historian, I have a vested interest in the significance given to discourse. Still I regret the weakening of our connection to the study of institutional power and the power of the state. Sometimes it seems we have exchanged the study of state power (and economic institutions for that matter) to pursue cultural domains too much disconnected from the older concerns.

I think we must connect what we have learned in those new areas to enrich our understanding of the state and economy and vice versa. How is that power acquired and deployed? As recent presidential elections demonstrate, the acquisition and deployment of power has enormous consequences at home and abroad. We must recognize that, wherever that illusive historiographical "mainstream" resides, it involves the state. To borrow a phrase from another discipline, it is time to bring the state back in, but in a way that makes its study richer and more significant. Social history and private life cannot be understood outside of their relation to the state, and the state cannot be understood without the social and cultural history in which it is embedded, a point brilliantly made by Nancy Cott in her *Public Vows: A History of Marriage and the Nation*.[6] We have certainly seen how cultural symbols have been deployed in the interest of state power and the way the issues addressed in these essays have been profoundly affected by various deployments of state power.

With these accounts of convention papers, articles, and book reviews and the question of special fields shaping the field as a whole, I am inclined to suggest the need for some serious thought about persistence and innovation in disciplines, and the historical discipline in particular. Many of my generation were deeply affected by the account of disciplinary change offered by Thomas Kuhn in *The Structure of Scientific Revolutions* (1962 *et seq*).[7] He portrays a powerful conservatism. Kuhn's brilliant work was mostly a thought experiment, with a few historical references, but historians may want a more empirical account of both stasis and transformation. For such a study, these essays provide a valuable starting point.

Such study is particularly important now, for it seems to be a no brainer to say that we are at the edge of a transformation in information technology. If we understand how scholarship moves from topical and specialized venues to the "mainstream," we may be able to usefully contribute to the restructuring that we will see in the next decade or so in a way that enhances the connection between specialized and "comprehensive" journals.

Even right now, with the existing technology of the *Journal of American History*, we might be able to make a first move in the direction of moving specialized scholarship more easily and directly into the mainstream. It would require only a shift in the way occasional reviews of fields are framed. Mostly they are internalist analyses of a field, making the case for the better work, warning against the wrongheadedness of other work, closing with a suggestion for future research in that field. Those articles have their value within the field and even for those outside it. But there could be another kind of review of the field that looks mainly to the implications of the work for the larger enterprise of American history. How might this work be integrated or brought into conversation with the larger themes of the mainstream narrative? Does it undermine that narrative? The question then is not where the subfield goes (as would be the case were we biologists), but rather what new research it might suggest for significant parts of the larger narrative of American history.

Depending how things go, the infrastructure for scholarly communication may encourage either more extreme specialization and fragmentation, or, perhaps with some creative thinking about linkages, cataloguing, and search engines, that default narrative may become more representative of scholarship than it has been. This might be a concern of the OAH as it moves farther into its second century.

NOTES

1. James C. Malin, "Ecology and History," *The Scientific Monthly* 70 (1950): 295–98; Malin, "Man, the State of Nature, and Climax: As Illustrated by Some Problems of the North American Continent," *The Scientific Monthly* 74 (1952), 29–37; Malin, "Soil, Animal, and Plant Relations of the Grassland, Historically Reconsidered," *The Scientific Monthly* 76 (1953): 207–20; Malin, "Space and History: Reflections on the Closed-Space Doctrines of Turner and Mackinder and the Challenge to Those Ideas by the Air Age, Parts I and II," *Agricultural History* 18 (1944): 65–74, 107–26.

2. Joan W. Scott, "Gender: A Useful Category of Historical Analysis," *American Historical Review* 91 (1986): 1053–75.

3. Richard White, *The Middle Ground: Indians, Empires, and Republics in the Great Lakes Region, 1650–1815* (New York: Cambridge University Press, 1991); Stuart B. Schwartz, ed., *Implicit Understandings: Observing, Reporting, and Reflecting on the Encounters Between Europeans and Other Peoples in the Early Modern Era* (New York: Cambridge University Press, 1994).

4. William Cronon, *Nature's Metropolis: Chicago and the Great West* (New York: W. W. Norton, 1991).

5. On this point of multiplying a heterogeneous chain or network of "actors" in explaining causation, historians may profit by exploring the ideas of Actor-Network Theory associated with the French sociologists of science, Bruno Latour and Michel Callon, not so much as a method but as a set of ideas about social life and historical change. A recent summary view is Bruno Latour, *Reassembling the Social: An Introduction to Actor-Network Theory* (New York: Oxford University Press, 2005). For a discussion of the usefulness of these ideas for studying urban history, see Thomas Bender, "History, Theory, & the Metropolis," at www.metropolitanstudies.de. It is in the Center for Metropolitan Studies Working Papers Series, 2006–2007, #005. 2006.

6. Nancy F. Cott, *Public Vows: A History of Marriage and the Nation* (Cambridge, MA: Harvard University Press, 2000).

7. (Chicago: University of Chicago Press).

Part III

EDITING THE JOURNAL

22

A Learned Journal Adjusts to Change

Lewis C. Perry

When first asked to speak at the 2007 meeting, I imagined standing at the podium as the "2000-year-old editor," recalling a pre-automation epoch when the *Journal of American Historians (JAH)* was edited and produced very differently from today. In reality, my editorial experience began in 1978, which was not so long ago, and ended in the mid-1980s. My memory goes back a little further, for I subscribed to the *Mississippi Valley Historical Review (MVHR)* sometime around 1963 or 1964, and as a graduate student I studied many articles from *MVHR* issues of previous years. It is regrettable that we cannot hear the voices of previous editors who are no longer among us. In particular, I wish we could hear the voice of my predecessor, Martin Ridge, whose highly successful editorship had spanned twelve of the first fourteen years of the *JAH*. I retained and followed most of the procedures he put in place in the editorial office. When I resigned the editorship in 1984, Martin was chosen to lead the search for my successor. His is an important voice to try to remember today.

I was glad to discover in my file of editing-days memorabilia a 1976 document that will let me present Martin's voice. It consists of his answers to questions sent by Professor Norris Hundley of UCLA concerning the *JAH*, "its purpose, philosophy, scope, the kinds of articles being sought, etc." These were intended to be shared in a graduate class introducing students to scholarly journals in the field. Martin began by pointing out that the *JAH* was "the organ" of the OAH.

> It is therefore a magazine with an owner constituency. Unlike a private magazine, where the readers have no relationship to the publication, the *Journal* is directly accountable. As the Editor, I am accountable to the Board of the Organization, not to my University for what appears in the magazine. . . . The Organization of American Historians has defined the purpose of the *Journal* as providing to the membership a learned publication dealing with the history of the United States, its foreign policy, and its dependencies.

After noting that he could not comment on "the philosophy of the *Journal* prior to his editorship," though various editors had obviously interpreted the organization's goals in different ways, Martin went on:

> It has been my purpose to publish a magazine that has no ideological or methodological biases. Therefore, any area of American history and any methodology or ideology is acceptable, provided the essay attains high standards of scholarship. This means that we are concerned not so much with what an author says but whether he is the best exponent of that position. From time to time, as a result, essays appear in the *Journal* which contradict each other. From time to time, also, essays approach the same subject with different methodologies and arrive at different conclusions, albeit not contradictory ones.

From Martin's point of view, there were "essentially" seven types of essays, which he called "edited documents, methodological essays, new material, revision [of] fact, revision of interpretation, surveys of literature, and essays on the state of the art." Generally, the *Journal* excluded documents [I certainly had one such rejection], methodological essays (which belonged in more specialized newsletters), and new material devoid of interpretation. This meant that most published essays were either "revisionist in character" or dealt with "the state of the art and the dialogue as it appears in the literature. I am not sure [said Martin] that this is always for the best, but, nevertheless, this is what we have been doing for ten years, and it seems to have met with some success." The editorial board had adhered regularly to a preference for articles dealing with broader subjects and, in addition, essays "where the ideology or methodology is not as important as the substance." To ensure breadth and fairness over time, the composition of the editorial board changed regularly, with a goal of representing "different historical schools" and giving "all elements in the profession" reason to feel that "they have an attachment to the magazine." The editor's role was "that of a servant of the profession who will try to bring to publication the scholarship of the practitioners regardless of where they stand in the historical spectrum."

Martin also wrote at length about the book-review section of the *Journal*, which he considered "as important as the articles." The key points he mentioned were these: he had eliminated the publication of unsigned book notes to avoid "anonymous slanders." The goal was to review "all serious scholarly work which should be of interest to the profession." Coverage had been broadened to include works in American Studies, political science, economics, and humanities in the broadest sense as well as "the narrowest kind of historical monographs." "The real question that has troubled us here," he added, "is to what extent we must involve ourselves with vanity publication." Reviewers were selected from files arranged analytically as well as chronologically. "Serious scholars" were invited to "let us know about their professional work so that we can use them as reviewers." The goal was to identify experts who would write informative, critical reviews, but sometimes unavoidably "we have permitted either a vendetta or mutual admiration society to function." There were word limits, but "this is far more flexible than one might imagine."

There are many issues we might discuss here. I doubt that the ideologies and methodologies characterizing "historical schools" or defining "the historical spectrum" look the same today. But there is still much to be said for the good old-fashioned fairness that Martin championed. In 1979, replying to the same questions from Professor Hundley and his graduate students, I began by reaffirming the principles Martin had outlined: not only fairness, but also accountability, high standards, a quest for excellence. The *MVHR* had been "the first scholarly journal to which I subscribed," and I, too, thought of the OAH as a learned society. (I'm not sure whether that would be a controversial stand today, but it might sound quaint or anachronistic to some.) In applying for the editorship, I had emphasized the many "interesting," and sometimes "indispensable," articles found in the pages of the *MVHR* and *JAH*. Though new historical journals were being launched every year, the *JAH* was still the only journal that a diverse audience of American historians and practitioners were likely to read. That audience expected "the most up-to-date, well informed, solidly researched articles in American history" and expected "these articles to be of more than passing importance and to speak beyond a narrow subdiscipline or specialty." "The strength of the journal," I pointed out, "lies in these three things; a proud tradition, a wide readership, and its standing as the journal of all Americanists." I would always take it as my responsibility to protect the *Journal*'s reputation as the outstanding scholarly journal in the general field of U.S. history.

Martin was around during my first semester in Bloomington. Some suggested that this was in case I needed his help or fell on my face (I was very inexperienced) but Martin, I'm sure, never expressed such doubts or encouraged them in others. He was supportive, helpful, and very careful not to interfere. I enjoyed getting to know him. To my initial surprise, there was virtually no interaction between the *JAH* and the *American Historical Review*, though both were housed on the same floor and in the same department. Perhaps the greatest help in my transition came from Robert Gunderson, who was serving as interim editor that summer, who had been close to Martin and, in his own right, was a former editor of the *Quarterly Journal of Speech*. Bob was one of the most joyous, gregarious, wittiest, and savviest senior colleagues I ever met, and he prepared me well for all the lessons in human nature I could expect by way of authors, reviewers, Indiana associates, and others in the profession. Bob explained the choices I had, and encouraged me to make whatever changes made sense to me and to have fun doing so. I hasten to add that the executive secretary of the OAH, Dick Kirkendall, also a professor in the IU history department, consulted with me regularly, listened to my plans and aspirations, gave lots of good advice, and never, to my recollection, tried to intervene in *JAH* policy. I had occasions in future years to say that he was my model for the kind of administrator I would like to be: clear, direct, open, supportive. Dick joined me in putting the printing contract out for bids, and in the process deriving savings from a new design, typeface, binding, and other changes that kept costs under control as I tried to make changes.

Every change of editors is an opportunity for change, and most candidates for the job have some agenda for change. My fixation was on the articles. Before applying for the position, I asked friends and colleagues their opinions about the *JAH*, and some described it as less exciting than it used to be. Martin Ridge had noted on several occasions that fewer senior scholars were submitting articles; most submissions came from recent PhD's. Although new developments in the profession were marked by articles in the *Journal of Social History*, the *Journal of Interdisciplinary History*, *Signs*, or the revitalized *American Quarterly*, the *JAH* seemed to be on the sidelines. I expressed a goal of finding and publishing more articles that represented the best of the current, lively moment in U.S. historical scholarship. It turned out that my views were shared by some on the editorial search committee and the executive board of the OAH. Martin Ridge had already made some nominations to the editorial board to reflect new fields of emphasis in American history. And once I was on board I felt a lot of support in the profession at large as I did my best to make the *JAH* better reflect the vigor of historical scholarship and the diversity of professional life in our times. Put simply, I never felt I was in a fight.

While avoiding the appearance of any abrupt break with our traditions, I did everything possible to signal a new spirit of openness and excitement. New nominations to the editorial board helped send out the message. A new design was introduced, with a cover symbolizing the refractions of our past in our current practices. I was delighted that many correspondents appreciated the symbolism and even the humor of the design. We had not retired the steamboat! Meanwhile, I took every opportunity to entice, solicit, and do whatever else I could to draw more exciting articles in a wider field of history, including some with public usefulness. I wrote letters and buttonholed senior scholars at conventions urging them to write and submit articles. I encouraged the authors of good papers to expand them for publication. I was very happy when the *New York Times* in June 1979 featured a story on one of our articles and its relevance to the ongoing second round of Strategic Arms Limitations Talks (SALT II).

I came to the *JAH* with an abiding love for the kinds of magazines that had been so important to intellectual culture in the United States for a long time. Obviously the tradition of the learned journal was foremost, but I envisioned a magazine that you could hold in your hand and read. I wanted to publish more articles—at least five each issue—to increase the odds that every reader would find at least one or two of interest. I also added some "commentary" features on recent and future directions in U.S. historiography. To accomplish these goals, we transferred some features from the back of the magazine—news and personals, obituaries, the convention report, and most other reports—to the OAH *Newsletter* and eliminated whatever seemed ephemeral. But I gave up on a scheme, my own and that of some of the people who interviewed me, to print fewer and longer book reviews. The replies to a questionnaire (circulated via the *Newsletter*) convinced me that such a change would be anathema to the readership. But if we reviewed about the same number of books, we resisted pressures to review more and more books. The principal controversy we faced concerned whether the *JAH* should review textbooks. I squelched any talk of being a "journal of record," if only because we did not work from a small stable of reviewers whose judgments we could stand behind, alter, or reject. We did add many potential reviewers to the files, many of them from public history or other groups that complained of being neglected by the OAH, and we deliberately tried to diversify our choices of reviewers. By 1983 over 50 percent of our reviewers were appearing in the *JAH* for the first time. I thought this had some good effects, but it's not clear that it made the reviews better or worse or less often complained about.

We certainly published more articles in issues with fewer pages than the *Journal* had done in the past. As I look back over the table of contents, I feel fairly good about the results. Readers said nice things. One compliment (I guess) arrived after the printer accidentally placed thirty-two pages of advertisements at the front of one issue, before the title page. On the sheet conveying the printer's apology, Bruce Kuklick, who had done so much to enliven and improve the *American Quarterly*, wrote to me:

> Lew
> This cheered me enormously.
> I have an album of errors like this, both public & private. I've been feeling so miserable about the "new" *JAH* that I'm consoled a bit to know you're fallible.

But reading back on things I wrote in 1978 about my goals and, later on, about our achievements, I smile at their confidence and excitement. How youthful they seem! And I am well aware that I did not go in directions that some advised and that have become commonplace in the *JAH* and elsewhere: previews and synopses in the editor's words of what the articles are about, special volumes of solicited articles, and symposia with critiques and an author's reply accompanying an accepted article. I thought good, well-titled articles should stand on their own; I preferred to have articles accepted in the traditional way, with "blind" readings and revisions. As I said in an editorial board meeting where these possibilities were discussed, I was most comfortable with a self-effacing style as editor.

Besides, I was definitely, if usually happily, overworked and just trying to keep up. I got terrific help, but with frequent turnover, from a staff of three graduate student assistants, a part-time associate editor, and a full-time secretary. A part-time copy editor joined the staff only at the end of my term. I read every submitted manuscript, as Martin Ridge had done, and like him, I took responsibility for all the copyediting and marking all corrections on proof. I taught half-time in the IU department and usually had a heavy committee load (not quite as heavy, though, as Dick Kirkendall's). I never could give as much time to competing for articles or promoting them as I would have liked. Then, too, I did think of the *JAH* as a learned journal and, by the end of my tenure, I thought of the editor as de facto spokesman in the OAH for those who still valued it as a learned society at a time when it was being transformed into a professional organization pursuing other missions and reaching out to new constituencies who were presumed, perhaps not always accurately, not to have that conception. Incorrigible if nothing else, I voiced the opinion when running for the executive board in 1996 that "I have always felt that the better we function as a learned society—with lots of room for honest criticism and intellectual exchange—the better we will do as a professional organization advancing our mutual interests in increasing support for scholarship, teaching at all levels, and public history."

In 1984 and 1985, when the OAH was searching for my successor, I had quite a few phone calls from finalists for the position. When answering various questions, I always stressed what a great job it was, especially because there was so much goodwill throughout the profession, so many people who wanted you to do well and were glad, even grateful, that you were working to uphold and advance the *Journal*. I loved working with the graduate students. Of many good friends who worked with me, I have to mention Ed McClellan, associate editor, acting editor, and later editor of the *History of Education Quarterly*. I loved working with younger authors and talking about writing and publishing with students and beginning scholars. (I did a lot of that, as Martin had before me.) I loved meeting senior historians, from all parts of the country, whom I might otherwise never have met. For me, in an age of specialization, it was wonderful to have a job that kept me in touch with all fields of U.S. history. I appreciated the regular cycle of bringing an issue to completion every three months. This is so different from working on a book or even an article that takes years; I thought of it as like going on with a play when the curtain rises. No more changes. Move on.

23

Editing and the Challenges of Specialization, Audiences, Sites of Practice

David Thelen

When he asked me to "explore your own experiences as editor," Dick Kirkendall suggested: "You could tackle such questions as how you saw the journal when you took the job, what you hoped to accomplish, what you believe you accomplished, and why you did not accomplish more." The questions assumed that I approached the editorship with goals and then spent fourteen years trying to accomplish those goals. As I thought about how to answer, I recognized that I fundamentally experienced the editorship as an ongoing process of questioning and discovery, of trial and error, a continuing, evolving, sometimes contested, process, with rising and falling confidence, attempting to figure out what the *JAH* could be and do. And since our product was a journal of record in American history, the quest to figure out what the *JAH* could do was simultaneously an exploration of what the content and practice of American history could be and do. Indeed, my memories of editing the *JAH* are inseparable from my evolving thoughts about historical practice and scholarship. Above all, editing the *JAH* was never an individual task; it was the work of a team or rather teams of individuals and indeed of the whole community of American historians who so generously responded to requests for all kinds of help. Evolving ideas of mission emerged, not in isolation or from afar, but from the everyday challenges of work: what to write to help an author bring more significance or clarity to a manuscript; what resources to seek to implement a new initiative; what about their work to ask museum curators or Russian scholars to bring to the attention of the *JAH*. As I was preparing this essay, I was torn between zeroing in on what I learned about editing the *JAH* or stepping back to reflect on what I learned about our discipline. What follows is a little of both.

Before I could decide whether I even wanted to do the job, I had to overcome real reservations I associated in advance with the word *editor*. I still hesitated when facing the choice between *lie* and *lay*, *which* and *that*. And during the on-campus interview, I realized how inadequately I had checked the accuracy of my footnotes before publishing my books. I feared that the title was both intimidating and a poor fit with my strengths. But during the interview I spent a morning with Otto Pflanze, editor of the *AHR*, and he helped me to see that editing was basically about organizing people and ideas. That was a familiar and enticing prospect. And a little while later, when Susan Armeny joined the *JAH* staff, I could breathe more deeply because I knew that the *JAH* had a real editor.

I approached the editorship with some interrelated assumptions about organizing that derived from how my scholarship had reinforced my experiences with community organizing. I'm not sure how fully developed these assumptions about organizing and practice were when I became editor in 1985 nor how widely I articulated them at the time, but I am sure in retrospect that they helped me make sense of what I was doing as editor. Growing up on Chicago's South Side in the home of parents who combined community organizing with their other roles, I was raised with models of practice that I remade on my own terms when I went to Antioch College, where we alternated a quarter of study with a quarter of work and where we were always pushed to interrogate theory with practice, study with activism. Organizing was about providing means for people from different backgrounds to explore and make things in common from which they could recognize and use a fuller range of their personalities and roles. In other words it was about empowerment. With these experiences and prejudices I assumed that theory emerged from practice, that practice was usually ahead of, more open-ended, and more creative than the capacity of theory to specify. Practice put ideas into motion; theory made them stand still.

Having gone to graduate school in Madison in the mid-1960s, I was immersed in the sense that history must somehow be able to advance a better world. But I can't now reconstruct just how I thought this would happen: Was it the topic? Method? Questions? Process? Audience? Lessons? Classroom? Publications? But I did know for sure that it was about the intersection between civic activism and scholarship.

In trying to contextualize how I would approach connections between scholarship and activism as editor I think I was part of a generation of people who became historians with a faith in an unlimited democratic future, propelled along by social movements with a vague hope to make history more democratic both in content and practice, from the bottom up, in a project that included scholarship, teaching, and civics. When those movements faded, and with them faith in a democratic future, faith that all things were possible, we were left unsure what we wanted the historical profession to look like, how we wanted to experience it, and above all how we should relate to people outside the academy. By the time I became editor in 1985, I thought the discipline (and the *JAH*) had already become significantly more democratic in its content. It embraced voices and experiences that would have been unthinkable a generation earlier. However, our grassroots initiatives to democratize practice through museums, films, or community oral-history projects had basically failed to transform the academic cultures of historical practice. Although we had succeeded in bringing previously invisible actors out of the shadows where they could contest established narratives and textbooks (and become new specialties in academic departments), and although we had pried open sites of practice to include women (and less successfully representatives of other groups), we had failed to fulfill the larger, if inchoate, vision for democratizing the practice of history. We had assimilated to rather than transformed existing practices, hierarchies, rewards, and privileges.

For me the key to widening horizons was to invite and encourage a wide variety of people to participate, to converse with each other, to keep things open for dialogue and for assembly in new ways so that individuals could be seen and heard by people they hadn't previously met, to explore different sides of their natures, different roles they inhabited or could imagine inhabiting, different perspectives. I hoped to create and nurture structures where people could bring concerns that they felt had been marginalized by privileged practices of professional production, where people could find and connect with people from other backgrounds, to discover new practices to widen horizons. In retrospect I marvel at how much open-endedness I seemed to thrive on, sometimes, I fear, to the discomfort of those who preferred more certainty, but I clearly liked ideas that were in motion, capable of meeting mutual and reciprocal needs, capable of helping people explore different sides of their natures, different roles they inhabited or could imagine inhabiting.

I basically brought the same approach to ideas when I became editor: seeking out voices, putting them in dialogue. From my identification with consumer roles in my scholarship and organizing I approached the *JAH* with the conviction that the *JAH* belonged to the readers. My first job, as a result, was to listen to how readers experienced the *JAH*, what they used it for and how, what they liked and disliked about it, what they wanted the *JAH* to be and do, what changes would make it more interesting and valuable to them. And so the first thing I did was to enclose in my first issue a detailed questionnaire that sought to find out what readers wanted. (Over the next years, I would send out four other surveys so that readers could advise on directions.) We ultimately got over 1,000 responses to that first survey, and I wrote up the results in the June 1986 issue in hopes of starting a dialogue about the *JAH* with readers. Pablo Picasso once defined a painting in a way that evoked for me how I was beginning to see my challenge as editor. A painting happens, Picasso said, at the place where the painter, who puts on canvas half of what it takes to create a painting, meets the viewer, who brings the other half, and in the exchange the painting takes place. I thought that way about the *JAH*.

While I was awaiting results from the survey I was learning how the people who made the *JAH* happen, the staff in Bloomington and also the editorial board (the painter side of the painting) could become places for exploring possible directions for the *JAH*. In those first months I was learning for myself what Lew Perry had told me had been a delightful surprise for him, the joy that comes from being part of a community working hard, creatively, intensely, sacrificing time and energy, to make a common product. I still remember fondly the feelings of connectedness and community I felt in our little houses on Atwater Street. And the staff discussions of article submissions were simply the best discussions of historical scholarship I have ever participated in. I'm sure all the editors would agree that this experience of a common mission that drew in individuals across the whole profession was one of the best parts of editing the *JAH*. And in my particular case, I needed intense engagement, to solicit ideas from others and try out ideas on others, to listen to how staff and board members made sense of what we were hearing from readers, in order to develop both new initiatives and the confidence and capacity to try them.

From more than 1,000 responses to this first survey we began to visualize outlines of what I later came to frame through other surveys and experiences in larger terms as the greatest challenge for the *JAH* during my editorship. As a journal of record for American historians, the *JAH* had first to recognize and address needs and uses readers wanted to make of a scholarly literature that was exploding in volume and specialties. With our central position in the field, the challenge for the *JAH* was whatever challenges readers experienced when they engaged that literature. By 1985 the challenge was not to recognize and include the new specialties in articles and reviews. Lew had already opened up the *JAH* to include new specialties. The real problem, readers seemed to be saying, was to engage and master this literature. They felt obliged, sometimes eager, to know everything new but, at the same time, they reported that it was an increasingly hopeless task for any individual to "keep up with the (my) field." In that first survey, most readers reported that they used book reviews and lists of recent scholarship but didn't read most of the articles.

Readers wanted book reviews, the most widely used part of the *Journal*, to be a place where they could feel that at a glance they could see the full range of new scholarship and get at least a preliminary sense of whether a new book was worth their attention. So we published over a hundred short reviews in each issue. Here in one place, if not through reviews then through lists of articles and dissertations that we also published, they could hope at least to see it all, to get a quarterly overview. To meet this need, we also sought out essays that tried to map the most important new developments in a field, such as environmental or diplomatic history.

From readers' comments, it grew increasingly clear that readers approached an article differently from its author. They brought different needs and criteria than specialized referees carried to their responsibilities. The same individual experienced the *JAH* in different roles, and those roles sometimes even clashed within individuals as well as among specialists in an article's subject and people with only a casual interest in its topic. In fact, I recall with a shudder even now how often participants in that first questionnaire called *JAH* articles "narrow, overspecialized, and boring." I learned that it was a mistake for the *JAH* to distinguish scholarship (what the *JAH* was supposedly about) from teaching, because many readers looked to the *JAH* when they thought about what they wanted to do in the classroom. The distinction between scholarship and teaching was not only strange and artificial, it was also foreign to the traditions of the *JAH* and its predecessor journal, the *MVHR*, for which teaching was a more visible and central concern than it had become in recent decades. Recognizing that the same person might be both a teacher and a scholar led me to recognize that readers brought other roles and lenses through which they approached articles: as family member, citizen, hobbyist, and above all as human being with different traditions of ethnicity, religion, race, community. Individuals became historians not simply to make and read published specialized contributions. The *JAH* was most successful when we could appeal to a variety of roles and expectations that people had brought to becoming historians.

Readers repeatedly told us they wanted the *JAH* not only to bring new work to their attention but also to help them tame and make sense of the exploding, sprawling, diverse literature. Over the years, mostly in the course of evaluating 250 article submissions each year, of reading and engaging not only an article but also multiple readers' reports, I came to blur what I heard from readers into my own emerging sense of what was best and worst, exciting and depressing, about scholarship in American history.

In making editorial decisions, I began with a commitment to the standard three criteria that I believe I inherited. We asked referees to judge articles by these criteria: soundness (are points documented? Is writing clear?), significance (does it adequately address these questions: So what? Who cares?) and originality (Is its contribution new, original?) I observed over the years that in practice the three criteria were not equal. Referees usually found submissions to be sound but rarely to be significant and so the criterion that really mattered was originality. An original contribution would usually be a specialized one, a new method, theory, fact, term that could best be appreciated by other specialists. Readers often said that they wanted the *JAH* to publish the newest, most original ideas and discoveries.

The problem was that readers also told us that they didn't read most of the articles. Any one article would, at best, appeal only to a few specialists. Of course we, as I'm sure other editors, tried all kinds of things in editing to try to widen the appeal of an article, but I think the implicit value of originality, particularly as it was taught in graduate school, worked against engagement with a wide range of people interested in American history. In a subsequent survey, readers said that the thing they liked most about the prevailing practice of American history was its embrace of originality, and the thing they liked least about it was its embrace of originality!

With what I heard as an injunction to look for ways of transcending or connecting content specialties, I came to believe that the mission of a journal like the *JAH* had to change from what it had been in the early days of professional scholarship. A century ago editors like J. Franklin Jameson of the *AHR* saw themselves (and were seen by new academics) as policemen, charged with advancing a profession against amateurs merely dabbling in history, trying to teach people how to make sound and original contributions. But when scholarship exploded in specialties and audiences, the initiative for advancing original knowledge passed to the graduate seminars where apprentices were taught the specialty, where the originality of contributions to that specialty could best be advanced and appreciated. A modern broad-gauged journal like the *JAH*, by contrast, has first to be a place where readers can confidently get an overview of the latest work. As long as book reviews and lists of recent scholarship did this well, I thought we could sometimes use the article section to experiment with ways of creating discussion across specialties and practices, about how to practice and tame literature.

This was hard conversation to present-day ears because the language of originality had strangely left our field without much thoughtful reflection on the practice of history and connections with audiences. We couldn't even name the problem. I am eternally grateful to a senior professor of American history at the University of Heidelberg for making this point vivid. It was a snowy February day in Bavaria, a meeting of the historian members of the German Association of American Studies, and I was talking about originality, significance, and soundness as criteria for judging scholarship. As soon as I finished speaking, this professor, Detlef Junker, raised his hand. Professor Thelen, he insisted, you don't understand. The most important criterion for scholarship is "whether it contributes to human wisdom." I stared at him, dumbstruck. In my whole career I had never heard anyone connect the word "wisdom" with academic scholarship. But I also sensed immediately that this man, coming from a university founded in 1385, was somehow right.

I decided to test whether he and I were alone in this. I was preparing another survey of members, this time listing various statements about what history should be, and asking readers to check whether they strongly agreed, agreed, disagreed, with the statement. So I added "History should contribute to human wisdom" to the forty-one other statements we asked readers to agree or disagree with. The result? It came in second of the forty-two! This is not the place or time to deconstruct "human wisdom" or the possibility of having any now, but this exchange made me realize that there were powerfully different conceptions of what history could be and do from the ones we had been employing.

Readers seemed to want not to listen to lectures—single voiced monographic articles—but to eavesdrop on and join in conversations that were already in progress. They wanted multiple perspectives on issues, multiple voices, which seemed to invite them to think about different ways they wanted to enter an issue, to figure out where they might jump in and what they wanted to add to the conversation. So we developed roundtables and special issues around a theme or perspective we hoped would have wider appeal than a monographic article. And indeed they generally got fuller reader response, even if in one memorable case it was a chorus of outrage, than the more typical scholarly articles.

I realize that, so far, I have been slighting the task that took most of my time, that is, evaluating scholarly submissions, and the content that took up most of the journal's article space, namely, monographic articles. I'm not dwelling on them because the *JAH* will inevitably receive a couple hundred submissions each year over the transom. I knew from personal experience why authors wanted to submit articles to the *JAH*. I got tenure at Missouri because the *JAH* had accepted my article in 1969. An editor can get enough good articles to fill the *JAH* without any special effort. The criteria for evaluation are pretty clear, and, in any case, specialized referees, not editorial staff, usually made the specialized application of those criteria. I will confess to ambivalence about this process. I really enjoyed engaging a variety of perspectives on any particular article, and I enjoyed thinking about how to help an author present a contribution more clearly. These were the times when I felt most immersed in the field. At the same time, reading all these articles sometimes left me sympathetic to many readers' criticisms of scholarship in general: too self-referential, too fashion-conscious, too specialized, too academic.

I thought that listening to historians think about engaging different kinds of audiences than specialized academics, different uses than original scholarly monographs, I might at once find what I could contribute to thinking about what historians do and, at the same time, perhaps, address the common concerns of our readers. The haunting paradox for history in the late 1980s and 1990s, one that beckoned to me as one the *JAH* could address, was that many people were complaining about a declining popular interest in historical scholarship, about popular historical illiteracy, at the very moment when popular interest in history was exploding in museums, films, oral history projects, historic sites, genealogy. If historians wanted to engage broader audiences, they clearly needed to look for them in some other arena than scholarly journals and academic presses. The problem was not that popular interests did not exist; it was that they were invisible to many academics.

I hoped that by shifting the focus from content to practice, and particularly from product to reception, from scholar to audience, from the painter to the viewer of the painting, we might simultaneously engage more readers and broaden the horizon of history and its scholarship. One way to meet this need was to seek articles that addressed issues of practice and method and audience, either explicitly or implicitly, even when they were apparently "about" specialized topics like gender in New Orleans in 1840 or U.S.-Pakistan policy in 1948. Articles that addressed practice and method seemed to engage both more readers and a fuller range of an individual reader's multiple roles than those that simply made an original contribution to a specialized topic of content. But routine article submissions were still understandably geared to what authors thought specialized referees would be looking for.

I came to believe that we needed other ways of explicitly addressing issues of practice. I thought we might broaden how we conceived historical practice, how we understood both *history* and *American*, if we looked at where and how an historian engaged a variety of people and groups: for example, museum visitors, or a community interested in making an oral-history project, or audiences for a film or TV program, or university students in Brazil, or television viewers in Germany interested in how an historian might frame a contemporary presidential election. The *JAH* could make a major contribution by widening the arenas in which we evaluated scholarship from specialized books and monographs to sites where historians engaged wider audiences—arenas like museum exhibits, historic sites, films, oral-history projects, and foreign scholars who had to introduce ideas to students and readers in different cultures. I expected that museum curators or Mexican Americanists could both contribute and model a wider range of ways of thinking about how to connect scholars and audiences, painter and viewer, the two worlds that had to come together to make the painting. I thought that the key to engaging different audiences was to zero in on the different sites of practice, to draw the *JAH* into the different conversations about history in these different sites.

When we imagined broadening the horizon of what appeared in the *JAH* to include new arenas—museums, films, archives, oral-history projects, web sites, international scholarship—we faced new challenges because we were entering areas where we in Bloomington lacked competence. We developed the title of "contributing editor" and recruited good people with these specialties to assume responsibility for those areas—whether it was arranging reviews of museum exhibits or reporting the best new scholarship in Argentina or Japan— under overall direction and final editing from Bloomington. The contributions of contributing editors were essential, not only because of the specialized competence they brought, but also because conversations with the contributing editors kept the *JAH* alive to other ways of practicing history, ways beyond printed academic scholarship published in the United States.

Stepping further back, I now believe that the *JAH*'s initiative to internationalize the practice of American history was responding to the ways that economic globalization, international cultural circulation, and postcolonial movements were challenging modern history's founding faith in the desirability and capacity of nation and state to meet people's needs, resolve their differences, solve their problems, and be a central object of their identify and allegiance. These larger developments eroded an earlier faith in coherent nation-states and national cultures and the nation-centered historiographies that advanced them. If nation and state were to collapse as the core narratives of history, what was left from the discipline's traditions or could be imagined in the future as organizing topics or themes, subjects, or narratives for history? At home New Left and New Right questioned the desirability and capacity of national government to solve problems. Seeking out help from Americanists all over the world who were far more sophisticated in thinking about transnational content and practice, I came to believe a journal of American history should demonstrate just how central the American nation or state or culture is to understanding people, ideas, and institutions. These had once seemed possible to explain in national terms but now seemed to make better sense in transnational perspectives: things like black consciousness, the creation of the Boeing 757 or Chevy Nova, pragmatism, novels, paintings, music, even neoconservatism, to say nothing of the human beings who lived their lives in circuits between countries. In retrospect, transnational perspectives on American history were clearly emerging in response to the same pressures I was responding to, but I am proud of three special issues in 1999 that illustrated possibilities of theory, content, and practice: one on translations of the Declaration of Independence, one on Mexican-American dialogue, and one on a variety of themes. I came to see American history, indeed the practice of history, in much broader terms. I became interested in the different ways historians in different cultures introduced history to the next generation of students and professionals when, whatever their own parochialisms, they were not driven by the hard-driving, self-enclosing professionalism of the American academy.

We tried to bring into focus, make more visible and explicit, different ways, beyond printed scholarship, where historians were using and practicing and connecting with more diverse readers, where they had to be broader or at least different in locating audiences and defining contributions. This quest would lead me ultimately to want to know more about audiences, about how people understood and used the past in their everyday lives. By the time my perspective on the painting had gravitated ever more toward curiosity about what viewers brought, I knew it was time for someone else to explore how the *JAH* could define and address the challenges of scholarly literature and practice in American history. But I will never forget the incredible, unique, and fun privilege the *JAH* presented for collaborating with such a wonderful range of generous people who have made American history the creative and exciting world that it is.

24

Putting Together American History

Joanne Meyerowitz

When I served as editor of the *Journal of American History* (*JAH*) (1999 to 2004), I learned, among other things, that editing differs, mostly in good ways, from what we usually do as academic historians. For one, editing produces a tangible product, a new issue every three months as opposed to a new book every five, ten, or fifteen years. It provides the pleasure, on a regular basis, of holding a new object in hand, admiring its craft, and taking pride in a task accomplished. Also, the nature of the collaboration, with editors, staff, editorial board, peer reviewers, and authors, creates a cooperative venture for those of us trained in graduate school to spend most of our work time solo. It serves as a useful reminder that a group of people can accomplish more together than any single person could possibly accomplish alone. And finally editing involves a different kind of creativity than does authorship. The creativity comes not just in the suggestions an editor might make to an author but also in the roundtables, commissioned essays, and special issues that allow us, at least occasionally, to shake up the genre of the scholarly journal article and to think about how we might benefit by doing so.

At various points during my tenure, I thought of editing the *Journal* in the same way one might imagine directing a play or a film. The editor is not the star; she does behind-the-scenes work. But what editing offers, at its best, is the chance to be an *auteur*. That, at least, is how I sometimes liked to imagine it. The trick, it seemed to me, came, not only in eliciting the best possible performances from the various authors, but also in bringing it all together in some striking way. In other words, the point was not simply to enhance the individual performances but to create a whole that was more than just the sum of all the individual parts. A more humble way to think of it, and what I think I emphasized when I interviewed for the job, was that the *Journal*, with all its individual articles, roundtables, and reviews, could create a conversation, in which all Americanists might take part, even if only by listening. I still like the metaphor: the *JAH* as a site of discussion or collective reflection.

At the end of the 1990s, when I took on the job as editor, the possibilities for such conversation seemed to be endangered. For around a decade, various historians had pointed to a problem that they sometimes called fragmentation. They worried that social and cultural history had undermined the narrative of the American past. Social history, it was said repeatedly, had spawned a proliferation of specialized subfields that had, through their sheer multiplicity, overwhelmed the writing of a coherent American history. According to some, the ragged margins had erased the solid center. Compounding the problem, cultural history called into question the narrative itself, not so much the narrow content of the traditional narrative but the very attempt to tell an overarching story at all. And then the internationalization and transnationalization of history challenged the nation as the default unit of analysis. In the midst of these perceived crises, various U.S. historians called for a new synthesis or a new attention to narrative, and at the same time their opponents denounced synthesis and narrative as exclusionary and simplistic endeavors, possibly even forms of nationalism or imperialism. Somewhat late in these debates, in the summer of 2000, historian David Oshinksy published an Op-Ed piece in the *New York Times* under the headline "The Humpty Dumpty of Scholarship: American History Has Broken in Pieces. Can It Be Put Together Again?"[1] And that question,"Can It Be Put Together Again?" or maybe "How Should It Be Put Together Again?" was something I pondered as editor.

By definition, the *JAH* attempted, in one way or another, to put it together again. It is nominally a journal of American history, and the title itself announces that there is an American history worth pursuing under that name. Taking on the job as editor of an unspecialized, broadly defined, national journal required thinking about what American history might mean. My own tendency is to let a hundred flowers bloom. My scholarly career is a product of social and cultural history, and I generally celebrate the specialized subfields rather than decry their centripetal force. However, even with my relatively high tolerance for multitudes of histories spinning out in multiple directions, and even with my general skepticism of overarching narratives, I still felt there had to be some kind of connection or at least a conversation. Why else have a *Journal of American History*? We could just content ourselves with all the specialized journals. But many of us still teach U.S. history, even if our research is specialized in some subset of it. We have a practical need to bring it all together, to talk to one another about what we do and what it all might mean.

What I soon realized as editor was that fragmentation was, most fundamentally, a myth. At the time of the initial fragmentation panic, social historians tended to write of discrete cultures, subcultures, semi-autonomous cultures, neighborhoods, communities, and cities. In that model, fragmentation pointed to all the discrete groups and locales that we treated as separate entities. But by the 1990s, the discrete units or separate entities approach had already declined, supplanted by negotiations, middle grounds, hybridities, and syncretisms, and then, by the middle of the decade, by translocal and transnational connections and circulations. Our own approaches had shifted in such a way that we now routinely connected the so-called fragments. And not just with the overarching narratives that still appear in every textbook, and not just with the shared methods and standards of evidence that characterize much of our historical writing.

The very shift from semi-autonomous cultures to middle grounds to translocal and transnational circulations suggested that something else tied it all together: the unacknowledged ways in which we all, in our various subfields, borrowed from and picked up on the same ideas at virtually the same time. When a way of thinking permeated the atmosphere, similar phrases and ideas seemed to appear almost simultaneously in parallel form in disparate fields. It seemed to me that a scholarly journal might acknowledge and publicize the deeper logic underlying these simultaneities, not in retrospect but as they occurred. This did not involve an attempt to forge a grand synthesis but instead to recognize how, at any given historical moment, historical actors, including historians, absorb and rework the ideas around them. What were the critical concepts that we historians shared and circulated as we worked on our disparate projects? If we now attended to the translocal and transnational circulation of ideas, then shouldn't we also attend to the transsubfield circulations within our own discipline?

When I read submissions to the *Journal*, I sometimes caught a glimpse of those circulations in motion. Over the course of a couple of months, for example, I noticed three different manuscript submissions, on strikingly different topics, that all dealt in some way with the history of the flow of information and disinformation, and how the spread of information depended both on technology and on (sometimes misplaced) trust. The new interest in the history of information and disinformation seemed to follow the rise of the Internet (and also the Enron debacle). To give another example, I read a number of manuscripts that grappled with alternative forms of history making; not just memory and memorials, but also examples from the past of popular histories, exhibitions, and artwork, especially those by amateur historians who related subaltern histories left out of traditional scholarship. I also noticed a shift away from local studies and toward biographical ones. I vetted surprisingly few community studies but lots of manuscripts that focused in on a single person, usually a minor celebrity whose career somehow illustrated a larger historical theme. This seemed to me a notable shift in the way we constructed our narratives. And then there were the buzzwords: Cosmopolitanism, borders (both permeable and shored up), and empires repeatedly showed up in diverse essays on the eighteenth, nineteenth, and twentieth centuries. These approaches, themes, and concepts were the thin threads that seemed to tie disparate topics together. I became interested in how a journal might highlight these threads and make them more visible. Ultimately I had less fear of silence (that is, less fear of a fragmented field in which no one talked to each other) and more fear of missing the threads of conversations that were already taking place.

But in some ways the editorial process hampered the attempt to capture the conversations. Early in my tenure as editor, Glenn Ellison, an economist at MIT, sent me copies of a couple of essays he had written. He was (and this is peculiar) studying the publication patterns of scholarly journals. That was his academic project, and he had included the *JAH* in some of his research, along with dozens of other journals, almost all from other disciplines. He had lots of indecipherable econometric equations, but the gist was this: Over the last quarter of the twentieth century, journal articles, in an array of fields, had gotten longer. They had longer introductions and more sections that elaborated on or extended the main results. The review process had also gotten longer. The average time between initial submission and acceptance or publication had increased, in some cases dramatically. Ellison came up with a model in which he distinguished between two dimensions of quality: q and r. Q represented the manuscript's main ideas or main contributions, which he presumed present (perhaps incorrectly) in the initial submission, and r represented the add-ons that came with rewriting and revising, such as elaborations on an argument or discussions of related literature. He posited that authors, at the request of peer reviewers and editors, now spent proportionately more time on r (or revisions) than they had in the past. This suggested a growing lag time between the advent of a new contribution and its appearance in print. Adding r value took time.[2]

It also suggested that, by the time the *Journal* highlighted the conceptual threads that tied subfields together, they would be yesterday's news. I remember wondering how, if it took months and months to review and revise, we could possibly publicize the shared approaches, themes, and concepts as they emerged. We almost never accepted articles without requiring fairly extensive revision and a second round of peer review. We prided ourselves on the value added by our meticulous reviewing and editing process. But maybe we spent too much time editing, and maybe we forced authors to spend too much time polishing their prose, filling out historiographic context, and tempering their arguments. Was there a way to strike a better balance, in which some articles underwent the ultimate editorial polish and others came out shorter and faster, washed and clean, yes, but without the detailed waxing and buffing? This involved speeding up our own review processes, which we did, and sometimes it also involved commissioning shorter essays on shorter order. In one such attempt at timeliness, we commissioned several short essays on September eleventh in the months of October and November 2001 and published them ten or eleven months later in September 2002. That was peak speed, and it required too much extra effort from authors, editors, and staff. It was not something we could do on a regular basis.

It soon became clear that the electronic world offered new possibilities. From my first days on the job as editor, I realized that I could not avoid the looming electronic revolution. I was not immediately taken with it, though I engaged in a crash course of sorts to bring myself up to speed, not in the technical aspects (which will always elude me) but in the opportunities offered by them. There was the obvious: the new software that could speed up and cut the costs of print production; the online publication that made articles fully searchable and more widely accessible; the databases that made it possible to upgrade, expand, and put online the recent scholarship section; and the opportunities to supplement and broadcast the print journal on our own Web site. With the help of creative full-time technical staff and astute volunteer advisors, we did the obvious: We upgraded in-house production and our public Web site; helped found and then went online with the History Cooperative; created Recent Scholarship Online (RSO) as a special service for OAH members; and started a project called Teaching the *JAH*, with online primary sources and teaching guides to accompany featured articles. But there were intriguing hints of other electronic ways of enhancing communications and exchanges among historians. The question became how to use the new technology to elicit the kinds of conversations that revealed the underlying logic of our historical practice.

During my tenure, the closest we came was an annual "Interchange" section of the *Journal*. This was an edited print version of a month-long online discussion among historians. For the inaugural conversation, we invited nine senior American historians to discuss current historical practice. Steven Stowe, who was associate editor, and I posted questions to a private web page, and our nine historians answered our questions and one another. It was not quite the lively conversation, revealing all the threads of connection, I had imagined. The participants had busy lives, and they hesitated, I think, to engage in free and easy conversation, when they knew it would eventually appear in print. They also were not all happy campers. I got a few behind-the-scenes e-mails, which included some virtual eye rolling about the comments of other participants. Nonetheless, with a little prodding, we got enough good discussion to edit it down into something interesting and worth trying again. It was at least a start, and the second attempt, the following year, in which public historians talked about genres of history, was easier (or maybe I had lower expectations). In any case, I was pleased to see recently that the *American Historical Review* has borrowed the method to start its own online "Conversations."

An electronic experiment in collaborative writing had more intriguing potential, but unfortunately we had to abandon it early on. The plan was to have a senior historian select images of the American Revolution, which we would post to a private web page. We would then commission two teams of historians, from diverse subfields, to use the online evidence to construct two separate narratives. Team 1, for example, might have included an art historian, a social historian, and a military historian, and Team 2 might have included a cultural historian, a political historian, and a historian of the British Empire. Each team would work with the same evidence, and each team would write collaboratively through essentially the same process of collective writing and editing now used by *Wikipedia*. We would post the images and the two competing (or overlapping) narratives online, with shorter edited versions in the print journal. We could see what ideas emerged in parallel form and also how different historians might construct different (or similar) narratives using the same set of sources. We discussed a few variants of this project, and we actually commissioned a senior historian to select the images and begin the project. But then it fell apart. At that early point, we were imagining possibilities that probably should have been undertaken by more tech-savvy historians, not by a senior scholar who was, it turned out, not yet on e-mail and found the whole thing confounding. I regret that the experiment failed, though, and I would love to see some version of it. I know *American Quarterly* and the *American Historical Review* have done somewhat different electronic experiments, and I wish the *JAH* had contributed its own distinctive version during my tenure.

All this is still worth pondering, in part because of ongoing opportunities to engage in electronic intellectual experiments and in part because the print journal may well be moving toward obsolescence. I was not convinced of this while I was editor. The print journal was (and still is) thriving along with its online incarnation. But back as a full-time professor, I find, to my own surprise, that I tailor my syllabi to avoid articles that are not available online. I am moving away from print course packets, even at the graduate level, and I am teaching my students how to access journals online without ever subscribing to them or even reading them in print. I used to make regular trips to the library's current periodical room. I rarely do that now; instead, I browse online. I subscribe to fewer journals than I used to, and I am more likely now to find an article through a search engine and read it isolated from its context in a print journal issue. And I am not saving all my old copies of journals. I no longer use the old copies that sit on my bookshelf. I go to JSTOR instead. I have also discovered that I hesitate to submit my own manuscripts to any journal that is not online because I suspect that no one will ever read them. (Will this volume, I wonder, appear in electronic form?) What all this means is that my students and I are less likely than ever before to hold a journal and thumb through it or to see an issue as a whole. I think the signs are clear; for short scholarly articles and book reviews (though not yet for books and not yet for archives or museum exhibitions), online publication is gradually taking over. We need to imagine new ways to put it together again that do not rely on the juxtaposition of pieces within a print journal.

In the not-too-distant future, we may give up the tangible hold-in-your-hands artifact that gives an editor pleasure, but we can still have (and still experiment with) the collaboration and creativity of journal editing. (And, I should add, Ed Linenthal, the current editor of the *JAH*, is doing a great job now.) The electronic possibilities may help us cut the lag time between when the light bulb goes on in some historian's head and when it appears in print for others to read. In any case, the electronic world should not stop us from putting it together again in new ways, looking for the connections, highlighting the conversations, and playing with the genre. We probably will not have a single grand narrative, but we will not have random fragments either or, worse, an ossified American history.

NOTES

1. David Oshinsky, "The Humpty Dumpty of Scholarship," *New York Times*, Aug. 26, 2000, B9. On fragmentation, see also, for example, Thomas Bender, "Wholes and Parts: The Need for Synthesis in American History," *Journal of American History* 73 (June 1986): 120–36; Carl N. Degler, "In Pursuit of American History," *Journal of American History* 92, supplement to volume 92 (Feb. 1987), 1–12; Fred Anderson and Andrew R. L. Cayton, "The Problem of Fragmentation and the Prospects for Synthesis in Early American Social History," *William and Mary Quarterly* 50 (Apr. 1993): 299–310.

2. Glenn Ellison, "Evolving Standards for Academic Publishing: A q-r Theory," unpublished paper, September 2001.

25

Becoming the Editor

Edward T. Linenthal

The Minneapolis meeting in 2007 gave me a chance to meet Lewis Perry and to spend time with David Thelen and Joanne Meyerowitz, both good friends, both instrumental in my decision to accept a 2005 invitation to become the thirteenth editor of the *JAH*. After accepting the position, I read all the editor's reports, beginning with the first issue of the *Mississippi Valley Historical Review* (*MVHR*) (called "News and Comments" in those early years). It was a most valuable way of tracking changes and continuities in the historical profession through the eyes of *JAH* editors. It was also instructive to read that some of the vexing issues with which we still struggle have been around for many years. It was reassuring to learn that the sense of awe I sometimes feel in the face of this huge responsibility was shared by those who preceded me. It was inspiring to feel their passion and to appreciate their deep sense of stewardship of the *JAH*.

Before the centennial session, I fantasized, not only about the four of us talking together, but about an imaginary world in which *all* former *JAH* editors gathered. What would we say to each other? What would former editors think of the evolution of the *JAH*, its radically expanded coverage of the sites and practices of history? My sense is that the thirteen editors, three interim editors, and one acting editor would easily find common ground. I imagine we would all agree that, in the words of my friend and colleague David Chidester, tradition is not only handed down, it is also picked up. Each editor builds on the rich legacy and support of her or his predecessors. This generosity of spirit is evident in Lew Perry's insistence on recalling the editorial legacy of Martin Ridge, who characterized the editor's role as "that of a servant of the profession who will try to bring to publication the scholarship of the practitioners regardless of where they stand in the historical profession." Who would argue with Perry's statement that "there is still much to be said for the good old-fashioned fairness that Martin championed"?

We would all agree that generations of *JAH* staff have been devoted to the excellence of the *Journal* in every respect, from the demanding evaluation and editorial processes to the quality of the paper, the print, and the visual images. We would all agree that creating each issue of the *JAH* is an effort made possible by, in Dave Thelen's words, "a community working hard, creatively, intensely, sacrificing time and energy, to make a common product."

No doubt we might differ on emphases. Some editors would be more inclined to emphasize articles and book reviews as vehicles for the presentation of the best in scholarship and be less interested in conversation about the significance of that scholarship. They might express qualms about the round tables in which we present essays on related topics, at times including short pieces accompanying and playing off a longer one and reflections on personal experiences in the profession. Some would see special issues in which all articles share a common topic or theme as perhaps too narrow for a general readership. Others—and here I find myself of like mind with Dave Thelen and Joanne Meyerowitz—view the *JAH* as, in Meyerowitz's words, "a site of discussion or collective reflection." I suspect that our editorial gathering would reveal sharp differences of opinion regarding the wisdom of the *JAH*'s engaging the history of the present. I think especially of Dave Thelen's "History and the Public: What Can We Handle? A Round Table about History after the *Enola Gay* Controversy" in the December 1995 issue of the *JAH* and Joanne Meyerowitz's September 2002 special issue, "History and September 11." Their rationale for focusing attention on these issues resonated deeply with me. "Precisely because the debate came from and led in so many different directions," observed Thelen, "precisely because the leading participants were unable to agree about how and where and when to engage each other, this controversy presents an extraordinary opportunity to inquire how history is, and might be, practiced in our culture and institutions." Introducing the *JAH*'s "History and September 11" issue, Joanne Meyerowitz wrote, "'Before' and 'after' are never entirely severed, even in the moments of greatest historical rupture. The discontinuities of the past remain within the whole cloth of the *longue duree*. As historians, we devote our careers to placing the seemingly new in historical contexts."

In this spirit, we are especially proud of the *JAH*'s special issue of December 2007, "Through the Eye of Katrina: The Past as Prologue?" We worked with Lawrence N. Powell of Tulane University and Clarence L. Mohr of the University of South Alabama to create this ambitious issue, which featured many wide-ranging essays. In our preview, we informed readers: "Chronologically, they touch on events from the building of the first Mississippi River levees in the early eighteenth century to the use of tattoos as expressions of civic identity in post-Katrina New Orleans. Topically, they encompass urban, environmental, architectural, and musical history, as well as analyses of politics in three centuries and of carnival as a shaper of world views." The *JAH* also created an accompanying online project that addresses "themes of race, the environment, tourism, and musical and visual culture." By integrating interactive and informational resources into the essays, it creates a compelling immersive reading of the Katrina disaster.

This digital project was a major exploration of ways to reach diverse audiences who would otherwise never pick up a print issue of the *JAH*. We continue electronic initiatives begun during Joanne Meyerowitz's tenure, "Teaching the *JAH*," and "Interchange." The Katrina online project, however, represented the first major online companion to a print special issue.

I would share with the editors the many challenges the *JAH* faces in the digital age. Is there a long future for print journals? How can we best use the Internet to expand our readership without sacrificing the *JAH*'s standard of scholarly excellence? Should the Hurricane Katrina Web component serve as a model for even more ambitious projects? On what basis do we make decisions about the wisdom or folly of free access to articles? To book reviews? To the entire *Journal*? How can electronic initiatives strengthen our long-standing commitment to include colleagues beyond the borders of the United States in our work?

I would also say to the editors that when I was hired, some colleagues thought that I might immediately make the voice of the public historian dominant in the *Journal*. However, as I would inform them, I did not think it my role as editor to privilege a part of the profession that I call home. In fact, what has become increasingly clear to me is the importance of bringing the richness of the *Journal* to a wider public. I care about it all: excellent articles that speak across the profession, that sometimes win prizes, an occasional special issue, the roundtables, reviews of books, museum exhibits, films, Web sites, important essays on the challenge of teaching American history. All the editors would understand this caring. And whoever is blessed to become the fourteenth editor of the *Journal of American History* will, no doubt, feel the presence and the support of us all in this challenging and rewarding endeavor.

Part IV

THE MVHA–OAH AND THE TEACHING OF HISTORY

26

The Shouldering of Responsibilities

Gary B. Nash

In trying to move forward, it is always useful to look backward, glimpsing the road we have traveled in reaching the place where we now stand. Such is the case with the Organization of American Historians' (OAH's) involvement in teaching history from kindergarten to doctoral programs. As Part IV points out, the road has been a crooked one, filled with bumps and potholes. However, five veterans of the history wars in the last two decades portray a generally favorable trend: the OAH's shouldering of responsibilities for teaching history in all its many venues.

OAH's members have never been of one mind on how the profession should concern itself with the quality of history teaching in the precollegiate schools. Nobody argues about the merits of inspired teaching at the college level, but it is much more difficult to get individual history departments, let alone a large organization such as the OAH, to take seriously such an elemental proposition as the need to provide first-rate training for those who aim to become K-12 history teachers. Leaving this to schools of education has been the norm. The cold truth is that the training of history teachers in United States stands in stark contrast to that in many European nations and elsewhere around the world, where a master's degree in history is often the basic requirement. This inattention to teaching history teachers effectively is changing slowly with scattered history departments creating programs for preparing students for teaching world and U.S. history in the schools. But in the main, most history teachers have very frail backgrounds in history, and the OAH has not been able to do much about this.

If preservice teaching training is still inadequate, in-service training has fared better. The project to write national history standards, which occupied hundreds of teachers and academic historians from 1992 to 1994 (with subsequent revisions) strengthened the contact and cooperation among history educators at different levels because it brought together people who had stood, figuratively, on opposite sides of a grand canyon for a very long time. The attack on the standards, mostly from conservatives, in fact reinforced this new alliance. The hostile critics, in challenging the importance of a history education that is at once inclusive and global, reflective and analytical, helped to repair the long-troubled relations between historians and social-studies educators. Thus, the history standards tempest, whatever damage it did, had a silver lining. At all levels, history educators have recognized more clearly their common goals and how much they need one another to protect the gains, however insufficient, that the field had made since World War II. In this bridge-building project, the OAH has played a prominent role.

The OAH leadership in recent years has also committed itself to reaching out to precollegiate schools, community colleges, and organizations such as the National Park Service that serve up history to the history-hungry public. Playing an important role in the Department of Education Teaching American History grants that have provided professional development for history teachers in the schools over the last decade, the OAH and its members have taken important steps toward creating a new professional ethic where history educators at all levels are seen as part of a common cause. This is not easy work. The gains in the acquisition of historical literacy, not only in the schools and colleges but in the public at large, occur only incrementally. However, in its second century of existence, the OAH dare not back away from continuing and intensifying this commitment.

27

The MVHA and Teaching
A Strained Relationship

Ron Briley

In the February 2007 issue of the Organization of Historian's (OAH's) *Newsletter*, Education Coordinator Siobhan Carter-Davis describes numerous OAH educational initiatives, including the partnership with the Gilder Lehrman Institute for American History, support for the Teaching American History grant program, and sponsorship of community college workshops. Carter-Davis concludes her piece by noting, "With the commemoration of one hundred years of service, we hope that you will also join us in celebrating our renewed commitment to exploring and enriching the craft of teaching American history."[1] Such a commitment to teaching, however, was not always at the forefront of OAH goals and activities.

In the beginning, the MVHA did not mention history teaching as one of its concerns, but by 1910 membership was growing among history professors in the Midwest, and the new organization expanded its focus to consider such issues as the teaching of American history in elementary and secondary schools and the inclusion of state history in the high school curriculum and the offerings of state universities. The teaching of national and state history was now on the radar screen of the MVHA.[2] In the colleges and universities, those who advocated the teaching of American history had to contend with those who believed the emphasis should be placed on European history, but the belief in American distinctiveness, widely held in the post–World War I years, favored increased attention to the United States and its history. According to Julie A. Reuben in the *OAH Magazine of History*, the increasingly popular American history survey course "emphasized themes such as the struggle for national unity, the expansion of democracy, economic and technological revolution, and social reform."[3]

Some years earlier, prominent voices had called for the study of American history in the elementary and secondary schools. In 1893, the prestigious Committee of Ten, chaired by Harvard President Charles W. Eliot and sponsored by the National Educational Association, recommended that history be included in the curriculum for grades five through twelve, with American history the focus for grades seven and eleven. Although some critics complained that the Committee of Ten attempted to impose an academic curriculum upon all students, an 1899 report from the Committee of Seven, a group of historians appointed by the American Historical Association (AHA), echoed the findings of its predecessor, maintaining that history be studied in all four years of high school, with American history reserved for the senior year. Both reports were critical of memorization and rote learning, advocating critical thinking and the use of primary documents.[4]

History's place within the curriculum of the nation's schools, however, proved insecure. Critical educators complained that history was too "elitist" for the immigrant masses crowding American classrooms. Social efficiency experts favored more utilitarian courses of study, such as industrial and citizenship education. In reply to these critics, the National Education Association created the Commission on the Reorganization of Secondary Education (CRSE). The final report of the CRSE was published in 1918 as *Cardinal Principles of Secondary Education*, concluding that academic courses, such as history, were only for the small minority of students who were college bound. In 1921, education professors at teachers' colleges established the National Council for the Social Studies (NCSS) to implement the recommendations of the CRSE study. Historians appeared to endorse this approach when the Commission on the Social Studies, chaired by historian A. E. Krey, argued in its 1934 report that history was of little value in fitting students for "effective participation in society."[5]

At the time, the weakening of history in the schools received little condemnation from historians, in or out of the MVHA, but more contemporary scholars have been highly critical of both the replacement of history with social studies and the silence of professional historians. "From the 1930s through the early 1950s, social studies courses incorporated studies of current events and problems of social living for teens," Diane Ravitch, a prominent education reformer, has written. "U.S. history survived in the high schools, and some states and districts continued to offer or require a European-centered history course. But no state established a coherent, sequential history curriculum."[6] Gary B. Nash, Charlotte Crabtree, and Ross E. Dunn of the National Center for History in the Schools strongly criticized university-based historians. Proponents of highly controversial standards for the teaching of history in elementary and high schools, they charged that the professoriate had focused "on well-rewarded research in more and more specialized university environments" and "closed its eyes to pre-collegiate education."[7]

Although the AHA endorsed the historical profession's abandonment of the schools to social studies, the MVHA, despite expressing interest in more regional history for school curriculums, also paid little attention to history in the schools. During its early years, the Association invited teachers located near the meeting site to attend the annual meeting, and in 1916, it accepted an invitation from the AHA to participate in a "Teachers' Conference" during its annual meetings. This link between the two associations became a regular feature of AHA meetings for many years.[8] Yet, as the MVHA attempted to make its *Review* the leading scholarly journal in the whole field of American history, the organization allowed the AHA, in alliance with the National Council for the Social Studies (NCSS), to assume a leadership role in questions of history education.

Nevertheless, as issues of democratic citizenship became increasingly imperative in a world drifting toward war in the late 1930s, the MVHA launched a new initiative by instituting a Teacher's Section in the *MVHR*. It would appear periodically between 1937 and 1949. A discussion during the inaugural meeting of the new section made apparent the close links between the historical profession and the social studies. Meeting in St. Louis, Katherine Clarke of Washington University provided a report on the Missouri social-studies program for the primary grades, and the section's editor, Wesley Clark, reported upon the activities of the NCSS and praised the organization for launching publication of *Social Education*. In the September 1937 issue of the *MVHR*, he introduced his plan for reviewing books, many of them tied to social-studies education and all of them capable of being of use by history teachers. The editor concluded his report by noting that continuing interest in contemporary social and economic affairs, a key element in the social-studies curriculum, contributed to a "greater emphasis upon community studies."[9]

Collaboration with the NCSS was also evident in the 1938 Indianapolis meeting of the new Teacher's Section. The topic for the session was "Historical Materials for Social Studies Teachers." Presenters called for more illustrations in history texts along with greater emphasis upon social history compared with political and diplomatic events. The conference highlighted the concentration of the social studies upon community studies, but, today, many history teachers would certainly endorse the meeting's call for the incorporation of more primary documents into the history curriculum.[10]

Some of the conflicts between history and the social studies were evident, however, in the work of Fremont P. Wirth of Peabody Teachers College, which was reported upon in the March 1939 Teacher's Section of the *MVHR*. Speaking at the 1939 AHA meeting, Wirth asserted that history courses "must have social significance to the learner." Since the junior or senior history course would be terminal for most students, he argued, "It should contribute rather directly to the pupils' understanding of present problems."[11] In response to the views of educators such as Wirth, who presided at the 1939 meeting of the-Teacher's Section, the contributions of history as a discipline were championed in the March 1939 Teacher's Section. Burr W. Phillips insisted that objections to the study of history in the schools were based upon a misunderstanding of the discipline and "ill-defined theories of functionalism." The current-events functional approach of some educators disturbed Phillips, who concluded that "merely studying the historical backgrounds incidental to the investigation of a few problems is usually a sketchy and incomplete approach, an unsatisfactory substitute for the fuller long-range view gained from a history course presented in orderly fashion."[12] Despite the disagreement between Wirth and Phillips, an emphasis upon regional studies continued to provide a common thread for many teachers within both the MVHA and NCSS.

Phillips, who assumed editorship of the Teacher's Section in 1940, acknowledged that many historians questioned whether a section on teaching was appropriate for the *MVHR*. Nevertheless, the editor maintained that the section might emphasize how secondary teachers could employ the "contributions of the *Review* and of the history of the West in general." Phillips also reiterated the alliance between history and the social studies, writing, "Since the National Council for the Social Studies is the professional organization for teachers in our field [and is] closely associated with the American Historical Association and Mississippi Valley Historical Association, it has seemed desirable to include information about the meetings and publications of the Council."[13]

The editor was considerably more strident in his column following the Japanese attack upon Pearl Harbor and American entrance into World War II. Now ignoring issues of conflict between history and the social studies, the section emphasized the contributions that history teachers should make to the war effort. While asserting that teachers must continue to foster qualities of objectivity and fairness in their students, Phillips, nevertheless, argued, "The teacher who is not convinced of the justice of our cause or who fears for the outcome of the war has no place in the classroom." The editor also had advice for young teachers who were products of the post-World War I disillusionment symbolized by the strength of the isolationist and pacifist movements during the interwar years. Phillips deplored revisionist and debunking interpretations of American entrance into World War I, which had gained influence in the universities and schools during the 1920s and 1930s. He vehemently concluded, "The attack on Pearl Harbor should by now have done much to restore a certain perspective and sanity in our thinking about the issues involved in both wars. No longer do we need to have any scruples as to the justice of our cause and the ideals which we and our allies are fighting to preserve."[14]

The enlisting of history in the war effort, however, was problematic if the American people had little knowledge of the nation's history. On June 21, 1942, the *New York Times* published a survey revealing that 82 percent of American colleges and universities failed to require the study of American history and only 28 percent required United States history as an admission requirement. In the Teacher's Section of the *MVHR*, new editor Philip D. Jordan acknowledged that the survey conducted by the *Times* "only confirmed what many historians had suspected for years in an educational environment where the study of history was often supplanted by the more 'utilitarian' concerns of the social studies." Jordan asserted that it was time for historians to "renew their faith in their own subject and work toward making American history more and more available to the younger generation."[15]

Building upon the exhortations of Jordan, Edgar B. Wesley added his voice to the chorus that organizations such as the MVHA take a leading role in history education. Writing in the *MVHR*, Wesley maintained that historical associations needed to reassert their role in the creation of curriculum and history professors must accept responsibility for modeling good teaching practices and training prospective high school teachers.[16]

The call by Jordan and Wesley for the MVHA to assume a larger role in history education within the context of national unity required for the war effort was supported by Theodore C. Blegen in his 1944 MVHA presidential address. He announced his agreement with the 1944 report, *American History in Schools and Colleges*, compiled by the Committee on American History in Schools and Colleges. Composed of representatives from the NCSS, AHA, and MVHA, the committee contended that "knowledge of our own history is essential in the making of Americans" and committed the MVHA to expanding and improving the teaching of history in the schools and colleges. In a rhetorical flourish, Blegen proclaimed that the organization's educational initiatives were "being carried forward in the faith that along with the privileges we must accept the responsibilities of our high task as historians not alone of the great valley of America but also of the American people."[17]

The MVHA's wartime idealism regarding its obligations to history education could not be sustained in the postwar period. At first, the initial enthusiasm for reform was present. It was evident in a Teacher's Section piece by high school teacher Lucile Gustafson, who insisted that the primary obligation of American history in the social-studies curriculum was "to help bring a security of spirit into the lives of our young people by helping them to discover their place in the continuity of history. In this way, may we as teachers foster a feeling of personal security that must precede a world security."[18] The section also included teaching innovations that would continue to resonate with history teachers in the early twenty-first century. Philip Jordan suggested that the use made of film in the instruction of military recruits during World War II demonstrated the pedagogical possibilities of the moving image as a teaching medium, while Robert O. Keohane reiterated the centrality of primary sources in history education.[19]

Nevertheless, the MVHA concluded that there were limits to the role that the organization might play in history education both within and outside the traditional classroom. At its April 25, 1947, meeting, the MVHA Executive

Committee authorized the appointment of a subcommittee "to study the relationship of the Association to the teaching of history, and to recommend to the executive committee appropriate action in this important matter." The subcommittee, chaired by Thomas D. Clark, reached some rather pessimistic conclusions about the influence that the MVHA might exert upon history education. Asserting that, as an organization of professional historians, it was difficult to reach "the secondary school teacher in such a way as to interest him in the broad field of American history," the report maintained that the MVHA lacked the appeal to teachers in the schools of a more specialized organization such as the NCSS. In language that comes off as somewhat elitist today, the subcommittee asserted, "Membership of the secondary school teaching profession is neither research-centered nor stable as a long-range personnel organization. The turn-over of teachers is rapid, and a continuous effort is necessary to maintain the support of an organized body which depends upon this type of clientele." The professional research-oriented historians, Clark's group assumed, could best serve teachers by producing scholarship accessible to the general public and might also volunteer as speakers for teacher and educational organizations. In addition, the subcommittee implored scholars to maintain their alliance with the NCSS and chastised them for missing an "opportunity to establish a happy rapport with the secondary teacher and student by failing to encourage full and intelligent use of the materials of local history."

Clearly, the MVHA perceived itself as primarily an organization of researchers rather than teachers, yet the organization was not prepared to abandon teaching. The subcommittee called for the continuation of the Teacher's Section and then concluded:

> We are a group of rugged individualists going our separate ways with our burden of teaching, and many of us are forced to enjoy the stolen sweets of research surreptitiously as we can. Yet we have much to offer the whole field of history in clear coordination of the profession with the secondary field of teaching. If such an effort is made it will doubtless bring the historian to closer realization of the larger objective of his profession.[20]

Essentially, this effort was perceived from a hierarchical perspective rather than a collaborative approach with history teachers in the schools. Despite the call for a continued dialogue regarding history education in the schools, the Teacher's Section of the MVHR was dropped in 1949, and, in his 1953 MVHA presidential address, James L. Sellers acknowledged the growing gap between the professional research-oriented historians of the organization and history teachers in the schools. Reporting that the MVHA membership included approximately 1,600 individuals, Sellers observed, "These members came chiefly from the departments of history and historical societies, the two groups that were mentioned in the first draft of our constitution. Efforts to draw in the public school teachers of history have not proved permanently successful."[21]

After considerable discussion in the 1930s and 1940s regarding the proper relationship between the organization and history education, the MVHA by the 1950s had apparently accepted a degree of separation between the professors of history in the universities and the teachers of history in the schools. This separation did not need to remain permanent. In the mid-1960s, MVHA testified to a willingness to become more than it had once been, doing so by approving proposals to change the *Review*'s name to *The Journal of American History* and the Association to the Organization of American Historians. Although conceding that aggressive efforts to recruit new members who were not professional historians had virtually ceased, William Aeschbacher, the OAH's secretary-treasurer, announced in 1967 that the OAH had broadened its definition of *historian* and encouraged membership among history teachers in the secondary schools.[22] From its sometime strained relationship with history teachers in the schools during the years of the MVHA, the group with a new name was pursuing new avenues of collaboration.

NOTES

1. Siobhan Carter-David, "History Education in Our Centennial Year," *OAH Newsletter* 35 (Feb. 2007): 17.

2. William D. Aeschbacher, "The Mississippi Valley Historical Association, 1907–1965," *Journal of American History* 54 (Sept. 1967): 339–53.

3. Julie A. Reuben, "Going National: American History Instruction in Colleges and Universities," *OAH Magazine of History* 21 (Apr. 2007): 34.

4. Diane Ravitch, "History's Struggle to Survive in the Schools," *OAH Magazine of History* 21 (Apr. 2007): 28–29.

5. Diane Ravitch, *Left Back: A Century of Failed School Reform* (New York: Simon & Schuster, 2000), 227–29.

6. Ravitch, "History's Struggle to Survive in the School," 30–31.

7. Gary B. Nash, Charlotte Crabtree, and Ross E. Dunn, *History on Trial: Cultural Wars and the Teaching of the Past* (New York: Alfred A. Knopf, 1997), 39.

8. James L. Sellers, "Before We Were Members—The MVHA," *MVHR* 40 (June 1953): 14.

9. Edgar B. Wesley, "The Teacher's Section," *MVHR* 24 (Sept. 1937): 216–17.

10. Elmer Ellis, "Teacher's Section," *MVHR* 25 (Sept. 1938): 265–68.

11. "Teacher's Section," *MVHR* 25 (Mar. 1939): 543–48.

12. Elmer Ellis, "Teacher's Section," *MVHR* 26 (June 1939): 71–73.

13. Burr W. Phillips, "Teacher's Section," *MVHR* 27 (Sept. 1940): 275–76.

14. Burr W. Phillips, "History Teaching and the War," *MVHR* 28 (Mar. 1942): 593–96.

15. Philip D. Jordan, "The *New York Times* Survey of United States History," *MVHR* 29 (Sept. 1942): 238–42.

16. Edgar B. Wesley, "History in the School Curriculum," *MVHR* 29 (Mar. 1943): 565–74.

17. Theodore C. Blegen, "Our Widening Province," *MVHR* 31 (June 1944): 19–20.

18. Lucile Gustafson, "Social and Personal Values of American History," *MVHR* 32 (Sept. 1945): 255.

19. Philip D. Jordan, "Social Studies and the Sound Film," *MVHR* 30 (Dec. 1943): 408–11; and Robert O. Keohane, "The Use of Primary Sources in the Teaching of Local and State History in High School," *MVHR* 33 (Dec. 1946): 445–60.

20. "The Relationship of the Association to the Teaching of History: A Committee Report," *MVHR Review* 35 (June 1948): 99–102.

21. James Sellers, "Before We Were Members," 18–19.

22. Aeschbacher, "Mississippi Valley Historical Association," 344.

28

Why a Focus on Teaching Day?

Marjorie Bingham

One sign of change in the new era of the Organization of American Historians (OAH) was the Focus on Teaching Day. Beginning early in the 1980s, the annual meeting opened a large portion of the program on Saturday for discussions of the methods and issues of teaching history. There are, I think, three major reasons for such a day in a group with such a name: (1) to encourage more teachers to participate in the OAH convention and organization, (2) to demonstrate good teaching, and (3) to provide opportunities for unintended outcomes.

Like any good historian, however, I'd like to begin with a little background. About every thirty years or so, the profession discovered that the schools were teaching the wrong history in the wrong way. Around 1900, John Dewey and the Progressive Movement pointed to the lack of American history in the schools and the predominance of classical studies. In the 1920s and 1930s, Charles Beard and others encouraged more social-science emphasis, with the resulting National Council of Social Studies (1921). Merle Curti and Howard K. Beale also worked to provide links between schools and the universities. In the 1970s and 1980s, with the creation of the Department of Education under President Jimmy Carter and then the leadership of Terrance Bell, education became the focus of many studies. A National Commission on Education published, in 1983, *A Nation At Risk*, a study highlighting the dismal state of American education. Looking at the people who testified before that Commission, I did not see a substantial presence of historians. But the cause of history reform was taken on by the Bradley Commission on History in the Schools, led by Kenneth Jackson, a historian at Columbia University. The Commission worked to re-center history in a curriculum of what might be called a free-floating curriculum era. (In my high school, we tried to replace a requirement that students take driver's training with a mandatory semester of world history.) The Focus on Teaching Day, then, was part of an era of reform designed to encourage more academically sound and creative history teaching.[1]

The sharp decline in student enrollment during the era also influenced the effort to establish the day. To use another example from my school, enrollment was cut in half. For the colleges, this also meant fewer students and fewer professors; for the OAH and AHA, fewer members. New historical societies emphasizing multi cultural topics or new techniques became the focus of historians' energies. The broadly based organizations, like the OAH and AHA, sought a new pool of members, namely, teachers.

Hopes of reforming the curriculum and the classroom and of gaining new members influenced major figures in both organizations and encouraged them to provide leadership. Individuals who had teaching background in the schools, like Kenneth Jackson, Leon Litwack, and Hazel Hertzberg, led reform. Historians of women, such as Joan Hoff, Noralee Frankcl, Arnita Jones, and Anne Firor Scott, saw parallels between women's history and the lack of representation of teachers. Within the OAH and AHA, there were many supportive people. I remember from the OAH Lou Harlan, Mike Regoli, Jerry Bobilya, Dick Kirkendall, Howard Mehlinger, Arnita Jones, and Joan Hoff.[2] One of the wisest measures coming from such leadership was the application for Rockefeller money to fund scholarships for teachers to come to OAH conventions and be part of the early Focus on Teaching days. The State Humanities Commissions of California, Minnesota, and New York also chipped in funds.[3] The teachers who attended formed a nucleus that had wide influence in the field of teaching.

Turning to the reasons for a Focus on Teaching Day, the first is to encourage teacher participation. What do teachers get from an OAH convention? Four benefits quickly come to mind: up-to-date scholarship and debate; informal discussion of history, a real boon for the often isolated AP teacher; displays of academically challenging books, often missing at NCSS conventions; and chances to share their talents at Focus on Teaching Day events.

A second reason for the day is to share skills in teaching. One of my long time criticisms of NEH seminars has been the format of a professor professing in the morning and teachers expected to do lesson plans in the afternoon. For me, teaching is the integration of method and subject matter. Professors profess—they inform—but teachers, whether in kindergarten or graduate seminars, engage. Such an engagement is an art, and to do it with creative scholarship is a joy.

But the third reason for a Focus on Teaching Day is to encourage unintended outcomes. The network of Rockefeller scholars had concrete and lasting influences. One was Terrie Epstein, a teacher from the Denver area who suggested a newsletter to the AHA, but they mulled it over too long.[4] The OAH took up her suggestion, applied for more funds, and, through some struggles, began the *Magazine of History*. It is an ongoing source of aid, supplying lesson plans, historiography, and more.

Another example is the camaraderie of the teachers. People like Ron Briley, Earl Bell, Gloria Sesso, Doris Meadows, Howard Shorr, Bill McCracken, Kathy Keene, Bill Everdell, Julia Stewart Werner, and others formed the Organization of History Teachers (OHT). This group acted as a pool for positions within the OAH and AHA. The push for teaching awards, workshops, and organizational changes often came from this group. Later, under the leadership of Kenneth Jackson, Elaine Wrisley Reed, and the first two Vice-Chairs from OHT (Bingham and Bell), the National Council for History Education provided another and more lasting way in which teachers and professors could act together for history education.

As teachers who showed up for OAH conventions, they were often selected for the National Standards of History committees. Without reviewing the whole history of the debate over the standards—and not having served on any of the committees—I'd just say that I think that the politicization of the standards was one of the real tragedies of American history education. The controversy shifted education away from subject matter into seemingly safer, innocuous testing. Those who participated in the National Standards did, however, do a fine job, and I, like many others I'm sure, mined the standards for both subject matter emphasis and teaching ideas.

This day, this Focus on Teaching Day, has, then, a tradition to uphold for good thought, creative ideas, and shared plotting.

NOTES

1. For more detailed information see Diane Ravitch, "History's Struggle to Survive in the Schools," *Magazine of History* 21 (Apr. 2007): 28–32.

2. In the AHA, Sam Gammon, Jim Gardner, and Jamil Zainaldin were also very helpful. I remember Jamil sitting me down after I'd been elected to the Teaching Division and saying, "What do you intend to do for teachers?"

3. The Rockefeller Foundation awarded the OAH a three-year grant of approximately $250,000 for teacher activities and the Fund for the Improvement of Post Secondary Education made a multiyear commitment of about $450,000. State Humanities Commissions provided $5000 each for conventions held in their state. Information provided by Jerry Bobilya: e-mail, December 5, 2006, to author.

4. In a November 24, 2006, e-mail, Terrie Epstein described her thinking to me. "The idea for the newsletter/magazine came from my having attended an AHA sponsored conference for teachers on teaching the Constitution. Linda Kerber gave a talk on the historiography of the Constitution, then handed out a number of primary documents and I thought wouldn't it be great to have these kinds of materials available to high school teachers and students. So I sent AHA a proposal for a newsletter which would have a historiographical essay on a topic and one or two primary sources. The

AHA held off in part because they were co-sponsors or thinking of becoming co-sponsors of *The History Teacher*. So I sent the proposal to the OAH and they picked up on it. They asked me to come to the meeting where we discussed the Focus on Teaching Day idea as well. I think most of the credit goes to Joan Hoff who took the idea and got it institutionalized."

29

The OAH and the Community College Professoriate

Charles A. Zappia

The Mississippi Valley Historical Association (MVHA) and the Organization of American Historians (OAH) have long recognized that the dissemination of historical knowledge through teaching is as important as the generation of historical knowledge through research. Although this priority has had ups and downs through the decades, not long after the MVHA became the OAH, the organization, without weakening its commitment to scholarly research and quality publication, again sharpened its focus on teaching in the four-year colleges and history education at the primary and secondary level.[1] However, not until the early 1990s did OAH officers and members expand their interests to include the purest teaching institutions in the world of higher education: the community colleges.

There are several reasons why community colleges became more visible to OAH leaders at that particular time. First of all, even though junior colleges, the earliest incarnations of community colleges, had been around since 1901, it was not until the 1960s that their numbers and enrollments exploded. By the early 1990s the nation's community college student body had grown so enormous that more than half of all Americans taking college-level history courses were doing so at a community college.[2] Second, because the OAH is necessarily concerned with the employment prospects of historians, changes in the academic labor market demanded a re-examination of realistic job possibilities. While tenure-track positions at traditional colleges and universities stagnated and even declined, more jobs were opening at community colleges. Whereas, in the past, most who applied for community college positions held terminal Masters degrees, increasingly, new hires held PhD's from the same universities that produced the rest of the higher education faculty.[3] In addition, the American Historical Association (AHA) had already taken some steps to expand its membership to include more two-year college faculty.

Last of all, several strong believers in integrating community college historians into the mainstream of our profession came together in the OAH in the early 1990s. Arnita Jones, who brought a more activistic orientation to her appointment as executive director in 1990, was well aware that there were too many historians laboring in isolation in the community colleges. Larry Levine, who was elected to the presidency of the OAH in 1992, had expressed strong respect for the professional competence and dedication of community college historians, in part because he was introduced to higher education at the City College of New York, then an open-admissions institution like most of today's community colleges. Nadine Ishitani Hata, an El Camino College historian already active in earlier AHA efforts to reach out to the community colleges, began prodding the OAH to devote more attention to those institutions. Toward the end of his presidency, Larry Levine, with the solid support of Arnita Jones and the executive board, decided to devote considerable time and resources to improving the OAH's relationship with community college historians. At the annual meetings of the AHA in December 1992 and the OAH in April 1993, Levine and Jones hosted information sessions for community college faculty who were already members of both organizations. I attended those meetings. The numbers were small, but the level of enthusiasm was high.

In early 1994, the Organization appointed an *ad hoc* task force on community colleges. The group was composed of community college and university faculty from around the country, who quickly agreed on three major goals: (1) increase contact between community college historians and those teaching at other institutions of higher learning; (2) increase opportunities for community college historians to engage in research and scholarship by finding and publicizing funding sources and by persuading community college administrators that ongoing scholarship strengthens college teaching at all levels; and, (3) identify and support appropriate standards of professional practices at the community colleges.[4] Larry Levine graciously accepted a spot on the committee, promising to use his influence as past president to strengthen our organizational efforts. Nadine Hata, already a veteran activist, was selected to chair the task force, and I was a charter member as well. We also benefited from the efforts of Elizabeth A. Kessel (Ann Arundel Community College), George Stevens (Duchess Community College), and Myron Marty (Drake University). Executive Director Arnita Jones was a constant presence.

In October 1994, the task force sent out an ambitious survey to community college historians across the nation, the first of truly comprehensive scope. It asked for responses that would provide a coherent description of the community college historian and her/his institutions, programs, and responsibilities. When we initially reviewed the survey data, we found some results I expected to see, including that most community college historians experienced considerable satisfaction in their professional lives. But we also encountered many complaints about poor working conditions and the troubling academic culture of the community colleges. Many of our respondents complained of a general sense of isolation from the historical profession at large. Many argued that teaching loads were so heavy that they made scholarship nearly impossible. Several noted that, instead of recognizing that this situation was counterproductive to higher education, some community college administrators (and some faculty) saw scholarship and teaching as opposites rather than as complements. Many complained of the ongoing commercialization of higher education, that is, a strong emphasis on models of efficiency and productivity that are ill-suited to academic enterprises.[5] When asked what the OAH might do for them, the most common response was "include us in the profession." More specifically, some suggested coordinating more cooperation across the ranks of higher education in planning and teaching the survey course in United States History. Others asked that the OAH consider the papers of community college historians for their conferences and journals, help find more opportunities and funding for research and scholarly activities, and advocate for changes in graduate programs to better prepare today's PhDs for community college and other undergraduate instruction.[6]

The scope of the 1994/1995 study has yet to be repeated. Nevertheless, more recent studies based on much smaller samples indicate that there has been little change in the satisfactions, needs, and professional expectations of community college historians since the mid-1990s. What has changed is that the percentage that holds the PhD has increased and continues to do so, and the percentage of historians who teach in the community colleges is increasing as well. In our study, 43 percent of all respondents held PhDs; at present, a bit over 45 percent of all community college faculty have earned PhDs, and the community colleges now employ roughly 30 percent of all working historians.[7]

In 1999, the OAH, the AHA, and the Community College Humanities Association (CCHA) collaborated to publish a status report, *Community College Historians in the United States*, which was widely disseminated, testifying to the new importance that teaching history at the two-year level had assumed. Since the publication of that report, the OAH has remained solidly committed to supporting history instruction in the community colleges. Two-year faculty have served consistently on the policy-making executive board over the past decade or so. They have also been elected and/or appointed to the nominating board, and a number of committees. The *ad hoc* task force became a permanent Committee on Community Colleges in 1997. The Committee has remained active in organizing sessions at the annual meeting, sponsoring and hosting a convention reception for community college historians, and developing a host of projects intended to service the community college sector. In addition, the executive office has secured funding for a "Community College Project," which launched a series of workshops for community college U.S. history faculty that hopefully will continue into the future. Lee Formwalt, as executive director, was aggressive in his support of all the various community college programs. In short, the commitment of the OAH to supporting those historians who teach in the community colleges has been magnificent.[8]

So, what are the results to date of the OAH's strong support for community college historians? I would argue that the most important result is the virtual destruction of the status wall that once limited our communication with the rest of the profession. At annual conventions, telling a colleague from a research university that you teach at a community college no longer automatically ends the conversation, as it certainly once did.[9] In addition, the number of panelists and presenters at annual conventions who are employed by community colleges has increased; two-year faculty have been active in attempts to fine tune the survey course in U.S. and World History, and they have contributed to the AHA's recent publication of *The Education of Historians for the Twenty-first Century*. That volume offers some suggestions on how graduate education needs to change to prepare the growing number of newly minted PhDs accepting positions at community colleges.[10]

In reference to the goals set by the *ad hoc* task force back in 1994, we have met our first goal, which, in essence, was the integration of community college historians into the profession. Likewise, we have made considerable progress toward our second goal insofar as we have increased research and scholarship opportunities, mostly through greater integration rather than by generating or even identifying any significant new sources of funding.

However, there have been some disappointments as well. The OAH community college faculty membership numbers remain abysmal. There are, perhaps, as many as 6,000 tenured/tenure-track historians (and far more adjuncts) teaching history in the community colleges. Though probably at least half of those are Americanists, a recent query revealed that only 221 OAH members (of approximately 9,500) list their employer as a two-year college.[11] More distressingly, these numbers have declined dramatically in recent years. In April 1999, there were 316 community college historians who were members of the OAH.[12] Not only is the community college membership cohort far smaller than those of four-year colleges and research universities, it is far smaller than the K-12 component.[13] Though I long ago urged community college historians to list their departments in the AHA's *Directory of History Departments* as a simple statement of membership in the broader profession, very few have done so: In the latest edition of the *Directory*, I found only 5 (of 825 history programs).[14]

Given the considerable efforts of the OAH over a period of nearly fifteen years, why do so few community college historians join the organization and participate in its professional programs? I believe the most likely answer is that the academic culture of the community college sector effectively (though never directly) discourages any engagement beyond the immediate responsibilities of the faculty member's position. For years, we bemoaned our isolation, a significant cause of which was the exclusionary behavior of our four-year college and research university colleagues. The support programs of the OAH and, I might add, of the AHA as well, have effectively opened the arms of the profession to community college historians. The fact that most remain aloof of broader scholarly engagement results, in my opinion, from the subtle and incrementally demoralizing effects of community college teaching. Many two-year faculty enjoy their sense of freedom from the rigors of publication expectations and an overemphasis on traditional methods of evaluating their professional worth, deeply appreciate the difficulties facing their students, and celebrate the special joy of instructing those who, more because of social circumstances than lack of ability, will never grace the campuses of this nation's elite universities and colleges. Still, after years of teaching fifteen-unit/semester course loads with little opportunity to develop curriculum beyond the basic survey, with administrative insistence on higher class sizes and greater student "success" (which generally translates only to course completion), with the truncating of tenure lines and an even greater reliance on contingent faculty than is the case in other sectors, facing more political pressure to validate our efforts through developing often perfunctory "student learning outcomes" measurements, parrying demands to do ever more with even less funding support, community college faculty are often *just plain exhausted*. Under such conditions, the intellectual curiosity and, in fact, the passion that led us into and through the graduate study of history, tend to take a back seat to simply surviving each week's immediate demands.[15] Again referencing the 1994 Task Force goals, we have had little contact with community college administrators and trustees, and have done little to encourage them to recognize scholarship as an appropriate standard of professional practice.

Nevertheless, we can't stop now, even though I have heard recently some voices suggesting that the OAH leadership concentrate its admittedly limited resources on more traditional efforts like the *Journal* and the annual convention.[16] I strongly urge the leadership and general membership of the OAH to continue the organization's strong support of community college history teaching, despite the probability that these efforts will not win the organization many new members. What is happening in the community colleges is affecting the entire world of higher education, most especially its critical public sector. Over the past twenty years or so, state financial support for public higher education has deteriorated. As more students expect to earn a college degree, stagnating family incomes, hyperinflationary college costs, and decreasing governmental fiscal support have made these expectations less realizable for all but the well off. This has happened, not because our country has lost its direction, but because it was too long directed by the most selfish economic interests in league with neoconservative political cabals that reject the notion that public education is a social good, and that remain dedicated to not only privatizing most public programs but to destroying government itself. All these pressures are pushing more middle-class students into community colleges. This phenomenon might please some, because overall student ability among community college students may improve, at least as far as basic skills are concerned. However, their swelling numbers will also exert a downward pressure: it will deny more non-middle-class students access to higher education opportunities. Worse yet, budget-conscious state legislators will rhetorically praise (while stingily funding) the community colleges as providing their preferred model for higher education: they process more students at the lowest possible public cost.

California, with the largest community college system in the nation, provides an example of what state government officials like most and like least about public higher education. When I was lobbying California State legislators on behalf of the American Federation of Teachers, Local 1931, in the 1990s, everyone, but most particularly the most conservative Republicans, had nice things to say about community colleges, usually after they disparaged the "wasteful and elitist" University of California. It was clear to me that what they found most attractive about the California community colleges was their very low cost to the state's taxpayers. In the budget year 2007–2008, California's taxpayers spent just under $8 billion to support 2,621,398 students in the Golden State's 109 community colleges. The California State University system, with roughly 16 percent of the community colleges' enrollment (417,000 students on 23 campuses), is budgeted at about the same amount. The prestigious University of California, with a total student body equivalent to only 8 percent of that of the community colleges (214,000 students on 10 campuses), had a budget nearly eight times as large.[17] For those most concerned with keeping state government costs as low as possible (except, perhaps, for prison construction) it is obvious why the higher education system that educates the most students with the fewest dollars gets such kudos. The problem is that those low costs and "efficient" instruction are borne on the backs of faculty expected to teach a five-course-per-semester load, often at the expense of expanding or even maintaining their scholarly skills.

Consequently, the OAH and other organizations of scholars *must* sharpen their efforts to make certain that the initial goals of the *ad hoc* task force on community colleges are pursued. We must insist on standards of professional practice that will keep control of curriculum and, at the very least, of effective advising on course loads and class sizes in the hands of academics. We must increase our efforts to persuade community college administrators that scholarship is integrally related to good teaching, and hence class sizes and course loads should be *reduced* to encourage more scholarly activity, *even though such changes will have to await economic recovery*. In short, the OAH must deliver a strong message to the nation's community college trustees and administrators: An education is far more than the vocational training of the young, streamlined to prepare them for lives as efficient, obedient corporate employees. In a world more dominated by concentrations of economic power than perhaps ever before in the history of humankind, education at all levels must prepare students to make a living in an unforgiving marketplace. However, it must also encourage students to understand the social relations shaped by today's economic forces, and it must provide students with the critical tools to evaluate whether this is the kind of world in which they want to live out their futures.[18]

NOTES

1. Organization of American Historians Records, 1906–2003, Ruth Lilly Special Collections and Archives, IUPUI University Library, Indiana University Purdue University, Indianapolis http://www.oah.org/about/archives.html. Accessed October 5, 2006.

2. James J. Lorence, "Teaching History at Two-Year Institutions: A Status Report and View of the Future," in *Community College Historians in the United States*, ed. Nadine Ishitani Hata (Bloomington, IN: Organization of American Historians, 1999), 31.

3. Nadine Ishitani Hata, "Perspectives on the Community College Job Market: What to Expect," in *Community College Historians*, ed. Hata, 55–57.

4. Nadine Ishitani Hata, "Introduction," in *Community College Historians*, ed. Hata, 13.

5. Charles A. Zappia, "Focus on Community Colleges: Improving History Teaching and the Status of Historians at Community Colleges," *Perspectives* (May/June 1996): 27–30.

6. Hata, "Introduction," in *Community College Historians*, ed. Hata, 12–13; Zappia, "Improving History Teaching and the Status of the Community College Historian," in *Community College Historians*, ed. Hata, 18–19.

7. Zappia, "Improving History Teaching and the Status of the Community College Historian," in *Community College Historians*, ed. Hata, 16; Emily Sohmer Tai, "Research and the Classroom: A View from the Community College," *Perspectives* (November 2006): 18.

8. Much of this information is drawn from Meeting Minutes of the Committee on Community Colleges, May 27, 1999, March 31, 2000, April 27, 2001, April 1, 2005. www.oah.org/about/cmte/activities.html. Accessed October 7, 2006.

9. Evelyn Edson, "Historical Scholarship and the Community College Teacher," in *Community College Historians*, ed. Hata, 41.

10. Thomas Bender, Philip M. Katz, Colin Palmer, and the Committee on Graduate Education of the American Historical Association, *The Education of Historians for the Twenty-first Century* (Urbana: University of Illinois Press, 2004).

11. There may be some imprecision in these statistics, since only about 53 percent of all OAH members supply information on employment status. E-mail from Ginger L. Foutz, Membership Director, OAH (February 20, 2007).

12. Organization of American Historians, "OAH Membership Statistics and Demographics," unpublished document, April 1999, not paginated.

13. As of February 2007, there are 395 regular members who are K-12 teachers, in addition to the roughly 1,900 members in the History Educators category, almost all of whom teach in K-12. Foutz e-mail (February 20, 2007).

14. Zappia, "Focus on Community Colleges," *Perspectives* (May/June 1996): 30; American Historical Association, *Directory of History Departments, Historical Organizations, and Historians, 2008–09* (Washington, DC: American Historical Association, 2008). The five community colleges are Glendale, Austin, Henry Ford, North Hennepin, and San Diego Mesa.

15. Elizabeth Kessel, "Part Timers Fare Little Better at Community Colleges," Organization of American Historians, www.oah.org/pubs/nl/97nov/kessel.html; Scott Rausch, "Challenges to Academic Freedom in Community College History Programs," Organization of American Historians, www.oah.org/pubs/nl/2005may/rausch.html. Accessed November 20, 2006.

16. Nell Irvin Painter, "Into the OAH's Second Century," *OAH Newsletter* 35 (Aug. 2007): 3.

17. Rick Wolff, "The Decline of Public Higher Education," *Monthly Review* (February 17, 2007), http://mrzine.monthlyreview.org/wolff170207.html; California Community Colleges, State Chancellor's Office, http://misweb.cccco.edu/mis/onlinestat/studdemo_annual_college; California Department of Finance, Enacted Budget, 2007–2008, http://www/ebudget.ca.gov/Enacted/StateAgencyBudgets/6015/age. Accessed April 16, 2007.

18. Charles A. Zappia, "Academic Professionalism and the Business Model in Education: Reflections of a Community College Historian," *The History Teacher* 33 (Nov. 1999): 55–66.

30

The Recent Years

Timothy N. Thurber

The Organization of American Historians' (OAH's) commitment to teaching has never been stronger than during the past twenty years or so. During that time, OAH has undertaken or become involved in numerous exciting efforts that reflect its dedication to the teaching and learning of history. The OAH has transformed from primarily a scholarly organization to a more broadly based professional body that views teaching history as central to its mission. Nearly 20 percent of current OAH members are K-12 teachers, that is, roughly triple the number in 1993. Moreover, numerous activities have sought to promote excellence in teaching and learning at all levels and to audiences that extend beyond a traditional classroom.

The *Magazine of History* constitutes perhaps the most visible and important sign of OAH's role in the promotion of teaching and learning of history. Begun with the financial assistance of the Rockefeller Foundation, the *Magazine* has grown from 382 subscribers during its first year to more than six thousand today. The *Magazine*, which is published quarterly, was one of several programs undertaken in the early and mid-1980s that reflected a new commitment by OAH to align itself with governmental organizations and foundations to advance pre-collegiate history education. The *Magazine* debuted in April 1985 with a focus on teaching the 1960s and, perhaps more notably, an interview with then-Indiana University basketball coach Bobby Knight, who spoke powerfully about the importance of learning history. Since then, the commitment of OAH presidents and executive directors, the hard work and extraordinary dedication of numerous editors, guest-editors, and various assistants, as well as the support of outside organizations such as The History Channel and the Gilder Lehrman Institute, has ensured that the *Magazine* remains central to what OAH does.[1]

The road was not always smooth, but the *Magazine* has come a long way from its beginnings. Initially aimed exclusively at junior-and senior-high-school teachers, (indeed, the phrase "For Junior and Senior High School Teachers" appeared on the cover for several years), the *Magazine* has evolved into a valuable tool for educators at all levels.

Looking back on a decade's worth of work, Howard Mehlinger pointed out in 1995 that four questions stood at the core of the *Magazine's* mission:

- Why should secondary school pupils study history?
- What history should they study?
- How can teachers become more effective instructors?
- Where can teachers obtain resources they need to teach better?[2]

Mehlinger's observation still holds true today. The *Magazine* has featured a rich diversity of articles, many of which remain relevant many years later. The *Magazine* has included insightful pedagogical articles dealing with topics such as teaching students how to make historical arguments, using computers to promote thinking historically, improving the writing of exams, and bringing literature and film effectively into the classroom. It has also served as a resource guide by providing primary sources for classroom use, bibliographies, and reviews of documentaries and textbooks.

Perhaps most valuable of all has been the thematic focus of each issue. These themes, which have centered on particular individuals, institutions, or eras, have reflected the rich expansion of the discipline over the last forty years. Topics explored in the *Magazine* have included the environment, business, witchcraft, Jim Crow, Abraham Lincoln, sexuality, imperialism, science and technology, disease, and the Progressive era, among others. Particularly noteworthy here is the July 2005 issue, which featured the theme of teaching history through music and included a CD featuring twenty musical pieces, such as "Oh, Susanna!," "This Little Light of Mine," and excerpts from Aaron Copland's "Appalachian Spring." The CD proved so popular that back issues are, regrettably, no longer available. A relatively recent feature in the *Magazine* is the "America on the World Stage" column, which reflects the increasing internationalization and comparative aspects of learning American history.

Overseen by a guest editor who specializes in the featured topic, individual issues of the *Magazine* offer readers strategies for integrating that topic into their classrooms, a solid overview of recent trends in that particular field, and occasional glimpses into areas of scholarly disagreement. As new fields of inquiry have opened up or traditional areas have shifted direction, the *Magazine* remains a valuable learning tool for instructors. In an age of academic specialization at the collegiate level and proliferation of state learning standards in the K-12 ranks, this thematic focus can provide quick but substantive guides to scholarly trends. The *Magazine* also offers insight into historiographical controversies that can stimulate further reading.

OAH's commitment to teaching has also been evident in several cooperative efforts. Sometimes OAH has worked with other professional organizations, such as the American Association for the History of Medicine, in putting together a particular issue of the *Magazine*. OAH has developed a relationship with the Gilder Lehrman Institute for American History, which provides important primary source material in each issue of the *Magazine* and offers a grant program for K-12 teachers to help defray travel costs to the annual convention. In the late 1990s, OAH teamed with the National Center for History in the Schools to publish several teaching units. Topics included "The Great Depression and the Arts," "World's Fairs and the Dawning of the 'American Century,'" "Commemorative Sculpture in the United States," and "Early Chinese Immigration and the Process of Exclusion," among others. These projects brought together precollegiate teachers and university-level researchers to craft units tied to the U. S. History Standards.

Efforts to promote the teaching of history received a significant boost in 2001, when Senator Robert Byrd of West Virginia led a successful fight to enact the Teaching American History (TAH) Grant Program. More than $600 million has been awarded since its inception, an unprecedented level of federal funding for history education. TAH has brought teachers from all levels and types of institutions as well as historians from museums and other organizations into a lively conversation about the teaching and learning of history.

OAH has played a central role in these ongoing programs in several ways. It was one of several partners, including the Oregon Public Broadcasting System, in a $2 million grant awarded to reach teachers nationwide to promote content knowledge, skills in thinking historically, and strategies for using multimedia in teaching and learning. Research specialists have given lectures at numerous TAH workshops around the country, and collegiate teachers have formed collaborative relationships with precollegiate instructors. In 2006–2007, there were twenty-seven OAH lectures scheduled with sixteen TAH programs in thirteen states and Puerto Rico. Members of OAH from the collegiate level have reviewed applications for the Department of Education and helped precollegiate teachers craft grant proposals. In the early 2000s OAH met several times with TAH program officials from the Department of Education; these meetings deepened the awareness of OAH staff regarding the opportunities offered by the grant program.

TAH has become a regular part of the OAH annual convention. The Organization sponsored a TAH symposium at the 2006 annual meeting in Washington, D.C., and held another such event in Minneapolis the next year. In 2006, 140 people attended the symposium, which explored the impact of TAH funds on teachers and students alike. In 2007, participants included teachers, curriculum directors, school district representatives, and representatives from nonprofit organizations. Featured topics included the impact of TAH grants on individuals and departments; ways to boost collaboration among researchers, teachers, and educational experts; the effect of TAH grants on student learning; and the future of the program.

In recent years OAH members have also found valuable teaching material in the *Journal of American History*. The *Journal* regularly features reviews of documentaries, films, Web sites, and museum exhibits that can help busy teachers decide the most effective way to convey an idea or promote historical thinking. In the mid-1990s, the *Journal* revived its "Textbooks and Teaching" feature. Each March, the *Journal* has included several articles on pedagogical topics, such as the treatment of slavery in textbooks, the role of assessment, and teaching how historians work and think. Since 2001, the OAH Web site has featured "Teaching the JAH." Intended to promote a closer connection between research and teaching, this initiative seeks to have teachers use articles from the *Journal* in their classrooms. Each article is supplemented by comments from the author, primary source documents, and links to Web resources on that topic. These exercises educate students about that particular topic, but, more important, they demand critical thinking and afford a glimpse into how historians work.

OAH has publicly acknowledged the importance of history education in several other ways. Each year it honors an outstanding K-12 educator with the Mary Kay Bonsteel Tachau Teacher of the Year Award. The OAH has long played a leading role in National History Day, which was founded in the late 1970s. In 2001, OAH signaled its openness to new ways of teaching and learning when it became a sponsor, and, then, a year later, a producer, of the weekly half-hour public radio program *Talking History*. Featuring interviews with historians on a delightfully eclectic range of subjects that included daylight savings time, women's basketball, the Negro baseball leagues, marriage, and Walt Disney, *Talking History* was heard on more than four hundred public radio stations nationwide.

Usually less visible, but still critically important to teaching and learning, are the numerous advocacy efforts undertaken by OAH in recent years. In the mid-1970s, OAH was a founding member of the National Coordinating Committee for the Promotion of History. This organization ceased operation in 2003 and was replaced by the National Coalition for History, which seeks to promote public awareness of the importance of history and influence policy outcomes among lawmakers regarding curricula and other matters of interest to historians. Similarly, OAH is part of the National Humanities Alliance.

Though OAH can take pride in many efforts over the years, much work remains to be done. History education is under assault thanks to the No Child Left Behind Act and other developments as K-12 educators face increasing pressure to emphasize other disciplines and skills. Likewise, collegiate teachers must remain vigilant to ensure that history remains central for undergraduates. It is vital that OAH remain a strong advocate to outsiders for preserving history's place at the heart of what it means to be an educated person. At the same time, OAH must work inside the profession to ensure that history remains a discipline that effectively promotes students' reading, critical thinking, and communication skills, and, more important, excites students in a way that stimulates their curiosity about the world.

NOTES

1. Joan Hoff, "The Origins of the *Magazine*," *Magazine of History* (Fall 1995): 5–8.
2. Howard D. Mehlinger, "History Teaching and the *Magazine of History*: A Janus Perspective," *Magazine of History* (Fall 1995): 9.

31

A Plea for Equality

Leon F. Litwack

I joined the Mississippi Valley Historical Association (MVHA) more than a half-century ago, as I completed my PhD at the University of California, Berkeley, and prepared to teach at the University of Wisconsin in Madison. Several years earlier, I had also acquired a secondary-school teaching credential at Berkeley and did my student teaching at public high schools in Oakland and El Cerrito. More recently, a graduate student, while using the University of California archives, found a letter from the Dean of the School of Education, dated June 20, 1951, to President Robert Gordon Sproul seeking to blacklist me from the teacher certification program because of my association with organizations whose loyalty to the United States was suspect. "All agreed that Mr. Litwack should be discouraged, but none was able to provide us grounds for doing so that would stand up in court." Not the Dean's letter (of which I was totally unaware) but the seduction of further graduate study led me to forsake high school teaching for a PhD and a career in the university.

Thus, I bring to these essays at least some experience with teaching in the schools. The essays provide a valuable overview and several examples of how the MVHA and the organization of American Historians (OAH) initiated and expanded its commitment to secondary school and community college teaching, culminating in active recruitment campaigns, the Focus on Teaching Day at the annual convention, and the OAH *Magazine of History*. Ron Briley forcefully reminded us that in the early years of the MVHA, the teaching of history was not "a major priority." The MVHA and teaching was at best a strained relationship. At the same time, all authors agree we have come a long way in the past half-century, from indifference and neglect to benign neglect to active engagement. Charles Zappia in his essay, and by example also, makes a compelling case for the increased role of the community college professoriate in OAH programs in history teaching.

Through World War II and much of the Cold War, the traditional history course, both in colleges and high schools, provided a patriotic view of the past designed to promote citizenship, cultural unity, and confidence in American progress. The confidence and optimism resonated in our triumphal phrases: the City on the Hill, Manifest Destiny, Rendezvous with Destiny, and the American Century. The course content and textbook served to validate the American experience, that is, we are a nation exempt from history, from the limits that other nations have been taught by suffering to respect. What passed for so many decades as our culture, as a number of historians have argued, was largely an Anglo-American culture, masking itself as our common culture. The history I learned in public school in Santa Barbara was largely the history of Anglo-Saxons and Northern Europeans: Pilgrims, Puritans, Founding Fathers. It was someone else's history, or so it seemed, with little relevance to my life, the lives of my immigrant parents, or the lives of my neighbors, many of them recent arrivals from Mexico.

No group of scholars was more deeply implicated in the miseducation of American youth than historians. They did not simply reinforce prevailing racial and ethnic biases; they helped to create and shape them. They miseducated several generations of Americans, including my generation. What dominated their perceptions of the past were the views of the exceptional, those who comprised the political, economic, and intellectual elites of American society, privileged individuals who left the records (journals, diaries, and correspondence) with which historians felt most comfortable. The history of working class men and women was thought to be irreclaimable, because traditional methods of historical scholarship emphasized the importance of records and documents that such people rarely, if ever, kept. It is not as though the great mass of people, working men and women, white and black, have been inarticulate; it is only that they expressed themselves in ways that historians ignored or knew nothing about. It was not a failure of the archives but a failure of historical imagination.

In the 1960s and 1970s and with even greater intensity after 1980, the new voices and the new experiences brought to the writing and teaching of history transformed profoundly how we think about the past. As my colleague Lawrence Levine argued at that time, the study of history had never been more exciting or challenging; it had never been more varied in its focus, more open in its approaches, more imaginative in its methodology, more sensitive to the complexities and varieties of cultural documentation.

To read the press and popular magazines, to listen to the racial and cultural bigots is to believe that, around this time, storm troopers of the politically correct laid siege to and, in many cases, captured or subverted faculties and textbook publishers. But what these critics called a profound crisis in America's universities reflected their alarm over demographic changes in our student bodies and faculties (the "corruption" of admission and hiring standards by affirmative action), a continuing skepticism about the inclusion of new histories and cultural perspectives in the curriculum, and a heightened, often a hysterical, resistance to the argument that in a more diverse world, the study of white, literate men—indeed of Western culture itself—might be too restrictive.

The way in which history is written and taught does have consequences. That realization, and the need to challenge cultural illiteracy, began to attract growing attention in the 1960s, reflecting no doubt the events and movements that dominated those years. Our written work, our curriculum, how and what we taught would be increasingly directed toward illuminating the struggles of peoples long marginalized in our history—the effort to communicate their lives, aspirations, and hopes in a language that would engage the public as well as our students.

It was against this background that I agreed in 1987 to serve on the Bradley Commission and worked with the OAH to implement the Commission's findings and goals. The Commission may have started under a cloud of suspicion (funded by a conservative foundation, perhaps with a different agenda in mind), but thanks to Kenneth Jackson (who insisted on appointing the members) and the even-handed leadership of Elaine Reed, it asserted its own agenda and broadened its reach. In affirming the critical value of history, the Commission broke with conventional wisdom. It refused to privilege European history over the history of the peoples of Africa, the Americas, and Asia. To overcome cultural illiteracy, every student needed to have an understanding of the world that was not confined to the historical present or to his or her own culture. We also made clear the need to incorporate peoples and experiences previously excluded, to bring to historical consciousness (utilizing a variety of cultural documentation) people ordinarily left outside the framework of the American experience.

What the Bradley Commission affirmed would be derided by critics as "politically correct." Fortunately, our report preceded the hysteria, paranoia, and sometimes downright bigotry perpetrated in the name of defending Western civilization. We tried to incorporate into our report the far-reaching changes in the writing and teaching of history over the previous two decades. We recognized, moreover, that the curriculum in history, as in other disciplines, has never stood still; it has constantly evolved in response to new needs and new knowledge.

With all the progress made in the last several decades, the relationship between teachers in K-12 and in colleges and universities has been strengthened. We have learned the need to work together to achieve our goals, to learn from each other's experiences. However, there is a problem that the historical organizations, including the OAH, the AHA, and the National Council for History Education, have not confronted directly, although it threatens to undermine our best efforts to improve teaching. Helping teachers build a history curriculum and, more debatable, the idea of national standards and testing are acknowledged to be a part of the educational agenda, but even our achievements in this area mask deep problems in our educational system. Do these problems lie within OAH's sphere of influence or do we move on, heedless of their far-reaching and immediate implications?

Public education has come under a sustained attack, in some ways unprecedented in our history. For nearly two centuries, in much of the nation, public education provoked a variety of reforms and reformers, ranging from the Progressive educators, to the "back-to-basics" fundamentalists, to the post-Sputnik "crisis" and the frantic efforts made at that time to remake the curriculum to match or surpass the Soviet Union in the physical sciences. Periodically, most recently in the 1950s, upsurges of patriotism made Americanism and anticommunism integral parts of the public school curriculum, even as many teachers were fired and blacklisted for harboring or communicating "disloyal" thoughts. But whatever the source and no matter how dire the "crisis" demanding reform, previous debates and proposed reforms have shared some common assumptions, none more fundamental than the idea that public education had a genuine place in American society, symbolized by the little red schoolhouse, that it was a valuable, an indispensable component of a hopeful and democratic nation, that all children (regardless of class, race, or gender) should have equal opportunities to learn.

But the very concept of public schools faces dangers that threaten to undermine those schools altogether and create in their place an educational system based largely on class and race. In the Reagan era, public schools came under attack as a public financial burden and, at the same time, as a potential market for private profit. Not coincidentally, domestic policies in the Reagan-Bush years propelled us toward a two-class society. To alleviate the "burden" of public schools, various proposals were made under the deceptive banner of "free choice" to divert public funding (tax money) to private schools. That would divert appropriations from already desperately underfunded public schools to subsidize parents who were already sending their children to private schools. As many educators argued, the effects of such a redistribution were self-evident: the benefits would mostly accrue to those with the most know-how and resources to purchase the most desirable education.

How does this affect the OAH? Any policy that results, whatever its rhetoric or good intentions, in dividing the school population between the chosen and the "others" has to concern us as teachers, educators, and citizens. We should be concerned about the possibility that education may become a consumer good, something purchased from a vender, citizens will be transformed into consumers of an educational product packaged and sold in a deregulated educational marketplace, and children may be transformed into commodities, schools into instructional delivery systems, turning out bland and compliant products to meet the needs of corporate America.

Unequal resources threaten to undermine public education. We seldom consider how vouchers, national standards, and national testing will be implemented in a system of instruction based on class and race. The subject has barely been mentioned in this part of the book. And yet, the enormous gap between wealthy and poor schools can no longer be avoided; it goes to the heart of everything we attempt to do in regard to K-12 teaching. In evaluating national goals, educator Jonathan Kozol made the necessary point: "No goal calls for equal education for rich and poor children. No goal breathes a whisper of the abiding American embarrassment of racial segregation. I feel bewildered, heartsick, that it is politically possible to omit what ought to be the two most pressing ethical goals of a just society."

We can no longer avoid these issues or simply pay lip service to the notion of equality. We must, as an organization, affirm two primary positions: (1) We contend that national standards and testing, if they are to have any meaning, must be rooted in an educational system that gives every child a chance to learn and to succeed. The American Historical Association recognized this fact in its reaction to national standards: "Our general responsibility to society forbids our endorsing any recommendations for national standards that do not affirm clearly and categorically—on both ethical and programmatic grounds— that progress in resolving the inequities in the resources available to schools is prerequisite to implementation." (2) We must repudiate unequivocally the use of public dollars to provide vouchers to private schools. Not only would vouchers drain money from and the commitment to the improvement of teaching in the public schools, but they threaten to subvert the democratic idea itself, replacing the public school with a commercialized, profit-driven educational marketplace. (3) As educators, we must do more than deplore the inequities. We must insist on the enforcement of the law of the land, that is, the Supreme Court's ruling that education "is a right which must be made available to all on equal terms."

The Supreme Court decided in *Brown v. The Board of Education* that "separate educational facilities are inherently unequal," that providing public education was fundamental to good citizenship, and that school segregation placed an ineradicable stigma of inferiority on black students, affecting their hearts and minds "in a way unlikely ever to be undone." Some fifty years later, more than 72 percent of African American students attend schools in which they and other nonwhites are in the majority; some 37 percent attend schools in which 90 to 100 percent of the students are nonwhite. In 1998, the cover of *Time*, along with the feature story, said it all: "Back to Segregation: After four decades of struggle, America has now given up on school integration." By this time it was abundantly clear that whites would rather abandon the public schools and cities than share power and community with nonwhites; even many of the urban white northern liberals (from Washington, DC, to Berkeley, California) who had mandated or supported integration in the South placed their own children in private schools, avoiding the integration to which they had once paid lip service. If the Supreme Court was correct in 1954, the private school is as unconstitutional as the private academies hurriedly established in the South in the wake of the court decision; the private school remains a lingering vestige of social and economic apartheid in the United States.

When we remain indifferent to benign neglect, when we accommodate to second rate education in bleak classrooms, with minority youth living in devastated urban zones attending inferior, underfunded schools in racial isolation, often learning from overworked and poorly paid teachers, using old textbooks, provided a limited curriculum, and leading separate and unequal lives, we pay a heavy price, as citizens and as educators. It mocks our well-intended efforts to improve the teaching of history or any other subject. Listen carefully to the cry from the bottom, from those whose lives were largely untouched by the civil rights movement, from those trapped in substandard homes and schools the refrain from rapper Grandmaster Flash, "It's like a jungle sometimes, it makes me wonder / how I keep from going under. / So don't push me, cause I'm close to the edge / I'm tryin' not to lose my head." Those words still resonate.

It may be time to assess the consequences of the end of integration, the betrayal or deferral of once heightened expectations. It may be time to reconsider how to achieve equal educational opportunities, that is, access to equal facilities, salaries, teacher-student ratios, and curricula. This may require a major social upheaval, a radical revision of the funding and organization of public education that most Americans are not prepared to embrace. Even as the Organization of American Historians over the next century works with K-12 and community college teachers to improve the teaching of history, we may be forced to make some hard decisions on the future of public education to determine if it has a future, if this nation remains truly committed to racial justice. In 1995, four decades after the *Brown* case, Kenneth Clark, an African American educator who played a critical role in the Supreme Court decision, was asked what he thought blacks should call themselves. He replied, "White."

Part V

THE MVHA–OAH AND PUBLIC HISTORY

32

Public History
Past and Present

Spencer R. Crew

Clio, the muse for history, has many children, but they do not always play together well. They see things in different ways, pass judgment on their siblings, and have different people toward whom they direct their work product. This especially has been the case with historians who work in the academy and those scholars working in the public sphere. In some ways it is surprising that there is dissonance between them. They share many similarities. They often are trained in the same classes by the same professors. They share the same quest for accurate, well-researched scholarship as the foundation for the work they produce. They believe in the lessons history can offer and want to share the fruits of their work with others. They take pride in their work and desire the respect and support of their colleagues.

Where they differ is in the primary audiences for their work. In the academy, those audiences are students in their classes and other scholars. The primary means of transmittal of their information is through articles, lectures, seminars, and books. In the public sphere the key audience is the general public who bring varying levels of knowledge and interest to the interchange. They also are an audience whose attention must be cultivated rather than arriving as captive listeners. The way in which information is presented is particularly critical for public historians. Their research results have to be comprehendible and accessible to a broad spectrum of possible recipients. Jargon and pedantic writing will not work for their readers or listeners. As a consequence, their end products at times take forms different from those of their colleagues in the academy. Historians in the public sphere utilize formats ranging from exhibitions to films, official federal agency histories, research aids, and cultural survey reports, to name only a sample. Because these formats and materials do not always undergo the same lengthy peer review process that journal articles and books undergo for academic scholars, they are not always given credit as historical scholarship of the same pedigree as that produced in the academy.

A classic example of this clash of values was an article published in the newsletter of Organization of American Historians in February of 1996, written by three faculty members at the State University of New York at Brockport. They wrote in opposition to an AHA report from the proceeding March entitled "Redefining Historical Scholarship," in which an ad hoc committee called for a new, more comprehensive, and inclusive definition of historical work. Among the ways the March report broadened the definition of the advancement of knowledge was to include original research presented, not only in traditional forms like monographs and journal articles, but also in exhibitions, policy papers, contract work, or other commissioned studies. It further noted specifically that the application of knowledge executed by public historians should also be recognized as important and legitimate contributions to the profession.

The Brockport professors took exception to the report, suggesting that following the recommendations would risk lowering the standards for historical research and writings and demoralizing those in the profession committed to academic excellence. For them, there was no comparison to be made between the quality of the work done by academic historians and historians working outside the academy. Their views mirrored those of historians who believed that the work of public historians was not on the same level as their academic colleagues. To argue otherwise was a semantic game that, they said, would be likened to pretending "a dog's tail was a leg rather than what it was, only a tail."

Attitudes similar to those of the Brockport professors, and a feeling of alienation from colleagues in the academy fueled in part the emergence in 1940 of the American Association for State and Local History (AASLH), for many years a subset of the American Historical Association (AHA). One indication of the interest of this group in presenting history in an accessible form to the lay public was their creation of the popular history magazine *American Heritage*. Featuring many illustrations and nonjargon texts, this periodical offered an alternative to the more academic and dry information provided by other history journals of the period.

A similar sense of separateness resulted in the 1979 formation of the National Council on Public History (NCPH), an institution for the growing numbers of public historians and the organizations they represented. The Council grew out of a conference on public history organized in 1978 by G. Wesley Johnson, which attracted public historians from across the country eager to spend time with other scholars who were doing similar work. A year later another meeting in Washington, DC, resulted in the creation of this new organization. The establishment and continued vibrancy of both the AASLH and NCPH pointed to an ongoing difference in point of view within the ranks of historians who plied their craft in different ways and in different venues.

Even with the formation of these separate organizations, conversations continued within the AHA and the Organization of American Historians (OAH) about the importance and place of public history within the profession. Public historians continued to join these organizations, participate in their conferences, and play an active role as members. It was the lobbying of these members and sympathetic colleagues along with a more supportive leadership that led to the creation of the ad hoc committee whose report provoked the rebuttal from the three SUNY Brockport professors.

The positive news is that their rebuttal to rethinking scholarship occurred more than a decade ago. Fortunately, since then, conversations about how to think more broadly about scholarship have moved in a more positive direction, although there have been some bumps along the way. One such challenge was the decision of the OAH initially not to endorse the ideas in the AHA committee report. This decision certainly was not encouraging to public historians, but it did not dissuade them.

An important forward step took place a few years later when, in 2001, the AHA created another task force charged with "identifying ways the AHA can more effectively address the interests and concerns of public historians both within the Association and at large, as well as ways of deepening an understanding of and appreciation for the activities of public historians within the profession." Under the leadership of Linda Shopes and Victoria Hardin, the task force generated a number of recommendations for the profession. One of their key goals in writing the report was to reposition the relationship between public historians and their colleagues in the AHA and OAH to one that was less estranged and more "balanced, respectful, and dialogic."

The task force report, *Public History, Public Historians, and the American Historical Association*, was issued in 2004 and offered recommendations that the AHA and the OAH could implement to more fully integrate public historians into their associations. There were fifty-one recommendations, six of which were identified as key. Two of the six suggested the AHA reexamine the body of acceptable and credit-worthy scholarly activities considered by history departments as they look at hiring, tenure, and promotion. The committee also strongly suggested a review of the content and format of the organization's annual meeting to more fully include and recognize public history and public historians. One of the concerns was that sessions highlighting public history were seldom scheduled at prime times or given priority focus. The spirit of the recommendations was endorsed by the AHA council and its professional division, which had the task of ensuring continuing progress in finding ways to address the issues raised in the report. In subsequent years, regular sessions have been sponsored by the professional division, with public historians attending the annual conferences to receive feedback and suggestions about the efforts of the AHA with regard to the recommendations. Although these actions did not constitute total victory, they were significant milestones in the struggle for recognition within the AHA and the profession generally.

One of the impacts of the task force report was the formation of the *ad hoc* working group on evaluating public history scholarship in 2007. The working group included representatives from The National Council on Public History, the OAH, and the AHA. Its task was to produce guidelines that would seek to aid academic institutions to define public history work, how to assess it, and how to appropriately reward it in the tenure and promotion processes. In its final report in 2010, the working group provided suggestions for administrators, department chairs, tenure committees, and public scholars seeking tenure concerning critical issues for consideration at hiring, during the period leading up to tenure review, and in the actual review process. For the working group, it was important that history departments find methods to create equitable ways to assess and credit publicly engaged and collaborative research. The adoption of this report by the OAH executive board and the AHA council in 2010 was a strong indication that these professional groups have become more appreciative of the work of public historians.

There have been other signs of progress with regard to recognition of the work and relevance of public historians. James Horton's election as president of the OAH (2004–2005) was an important step in raising the profile of public history in the profession. Although he was primarily based in the academy, Horton's choices as a historian regularly had him working as a public historian. He spent many years involved with the Smithsonian Institution at the National Museum of American History, served as one of the lead historians in the creation of the National Civil Rights Museum in Memphis, Tennessee, took a year leave of absence to work at the National Park Service to help improve their historical interpretations, worked closely with the History Channel hosting a regular show on history, and has worked regularly with secondary level educators to support them in their work. As OAH president, one of his key goals was to promote the place of public history in the organization and extol the importance of history outside the academy. As president, he strongly endorsed the idea that historians had a responsibility to get accurate and well-presented history before the public to enable them to better navigate the complexities of the modern world. These were sentiments any public historian would heartily embrace.

The election of Pete Daniel as president of OAH in 2008 lifted recognition of the validity of public history even further. Daniel has been a curator at the National Museum of American History for more than two decades and a part of several exhibition teams. He left a tenured position to begin working at the Smithsonian. As OAH president, he has spoken about the importance of public history and the impact it can have upon the public. His election was seen by many as an important positive step for the status of public historians within the profession.

Although it is good to appreciate the changing atmosphere with regard to public historians, it also is important to take the time to reflect on how we have reached this point. It has not always been an easy path, but neither has it been one without moments of satisfaction. As a discipline, public history has flourished over the years. Public history training is a part of the graduate options for rising numbers of history programs. More recently public history has gained increased attention as the job market for historians stiffened and opportunities outside the academy offered important alternatives for historians seeking employment. As the interest in public history grows, a better sense of what the work entails, along with historical perspective, is crucial.

There is no better way to understand the history, the challenges, and the satisfaction connected to public history than to allow practitioners the opportunity to reflect on their work. Their passion and dedication to the discipline can be both engaging and enlightening. They also can offer a sense of the breadth of activities that are encompassed under the rubric of public historian. The essays that follow provide a retrospective look at public history. The authors are veteran public historians who share a passion for public history but bring different perspectives about its relationship to the larger field. They also provide insights into the many different ways public historians perform their work. In their presentations, these historians provide perspective on how public history has evolved, insight into the contributions public historians have made to the field of history, and analysis of their past and present relationship with other historians. In the end, the goal is not to unearth past divisive issues but to affirm the value of public history to the historical profession. They also look to remind us of the pertinence of public history to one of the goals of all historians, which is to offer perspectives that help their fellow citizens navigate a complex and often confusing world. It is a reminder that they, too, embrace Clio as their muse and are dedicated to honoring her spirit through their work.

33

Historians in the Federal Government

Donald A. Ritchie

In 1974, research for a chapter in my dissertation took me to the Federal Records Center in Suitland, Maryland, to consult the files of the Office of Civilian Defense from 1941 to 1943. Since no one had requested them before, the records remained classified, but the Archives' staff arranged to have all 3,000 cubic feet of material opened by the next day. This was both good news and bad news, since I now faced the daunting prospect of combing through 3,000 cubic feet of records. From the first box, the first item I removed bore the title "Narrative Account of the Office of Civilian Defense," by Robert McElroy, dated November 1944. It was an on-the-spot history of the Office of Civilian Defense (OCD), compiled in response to President Franklin D. Roosevelt's 1942 executive order that all wartime agencies document their missions and prepare "an accurate and objective account" of their experiences. As a wartime government historian, McElroy had examined the agency's files and interviewed key personnel, including the secretary who later married the OCD's director, James M. Landis, the man whose career I was studying. Needless to say, that official history guided my research through those many boxes of records, expediting the process and enhancing the chapter.[1]

That experience highlighted several important points about historians in the federal government. One was that they have been working inside the government for a long time. In fact, the first federal historical project got under way nearly a half century before the founding of the Mississippi Valley Historical Association (MVHA). Back in 1861, staff of the State Department began to compile, edit, and publish the Foreign Relations of the United States. The Foreign Relations Series hired its first PhD historians in 1924, and has continued to produce hundreds of volumes, having now reached the Nixon-Kissinger era. The second point was that federal historians, in countless ways, have facilitated historical research, even if researchers were unaware of their efforts and were surprised to discover it. That point was reiterated in 1999, when the distinguished Princeton historian Robert Darnton, as incoming president of the

American Historical Association (AHA), asked curiously, "What do federal historians do?"[2]

Such fogginess has a long history in the profession. The MVHA owed its start to a former federal official, Secretary of Agriculture J. Sterling Morton. As a Nebraska newspaper publisher, Morton campaigned for an authoritative history of Nebraska, and his initiative prompted the first meeting of the MVHA. The new organization also attracted college professors, who quickly formed its core membership.[3] By the time the association had changed its name in 1965, its members and its services were firmly planted in the academy. When I entered graduate school in 1967, the journal, programs, and mind-set of the OAH were exclusively oriented toward academic careers in history. When I earned my PhD in 1975, however, that world had fallen into crisis. For historians, 1975 served as the functional equivalent of 1929, producing an oversupply of new doctoral degrees facing an undersupply of academic job openings. Some quit the history profession altogether, some fell back on the breadline of adjunct teaching, and some discovered the federal government and other employers of public historians. By chance, the government was then in the midst of augmenting its historical operations in anticipation of the National Bicentennial in 1976. Existing federal historical offices expanded and new offices emerged. In 1975 the Senate fortuitously created its Historical Office, appointing Richard Baker as the first historian; six months later, I joined the office as associate historian.

In graduate school, I had the advantage of contact with Walter Rundell, then chairman of the history department at the University of Maryland. Rundell had devoted his attention to rethinking the traditional definitions of the professional historian, and had produced an important survey, *In Pursuit of American History: Research and Training in the United States*.[4] As chair, he took advantage of the university's proximity to the capital by arranging for the historian in the Department of Labor to exchange places for a year with the faculty's labor historian, and in various other ingenious ways exposed the green graduate students in his department to the possibilities of careers as historians outside a university. We discovered that professional historians were embedded throughout the government, bearing the titles of archivists, editors, researchers, park rangers, museum curators, and even historians.

Although relieved to have found gainful employment that put their historical interests and research training to good use, many of the new federal historians suffered what Richard Hofstadter would have deemed a "status anxiety" over the way the rest of the profession viewed them. A fellow graduate student, who had been hired as one of the first curators at a new historical museum, described to one of his professors the immense satisfaction he gained from watching crowds of visitors read his text from the walls of the exhibit halls. The professor nodded but afterward commented, "It's too bad, because he would have made such a good historian." His definition of *historian* did not include a museum curator, no matter how historical the subject or large the audience. This was a time when the membership committee of the OAH was still divided into two-year institutions and four-year institutions. (I pointed out that I worked for a six-year institution.) In capsule, it represented a way of thinking that tended to marginalize federal historians.

Uncertainty about their professional standing led federal historians in 1979 to create the Society for History in the Federal Government (SHFG). Note that its title is "for History in," not "for Historians of," because the Society included independent contractors, academics among them, as well as those employed within the government, and because not all federal historians write about the government. Members of the Society included historians, archivists, curators, librarians, editors, and preservationists, for whom it served as a professional network to promote common interests.[5] Neither the SHFG nor the National Council on Public History (NCPH) advocated that federal historians secede from the OAH or the AHA, and both of those professional associations eventually redrew their boundaries to make their meetings more accommodating to the new field. They created prizes to recognize significant publications and other contributions by public historians, including federal historians, and appointed committees to deal with issues that concerned them. Capping this enhanced professional recognition of federal history was the choice of Pete Daniel, a curator in the Smithsonian's National Museum of American History, as president of the OAH in 2008–2009.[6]

The OAH has also co-sponsored a number of its annual meetings with the NCPH, for which federal historians have served on the program committees. Being the larger organization in the partnership, the OAH chose the conference themes for these joint meetings, some of them being on the abstract side. The joint conference that met in Washington in 2002, for instance, had the theme of "Overlapping Diasporas: Encounters and Conversations," which did not easily fit the interests of public historians. But program committee members from the two organizations worked together harmoniously, and the final program was fully interlaced with public history sessions. Federal historians provided many of the political- and military-history sessions that appeared on that program, aptly suited to the meeting's location in the national capital, and at a time when the government was going to war. The OAH's innovation of state-of-the-art sessions has also given program committees the opportunity to create panels rather than simply pick from proposals submitted independently. This device helped focus attention on areas that had been previously neglected or underrepresented, to the benefit of both academic and public historians.

The OAH's Research Committee regularly addressed issues of recordkeeping, declassification, and access to federal documents, allowing government and university-based historians to work cooperatively rather than to polarize.

Researchers have long been fighting battles with federal agencies to release historically significant material. Although historians within those agencies can appreciate why some safeguards are necessary for more sensitive records, historians both inside and outside the government ultimately want more government documents opened at a faster pace. Federal historians have helped to write the guidelines for access to the records of their agencies. The Senate, for instance, had no standard policy for releasing the official records generated by its committees, whether from recent times or the distant past, until 1980 when it adopted a resolution, drafted by its Historical Office, to open most records automatically after twenty years (the more sensitive records dealing with national security, personal privacy, and investigations could be closed for up to fifty years). Federal historians have suggested strategies for their academic colleagues in approaching agencies for access to records, have assisted OAH officers with their testimony about these issues before congressional committees, and have alerted historians to the potential problems that may emerge from changing public policy between one administration and the next.

By the 1980s, public historians, and particularly federal historians, were enjoying higher visibility in the publications of the leading historical associations. The *OAH Newsletter* began to include more regular reports on federal historians and the issues that most concerned them. The *Newsletter* also began running reports from the director of the National Coordinating Committee for the Promotion of History (NCC)—later the National Coalition for History (NCH)—who has kept the profession informed of the government's historical activities, from appropriations to declassifications and court rulings. At the same time, the *Journal of American History* expanded its review section to include documentaries, museum exhibits, and Web sites, which often highlight the work of federal historians who also serve as reviewers. In 1987, the *JAH* launched an annual section of articles on oral history as a methodology, and from the start it included pieces on federal oral history programs. In some issues, the section was the only place to find a contribution from a federal historian. It flourished for a decade, but it occupied a prime piece of real estate in the journal that was coveted for other purposes and, consequently, it was eventually discontinued.

Because federal historians are not subject to publish–or- perish pressures for attaining tenure, few have submitted the type of analytical essays generally published in the *JAH*. Their articles, which tend toward case studies and methodologies, have been more likely to appear in *The Public Historian* or other more specialized journals. Nor has the *JAH* included many public or federal historians in its roundtables on specific issues. Even in military history, an area that has attracted a high concentration of federal historians, the roundtable consisted entirely of academic contributors, although one had previously directed the Naval Historical Center.[7]

What exactly have historians accomplished in the federal government that should gain the attention of the historical profession? This is not an easy question to answer, because there is no typical federal historical office. Federal historical offices range from large operations, such as those in the military or the National Park Service, to one-person shops. Federal historians write histories, prepare documentary editions, put out pamphlets, run Web pages, conduct interviews, mount exhibits, produce videos, create curriculum guides, sponsor conferences, and provide historical reference for their agencies, the public, and the media. They administer internships, travel grants, and fellowships for historians and students. Many of them speak regularly about the history and operations of their agencies to groups inside and outside the government. Some have long shelves of books to their credit. The historians in the Office of Secretary of Defense, for instance, are producing a series of detailed studies of each defense secretary, drawn from a mountain of primary sources. Historians at the Supreme Court recently completed a thirty-year project to collect and publish the records of the court's early history, a documentary record that jurists and historians believed to be lost. And the Nuclear Regulatory Commission authorized a history of the events at Three Mile Island, released on the twenty-fifth anniversary of that chilling event. Their painstaking work in discovering, declassifying, and describing previously unavailable resources will benefit future researchers and stand as reliable reference sources on their own.[8]

Anyone tempted to dismiss these works as official history should read William Hammond's two-volume history of the military and the media during the Vietnam War, *Reporting Vietnam: Media and Military at War*. As an official historian for the U.S. Army Center for Military History, Hammond obtained unparalleled access to military and civilian government records, interviewed key personnel, and surveyed the burgeoning literature on Vietnam. He concluded that the military, rather than the media, bore responsibility for that war's public relations quagmire. No researcher outside the government could have competed with Hammond's security clearances and ability to pry open still-classified records, nor would an outsider's account have been as convincing for Hammond's intended audience: the generations of military officers who will deal with the media in future conflicts.[9]

Such historical narratives have connected current civilian and military officers and staff with their own history, detailing how policies developed, how procedures changed over time, and what worked best, or failed, in the past. Through publications, reports, and reference works, federal historians serve as the institutional memory for their agencies. When the Space Shuttle Challenger exploded in 1986, NASA's historical office came to the aid of stunned agency officials by providing a detailed report about how NASA had responded to previous catastrophes. Historical offices prepare reports and briefing books in response to specific requests from administrators seeking comparisons between past policies and pending initiatives. Of course, not all administrators make use of such studies. As the United States prepared for war in Iraq in 2002, the Department of State commissioned the historian Drew Erdmann, who had studied under Ernest R. May, a leading proponent of making history available for policy makers. The department wanted a report on the outcome of twentieth-century postwar reconstructions. Erdmann compiled enough historical analogies to conclude that chances of long-term success depended on international support from the outset, and on sufficient numbers of troops to ensure stability in the postwar phase. The Secretary of State admired the report and circulated it to the vice president, the secretary of defense, and the national security adviser. Later, when asked why his report had no effect on their decisions, Erdmann responded, "Maybe it wasn't read."[10]

The media is a hungry consumer of the kind of information that government historians provide. In many executive departments, federal historians are discouraged from talking directly to reporters, and media requests are channeled through press offices. Sometimes, however, federal historians provide timely reference to reporters, who are pressed by deadlines. They dispel confusion, discourage hyperbole, and set the record straight without taking sides in any policy or political dispute.

The Senate Historical Office has spent a considerable amount of time taking calls and answering e-mail messages from reporters, trying to furnish factual answers to their questions. The presidential impeachment trial in 1999—the first since 1868—besieged the office with questions from reporters, some of whom apparently had gone through college without taking a history course. "Who is Andrew Johnson and why was he impeached?" a perplexed reporter asked at the Clinton trial's outset. The illness of South Dakota Senator Tim Johnson in 2006, which jeopardized his party's slender majority in the Senate, also generated a slew of questions on historical precedents. After thirty years of operation, the office has compiled multiple volumes of Senate facts: how many did what, when, and under what circumstances. We can provide comprehensive lists to reporters over the phone, by e-mail, or on the Web site. A reporter based in New York, who recently needed help on short notice on precedents about senators who ran for president, responded gratefully: "The Senate historian's office is seen as a treasure in Washington, and I can see why."[11]

Federal historians have influenced their agencies' records management policies, convincing those agencies to preserve more records and open documents for research. Some historical offices maintain their own records collections, whereas others serve as conduits for the transfer of agency records to the National Archives. They are often consulted over FOIA requests from historians and journalists. Historians operate within all the intelligence agencies, where almost everything is classified and is likely to remain closed for decades. In such cases, their research serves as an advance guard for historians. This is especially critical when it comes to conducting oral history interviews with intelligence agency staff forbidden by law from talking about what they do without authorization. Many of these staff may no longer be around to interview when the documents have finally opened, so it is crucial to have trained historians on site to conduct timely interviews.

Oral history methodology has been employed within the federal government for a long time. Federal historians were interviewing combat troops at Normandy Beach in 1944 and are interviewing troops in Iraq and Afghanistan today. Historians in Congress, the Supreme Court, the cabinet offices, and many other federal agencies have been recording the memories and perspectives of a broad cross section of federal personnel, from cabinet secretaries, federal judges, and Foreign Service officers to scientists, managers, and office secretaries. The interviews have dealt with everything from medicine and international finance to the drive for equal opportunity for women and minorities in government employment. Some federal oral histories are now available on the agency Web sites, and many of the recordings and transcripts are deposited at the National Archives and the Library of Congress. In addition to the oral histories conducted by federal historians, the Veterans History Project at the Library of Congress has solicited and accepted more than 45,000 interviews from the general public, after providing them with information about how to conduct, record, and preserve interviews with war veterans and civilians from the home front.[12]

Interviews do not just happen; someone needs to carry out the program and to convince potential interviewees to participate. In the 1980s, federal historians found that some federal officials were reluctant to give interviews unless they could close those interviews for a set period of time, and not have them opened prematurely because of a Freedom of Information Act request. The Society for History in the Federal Government worked with the National Archives, the Justice Department, and the Copyright Office to determine that those who participate voluntarily in a federal oral-history project do not automatically waive their copyright. They can choose to donate the transcript to the public domain at a later date, keeping the interviews closed until then. As donated material, interviews fall under Freedom of Information Act's (FOIA's) gift exemption, comparable to the donation of a manuscript collection. In the quarter century since that policy was formulated and disseminated, numerous federal oral histories have opened for research, but none of those that followed the recommended procedures opened any earlier than their donors requested. Federal historians thus avoided a "chilling effect" that might have discouraged the collection of candid interviews.[13]

Federal historians devote a great deal of effort to the public presentation of history, reaching audiences that neither exclude nor are limited to fellow professional historians. Their audience includes their agencies, the media, scholars, students, tourists, and Web browsers. Federal historians present history in many formats, including museums, traveling exhibits, national parks, historical sites, documentaries, and Web sites. Since the 1980s, the "culture wars" have made it more difficult to mount exhibits, as the curators of the Enola Gay, the West in American History, and Science in American Life exhibits can readily testify. With federal funds declining, museums have turned to private donors to underwrite exhibits, and some of those donors have sought to influence the content and interpretation of the exhibit. Citizens groups have taken offense over museum interpretations, and politicians have had conniptions over exhibits they considered too critical of American life. Despite some well-publicized battles and defeats, curators and historians continue to maintain professional standards, and have fought the good fight to keep historical presentations accurate, challenging, and relevant.[14]

Many federal historians, not just museum curators, have been involved in presenting exhibits inside their own agencies, to enlighten those who work at or visit the headquarters. During the last decade, such efforts have expanded to include online exhibits, adding narratives, reference material, documents, and data to agency Web sites, expanding the audience well beyond agency insiders. The historians at the National Institutes of Health, for example, had rarely been able to mount an exhibit off their own campus in Bethesda, Maryland. The Internet has enabled them to post educational materials and other exhibits of interest to students across the country. The National Museum of American History records ten million online visitors every year, which is triple the number of people who physically enter the museum during the same period. When the museum was closed for renovation, the Web site served as a substitute, allowing its vast collection to remain available to an international audience. The National Archives has been constantly adding a vast amount of federal data to its online resources. You can read the oral history transcripts of the presidential libraries online, without traveling to West Branch, Iowa, or Independence, Missouri. The Senate Historical Office is posting full oral history transcripts, historical essays and statistics, and the entire *Biographical Directory of U.S. Congress*, with accompanying bibliographies and location of manuscript collections for everyone who served in Congress. An "In the News" feature on the Senate Web site includes information and historical context for whatever events are transpiring at the moment: advice and consent on a nomination or treaty, the State of the Union address, a filibuster, or some other parliamentary maneuver. The availability of online resources has reduced the number of phone calls to the office from the public and the press, who have grown used to searching the Web site, freeing staff time for other projects. The monthly statistics on the number of hits on the Senate Web site show a phenomenal number of users, and e-mail requests indicate that a large percentage of them are students working on papers.[15]

The greatest public outreach program among federal historians occurs in the National Park Service (NPS) that currently operates 391 park areas and historical sites. The NPS employs staff that specializes in the history of every region, ethnic group, and time period represented in its vast holdings, reasoning that collectively these historical sites and parks represent "an American history textbook" that can educate the visiting public about the people, events, buildings, objects, landscapes, and artifacts associated with each location. Across the country, from the cotton mills in Lowell, Massachusetts, to Central High School in Little Rock, Arkansas, and the Klondike Gold Rush National Historical Park in Skagaway, Alaska, NPS historians study sites being preserved; prepare reports, pamphlets, and other publications; assist in producing orientation films for visitors; and often work on site as ready sources of information.[16]

Despite all these accomplishments among federal history offices, there have been some unsettling trends. Several federal agencies have closed their libraries and outsourced their reference work. Elections and internal reorganizations have taken place, supportive agency heads have departed, and federal historians have found themselves forced to justify their existence. Budget deficits and antigovernment sentiments have reduced or eliminated some historical programs. Many of those historians who entered government service in the 1970s are on the verge of retirement, uncertain over whether their positions will continue after they depart. The National Coalition for History, the historical profession's Washington lobbyist, continues to do yeoman duty in alerting historians about potential cutbacks in jobs and services, but the profession and its membership organizations need to remain vigilant to preserve existing historical programs and find opportunities to create new or expanded programs in agencies that have neglected their history.

In several agencies without historians on staff, current and former employees have banded together to form private historical societies to replicate their work. These nongovernmental, nonprofit organizations sponsor lectures, conduct interviews, collect photographs and other memorabilia, and maintain Web sites. The Society of Former Agents of the FBI, for example, has sponsored an FBI Oral History Heritage Program, hiring the FBI's former official historian to run workshops and supervise the product of its volunteer interviewers. The Securities and Exchange Commission Historical Society sponsors a virtual museum and archive of SEC and securities history, to preserve the commission's collective memory and to make its history more available to the SEC staff and the public. Such efforts, though not desirable substitutes for agency historical offices, demonstrate the value that those within the government place on preserving and disseminating their histories.[17]

This brief summary hardly does justice to the activities of the hundreds of federal historians who have operated out of scores of offices and museums, working on a myriad of projects. Those who have tapped federal historical resources can name many other creative efforts that assisted their research and furthered their understanding of historical events and personalities. For some researchers, however, it will take more time to discover and appreciate these contributions, like the one I came across by chance in Robert McElroy's narrative history of the Office of Civilian Defense.

NOTES

1. Donald A. Ritchie, *James M. Landis: Dean of the Regulators* (Cambridge, MA: Harvard University Press, 1980), 103–19.
2. Victoria A. Hardin, "What Do Federal Historians Do?" *AHA Perspectives* 37 (May 1999), 19–24.
3. John R. Wunder, "The Founding Years of the OAH," http://www.oah.org/pubs/nl/2006nov/wunder.html.
4. Walter Rundell, *In Pursuit of American History: Research and Training in the United States* (Norman: University of Oklahoma Press, 1970).
5. "About the Society," http://shfg.org/target.html
6. "Forrest C. Pogue Award Interview—Pete Daniel," *Oral History in the Mid-Atlantic Region Newsletter* (Summer/Fall 2003): 5–10.
7. Donald A. Ritchie, "Oral History in the Federal Government," *Journal of American History* 74 (Sept. 1987): 587–95; "American Military History: A Round Table," *Journal of American History* 93 (Mar. 2007): 1116–62.
8. Lawrence S. Kaplan, Ronald D. Landa, and Edward J. Drea, *The McNamara Ascendancy, 1961–1965* (Washington, DC: Office of the Secretary of Defense, 2006); Maeva Marcus and James R. Perry, eds., *The Documentary History of the Supreme Court of the United States, 1789–1800* (New York: Columbia University Press, 1985–2006); *New York Times*, December 30, 2006, A15; J. Samuel Walker, *Three Mile Island: A Nuclear Crisis in Historical Perspective* (Berkeley: University of California Press, 2004).
9. Originally published as William M. Hammond, *Public Affairs: The Military and the Media, 1962–1978* (Washington, DC: U.S. Army Center for Military History, 1988), and *Public Affairs: The Military and the Media, 1968–1974* (Washington, DC: U.S. Army Center for Military History, 1996), a condensed version appeared as *Reporting Vietnam: Media and Military at War* (Lawrence: University Press of Kansas, 1998).
10. George Packer, "War After the War: Letter from Baghdad,' *New Yorker* 79 (Nov. 24, 2003): 58–85; see also Richard E. Neustadt and Ernest R. May, *Thinking in Time: The Uses of History for Decision-Makers* (New York: Free Press, 1986).
11. Donald A. Ritchie, "The Past Meets the Press: Historians and the News Media," *The Maryland Historian* 30 (Spring 2006); Sewell Chan, e-mail to the author, January 22, 2007.
12. Donald A. Ritchie, *Doing Oral History: A Practical Guide* (New York: Oxford University Press, 2003), 41–44.

13. See the "Oral History in the Federal Government" special feature in the *Oral History Review* 30 (Summer/Fall 2003), 77–128.

14. See Edward Linenthal and Tom Engelhardt, eds., *History Wars: The Enola Gay and Other Battles for the American Past* (New York: Metropolitan Books, 1996).

15. See Lee Ann Potter, "From Information to Engagement: Online Resources for Educators from the National Archives," Amy Bartow-Melia and Matthew MacArthur, "Electronic Outreach at the National Museum of American History," Sarah A. Leavitt, "Educational Outreach Programs at the Office of NIH History," and Beth Boland, "Give the People What They Want: Using the Internet to Inform the Public," all in *Society for History in the Federal Government Newsletter* 11 (Fall 2006): 3–10.

16. "History," http://www.nps.gov/history/history/hisnps/; *Directory of National Park Service Historians, 2006–2007* (Washington, DC: National Park Service, 2006).

17. Brian R. Hollstein, "Former FBI Agents Document Secretive Careers," *Oral History Association Newsletter* 41 (Fall 2007): 5–6; Virtual Museum and Archive of SEC and Securities History: http://www.sechistorical.org/.

34

Discovering Public History in an Unlikely Place

UC, Santa Barbara, 1976 and After

Otis L. Graham Jr.

One afternoon in 1976 Robert Kelley came into my office and asked me to join him, and G. Wesley Johnson, in establishing a new graduate program to train young historians to practice their craft off campus. I was a full professor, but my reaction, as I look back, deserved a grade of F. I questioned whether this initiative to find historical careers for our students would work, as there was little off-campus opportunity for historians. Bob gently reminded me of the many historians pursuing careers in historic preservation, museums, state and local historical societies, archives. He also told me, with some excitement, of his service as an historical consultant in extensive litigation on California water rights cases, and expressed confidence that historical expertise had an expansive future with governments, courts, businesses.

I agreed to try to help, though impressed that we did not know precisely what we were doing. Only looking back can I see that in the late 1970s we had entered an era of an unexpected convergence of two streams of historical professionalism that had taken different paths a century earlier. As university-based historians became professionals in the late nineteenth and early twentieth centuries, they lost interest in, and sometimes even alienated, off-campus historians. This led to the formation in 1940 of the American Association of State and Local History (AASLH), as well as separate professional organizations for archivists and preservationists.

In my graduate-school years at Columbia in the early 1960s nobody told me that there were working historians in other places than campuses. No one informed me that there were historians practicing their craft not only in state and local historical societies, historic preservation, and museums, but also in the Army, Navy, and Air Force, the Departments of Agriculture and State, the Atomic Energy Commission, Wells Fargo Bank, and in the government of the city of Rochester. I did not hear that someone in Iowa named Benjamin Shambaugh had, long before my time, led a state-financed applied-history research program designed explicitly to serve the policy needs of Iowa legislators. Only much later did I learn that Darlene Roth and other historians in 1976 had established "The History Group" in Atlanta to do contract work and Alan Newall had set up in 1979 a consulting firm in Montana, and they paid themselves salaries. No, to me and everybody I met in my world of history, a historian was a professor. We were taught this from the books we read, in hallway talk, in the meetings of the OAH, the Southern, the AHA.

Now, Bob Kelley, an academic, was proposing that the academy get into the business of training some of our students to enter those unknown worlds beyond the ivory towers, since the sudden arrival of a severe job crisis had created in history graduate programs a spirit of dismay and urgency, but few remedial ideas. Wes Johnson, in the first issue of a journal published by the History Department at the University of California-Santa Barbara (UCSB), *The Public Historian*, hailed our program and others we soon heard about back at Carnegie Mellon and down the road at UC Riverside as "the birth of a new field," which it wasn't. It was the birth of graduate programs for an old field.

Bob proposed to call this new field Public History, because the word *applied* was anathema at the University of California and all research universities. There was resistance to the term. As Rebecca Connard, a graduate of the Santa Barbara program, once put it, kindly, "Public History is not a term that explains itself." But somehow the term stuck.

We had a lot to learn, and fast. With the public history graduate program in place at UCSB, Bob found a sympathetic executive at the Rockefeller Foundation, and we hosted in April 1979 a conference on this "new field" at a retreat in Montecito. New field! My god, eighty people from all parts of the country showed up on little notice, and three days were stoked with the excitement of discovering like-minded people with a common understanding that something rather old, off-campus history, was now re-discovered and re-appreciated and ripe for expansion and the attention of all historians—even the academics who hardly knew that this working base was out there at all. We learned that public history had been around for a long time without the name, and was currently flourishing, even though it did not run under that particular label, or any other. Lots of public historians were busily plying their trade off campus, and now Kelley and others had convened a meeting to name them, make plans to train their next generation, and organize the lot of them for mutual advancement and public service.

At the Montecito meeting, a steering committee was appointed to convene another gathering for purposes of forming an association, and the National Council on Public History (NCPH) came out of a series of meetings in Washington in September and December 1979 and at Carnegie Mellon University the next spring. The NCPH founders first considered an organizational formula such as a council of "constituent groups" but soon wisely settled on a membership organization that thrives today.

A lot of the historians who came to the Montecito, DC, and Carnegie Mellon meetings to establish the NCPH were professors. They included Kelley, Johnson, Peter Stearns, Joel Tarr, Noel Stowe, and Barbara Howe. We were professors joining hands with public historians from federal agencies and historical societies to make the public history social movement, if I may call it that, grow and prosper. All of us who taught public history graduate courses on university campuses turned ourselves into public historians by doing some contract research. That is, we practiced what we taught.

At the time of NCPH's founding and early years, we public historians did not regard our relationship to the OAH as the central question. America's public historians, though not yet using that term, had seceded long ago from the American Historical Association (AHA) and the OAH. Yes, some public historians in museum and historical-society work who belonged to the American Association for State and Local History (AASLH) surely also had membership in the AHA and OAH, but they were sufficiently professionally estranged to have formed their own associations, which they looked to for the services historians need from their trade associations. They felt that their client-oriented work and their concerns had long been ignored by the AHA and OAH. It is also true that we few academics caught up in public history in the late 1970s had strong ties to the AHA, where I served a term on the Council, and to the OAH, where I have been a member since 1960. But in 1978–1980 and after, we were thinking of how the NCPH could serve public historians, not how to persuade the OAH to respond to us.

The public history movement did need a base in some universities, to be sure, twenty five or thirty of them where public history graduate programs could be located, but as for the two flagship historical societies, public historians at the Montecito meeting realized that we were beyond the secession stage and were forming our own government! We were thinking about what we could do for ourselves with our new organization—hold annual meetings, publish a journal and a newsletter that would, in their different ways, explore and illuminate our particular issues, including peer reviewing public historical work, which would include the unpublished gray literature delivered to the client, consider a code of ethics, explain ourselves to potential students and clients, promote exchange of syllabi among graduate programs, establish best practices in public-history graduate training, explore the pros and cons of some forms of certification, and much else. The OAH could not do this for us.

In those early, institution-building days, all I heard from public historians with respect to the OAH was the complaint that an occasional breeze of contempt blew our way or, at best, snide remarks like "You folks are doing second-rate work." I never saw much hard evidence for these complaints of open, verbalized snobbery, but, then, I was an academic and might not hear it. Anyway, public historians' attitude in those days was: Ask not what the OAH can do for you, but what you can do for yourselves. That was the question, and the NCPH, *The Public Historian*, and the Society for History in the Federal Government were some of the answers.

That said, here are some brief thoughts about the relationship, because there is a story there, if not exactly what you might expect. It is my distinct recollection, backed by some research facilitated by documents and information supplied by Brenda Burk of the Indiana University-Purdue University Indianapolis Library and Susan Ferentinos, Public History Coordinator for the OAH, that the OAH reached out to us, early and often, not the other way around. The OAH was not unaware of the public history uprising. The January 1979 *OAH Newsletter*, months before the Montecito meeting, carried an article on this new identity among historians. When the Montecito meeting was held, Richard Kirkendall, the OAH Executive Secretary, was there. I have never asked whether he invited himself and assume that conference planners invited him out of respect and may have been a bit surprised when he showed up. He did not come as a spy or saboteur but was curious, open-minded, sympathetic, and eager to have the OAH respond constructively to this insurgency, as soon as they figured out what it was. Everything that happened thereafter suggests to me an organizational open mind and sympathetic if somewhat puzzled stance by the OAH bureaucracy. They appointed committees, and a relationship was forged.

The National Coordinating Committee for History had been established in the mid-l970s to lobby for history, and, under Arnita Jones's leadership, representatives attended many of the founding meetings of the public historians and could hardly have been more helpful. In l981 NCC published A *Directory of Historical Consultants*. The OAH had established a Committee on Historic Sites in 1966, which became the Historic Preservation Committee in 1975, and the Public History Committee in l981. But this understates the fecundity of OAH committee formation, something the Organization is good at. At the business meeting of the association in 1979, as the public-history rebels encamped across the Brandywine in Montecito, President Carl Degler proposed, and the membership adopted, a resolution establishing a special committee to "study the question of how to include nonacademic members." Degler appointed three nonacademic historians to that committee, chaired by Larry Tise, and, in early fall, it sent a questionnaire to 650 historians working within the federal government, as well as historians in state historical societies and archives, and others in private consulting, asking about "their professional needs" and what type of organization might best fulfill them. I have no space to go into the interesting results, except for two highlights. One was the report that a few public historians stubbornly disliked the new term *public history*. And, in the committee's words, "relatively few historians in the public and private sectors now belong to the OAH (31% of federal and 21% of non-federal public historians.")

The OAH had a problem, and now they knew it, with supporting evidence. The committee made thirteen recommendations for meeting the needs of this constituency. The executive secretary vetted this report with another OAH committee which passed on the recommendations to the OAH board, and the tone of all this communication is one of receptivity, and a positive intent to supply desired services and open the association's conferences and publications to this new, or old and almost lost, constituency. I would call all this very quick action in an inclusive spirit by a professional bureaucracy. There was also some wisdom along the way. The Tise committee's recommendations included two conveying the idea that "the term public history not be used by the OAH, without other qualifiers." The OAH was being asked to throw the very name of the new segment of the profession into question. Kirkendall knew a hornet's nest when he saw it and advised the board to pass on that one. Terminology must be fought out among the people who care about it. The OAH would not referee that fight.

So, while we were starting up a new organization, the old one asked a large number of public historians what the OAH could do for them, even suggesting some ideas: review museum exhibits in the JAH; make a public history category when listing Recent Scholarship in the JAH; schedule public history sessions for every annual meeting; give considerable newsletter coverage to public history issues and developments; and, an even better idea, meet jointly from time to time at annual meetings. It is my impression that the OAH moved with reasonable promptness in all these directions. The organization was slower to appoint and nominate public historians for service on committees and to nominate them to run for top offices. There has been some progress here, which I documented in an Editor's Corner in *The Public Historian (TPH)*(Summer, 1996).

These tangible responses by the OAH, this reaching out to a wayward constituency, represent the part of the relationship one can document. There is another dimension that I do not think can be captured in documents but can be only in oral histories. Inside the ranks and meeting halls of public historians, there has been from the beginning, or the beginning I know anything about, a repeated complaint that the AHA and OAH professors saw the off-campus historians as second-class citizens, the people who couldn't land a university job. This is surely impossible to document, measure, and assess. So I will give you three anecdotes.

Two convey open expressions of fundamental ignorance of what public history was. Ignorance is not exactly dismissal or contempt, but it surely reflects a certain lack of respect. In one of my conversations with a good friend, John

Higham, one of the foremost historians of America and also a former president of the OAH, he turned to me and bluntly asked: "Otis, what is public history?" He asked this in the 1990s, in my eighth year as editor of *TPH*, a journal almost twenty years old that few academic historians subscribed to or read. Another former president of the OAH offered in the 1990s to address the annual meeting of the NCPH, and his offer was accepted with gratitude. He came, and told about the many times he, too, had been a public historian, advising Ken Burns and other filmmakers as they created historical documentaries for the public. He had also done much public history in the form of consulting with congressional committees, or commenting on the historical aspects of the impeachment proceedings against Nixon and Clinton. He thought *that* was public history, when it was being a public intellectual, and they are different things. After the talk, some of my public-history friends were downright angry at this misconception. So I would say, on the matter of OAH and the public historians, that OAH elected leadership and staff have been paying attention and responding. Too many of the professors who make up the membership have not been paying much attention.

There are many reasons to do so, not least that there are careers for historians there. Further, academic historians have developed a problem that public historians might well help them with. Public historians *have* to reach their audiences, and they give this challenge a lot of thought and self-assessment. There is no tenure, and they are out of work if they talk down to or around their audiences, or use the opaque language of postmodernist theory. Academics, to a great degree, have lost their audience—the American people. Public history is a place where that has not yet happened, and the ivory-tower residents should come down, learn, and plunge in.

Perhaps this is what lay behind another anecdote that is more encouraging. At the 1989 meeting of the OAH jointly with the NCPH in St. Louis, I turned a corner to see longtime *Journal of American History* editor David Thelen, who hailed me with these words: "Otis, public history is where it's at!" The public history/OAH relationship has been a mixture of my three anecdotes, and I like to think that the third one projects the future.

35

Public History and the Academy
A Continuum of Practice

Marla R. Miller

An image kept coming to my mind as I was reading what my fellow authors in this public history part had to say. Somewhere, though I can no longer recall where, I have seen a photograph of a meeting in progress; four or five people are in the frame, sitting around one of those cookie-cutter corporate conference tables, with those blank expressions you would expect to find in such a photo. It accompanied (in my dim memory) an essay about how the heroism of community activism occurs not in rallies or marches but in the tedium of committee work. Given the notable presence of joint, advisory, ad-hoc, membership, and prize committees; joint conference planning; budget studies; task forces; and other reports scattered throughout these essays; it strikes me that the success or failure of collaborations around public history involve a high tolerance for administrivia.

That theme is something to which I'll return, but at the outset, I want to say something about the continuum on which all historians practice. Implicit throughout these essays is the assumption of a gap or divide separating public and conventional historians, and before I go on, I would like to challenge that premise. It is simply not the case that some historians are altogether public historians and some are altogether not; perhaps it is an artifact of my own generational perspective, but I have met very few university or college-based historians who are in no way public historians, regardless of whether they see themselves that way, and, of course, all public historians embrace the values and training of the discipline writ large. In many ways, these chapters are less about two discrete categories of historians in tension, but about clashing institutional cultures. Put another way, sometimes it is not larger values or principles but small matters of habit, practice, and paperwork that prove obstacles to co-operation. Other contributors have assumed an enduring sense of estrangement between two camps of practitioners, but in truth each one contains evidence of both unity and division, as well as areas in which the lines separating practitioners are blurry at best.[1]

Germane to our purposes, we have certainly learned that the OAH has been involved in public-history initiatives from its inception. Otis Graham's remarks in particular, which track public history's consolidation in the 1970s, after decades of practice beyond the view of academe, nevertheless remind us that such divisions are too facile: from the outset, many of the founders of the modern public history movement were professors, and the OAH, even though, early in its life, it had quickly became dominated by historians based in institutions devoted to higher education, showed early and ongoing interest in supporting and advancing the public-history uprising or social movement—terms I quite like. Although it is true that practicing public historians withdrew from OAH and other professional associations less actively engaged in the on-the-ground issues they faced, the break was never complete. The OAH was present at the now-famous Montecito meeting, in the form of Executive Secretary Dick Kirkendall, and, well before that, established its Committee on Historic Sites in 1966. Don Ritchie notes the productive series of joint meetings between the OAH and the National Council on Public History, as well as the efforts of the OAH Research Committee, particularly around issues of access to sensitive records. Otis reports that an OAH subcommittee formed to assess ways that OAH could serve public historians found that "relatively few" such historians maintained OAH membership, but the figure—31 percent of federal historians, or nearly 1 in 3—seems surprisingly robust to me. And yet OAH sought to do still better. As these papers note, in newsletter articles, *Journal of American History* features, new committees, and studies, OAH worked (if modestly, also consistently) to respond to the needs of this constituency.

The themes of division or at least dissonance that trace through these chapters, to my mind, tell stories about diverging institutional cultures, needs, and priorities, and about disjunctions, too, between the OAH as an organization and the individual members it represents as well as the discipline for which it advocates. Institutional cultures matter, and have, over the past century, introduced and exacerbated gaps among historians who view our shared enterprise from different institutional perspectives. Even when public history was not well understood by most working historians, typically employed by colleges and universities, and so marginalized in the professional culture of the discipline, the OAH as an organization continued to support public history practice, but both the organization and its members have at times been hampered by a seemingly ineluctable undertow generated by their home institutions.

To put that another way, the spirit may be willing, but institutional bodies are often weak vehicles for functional partnerships. Heather Huyck, in her paper presented at the 2007 meeting, pointed out how the uncompromising calendar of the academic year and the comparatively extended timetables of the National Park Service complicate and sometimes undermine attempts to collaborate—something I know to be true from first-hand experience. Don Ritchie reminds us that the OAH membership structure assumed employment in two- and four-year institutions, assumptions that marginalized many others. David McMillen, the most pessimistic among the presenters at the meeting, went so far as to call the relationship between the OAH and the National Archives "antagonistic." Describing the sometimes tense relationship between them and portraying them as seeming to work at times at cross purposes, he suggested that this stemmed from the administrative need of federal employees to obtain external approval and support from their most obvious constituencies bumping up against the assumption of university and college-based historians that their most effective contribution involves flexing their analytical muscle.

Yet these chapters all note that the OAH is deeply rooted in public history practice, and has sustained an ongoing (if sometimes comparatively marginal) interest in public history issues over its entire hundred-year history. To be sure, the writers draw our attention to less tangible tensions, including the struggle among public historians to forge a professional identity within a discipline that had become so focused on university and college-based practice, and these concerns and experiences are not to be dismissed lightly. Ritchie calls it "status anxiety," a term I think all the presenters would accept. Huyck's presentation contained no shortage of quotations from leading Park Service officials who reported being dismissed or overlooked by their counterparts in higher education, and Graham describes frustrating exchanges that reveal widespread ignorance about public-history practice among colleagues whose practice is narrower in scope. Those unpleasant moments, as they accumulate over the course of careers, do obtain the power to shape the realm of the possible, and we cannot fail to appreciate the ways they have shaped past practice.

But everyone has those stories, and to be perfectly candid, I'm going to stop telling mine, because what is also clear from what my colleagues offer here is that there's little to be gained by reiterating them when there's also a history of productive collaboration on which to draw for our conversation. Each of these authors, as they seek to consider how the OAH has figured into their own corner of public-history practice, finds evidence of fruitful cooperation, and as our discipline, which is no longer taken for granted as an essential element of sound education or insight, struggles to make a case for itself in the wider currents of American culture, it's that common ground that matters. As my friend and colleague Anne Whisnant has said, "The broad public importance of history needs to be articulated—everywhere, by everyone."

We need to focus on the common ground that unites historians across occupational settings, because the crisis that faces the discipline is shared by all of us. As Graham suggests, academic history has already lost its audience, and public history offers a "place where that has not yet happened." But even there, while history thrives in documentaries and popular nonfiction, today's history museums and historic sites struggle to retain their once-large audiences. The historic house museum format in particular seems no longer to seem relevant to the visitors who once sought them out. Ritchie notes alarming trends within federal agencies: libraries have closed, positions have been eliminated, and programs discontinued. He also reminds us that shrinking public funds have forced the nation's museums to look to private donors for support, a development with serious consequences for the content of future exhibitions. McMillen, the representative of the National Archives, reminded us at the conference that an urgent situation continues to evolve in the retention of electronic records, one of several issues concerning the preservation and access of government documents that archivists and historians will confront together in the coming years. The discipline, writ large, has to become as invested in the selection of direction-setting historians at the federal level as they would in the selection of their own next Dean or Director. As the position of the humanities in general declines in American educational systems, it has become easier and easier to eliminate funding for history education everyplace, from the K-12 and higher education systems to the Smithsonian Institution and the National Park Service.

It's a lot for all of us, already too busy to keep up with the administrivia of our own lives, to keep track of, but that's where professional organizations like OAH are most essential and most effective, helping all of us stay connected to the challenges facing our colleagues in other places, and doing what we can to support them in their own corner of our shared enterprise.

Huyck made a number of specific recommendations that are well worth considering for the future of the OAH, including the integration of public-history courses in graduate curricula, reviving something like the AHA's former congressional fellowship, cultivating mentorship and networking opportunities, and engaging university and college-based faculty more actively in advocacy for history in the federal government. Ritchie's mention of the service that historians in the federal government provide to journalists suggests a potentially fruitful area of collaboration that is close to my own heart. Clearly, there's a great need for historians to improve their public profile, and one way is for the general public to begin to expect the treatment of events in the national media to include historical perspective, something that the federal historians already offer. The OAH is already active in many initiatives aimed at thickening ties among a wider range of historians than recent decades have encouraged, and their efforts will only continue to grow. Such efforts help draw connections between the past and the future, and it's the latter to which historians, wherever their practice is based, must urgently attend. Public history still has, in my view, the "expansive future" that Bob Kelley described to Otis Graham in 1976, and the OAH will continue to be a steady partner in that work.

NOTES

1. As an aside, I await the day when guides to graduate school look more like guides to state parks; instead of columns for campgrounds and boat docks we will have columns indicating strengths in the curriculum, including "Historiography" and "Writing the Monograph," but also "Documentary Filmmaking," "Museum Interpretation" and so forth—the best programs will be those with the widest array of offerings.

Part VI

PRESIDENTIAL MEMORIES

36

The Sitting President Looks On—Uncomfortably

Richard White

A year as president of the Organization of American Historians (OAH) cannot help but make a person acutely aware of his own inadequacies. At least that is the effect that it had on me. The only consolation I ever felt was that maybe I did not do any worse than others who went before me, but I was president of the organization during its centennial year, which meant that this particular illusion could probably not survive my last act as president, presiding over the Presidential Memories session at the annual meeting in Minneapolis. I had to come face to face with a set of people whose accomplishments could only make me feel more badly about myself.

The session was organized by Richard Kirkendall, a colleague of mine when I taught at the University of Washington, and I was dazzled, or at least as dazzled as a middle-aged academic can be. I had met many of the people that I introduced, figuratively at least, during my own graduate education, and I had introduced others to another generation of graduate students and undergraduates in my own classes. These were people whose ideas I had stolen shamelessly. And they were people whose thinking about the American past had burst the bounds of the academy and influenced popular culture in ways that I admired.

And they all were, as I expected, graceful in their comments, often funny, and generous in their assessment of the organization and their colleagues. The only guilt that I had in listening to them was in their accounts of the problems that they faced as president, and most particularly in the problems they failed to solve. In this I took comfort.[1]

NOTES

1. Editor's note: In addition to the contributors to this part of the book, two other former presidents, John Hope Franklin, who died in 2009, and Mary Frances Berry, also shared their memories with us during the centennial conference, but they could not join in this stage of the project.

37

The Transformation of the Annual Meeting

Richard W. Leopold (1912–2006)

As the person who has been a member of this organization longer than anyone still alive, I thought it appropriate to recall the first meeting that I attended, the thirty-first, in Indianapolis in April 1938.[1] Because I was then only in my first year as an instructor at Harvard, and because Harvard faculty were conspicuous by their absence from such gatherings, I should explain why I happened to be there.

I had joined the Mississippi Valley Historical Association (MVHA) in April 1937, but knew few, if any, of its members. I had, however, spent more than two months in Indianapolis during the fall of 1935 doing research on my dissertation, a biography of Robert Dale Owen. At that time, I became acquainted with Christopher B. Coleman, president of the Indiana Historical Society, and Esther U. McNitt, chief of the Indiana Division of the State Library, who just happened to be, respectively, chairman of the 1938 meeting and a member of the local arrangements committee. One or both was responsible, I am sure, for a letter of September 10, 1937, from James G. Randall of the University of Illinois, chairman of the Program Committee, inviting me to present a twenty-minute paper on some phase of Owen's career. After some hesitation, lest I divulge my findings to two other scholars, one a tenured professor and the other a doctoral candidate at Columbia, both of whom had assured me a year before that they had begun writing about Owen, I accepted. I believed that my appearance would broaden my acquaintances within the profession and facilitate finding a position elsewhere when my three-year appointment as an instructor at Harvard expired.

A glance at the printed program reveals how the meeting in 1938 differed from those of recent times. Registration was fifty cents and a single room with bath cost $2.50 a night, while the price for the presidential banquet was $1.50. There were twelve sessions, typically two on each day, one with two papers and a second with three. No one served as discussant, although the chairperson was expected to comment briefly. Everyone followed this practice, except for Howard K. Beale, whose remarks, not surprisingly, ran the length of the three papers over which he was presiding. As was customary, the Executive Committee met after lunch on the first day and again following the business meeting on the second. Clarence E. Carter's presidential address, "The United States and Documentary Historical Publication," took place on the evening of the first day. Finally, it is impossible to provide the precise attendance figures. The summary provided by the Program Committee is silent on that matter, and my quest for information in the organization's archives proved fruitless. I do know that there were forty-three participants and perhaps thirty-four more who served as members of several committees. I would have to guess that the total number in attendance was under 200. To the best of my recollection, there were no African Americans and only two somewhat elderly women who were chosen to be commentators, one of whom was a last-minute substitute.

On Wednesday, April 27, I had left Boston on the Ohio State Limited and reached Indianapolis in time to register, obtain quarters, and still attend one of the opening sessions. It dealt with government and the historical profession. Paul M. Angle of the Chicago Historical Society was chairman, and speakers dealt with the National Archives, the Library of Congress, and the National Park Service. The luncheon that followed had the same theme. Dwight L. Dumond of Michigan presided, and the sole speaker was Luther H. Evans, head of the Historical Records Survey. Here, at last, was a familiar face, for Evans had taught me in my sophomore year at Princeton. I enjoyed several conversations with him during the remainder of the meeting; little did I realize that he would become Librarian of Congress in 1945. I think I attended the afternoon session dealing with the problems of the South in relation to other sections. In the evening, I heard Carter's presidential address. It is a comment on the times that there was a complimentary tea that afternoon and a complimentary smoker that evening.

Jim Randall had to use his imagination to come up with the title for my session. It was called, "Education and Reform," with Louise B. Dunbar of Illinois in the chair. My paper, "Was Robert Dale Owen a Reformer?," was the first of three. For those unfamiliar with Owen, and there were many then as now, he was, and remains, a second-rank historical figure who was quite prominent during the nineteenth century. His letters on emancipation were thought to have influenced Lincoln's thinking.

The other two papers presented in my session dealt with "Calvinism and the Anti-Slavery Movement at Miami University" and "Grahamism at Oberlin." I do not remember any searching comments on these three papers, although the chairperson offered a few innocuous remarks on all of them. The one thing that I do recall is that, in the corridor after the session, Raymond P. Stearns of

Illinois and George W. Adams of Lake Forest, both of whom had received their doctorates at Harvard, warned me that it was unwise to use the French language, as I had done in a quotation from Owen, before such an audience.

I missed the complimentary luncheon on Friday and the afternoon sessions that day to meet with the President of Bobbs-Merrill, David Chambers, who said he could not publish my dissertation as a trade volume, but, if it were condensed, he would consider it as a textbook. I was free, however, to take an automobile tour of the Hoosier capital in the company of Howard K. Beale and Francis B. Simkins, two of the most voluble members of the profession. After listening to the evening session, I caught the midnight train to Chicago to spend the weekend with my favorite cousin.

Almost twenty years later, in 1956, I found myself in Randall's position as program chairman for the Pittsburgh meeting. The registration fee was $1.00, and single rooms ranged from $4.00 to $9.00. Lunches were $2.50, and dinners were $3.50. The format had changed very little, although the number of sessions had increased over the years. My major contribution was to schedule several sessions with a single speaker of great distinction, such as Samuel F. Bemis, Elting E. Morison, Edmund S. Morgan, and Kenneth M. Stampp, with two or three commentators. I believe that John Hope Franklin was the only African American on the program, and Katherine E. Brand, the only woman scheduled to appear, was unable to attend. In contrast to 1938, we know the precise attendance: 597.

The most delightful session in Pittsburgh was one with which I had nothing to do because it involved the presidential address of Edward C. Kirkland, who was introduced by Thomas D. Clark. It was then that my long and valued friendship with Tom really began. In meeting after meeting, we would assess and eventually bewail the changing state of the profession, particularly the growing number of participants and sessions that seemed to go nowhere.

Twenty years after Pittsburgh, I was proud to be your president. Interestingly, the topic of my address in 1977 was "The Historian and the Federal Government," with many of the themes roughly identical to those in Clarence Carter's address of 1938. However, the Atlanta meeting differed markedly from the one in Indianapolis. There were sixty-three sessions embracing 269 participants; the registration fee had risen to $5.00. The registered attendance was 1,560. The executive secretary was Richard S. Kirkendall, who is responsible for organizing the present session and whose services I found indispensable for the Atlanta meeting.

Now, as I look back on my seventy-year relationship with the OAH, it is not surprising to me that my fondest memories cluster around the years from 1955 to 1970, when collegiality was at its height. The expansion of membership and the balkanization of the profession have created challenges to continued camaraderie. And I think of the many meetings since then, at which, seated with that grand old man, the late Tom Clark, we together moaned about the loss of the good old days. Let us hope that they are not gone forever.

NOTE

1. Editor's note: As Professor Leopold had died on Thanksgiving evening, November 23, 2006, his friend, former student, and biographer, Steven Harper, read the paper. In remarks during the reading, Harper said, "I am honored to voice the final public comments of one of the organization's finest sons" and "am especially privileged to share the floor with such an illustrious group. . . . Suffice it to say that my connection to Dick Leopold has taken me to the center of remarkable and historic relationships and places, including this event tonight. Although Dick did not know it at the time he and I prepared them during the weeks before his death . . . , what I read have become his last words to all of you. And those of you who knew Dick also know that he always had the last word."

38

The Warm Memories of a Life Member

Carl Degler

I may not be a fifty-year member yet, but I am a Life Member. That recollection reminds me of what I have gained over the years from this Organization. Even that Life Membership was one of those benefits. At my time and income, it seemed costly, so much so that I had to justify it to my wife. I told her that it would not only save my paying annual dues for years but that even in retirement, I would always receive some interesting mail, as has surely been a gain for me for two decades.

So now I have a chance to recall some more thoughts about what the OAH was like over the course of my years as an enthusiastic member. That takes me back to my days in the Mississippi Valley Historical Association (MVHA).

Few people today remember the usual job-seeking practices in historical conventions as I recall them. Today, a number of organizational arrangements, advertisements in the newletters, and so forth have helped job seekers and job providers to communicate more easily and practically. That is something the OAH achieved only over the years. In the early days of the MVHA, however, the practices at the job market were largely unorganized. The common procedure in those early days was not through services provided by seekers and sellers but through word of mouth among senior men meeting with other senior men, who might exchange offers for candidates, with the seeker of a job learning only later how to gain even an interview. Or, as in my own case, an old friend who had a beginning job told me of an opportunity, and when I was given the right information, I could write a letter to a possible job provider. Writing numerous personal letters to heard-about or hoped-for job opportunities was also a usual practice.

Yet, once inside the MVHA, I quickly gained a great sense of friendship and comraderie, if only because we were all in the same field at a time when the United States was a center of world concern and with a great sense of optimism and achievement. That was during the 1950s, of course. The MVHA met once a year, then, as now, but, then, you could easily meet fellow members and acquaintances and newcomers and see them again and again, establishing friendships over time, and looking forward to lunches, talks over beer, or before and after and even during paper sessions, not unlike today, except for one thing. In those old days, attendance was no more than a few hundred. As late as the Fiftieth Annual Convention in 1957, for example, registration was less than 600. By 1964, registration had more than doubled. Yet those were conventions at which you could relatively easily seek out familiar or new faces at the book stalls or in the corridors, just as you could find places to sit, drink, or talk at the bars, coffee shops, and restaurants in the hotel. Today, of course, our numbers require us to hope for the best in making contacts in the hotel and so we spread around town. Success, in short, paid a price. Speaking of registration, during my time in the 1970s and early 1980s, OAH registration numbers came close to those of the AHA, which, of course, included many Americanists. Still, those earlier meetings were actually more like old-boy networks. Women members were few and far between, as, I am sure, Anne Scott well remembers. Wives, however, were sometimes provided with tea! Who of us then knew of Louise Kellogg, who in 1930 became the first woman president of the Mississippi Valley Historical Association?

Our meetings were then located generally in the Middle West, where the founding began. At the first Pittsburgh convention, for example, it was officially announced as being the most eastern convention yet! Either by location or intension, the MVHA escaped the problem of holding conventions at segregated hotels, where housing and dining facilities were denied to Negro members.[1] The Southern Historical Association, of which I was also a member, was not able to follow the openness of the MVHA until several years after heated internal agitation.

A measure of the seriousness of the MVHA was that each year the paper sessions at the convention were reported in the June issue of the *Review*. Those reports provided the names, titles, and other details of each session of the annual program, often occupying as many as twenty pages of the *Review*. That practice ended after, apparently, the sessions became too numerous to report.

That was also the time when the MVHA transformed its name. I rather liked the title "Mississippi Valley," even though, in my early days, I had not been sure, as a resident of New Jersey, where or what the Mississippi Valley was. But I surely liked what I read in the journal of that name. Fortunately, our friendly and convivial meetings continued with the new national title.

About the same time, that change also introduced another gain for the association. From the beginning, the officers were largely, as far as I knew, designated by committees. But in the course of social changes in the country in general, historical associations turned to elections by members. I rather resisted it at first, but, as things turned out, it was surely a gain for the Association and lucky for me as well.

During the 1960s, opening opportunities became a habit of the Organization of American Historians (OAH). Perhaps the most vigorous form it took was the mounting interest in and recognition of black history, which soon broadened into radical history, which, in turn, was frequently shaped by a rising interest in Marxist thought. At the time, Marxism was hardly a broad aspect of thought in this country, which had never had much of a socialist past. Yet for many young people, like me, living in the late 1930s and after, Marxism was challenging, if not a necessity. As a result, the spread of Marxism among many members of the MVHA was simply another opportunity for me and, I think, for this organization. Marxian thinking was especially pronounced in the profession as a whole and, in the OAH, in black history and also the history of American foreign policy, both, of course, broadly relevant to changes then shaping up in American society at large and in the history of the Cold War.

Two presidents of the OAH in the late 1970s represented those aspects of radical thought. The two presidents were the late William Appleman Williams, a historian of American foreign policy and American history in general, and Eugene Genovese, a major historian of the antebellum South and comparative slavery. I knew both of them well and occasionally reviewed their books. I doubt that they ever reviewed any book of mine. All three of us, however, were accidentally connected by the election process. I became president between their terms. As an incoming president, my job was to introduce Gene Genovese and his wife, Betsey Fox-Genovese, for their joint presidential address. My remarks seemed more than acceptable since Betsey, at the end, came up to kiss my cheek! William Appleman Williams, a year later, briefly introduced me for my presidential address, which surprised me. As a graduate student of mine laughingly remarked at the time — a Liberal boxed in by two Radicals! I rather relished that opportunity myself.

The radical change in the organization from which I gained great satisfaction also emerged out of radical thought and agitation. It was the full opening of the OAH to the recognition and participation of women. In 1981, Gerda Lerner was elected the first woman president in fifty years; that same year Joan Hoff became the first to serve as executive secretary.

The push for openness and inclusion, which I have been recalling, was further reflected in the inclusion of public historians in the electoral processes of the OAH, itself a reflection of the broad role professional historians now play outside teaching. I met a professional historian whose work was at a Wells Fargo Bank, and his research is not about stagecoaches. Another professional historian has established a company that provides historical research for businesses and other enterprises. We now have historians of the Senate and the House in Washington.

As I reach these gains of the OAH, I have one more, which was a special gain for me. It was the OAH's creation of a program of distinguished lecturers.

I joined that program, from which the lecturers contribute their fees to the OAH. For me, though, the gain was my opportunity to speak publicly and persistently about a subject generally far removed from the minds of historians. If it had not been for that program, I would never have gained joyful opportunities in Texas, Utah, Kansas, and elsewhere to spread my eager message in trying to explain how Darwinian evolution helps shape human nature.

Let me close by noting that, two years after our centennial meeting, we celebrated the bicentennial anniversaries of Charles Darwin and Abraham Lincoln, both born on February 12, 1809.

NOTE

1. Editor's note: Professor Degler began attending meetings of the MVHA several years after the hotel issue had been settled.

39

The Third Woman in the Presidency

Anne Firor Scott

Of the seventy-seven presidents of this organization and its predecessor, I was the third woman. The first, a remarkable woman named Louise Kellogg, held the office in 1930. Fifty-two years later came the second woman. Between the second and the third, there was only a single year. Change was beginning, although I came into office with the overheard comment of a colleague "but we just HAD a woman!" ringing in my ears.

Not long after I turned over the gavel to Arthur Link, my husband asked: "So, was it worth all the pain and strain of being OAH president?" My reply was the story you may have heard of the legendary Charlestonian who, after being tarred and feathered and ridden out of town on a rail, said "If it hadn't been for the honor of it all I would just as soon have stayed at home."

My answer reflected the crisis-ridden year I spent trying to ride the somewhat unruly tiger called the Organization of American Historians (OAH). The treasurer was retiring, the organization was broke and maybe in debt, there was a profound difference of opinion between the executive board and the executive secretary about who spoke for the organization in such venues as congressional committees, the editor of the *Journal* was retiring, and there were several different perceptions of what the OAH was all about on the board and among the staff. None of this had anyone warned me about when I was nominated.

No one, as far as I knew, nor any written document, defines the president's duties or, for that matter, defines the qualifications for that office. Was it scholarship? Or service to the organization? Or presumed administrative ability? Or all of the above?

Tradition demanded a proper presidential address. I could not find any discussion about the purpose of the address: Was it to prove that the person elected could indeed conduct serious scholarship (a sort of super-PhD oral, so to speak) or should it be concerned with the state of the discipline, the state of the organization or, heaven forbid, the state of the world? So far, laissez-faire has ruled.

The invitation to be part of this conversation has led me into some reflection that might well have taken place twenty-three years ago when I reluctantly pondered accepting the nomination, but perhaps better late than never.

Though I had been a member of the Mississippi Valley Historical Association (MVHA) at the time the name was changed, I did not know much about its history. If I had I would have known that it was founded not by scholars but by archivists who were anxious for more support for their archives and for improvement of the teaching of American history in the schools.

I would have known, too, that crisis periods were nothing new. The first president, for example, had not only announced that he would not come to the annual meeting but that he doubted that the new organization would survive. In the meantime the AHA, apparently worried about competition and dripping condescension, suggested that if the Americanists simply must organize, they could be a subgroup of that organization. Relations between the two groups became so strained that the AHA refused to answer letters. A businessman and an archivist leapt into the breach and decided that affiliation with the AHA was *not* a good idea; he managed somehow to put together a program on short notice, and thus the beginning.

Nearly a half century later, the author of a fine article that appeared in the *JAH* in 1967 diplomatically described another crisis. He wrote, in part:

> A transition in the business office . . . caused a period of unsatisfactory handling of the finances of the Association that culminated in the disappearance of several thousand dollars--—a problem that was resolved amicably without legal action. . . . [He continues:] contention among members on the issue of racial discrimination and about the proposal to change the name, plus disillusion with the business problems coincided with the need to find a new editor of the Review . . . , a most critical period.

My own journal gives evidence of another bad time, not so much from crisis but from lassitude. I was first elected to the board in 1972 and at one point wrote that I had been bored to tears at a meeting. I quoted Bill Aeschbacher as saying he had been a member of the board for twenty years and had never seen such a useless meeting. In all my early meetings I had been astounded by the nature of our concerns. Once we spent two hours debating whether obituaries should be printed in the *Journal*. I wonder now that I didn't undertake to start a revolution rather than risk death from boredom.

It is clear, in retrospect, that by 1984 the OAH was on the verge of twenty years of considerable change of which the leaders were only as yet dimly aware. With a certain amount of starting and stopping, the ensuing years have indeed witnessed a revolution, one which is still in progress.

I suspect that a careful study of the past century would identify a series of cycles, smooth sailing alternating with stormy weather. Periods when almost nothing changed were often followed by spells such as the present one, when we are in the midst of redefining the nature and purposes of the organization and indeed of the discipline.

One repeated cyclical subject is that of cooperating with schools to improve the teaching of American history, a subject that was high on the first platform and has come and gone ever since. Its present manifestation is the enthusiastic endorsement by the board of work with community colleges.

One of the oddest things about historians is our lack of attention to our own history. It is odd, too, that this organization seems never to have addressed the question of the criteria for the presidency. Should the presidency be simply a reward for what is generally agreed to be good scholarship? Or should it be for innovative thinking about the future of the discipline, of the profession, or of the humanities? Or should it recognize a commitment to diversity? Or all of the above? Should a president have an agenda or is that the job of the membership? If so, how are the members to register their thinking? One former president whom I consulted before taking on the job said, "You can't accomplish anything in one year. Take it as an honor and let it go at that." Shocked by his advice, I decided first to make sure that the program in 1984 would be first rate, and thanks to Ira Berlin and Dorothy Ross, this happened. They set a high standard that has influenced subsequent Program Committees.

Then I struggled to write a presidential address that would combine scholarship with a general proposition about the nature of historical research. I have seldom seen that essay, called "On Seeing and Not Seeing: A Study in Historical Invisibility," cited. It appears to have dropped into a black hole. (I am reduced to treasuring the comment of one colleague who will be forever high on my list: "First presidential address I ever heard that didn't bore me.")

I failed utterly to find a replacement for the treasurer, a task that Arthur Link accomplished on his first day in office when he recruited the remarkable Cullen Davis, who not only got us out of debt but built up a reserve fund that has been our salvation in recent crises. The search for a new editor was painful but wound up well. Taking it all in all, I would give myself a B-.

As we continue in this period of rapid change, I suggest that some of the issues I have raised here might merit a committee or two to examine them, and I warn my successors that "you don't know nothing yet, baby."

40

The OAH in Philadelphia
The Musical

Leon F. Litwack

Some fifty years ago, as a junior faculty member of the University of Wisconsin, I made my way to the annual meeting of the Organization of American Historians (OAH), then known as the Mississippi Valley Historical Association (MVHA). I was in good company, driven by Tom Clark (a visiting historian that year) and my colleague Vernon Carstensen. My fellow travelers introduced me, a recent arrival from California, to the Midwest and its agriculture.

To read the program of the centennial meeting of the OAH in 2007 is to be impressed with how far we have come in the fifty years since I first attended an annual meeting. The study of the past has never been more dynamic, exciting, or challenging. It has never been more sensitive to the complexities and varieties of cultural documentation and expression. The new voices, the new experiences, the new cultural perspectives have transformed profoundly how we think, talk about, write, and teach American history. Robert Palmer, the blues historian, said it best: "How much thought can be hidden in a few short lines of poetry? How much history can be transmitted by pressure on a guitar string?" and he answered, "The thought of generations, the history of every human being who's ever felt the blues come down like showers of rain."

That is the idea, the spirit I wanted to communicate when I served as president of the OAH in 1987 and prepared for the convention in Philadelphia that would commemorate the bicentennial of the United States Constitution. To open the convention, I proposed a plenary session called American History, American Music, to underscore the importance of music in understanding the diversity of expression in America. To further this objective I sent this letter to Pete Seeger, who had come to personify folk music in contemporary American society and had just published, *Carry It On! A History in Song & Picture of the Working Men and Women of America*.

The OAH in Philadelphia

Dear Mr. Seeger,

I am writing to you as the newly elected president of the Organization of American Historians. With approximately 13,000 participating members and institutions, the OAH is the largest association dedicated solely to serving the interests of the scholars, teachers, and researchers specializing in United States history. The bulk of the membership consists of college and K-12 teachers, as well as trained historians who work in media, museums, libraries, archives, and research institutes. The OAH will be holding its annual meeting in Philadelphia on April 2–5 at the Wyndham Franklin Plaza Hotel. It is, of course, the bicentennial of the Constitution, and the fact that we are meeting in Philadelphia is hardly coincidental. In appointing the Program Committee, I discussed with them how we might best observe the bicentennial. My suggestion was adopted, and the theme of the meeting will be "Dissent in American Society." For the opening plenary session on the evening of April 2, we discussed various possibilities, including an invitation to Justice William Brennan of the Supreme Court, who has been one of the more vigorous critics of the efforts of the Reagan Administration to undermine and distort the very meaning of the Constitution. He may speak at a different time if he is available. Our clear and unanimous choice for the opening night would be your appearance in a musical tribute to dissent, from the American Revolution to the Civil War and Emancipation, to the labor, civil rights, and feminist struggles of the late nineteenth and twentieth century. The points we wish to make clear: This nation has flourished on dissent, few people have cared more deeply about their country than those who have questioned its pretenses and occasionally unmasked its leaders. Throughout our history, the movements of dissent and protest, though unpopular in their own time, have usually had a firmer grasp of what was happening to their country, a truer dedication to the idea on which it was founded than the official voices of power and prestige. Still another point that needs to be made is that, throughout our history, individuals and groups have found ways to relate their experiences and to communicate their feelings about matters of daily concern to them, and they have often done so in their music, folklore, and humor. The history of ordinary people was once thought to be irreclaimable, but only because traditional methods of historical scholarship emphasized the kinds of records and documents working class people and ethnic communities seldom preserved.

Unfortunately, we are not a wealthy organization, and we are unable to pay the usual honorariums for guest appearances. We would, of course, cover the cost of transportation, hotel, and meals. I am hoping that the idea alone might be sufficient to seize your interest—a musical celebration of two hundred years of dissent and struggle in America. I can assure you of a grateful and enthusiastic audience.

We did meet briefly several years ago. I am a consultant to the series of films and slide shows being produced by the American Working Class History Project at the Graduate Center of the City University of New York. Steve Brier, one of my former students at Berkeley, and Herb Gutman, a close friend and fellow historian, were also present at that meeting, and I believe you were working at that time on your own book on American history through song.

I look forward to hearing from you.

On the evening of April 2, 1987, the OAH convention opened with the session, American History, American Music: The Legacy of Dissent. Chaired by William Ferris, then of the University of Mississippi, the performers were Son Thomas, Mississippi Delta blues singer; Tracy Nelson, country blues singer; and Pete Seeger. The concert set the tone for the meeting, a unique event in the history of the MVHA and the OAH. How many times did people come up to me and exclaim, "The OAH will never be the same again." They were wrong, but it was truly a night to remember. The presidential address two nights later was devoted to the bicentennial and the black struggle for freedom, ending with Sterling Brown's eloquent tribute to Nat Turner. After the address, hundreds of historians took to the floor, rockin' and rollin' to the finest R&B and rock 'n' roll—on tape. That, too, was a night and a convention to remember!!

41

History's Public Function

Eric Foner

My presidency occurred during a period of transition for the Organization of American Historians (OAH), a time when it took on increasingly public functions. Its core activities remained purely scholarly—the journal, annual meeting, recognition and promotion of scholarship, and so on. But the officers, including Executive Director Arnita Jones, had to devote increasing time and energy to public issues, such as access to documents; declassification; the Freedom of Information Act; and the reluctance of administrations, Democratic or Republican, to allow full openness. I well remember problems with the Clinton administration about the declassification of government documents. After twelve years of rather secretive Republican administrations, we had expected better. As I remarked at one executive-board meeting, this wouldn't be happening if a Democrat were president.

But behind these specific questions lay a larger issue: history's sudden emergence as a "wedge issue" in the so-called culture wars. During the decade of the 1990s, it sometimes seemed, one could scarcely open a newspaper without encountering bitter controversy over the teaching and presentation of the American past. One acrimonious dispute centered on whether the "new history" was producing a sufficiently uplifting version of the nation's development. The Columbus quincentennial of 1992 was all but ruined by debates about whether the anniversary of his "discovery" should be recalled as a source of national pride (the birth of a New World) or shame (the decimation of native populations and the introduction of slavery). A planned exhibit at the Smithsonian Institution to mark the fiftieth anniversary of the dropping of the first atomic bomb was denounced by veterans' groups for suggesting that the use of the weapon may not have been necessary. In the end, the museum was forced to remove virtually all historical material that was to have accompanied the display of the Enola Gay, the plane that bombed Hiroshima. Proposed national standards for the teaching of history, developed in a project headed by my successor as OAH president, Gary Nash, were denounced by critics like Lynne

Cheney, former head of the National Endowment for the Humanities, for devoting too much attention to obscure members of minority groups, slighting more prominent American leaders, and offering an uninspiring account of the nation's development.

These debates achieved a remarkable level of vituperation and oversimplification. One letter to the editor likened the National History Standards to distortions of the past "developed in the councils of the Bolshevik and Nazi parties." The high, or low, point of my career, soon after my presidency, came when I debated Ms. Cheney about the history standards on Pat Buchanan's TV show *Crossfire*. This was not the site for high-level discourse. She accused historians of being "depressing" and failing to instill patriotism. I replied, "If you want to stop being depressed, go to a psychiatrist. If you want to understand the past, go to a historian."

Although they generated far more heat than light on the study of the past, the history wars did underscore the basic differences between historians' understanding of their task and what much of the broader public thinks the writing of history entails. (Nietzsche distinguished three approaches to history—the monumental, antiquarian, and critical, the first two being history that is celebratory and nostalgic, the third being history "that judges and condemns.") Among other things, the 1990s debates revealed that the desire for a history of celebration is widespread and knows no political boundaries. Historians view the constant search for new perspectives as the lifeblood of historical understanding. Outside the academy, however, the act of reinterpretation is often viewed with suspicion, and "revisionist" is invoked as a term of abuse.

At a Senate hearing on the Smithsonian controversy, Senator Dianne Feinstein of California remarked that when she studied history as a Stanford undergraduate, her professors confined themselves to presenting facts. Now, she complained, historians were engaged in interpretation. I found this difficult to believe. Was it really true that such Stanford historians as David Potter and Don Fehrenbacher simply presented facts to their students? Surely, her Stanford classes must have introduced Senator Feinstein to the writings of giants of scholarship like Carl Becker and Charles Beard, who nearly a century ago demolished the notion that historical truth is fixed and permanent and that fact and interpretation can be sealed off from one another. The very act of selecting and ordering some facts while ignoring others is itself an interpretation. I am reminded of my conversation during the history-standards debate with an eager young reporter from *Newsweek*. "Professor," she asked, "when did historians stop relating facts and start all this revising of interpretations of the past?" Around the time of Thucydides, I told her.

Other memories of my term in office are less weighty. My predecessor as president was Lawrence Levine. Years before, I had purchased a nice down winter coat from a shop in Berkeley. It needed repair and the company told me this would be done without charge if I could get the coat to them. Seeing the opportunity to save the cost of shipping, I asked Larry if I could bring the coat to Anaheim, where the OAH annual meeting in which I became president was to be held, and he could then deliver it when he returned to Berkeley. At the end of the convention, I gave him the coat, and he remarked, "I came to the convention as president; I am leaving as president's valet."

The convention where I delivered my presidential address and ended my term in office was held in Atlanta in the spring of 1994. One highlight was the appearance of former president Jimmy Carter before around 1,000 historians for an hour of questions and answers—questions unfiltered and unrehearsed. Whatever one thinks of his record as president, Carter impressed us all with his wit, articulateness, and command of the language. Yes, there once was a time when presidents of the United States could speak in grammatical English sentences, respond intelligently to unanticipated questions, and speak in developed thoughts, not rehearsed sound bites.

I had actually spent part of my term as OAH president in England, where I was teaching as Harmsworth Professor of American History at Oxford. That the organization did not seem to suffer in my absence is a tribute to our hard-working, professional staff. Or, it may suggest that we don't really need a president. My daughter Daria, then six, insisted that she wanted to fly to Atlanta with me for the convention. However, because my wife had to remain in England, this wasn't possible. But Daria refused to take no for an answer. In our Oxford home, she put up little signs on the walls, with themes she thought would be persuasive: "Am I not free in my own house?" "Women should have their rights." When I asked her what was going on, she replied: "This is my demonstration." I had to resist even though I admired her assertiveness.

The OAH has never surrendered the public role it assumed in the early 1990s, nor should it. Indeed, the need for historians' engagement with the public is more pressing today than ever. In the early twenty-first century, we live in a world where fundamentalism—religious and secular—too often overrides reasoned analysis, where scientific knowledge is subordinated to doctrine, where intellect and expertise are denigrated in favor of blind loyalty, where arts and humanities programs, whether in underfunded high schools or national cultural institutions, are the first to suffer from budget cuts.

Given the partisan exaggerations and intellectual distortions so evident in the debates of the 1990s and in public discourse today, it would be perfectly understandable if historians retreated altogether from the public sphere. This, I believe, would be a serious mistake. A century ago, in his presidential address to our sister organization, the American Historical Association (AHA), Charles Francis Adams called on historians to engage forthrightly in public debate. The study of history, he insisted, had a "public function," and historians had an obligation to contribute to debates in which history was frequently invoked with little genuine understanding or knowledge. "The standard of American political discussion," Adams remarked, "is not now so high as not to admit of elevation," and invocations of history should not be left to "the journalist and the politician." These observations are as relevant today as in 1900, when Adams spoke.

42

The OAH in St. Louis
The Protest

David Montgomery

The St. Louis convention in 2000 was a truly memorable occasion. The Organization of American Historians (OAH) staff, executive board, and countless members had made common cause to rescue a convention that three months earlier had seemed threatened with disaster, and their efforts had enjoyed the creative support of the city's government and citizenry.

Almost five years earlier the OAH had contracted with the Adam's Mark hotel chain (HBE) to hold the 2000 convention at the chain's St. Louis hotel. By December 1999 everything appeared to be in order for a fine meeting, until we learned that the National Association for the Advancement of Colored People (NAACP), the Attorney General of Florida, and the United States Justice Department had all brought suit against the Adam's Mark for discrimination against African American patrons during a Black Colleges Reunion at the hotel's Daytona Beach facility the previous spring. Five students attending the reunion accused the hotel of placing them in rooms from which furnishings had been stripped, of charging more for those rooms than was asked of white patrons, and of requiring the students to carry their own luggage and to wear color-coded armbands for identification. The Justice Department had the case extended to six Adam's Mark hotels in all and had noted that this was the first instance involving the 1964 Civil Rights Act in which it had found it necessary carry a discrimination case against a hotel to trial.[1]

As news of the lawsuits against the hotel spread across the country, more than twenty-five organizations canceled contracts for meetings at various Adam's Mark hotels, among them the Episcopal Church, the Lutheran Rocky Mountain Synod, and the U.S. Post Office (all of which had contracted for the Denver Adam's Mark). By early January, a growing number of OAH members who were listed on the program for the pending convention had notified the executive board that they would not participate in a meeting held at the Adam's Mark. Other members notified us that they simply would not attend the convention: they found outrageous the discriminatory conduct with which the hotel's managers had been charged, thirty-five years after the passage of the federal law banning racial discrimination in public accommodations.

The executive board and Executive Director Lee Formwalt (then scarcely three months in office) devoted much of January to conference calls. Although the discussions were fervent, absolutely no one engaged in posturing. They soon produced agreement on three basic principles to guide the organization's response. First, canceling the convention was out of the question. Hundreds of members had already made intellectual and often financial commitments to take part.

Second, the OAH should protest publicly against the racism with which the hotel had been charged and, at the very least move major public sessions out of the hotel. We could not fulfill our mission of encouraging the open exchange of various points of view found among members, if we met under circumstances that made any members feel unwelcome or unwilling to participate because of racial discrimination.

Third, the OAH was not in a position simply to cancel its contract with the Adam's Mark hotel. The financial penalties to which we would be liable for canceling the existing contract would have crippled our organization for years to come. The question faced by the officers, therefore, was how to reconcile these somewhat conflicting goals.

In search of an answer to that question, the Board and the Bloomington office established close contact with the membership. I received especially helpful advice from Mary Frances Berry, Eric Foner, Ralph Luker, Robin Kelly, Michael Frisch, Gerda Ray, and William Preston. Lee Formwalt and I received a flood of letters from members. A poll of members revealed that 77 percent of the respondents favored a protest against racism and believed that all members had to feel free to participate, 11 percent wanted to cancel the convention, and 9 percent thought it should proceed as planned, because the conduct of the hotel was none of our business.

Difficult as our situation was, it was very different from our organization's confrontation with racial discrimination in the 1950s. The Mississippi Valley Historical Association (MVHA), precursor of the OAH, had designated New Orleans as the site for its 1952 convention, when segregation was still unequivocally the law in that city. African American members, few as they then were, were permitted to attend sessions at convention hotels, but they could not sleep, dine, or socialize there. President Merle Curti informed the executive committee a year in advance of the scheduled meeting that he refused to deliver his presidential address in such a setting. He proposed to move the forthcoming convention from New Orleans to Chicago.

In marked contrast to the executive board's unanimity facing the St. Louis decision, in 1951 an adamant minority of the organization's officers resisted the proposal to move, though without success. The battle over segregated facilities was not over, however, but continued for another two years. The culmination was an ambiguously worded referendum, which was phrased so as to evade the question of whether black members could reside at a convention hotel, and the response to it revealed a sharply divided membership. The executive committee then unilaterally settled the issue by voting to accept no invitations for convention facilities unless providers guaranteed that there would be no discrimination in meals or housing. The hotel under discussion at that time was in Topeka, Kansas. One month later, the United States Supreme Court handed down its historic decision, *Brown v. Board of Education of Topeka*.[2]

Despite the unanimity of the OAH's leadership in early 2000, however, its quest for a way to adhere to the principles on which all had agreed still proved elusive in early February. When the executive board addressed a letter to President Fred S. Kummer of the Adam's Mark calling for prompt settlement of the dispute, the reply was a curt denial that there was anything to be negotiated. When the officers then arranged a meeting with Kummer, he canceled on the eve of the scheduled date.

During the same week, Mark Naison, Jeffrey Sammons, Donald Spivey, Timothy Tyson, and other members formed a Committee for a New Convention Site, demanding that the OAH either cancel the forthcoming convention or face protest actions during the meeting. When I contacted those members and informed them of the then-pending meeting with Kummer, however, they readily agreed to address their protests directly to him. From that point on, the Committee's members worked closely with OAH officers in helping make arrangements for the convention that did take place.

The breakthrough came from the city of St. Louis itself. Lewis Perry, former editor of the *Journal of American History* and then on the history faculty at Saint Louis University, had approached its President, Father Lawrence J. Biondi, S.J., to inquire whether sessions from the convention program could be moved from the hotel to the university. On February 20 the clouds lifted. Father Biondi spoke with me by phone and informed me that the campus was ours.

With little more than a month to go before the convention was scheduled to begin, our members in St. Louis joined with the staff in Bloomington and members of the city government in a blaze of activity. The OAH headquarters in Bloomington was converted into a veritable war room, from which Lee Formwalt, Sheri Sherrill, Amy Stark, John Dichtl, Damon Freeman, and others toiled often into the night arranging bus transportation to and from Saint Louis University, book exhibits at the new location, scores of meeting rooms in other parts of the city. They did not cancel the contract with the

Adam's Mark or ask members who already had reservations there to move their accommodations, but they relocated all OAH business elsewhere.

Of all members determined to make the convention a success and also to protest the actions of the Adam's Mark, those in St. Louis itself were the most adamant. The local Special Events Committee, Kathy Corbett, Leslie Brown, Juli Jones, and Gerda Ray, converted themselves into a large action committee and received vigorous support from the regional NAACP. When Lee Formwalt and Damon Freeman of the Bloomington staff visited the city in mid-February they found welcome mats everywhere. My calls to Lars Negstad of the Hotel Employees and Restaurant Employees and to Bill Fletcher, then of the AFL-CIO staff, had established contacts who cleared the decks with the Board of Aldermen. Our legal counsel in the city, Lisa van Amberg, was more than eager to take on the Adam's Mark. She had successfully pressed charges of discrimination in employment at the St. Louis hotel itself, only to have a higher court reduce the imposed fine to an insignificant amount.[3]

The Board of Aldermen arranged for a resolution welcoming the OAH to be passed as our delegates arrived, and it put the convention bureau at our disposal, so that guides would greet OAH members at the airport and signs announcing our presence would be posted at street corners. The welcome was seconded by editorials of the St. Louis *Post-Dispatch* and programs on local television.

The reconstituted special arrangements committee organized a public rally in the open square before the courthouse where the Dred Scott case had first been heard (and adjacent to the hotel) under the slogan coined by Kathy Corbett: "Make Racism History." James Buford, Chief Executive Officer of the Urban League of Metropolitan St. Louis, spoke the most memorable words of the occasion. He did not have the keys to the city, said Mr. Buford, but the OAH had won the hearts of African Americans in St. Louis.[4]

Many convention delegates joined local citizens in a candlelight march to "Make Racism History," which was led by the Albany, Georgia Civil Rights Museum Freedom Singers. The procession crossed the city from that square to the city's Episcopal cathedral, where we gathered for my presidential address. It was in that splendid cathedral that several members who had won awards for their new books returned to the podium to donate the money they had just received in order to help the OAH defray the extraordinary expenses of the convention.

For a finishing touch, balmy sunshine greeted historians every day of the convention (March 30 to April 2). It was also Parents' Weekend at Saint Louis University, and university administrators happily told us about the favorable comments they had received about all the famous historians on campus.

What of the suits against the Adam's Mark? During the week before the historians assembled, the hotel management had agreed to a consent decree providing for nondiscrimination policies to be monitored by Project Equality of Kansas City, Missouri, and for monetary relief totaling $8 million.[5]

That agreement did not end the difficulties facing the OAH by any means. After the St. Louis meeting, the Adam's Mark Hotel sued the OAH for the cost of meeting rooms for which we had contracted but which we did not use. The total amount came to a little over $100,000. OAH staff members Lee Formwalt and Sheri Sherrill flew to St. Louis and joined me in being deposed by the Adam's Mark's attorney.

The following summer, however, an appeals court threw out the award made to the students discriminated against in Daytona Beach on the basis of recent court decisions limiting class action suits, though it upheld the Justice Department's settlement concerning steps to prevent future discrimination at HBE's twenty-one hotels.[6] The NAACP renewed its court action in the form of individual suits, and at the beginning of December it reached a settlement of those claims out of court. As part of the settlement, the Adam's Mark agreed to dismiss all monetary ("attrition") claims against the OAH for failing to use contracted rooms or eat food that had been purchased for delegates' use. The NAACP's attorneys had been adamant on behalf of the OAH, refusing to accept a proposed settlement that would have excused from financial penalties all institutions that had canceled their contracts in protest, but not the OAH, which had *not* canceled. President Julian Bond provided a statement for our press release: "The NAACP is thankful for OAH's principled stand against bigotry at great potential cost. In the end, justice prevailed and right triumphed—as history teaches us it often does."[7]

The St. Louis convention was truly an occasion to remember. It was a lesson in what cooperation can accomplish.

NOTES

Note: I am indebted to Lee Formwalt for his comments on an earlier version of this essay.

1. "Justice Department Files Lawsuit against Adam's Mark Hotel Chain," *United States v. HBE Corporation* (M.D. Fla. 1999), http://www.usdoj.gov/crt/housing/caselist.htm.

2. Ray Allen Billington, "From Association to Organization: The OAH in the Bad Old Days," *Journal of American History (JAH)* 65 (June 1978): 78–83; Thomas D. Clark, "Our Roots Flourished in the Valley," *JAH*, 93–97; Howard K. Beale to Thomas D. Clark, Feb. 2, 1954 (in David Montgomery's possession). I am grateful to professors William Preston and Gerda Ray for bringing the articles to my attention and making Beale's letter available to me. See also Howard K. Beale, "The Professional Historian: His Theory and His Practice," *Pacific Historical Review* 12 (Aug. 1953): 227–55. I am grateful to Professor John Higham for bringing this article to my attention.

3. *Equal Employment Opportunities Commission v. HBE Corporation*, 135 F. 3d 543 (8th Cir.,1998), section V B, point 38.

4. Marty Blatt, "NCPH and OAH—The St. Louis Conference and Future Joint Meetings," *Public History News* (Summer 2000): 21.

5. "Justice Department Settles Lawsuit against the Adam's Mark Chain," press release, March 21, 2000, http://www.usdoj.gov/opa/pr/2000/March/134ct.htm; David Montgomery, "We Met in St. Louis," *OAH Newsletter* 28 (May 2000): 1, 10.

6. E-mail from Lee Formwalt to David Montgomery, Nov. 19, 2000, citing AP news story of Oct. 18, 2000.

7. Quoted in e-mail Lee Formwalt to executive board, Dec. 4, 2001.

Afterword

Katherine Mandusic Finley

Since 1907, the Organization of American Historians (OAH) has experienced an illustrious career. The organization has seen considerable change over time, including a change of name, its headquarters' location, and a change in direction. It has evolved from a very small association run by dedicated volunteers to a very large one with a fulltime, paid staff working for a volunteer board of directors. It has emerged from a regional association to an international one. The publications have increased in both number and size. The annual meeting has grown from one with a few hundred attendees to one with over two thousand. Although founded by directors of state historical societies who were concerned at the outset with the state of historical scholarship and the teaching of American history, the OAH has struggled with the multifaceted complexities of these and other weighty issues. The organization also faced questions concerning its core constituencies and whether it was merely an association of members sharing common interests, or an organization whose purpose was to shape the field of history itself and represent the profession by taking a stand on issues of public interest. The OAH has taken a number of steps to ensure that teaching of and research in American history remain central to its mission, whether in the high schools, community colleges, universities, or public spaces (i.e., museums, historical societies, and national historic parks and sites).

Membership associations are as old as this nation, and some even consider them "the oldest nonprofit form."[1] When the French political theorist and historian Alexis de Tocqueville traveled to the United States in the 1830s, he noted that "Americans of all ages, all stations in life are forever forming associations."[2] The American Society of Association Executives presently estimates that there are 86,054 trade and professional associations (including learned societies) in the United States.[3] For an association, the OAH is middle aged since a number of well-known learned and professional societies (e.g., the American Statistical Association, the American Psychiatric Association, and the American Medical Association) are beyond their sesquicentennial anniversaries. As with many older and established nonprofit organizations and learned societies, the OAH has faced its share of crises. Some of them were financial in nature; others dealt with substantive threats to the field of American history and how it is taught, presented, or practiced in the United States and abroad. However, as with many older scholarly association or learned societies, the OAH has survived to become a strong, more efficient organization.

Yet, even with its growth and maturity over the years, like many other nonprofit organizations today, the OAH faces many challenges. Some of these recent challenges are not new to the OAH, such as a crisis in the teaching of history, a serious reduction in the demand for history graduates, and the reduction in tenure-track teaching positions at colleges and universities. New challenges facing the organization involve the increasing use of and reliance on digital technologies for scholarly communication, the migration from print to online publishing of academic journals, the global economic downturn that has resulted in slashes to state budgets used to support travel funds for professional development, political challenges from state and local school boards influencing how history is taught in the schools, and the growing impact of specialty history associations. All of these have led to a decline in membership and revenues.

Fortunately, the leadership of the OAH is addressing these challenges. As a result, the OAH's Strategic Planning Committee was formed in 2007.[4] Initial discussions about the strategic plan began that year and continued in full force in 2008 and 2009. During that time, committee members gained input into the plan and the planning process from the OAH executive board, the OAH committees, and the general membership. As part of that process, the Strategic Planning Committee identified eight major areas of concern for the OAH: membership, activities and programs, finances, development and marketing, new media, public history, internal organization, and advocacy. After discussing these concerns with the executive board and surveying the membership on key issues, the planning committee drafted a plan, which was presented to the board and to the membership. Following a period of open comment, the committee refined the plan and presented it to the board, which approved it in November 2009.[5]

The plan contained six major goals designed to address the various issues facing the OAH and to ensure that the association continues to meet the needs of its member, the profession, and the discipline of American history. These goals include:

1. Sustaining and strengthening the OAH's support for the production and dissemination of historical scholarship of the highest order in all fields of American history.
2. Continuing and expanding efforts to create a larger and more inclusive OAH, attracting a membership that reflects the broad community of American historians.

3. Creating an integrated, sustainable and efficient organization for the twenty-first century.
4. Meeting the challenge of the revolution in information technology.
5. Broadening and deepening the OAH's commitment to outstanding instruction in American history.
6. Advocating for and communicating the OAH's mission, programs, and achievements, as well as the accomplishments of its members, to both the profession and the larger public.

Upon approval of this plan, the OAH began immediately to focus on reorganization of the staff along functional lines to make a more efficient and effective organization. Along with this reorganization came recognition of the need for increased fiscal responsibility. In devising the strategic plan, it became apparent that the OAH needed to become more sustainable, and it has taken the necessary steps to ensure a healthy financial future for the OAH.

Embedded in these broad goals are a number of objectives. To promote historical scholarship, the OAH is committed to continuing and further developing the *Journal of American History*, the *Magazine of History*, the Distinguished Lectureship Program and collaboration with the National Park Service. To increase membership and better represent the entire history profession, the OAH will redouble its efforts at being more inclusive by creating a "big tent" for all practitioners of American history. In a survey to the membership as part of the strategic planning process, the major reason individuals joined the OAH was "to be part of a community of historians." The OAH Strategic Planning Committee has outlined steps to ensure that current members continue to view themselves as part of this community, and that we will continue to encourage the involvement of all historians who want to become part of this larger community.

The environment for nonprofit organizations has definitively changed over the past several decades. How will the OAH fare in this new environment? No one has a crystal ball to see the future, but the OAH executive board's acceptance of a strategic plan that directly addresses the challenges faced in today's competitive situation is a first step toward success. In 2006, the American Society for Association Executives and the Center for Association Leadership (the Center) published a study to determine what successful associations have in common. Entitled *7 Measures of Success: What Remarkable Associations Do that Others Don't*, the study gathered data over three years from the top five nonprofit associations. It was based on a research methodology set forth by Jim Collins, author of *Built to Last: Successful Habits of Visionary Companies* and *Good to Great: Why Some Companies Make the Leap and Others Don't*. The study indicated that outstanding associations: (1) were highly engaged in membership services; (2) aligned their mission with the membership benefits and the programs; (3) relied on data and analysis to make decisions; (4) conducted frequent and open communication among its members, stakeholders, volunteer leaders, and staff; (5) had leadership that exhibited visionary thinking and encouraged it at all levels; (6)readily adapted to change; and (7) had built fruitful partnerships, alliances, and collaborations.[6] Much of OAH's Strategic Plan embraces these "measures of success."

The OAH has survived for more than one hundred years because of its ability to adapt and to connect with its many constituencies. More than ever in today's complex political and global environment, an understanding of history is an important part of ensuring a strong democratic nation. As a community of historians, the OAH must ensure that it lives up to its mission of "promoting excellence in scholarship, teaching, and presentation of American history, and encourages wide discussion of historical questions and the equitable treatment of all practitioners of history." The Organization of American Historians has a promising future with every opportunity to be a truly remarkable and visionary learned society.

NOTES

1. O'Neill, Michael, *The Third America: Emergence of the Nonprofit Sector in the United States* (San Francisco: Jossey Bass, 1989).

2. Alexis de Tocqueville, *Democracy in America.*

3. http://www.asacenter.org/About Us/content.cfm?ItemNumber=16309.

4. Strategic Planning Committee members included Pete Daniel (chair, OAH president elect at the time and subsequently president); board members Elaine Tyler May (subsequently president elect and president), Linda Shopes, and David S. Trask; Steven D. Andrews, *JAH* staff member; Jay Goodgold, chair of the Leadership and Advisory Council, and Alice Kessler-Harris, past OAH board member and subsequent president elect. Ex-officio members included Lee Formwalt (executive director through July 2009); Katha Kissman, interim executive director (August 2009–March 2010); Edward T. Linenthal, *JAH* editor; and Robert Griffith, OAH treasurer.

5. The complete plan can be found at http://www.oah.org/strategic/final.html.

6. ASAE Center for Association Leadership, *7 Measures of Success* (Washington, DC: 2006).

Appendix
The Officers, 1907–2012

PRESIDENTS

Francis A. Sampson (1907)
Thomas M. Owen (1907–1908)
Clarence W. Alvord (1908–1909)
Orin G. Libby (1909–1910)
Benjamin F. Shambaugh (1910–1911)
Andrew C. McLaughlin (1911–1912)
Reuben G. Thwaites (1912–1913)
James A. James (1913–1914)
Isaac J. Cox (1914–1915)
Dunbar Rowland (1915–1916)
Frederic L. Paxson (1916–1917)
St. George L. Sioussat (1917–1918)
Harlow Lindley (1918–1919)
Milo M. Quaife (1919–1920)
Chauncey S. Boucher (1920–1921)
William E. Connelley (1921–1922)
Solon J. Buck (1922–1923)
Eugene C. Barker (1923–1924)
Frank H. Hodder (1924–1925)
James A. Woodburn (1925–1926)
Otto L. Schmidt (1926–1927)
Joseph Schafer (1927–1928)
Charles W. Ramsdell (1928–1929)
Homer C. Hockett (1929–1930)
Louise P. Kellogg (1930–1931)
Beverley W. Bond, Jr. (1931–1932)
John D. Hicks (1932–1933)
Jonas Viles (1933–1934)
Lester B. Shippee (1934–1935)
Louis Pelzer (1935–1936)

Edward E. Dale (1936–1937)
Clarence E. Carter (1937–1938)
William O. Lynch (1938–1939)
James G. Randall (1939–1940)
Carl F. Wittke (1940–1941)
Arthur C. Cole (1941–1942)
Charles H. Ambler (1942–1943)
Theodore C. Blegen (1943–1944)
William C. Binkley (1944–1946)
Herbert A. Kellar (1946–1947)
Ralph P. Bieber (1947–1948)
Dwight L. Dumond (1948–1949)
Carl C. Rister (1949–1950)
Elmer Ellis (1950–1951)
Merle E. Curti (1951–1952)
James L. Sellers (1952–1953)
Fred A. Shannon (1953–1954)
Walter P. Webb (1954–1955)
Edward C. Kirkland (1955–1956)
Thomas D. Clark (1956–1957)
Wendell H. Stephenson (1957–1958)
William T. Hutchinson (1958–1959)
Frederick Merk (1959–1960)
Fletcher M. Green (1960–1961)
Paul W. Gates (1961–1962)
Ray A. Billington (1962–1963)
Avery O. Craven (1963–1964)
John W. Caughey (1964–1965)
George E. Mowry (1965–1966)
Thomas C. Cochran (1966–1967)
Thomas A. Bailey (1967–1968)
C. Vann Woodward (1968–1969)
Merrill Jensen (1969–1970)
David M. Potter (1970–1971)
Edmund S. Morgan (1971–1972)
T. Harry Williams (1972–1973)
John Higham (1973–1974)
John Hope Franklin (1974–1975)
Frank Freidel (1975–1976)
Richard Leopold (1976–1977)
Kenneth M. Stampp (1977–1978)
Eugene D. Genovese (1978–1979)

Carl N. Degler (1979–1980)
William A. Williams (1980–1981)
Gerda Lerner (1981–1982)
Allan G. Bogue (1982–1983)
Anne Firor Scott (1983–1984)
Arthur S. Link (1984–1985)
William E. Leuchtenburg (1985–1986)
Leon F. Litwack (1986–1987)
Stanley N. Katz (1987–1988)
David Brion Davis (1988–1989)
Louis R. Harlan (1989–1990)
Mary Frances Berry (1990–1991)
Joyce Appleby (1991–1992)
Lawrence W. Levine (1992–1993)
Eric Foner (1993–1994)
Gary B. Nash (1994–1995)
Michael Kammen (1995–1996)
Linda K. Kerber (1996–1997)
George M. Fredrickson (1997–1998)
William H. Chafe (1998–1999)
David Montgomery (1999–2000)
Kenneth T. Jackson (2000–2001)
Darlene Clark Hine (2001–2002)
Ira Berlin (2002–2003)
Jacquelyn Hall (2003–2004)
James O. Horton (2004–2005)
Vicki L. Ruiz (2005–2006)
Richard White (2006–2007)
Nell Irvin Painter (2007–2008)
Pete Daniel (2008–2009)
Elaine Tyler May (2009–2010)
David A. Hollinger (2010–2011)
Alice Kessler-Harris (2011–2012)

FOUNDERS

William S. Bell, Montana Historical & Miscellaneous Library
Edgar R. Harlan, Historical Department of Iowa
George W. Martin, Kansas State Historical Society
Clarence S. Paine, Nebraska State Historical Society
Francis A. Sampson, State Historical Society of Missouri
Benjamin F. Shambaugh, State Historical Society of Iowa
Warren Upham, Minnesota Historical Society

SECRETARY-TREASURERS

Clarence S. Paine (1907–1916)
Clara S. Paine (1916–1952)
James C. Olson (1953–1956)
William Aeschbacher (1956–1969)

EXECUTIVE SECRETARIES/DIRECTORS

David Miller (1970)
Thomas Clark (1970–1973)
Richard Kirkendall (1973–1981)
Joan Hoff-Wilson (1981–1989)
Arnita A. Jones (1990–1999)
Lee Formwalt (1999–2009)
Katherine Mandusic Finley (2010–)

TREASURERS

William Aeschbacher (1969–1976)
Robert K. Murray (1977–1984)
Cullom Davis (1984–1993)
Gale Peterson (1993–2003)
Robert W. Cherny (2003–2008)
Robert Griffith (2008–)

EDITORS

Benjamin F. Shambaugh (1908–1914) (*Proceedings*)
Clarence W. Alvord (1914–1923)
Lester B. Shippee (1923–1924)
Milo M. Quaife (1924–1930)
Arthur C. Cole (1930–1941)
Louis Pelzer (1941–1946)
Wendell H. Stephenson (1946–1953)
William C. Binkley (1953–1963)
Oscar O. Winther (1963–1966)
Martin Ridge (1966–1978)
Lewis Perry (1978–1984)
Paul Lucas (1984–1985)
David Thelen (1985–1999)
Joanne Meyerowitz (1999–2004)
Edward T. Linenthal (2005–)

Notes on Contributors

Thomas Bender is University Professor of Humanities and Professor of History at New York University. His recent publications reflect his several interests: *Rethinking American History in a Global Age* (2002), *The Unfinished City: New York and the Metropolitan Idea* (2002), *The Education of Historians for the Twenty-First Century* (2004), *A Nation Among Nations: America's Place in World History* (2006), *The Urban Imaginary: Locating the Modern City* (2007), and *The Transformation of American Higher Education, 1940–2005: Documenting the National Discourse* (2007).

Marjorie Bingham taught Advanced Placement history at the St. Louis Park High School in Minnesota for more than thirty years and served as adjunct professor in Graduate Studies at Hamline University. Her publications include thirteen books in the *Women in World Cultures* series and, most recently, *Moving Forward: Minneapolis Woman's Club* (2007). A founding vice president of the National Council for History Education, she has been elected to committees in both the OAH and the AHA, served as a Bradley Commissioner, received the AHA's Nancy Lyman Roelker Mentorship Award, and is now serving as an OAH Distinguished Lecturer.

John Bodnar is Chancellor's Professor of History at Indiana University, Bloomington. His books include *Workers' World: Kinship, Community, and Protest in an Industrial Society, 1900–1940* (1982), *Transplanted: A History of Immigrants in Urban America* (1985), *Remaking America: Public Memory, Commemoration and Patriotism in the Twentieth Century* (1992), *Bonds of Affection: Americans Define Their Patriotism* (1996), *Our Towns: Remembering Community in Indiana* (2000), and *Blue-Collar Hollywood: Liberalism, Democracy, and Working People in America* (2003).

Ron Briley is a history teacher and assistant headmaster at Sandia Preparatory School in Albuquerque, New Mexico, and teaches also at the University of New Mexico—Valencia Campus. He has received teaching awards from the

Society for History Education, the OAH, and the American Historical Association. His publications include *Class at Bat, Gender on Deck, and Race in the Hole: A Line up of Essays on Twentieth Century Culture and America's Game* (2003), *James T. Farrell's Dreaming Baseball* (2007), and *All Stars and Movie Stars* (2008).

Karl Brooks is an associate professor of history and environmental studies at the University of Kansas. He was trained in law at Harvard as well as history at Kansas and worked in Idaho as a lawyer, a state legislator, and with an environmental group before becoming a historian. He teaches environmental history, environmental law, and legal history. His publications include *Public Dams, Private Dams: The Hell's Canyon High Dam Controversy* (2006). On leave from his university, he is now regional administrator in Kansas City, Kansas, for the U.S. Environmental Protection Agency.

William H. Chafe, a former president of the OAH, is the Alice Mary Baldwin Professor at Duke University. Although he has accepted heavy responsibilities in administration at Duke, he has published eight books, most recently *Private Lives/Public Consequences: Personality and Politics in Modern America* (2005). He received the Robert F. Kennedy Book Award for *Civilities and Civil Rights: Greensboro, North Carolina and the Black Struggle for Freedom* (1980) and the Sidney Hillman book award for *Never Stop Running: Allard Lowenstein and the Struggle to Save American Liberalism* (1993).

Edward M. Coffman retired in 1992 from the University of Wisconsin-Madison. He also taught, as a visitor, at several institutions of large importance in American military history: West Point, the Air Force Academy, the Army Command and General Staff College, and the Army War College. His publications include *The Old Army: A Portrait of the American Army in Peacetime, 1784–1898* (1986) and *The Regulars: The American Army, 1898–1941* (2004).

Spencer R. Crew is the Clarence J. Robinson Professor of American, African American, and Public History at George Mason University. Working in public history for more than twenty-five years, he has served as director of the National Museum of American History and president of the National Underground Railroad Freedom Center. His major exhibitions include "Field to Factory: Afro-American Migration 1915–1940," and his publications include *Black Life in Secondary Cities: A Comparative Analysis of the Black Communities of Camden and Elizabeth, N.J. 1860–1920* (1993) and *Unchained Memories: Readings from the Slave Narratives* (2002).

Notes on Contributors

Carl Degler has held presidencies of the OAH, the AHA, and the Southern Historical Association and is now the Margaret Byrne Professor of American History Emeritus at Stanford University. His books include *At Odds: Women and the Family in America from the Revolution to the Present* (1981) and *In Search of Human Nature: The Decline and Revival of Darwinism in American Social Thought* (1991). His *Neither Black nor White: Slavery and Race Relations in Brazil and the United States* (1972) was awarded a Pulitzer Prize.

Katherine Mandusic Finley is the executive director of the OAH. Finley holds undergraduate and graduate degrees in history from Ohio Wesleyan University and Case Western Reserve University (respectively), an MBA from Indiana University, and a PhD in interdisciplinary studies from Union Institute and University, and has worked for history museums and for associations for more than thirty years. While in museums, she published two books and several articles on medicine in nineteenth-century Indiana. Since receiving her PhD (with a concentration in organizational development and association management), she has written a number of articles on nonprofit management and executive succession. Finley holds certifications in association management, fundraising, and meeting planning.

Eric Foner, past president of the OAH, the AHA, and the Society of American Historians, is the DeWitt Clinton Professor of History at Columbia University. His books include *Free Soil, Free Labor, Free Men: The Ideology of the Republican Party Before the Civil War* (1970), *Tom Paine and Revolutionary America* (1976), *The Story of American Freedom* (1998), and *Who Owns History? Rethinking the Past in a Changing World* (2002). His *Reconstruction: America's Unfinished Revolution, 1863–1877* (1988) received several awards, including the Bancroft and Parkman prizes.

Otis L. Graham Jr. is professor of history emeritus at the University of California, Santa Barbara, and visiting scholar at the University of North Carolina, Chapel Hill. He has served as editor of *The Public Historian* and director of the Graduate Program in Public Historical Studies at Santa Barbara and received the Robert Kelley Memorial Award from the National Council on Public History. His books include *Losing Time: the Industrial Policy Debate* (1992) and *Unguarded Gates: A History of America's Immigration Crisis* (2004).

Stephen J. Harper is an attorney with degrees from two universities, Northwestern and Harvard. A former student of Richard Leopold, he drew heavily on weekly conversations with him during the final two years of his life to write

Straddling Worlds: The Jewish-American Journey of Professor Richard W. Leopold (2008). He is also the author of *Crossing Hoffa: A Teamster's Story* (2007).

Joan Hoff, executive director of the OAH from 1981 to 1988, has been contributing books on American politics and foreign policy since the 1960s. The books include biographies of Herbert Hoover and Richard Nixon and, most recently, *A Faustian Foreign Policy from Woodrow Wilson to George W. Bush: Dreams of Perfectibility* (2008). She has also published *Law, Gender and Injustice: A Legal History of U.S. Women* (1991). Her academic posts include professorships at Indiana University, Ohio University, and Montana State University.

David Hollinger is the Preston Hotchkis Professor of American History at the University of California and a Fellow of the American Academy of Arts and Sciences. His recent publications include *Cosmopolitanism and Solidarity* (2006) and *Postethnic America: Beyond Multiculturalism* (2006) and articles in *Daedalus*, *Journal of American Ethnic History*, *Church History*, *Modern Intellectual History*, and *American Historical Review*. He is the president of the OAH for 2010–2011.

Frederick E. Hoxie was for many years the director of the Newberry Library's D'Arcy McNickle Center for American Indian History and has been since 1998 the Swanlund Professor of History at the University of Illinois, Urbana-Champaign. His publications include *Parading Through History: The Making of the Crow Nation in America, 1805–1935* (1995), *Talking Back to Civilization: Indian Voices from the Progressive Era* (2001), *The People: A History of Native America* (2007), and *Lewis and Clark and the Indian Country: The Native American Perspective* (2007).

Arnita A. Jones served as acting executive secretary, executive secretary, and executive director of the OAH from 1988 to 1999. Becoming executive director of the American Historical Association in 1999, she continued in that role until her retirement in 2010. Prior to her work with the OAH, she was staff associate for the National Coordinating Committee and then Program Officer for Planning and Assessment Studies at the National Endowment for the Humanities and senior historian at History Associates Incorporated.

Michael Kammen is the Newton C. Farr Professor of American History and Culture (emeritus) at Cornell University. He has held a visiting professorship at the École des Hautes Études, is an elected member of the American Academy of Arts and Sciences, served in 1995–1996 as president of the OAH, and received the AHA Award for Scholarly Distinction in 2009. His books include *People of Paradox: An Inquiry Concerning the Origins of American Civ-*

ilization (1972), awarded a Pulitzer Prize; *A Machine That Would Go of Itself: The Constitution in American Culture* (1986), awarded the Francis Parkman Prize and the Henry Adams Prize; and *Digging Up the Dead: A History of Notable American Reburials* (2010).

Stanley N. Katz, a former president of the OAH, is a lecturer with the rank of professor in the Woodrow Wilson School of Princeton University and president emeritus of the American Council of Learned Societies. A scholar of American legal and constitutional history and of philanthropy and nonprofit institutions with many publications, he is the editor of the Oliver Wendell Holmes Devise *History of the Supreme Court of the United States* (1990–) and the *Oxford International Encyclopedia of Legal History* (2009).

Alice Kessler-Harris is the R. Gordon Hoxie Professor of History at Columbia University. Her publications include *Out to Work: A History of Wage-Earning Women in the United States* (1982), *A Woman's Wage: Historical Meanings and Social Consequences* (1990), *In Pursuit of Equity: Women, Men and The Quest for Economic Citizenship in Twentieth Century America* (2001), and *Gendering Labor History* (2007). She has received a Bancroft Prize, among other awards, served as president of the Labor and Working-Class History Association and as an elected member of the AHA Council, and is now president elect of the OAH.

Richard S. Kirkendall, a former executive secretary of the OAH, is the Scott and Dorothy Bullitt Professor of American History Emeritus at the University of Washington. His books include *Social Scientists and Farm Politics in the Age of Roosevelt* (1966), *Uncle Henry: A Documentary Profile of the First Henry Wallace* (1993), and *Harry's Farewell: Interpreting and Teaching the Truman Presidency* (2004). He served as vice-president of the AHA's Professional Division and received an honorary doctorate from Gonzaga University and a Distinguished Service Award from the OAH.

James T. Kloppenberg is the Harvard College Professor and the David Woods Kemper '41 Professor of American History at Harvard University. His interests are in American and European democratic theory and practice since the seventeenth century and the relation between history and critical theory, and his books include *Uncertain Victory: Social Democracy and Progressivism in European and American Thought, 1870–1920* (1986), *A Companion to American Thought* (1995), and *The Virtues of Liberalism* (1998). The OAH awarded him the Merle Curti Prize for *Uncertain Victory*.

Richard W. Leopold was the William Smith Mason Professor of History at Northwestern University from 1963 to 1989. He served the OAH in several posts, including the presidency, and the OAH has awarded the Leopold book prize biannually since 1984. His books include *The Growth of American Foreign Policy: A History* (1962). He served on numerous governmental advisory committees, was a president of the Society for Historians of American Foreign Relations, and later received its Norman and Laura Graebner Award for his contributions to the field. He died in 2006.

William E. Leuchtenburg, past president of both the OAH and the AHA, taught at Columbia University for thirty years before moving to the University of North Carolina, Chapel Hill, in 1982. He is a major contributor to the literature on F.D.R., and his 1963 book, *Franklin D. Roosevelt and the New Deal, 1933–1940*, earned the Bancroft and the Francis Parkman prizes. More recent books include *In the Shadow of FDR: From Harry S. Truman to George W. Bush* (2001) and *The White House Looks South: Franklin D. Roosevelt, Harry S. Truman, Lyndon B. Johnson* (2005).

Edward T. Linenthal is editor of the *Journal of American History* and professor of history at Indiana University. His books include *Symbolic Defense: The Cultural Significance of the Strategic Defense Initiative* (1989), *Americans and Their Battlefields* (1991, 1993), *Preserving Memory: The Struggle to Create America's Holocaust Museum* (1995, 2001), and *The Unfinished Bombing: Oklahoma City in American Memory* (2001). He has enjoyed a long-time working relationship with the National Park Service and is an adjunct professor in the Department of Religious Studies at IU.

Leon F. Litwack, a former president of the OAH, is the Alexander F. and May T. Morrison Professor of American History Emeritus at the University of California, Berkeley. His books include *North of Slavery: The Negro in the Free States, 1790–1860* (1961), *Been in the Storm So Long: The Aftermath of Slavery* (1979), *The Enduring Struggle: Tom Joad's America* (1991), and *Trouble in Mind: Black Southerners in the Age of Jim Crow* (1998). His awards include a Pulitzer Prize, a Francis Parkman Prize, an American Book Award for his research and writing, and a Golden Apple Award for Outstanding Teaching.

Joanne Meyerowitz, a former editor of the *Journal of American History*, is a professor of history and American studies at Yale University. There she co-directs (with George Chauncey) the Yale Research Initiative on the History of Sexualities. Her most recent book is *How Sex Changed: A History of Transsexuality in the United States* (2002).

Marla R. Miller is a member of the history department of the University of Massachusetts, Amherst. There she serves as director of the public history program, teaches courses in public history, material culture, and museum and historic site interpretation, and consults with museums and historic sites. Her primary research interest is women's work before industrialization, and her book *The Needle's Eye: Women and Work in the Age of Revolution* (2006) won the Costume Society of America's award for the best book in the field for that year. More recently, she published *Betsy Ross and the Making of America* (2010).

David Montgomery, a former president of the OAH, is Farnam Professor of History Emeritus at Yale University. His contributions to a "new labor history" include *Workers' Control in America: Studies in the History of Work, Technology, and Labor Struggles* (1979), *The Fall of the House of Labor: The Workplace, the State, and American Labor Activism, 1865–1925* (1987), *Citizen Worker: The Experience of Workers in the United States with Democracy and the Free Market During the Nineteenth Century* (1993), and *Black Workers' Struggle for Equality in Birmingham* (2004).

Gary B. Nash is professor emeritus at the University of California, Los Angeles, and director of the National Center for History in the Schools. He is an elected member of the American Academy of Arts and Sciences, the American Philosophical Society, the American Antiquarian Society, and the Society of American Historians and a past president of the OAH. His most recent books are *The Forgotten Fifth: African Americans in the Age of Revolution* (2006) and *Friends of Liberty: Three Patriots, Two Revolutions, and a Tragic Betrayal of Freedom in the New Nation* (2008).

James T. Patterson is the Ford Foundation Professor of History Emeritus at Brown University. A specialist in American political history in the twentieth century, he published his first book, *Congressional Conservatism and the New Deal*, in 1967. His most recent ones are *Restless Giant: The United States from Watergate to Bush v. Gore* (2005) and *Freedom Is Not Enough: The Moynihan Report and America's Struggle Over Black Family Life—from LBJ to Obama* (2010).

Kathy Peiss is the Roy F. and Jeannette P. Nichols Professor of American History and chair of the History Department at the University of Pennsylvania. Her publications include *Cheap Amusements: Working Women and Leisure in Turn-of-the-Century New York* (1986), *Hope in a Jar: The Making of America's Beauty Culture* (1998), and *Major Problems in the History of American Sexu-*

ality (2001). She is currently working on a project on librarians, books, intelligence gathering, and cultural reconstruction in the World War II era.

Lewis C. Perry, a former editor of the *Journal of American History*, recently retired from the history faculty of Saint Louis University. He earlier taught at the State University of New York at Buffalo, Indiana University, Bloomington, and Vanderbilt University. His publications include *Intellectual Life in America* (1989) and *Radical Abolitionism: Anarchy and the Government of God in Antislavery Thought* (1995).

Donald A. Ritchie is the director of the U.S. Senate Historical Office. He has run that agency's oral-history program, served as president of the Oral History Association, and published *Doing Oral History: A Practical Guide* (2003). His other books include *James M. Landis: Dean of the Regulators* (1980), *Reporting from Washington: The History of the Washington Press Corps* (2005), and *Electing FDR: The New Deal Election of 1932* (2007). His *Press Gallery: Congress and the Washington Correspondents* (1991) won the OAH Leopold Prize.

Anne Firor Scott, a former president of the OAH, is often referred to as the pioneer of modern women's history. Her first book, *The Southern Lady*, was reissued in a twenty-fifth anniversary edition in 1995 and is still in print, forty years after its initial publication. A past president of the Southern Historical Association, she has also received a lifetime achievement award from the American Historical Association.

Stephanie J. Shaw is an associate professor of history at Ohio State University. Her publications include *What a Woman Ought to Be and to Do: Black Professional Women during the Jim Crow Era* (1996), which won the Association of Black Women Historians' Letitia Woods Brown Prize; her article "Using the W.P.A. Ex-Slave Narratives to Study the Great Depression" received the Southern Historical Association's Green-Ramsdell Award. She has served on committees in the OAH and is the Second Vice President of the Southern Association for Women Historians.

Arvarh E. Strickland is professor emeritus of history at the University of Missouri, Columbia. His publications include *The History of the Chicago Urban League* (1966), *Working with Carter G. Woodson, the Father of Black History: A Diary, 1928–1930, Lorenzo J. Greene* (1989), and *Selling Black History for Carter G. Woodson: A Diary, 1930–1933, Lorenzo J. Greene* (1996). He served the University of Missouri in a variety of ways, and in 2007, it recognized his contributions by naming a classroom building Strickland Hall. In 2010 the Southern Historical Association gave him its John W. Blassingame Award.

Notes on Contributors

David Thelen is the Distinguished Professor of History Emeritus at Indiana University, Bloomington. His publications include *Becoming Citizens in the Age of Television: How Americans Challenged the Media and Seized Political Initiative During the Iran-Contra Debate* (1996) and *The Presence of the Past: Popular Uses of History in American Life* (1998). Following his service as editor of the *Journal of American History*, the OAH established the Thelen Prize for the best article on American history published in a foreign language. Since 2008, he has been visiting professor of history at the University of Johannesburg, where he co-directs a civic engagement–oral history project in that city's Sophiatown neighborhood.

Timothy N. Thurber is an associate professor of history at Virginia Commonwealth University. Interested primarily in post–World War II political history and civil rights issues, he is the author of *The Politics of Equality: Hubert H. Humphrey and the African American Freedom Struggle, 1945–1948* (1998), and he is currently exploring the Republican Party and African American civil rights after World War II.

Richard White, president of the OAH in 2007, is the Margaret Byrne Professor of American History at Stanford University. His books include *The Middle Ground: Indians, Empires, and Republics in the Great Plains Region, 1650–1815* (1991) and *It's Your Misfortune and None of My Own: A New History of the American West* (1991). He has also published a book about his mother: *Remembering Ahanagran* (1998). His awards include the AHA's Albert J. Beveridge Award, the OAH's James A. Rawley Prize, the Francis Parkman Prize, and a MacArthur Foundation Fellowship.

Gavin Wright is the William Robertson Coe Professor of American Economic History at Stanford University. He has a longstanding interest in the economic history of the American South, has published *The Political Economy of the Cotton South* (1978), *Old South, New South* (1986), and *Slavery and American Economic Development* (2006), and is currently working on the economic causes and consequences of the Civil Rights Revolution.

Charles A. Zappia, currently the Interim Dean of the School of Social/Behavioral Sciences and Multicultural Studies and a professor of history at San Diego Mesa College, has participated for over fifteen years in attempts to integrate community college historians more fully into the mainstream of the profession and has held positions in both the AHA and the OAH. He has published essays in *Community College Historians in the United States* (1999), *The Italian American Experience* (1999), *The Lost World of Italian American Radicalism* (2003), and *The Encyclopedia of the Vietnam War* (2003), among other publications.